CENTENNIAL
BUCKEYE
COOK BOOK

Compiled by

the Women of the First Congregational Church,
Marysville, Ohio.

With Introduction and Appendixes by

Andrew F. Smith.

Ohio State University Press
Columbus

Reprinted from the Szathmary Family Culinary Collection, Culinary Archives & Museum at Johnson & Wales University, Providence, Rhode Island.

Introduction and Appendixes copyright © 2000 by Andrew F. Smith

First Ohio State University Press edition published 2000.

Library of Congress Cataloging-in-Publication Data

Centennial buckeye cook book / compiled by the Women of the First Congregational Church, Marysville, Ohio ; with introduction and appendixes by Andrew F. Smith.
p.   cm.
Includes bibliographical references and index.
ISBN 0-8142-0836-3 (cl. : alk. paper).—ISBN 0-8142-5039-4 (pa. : alk. paper)
1. Cookery, American.   I. Women of the First Congregational Church (Marysville, Ohio)
TX715.C4357 1999
641.5973—dc21   99-36683
CIP

Jacket design by Gore Studio.
Type set in Fournier by Graphic Composition, Inc., Athens, Georgia.
Printed by McNaughton & Gunn.

9 8 7 6 5 4 3 2 1

CENTENNIAL
BUCKEYE
COOK BOOK

CONTENTS.

Introduction by Andrew F. Smith.   vii

CENTENNIAL BUCKEYE COOKBOOK.   I

Appendix 1: Short-Title List of Ohio Cookery Works
            Published or Written through 1900.   335
Appendix 2: List of Buckeye Cookery Books.   349

INTRODUCTION.

Andrew F. Smith.

THE CENTENNIAL.

When the United States commemorated the one hundredth anniversary of the signing of the Declaration of Independence, celebrations were held across the nation. What particularly captivated Americans and foreigners alike were the festivities surrounding the Centennial Exposition in Philadelphia. President Ulysses S. Grant opened the Exposition on May 19, 1876, and fairgoers flocked to the 236-acre site with its 180 buildings filled with exhibits—fifty of which were sponsored by other nations. When it closed six months later, over ten million visitors had passed through the gates.

The Centennial Exposition, like many world's fairs, featured foods and beverages that were new to many Americans. In the Horticultural Hall, for instance, a forty-acre display of exotic tropical fruits exhibited bananas. While bananas had been imported into the United States since the 1840s, they were mainly consumed in coastal ports. Recipes containing bananas did not regularly pop into cookbooks until the early twentieth century. At the Centennial Exposition a guard was posted near the banana tree to prevent visitors from pulling them off. Outside the hall bananas sold in foil wrappers for ten cents apiece.[1]

In the Machinery Hall the process of manufacturing red and white popcorn balls was demonstrated. Popcorn creations had been a fad food since the 1840s, but popcorn recipes commonly did not find their way into cookbooks until toward the end of the nineteenth century. The booth at the Centennial Exposition "was crowded all day, and thus showed the attractiveness of the exhibitor's peculiar wares and machinery." I. L. Baker, who sponsored the exhibit, had paid the high price of

$8,000 for the exclusive popcorn concession throughout the grounds. Baker set up several of the "curious and attractive furnaces and selling-booths" and sold popcorn for five cents a bag.[2]

Another unusual culinary feature of the Exposition was soda, which had been used since the 1840s as a chemical leavening agent for making bread. While the process for using soda to make carbonated water had been known for centuries, it had been rarely used commercially. At the Centennial Exposition temperance supporters had managed to ban the sale of hard liquors. James W. Tufts and Charles Lippincott risked the astronomical fee of $50,000 for the privilege of selling soda water at the Exposition. Tufts and Lippincott constructed a three-story edifice with a thirty-foot soda fountain as their feature attraction and set up counters around the grounds to service other fairgoers with soda, syrup, and ices. Luckily for their venture, the summer of 1876 was hot. The counters were crowded throughout the life of the Exposition. Still, Tufts and Lippincott lost money at the Exposition; but it proved to be a wise financial investment, for they made a fortune selling soda fountains or dispensers to drugstores around the nation afterward. With the soda fountains went counters for customers, which soon became social gathering places in towns throughout America.[3]

Three cookbooks celebrated America's Centennial. Two were connected directly with the Exposition: Ella Myer's *The Centennial Cook Book and General Guide* and the Women's Centennial Committee's *National Cookery Book*. These were professionally written cookbooks worthy of acquisition, and copies sold briskly as souvenirs. The Women's Committee added an interesting dimension to the development of cookbooks. Intending to address the question asked by foreigners as to what were America's national dishes, the committee sent a request for recipes to every "State and territory in the union" and the results were presented in their *National Cookery Book*.

The third cookbook, the *Centennial Buckeye Cook Book,* was compiled by a committee of women at the Congregational church in Marysville, Ohio, and was dedicated to the "plucky housewives of 1876 who master their work instead of allowing it to master them." As the *Centennial Buckeye Cook Book* was not connected with the Philadelphia Centennial Exposition, it did not receive the national visibility that the other two enjoyed. The *Centennial Buckeye Cook Book* had been scheduled for release before the festivities scheduled for July 4, 1876, in Marysville, but it was not published until the fall—months after the centennial hype had died down. At the time, charity cookbooks sold a few thousand copies. However, the *Centennial Buckeye Cook Book* sold well, and its successor editions sold even more. Revised nine times, full of innovative recipes, the work survived and thrived throughout the rest of the century. By 1900, it had sold over one million copies, which made it the largest-selling American cookbook in the nineteenth century and one of the most widely distributed books in United States.[4]

THE ROOTS.

Marysville, Ohio, is a small town about thirty miles northwest of Columbus. While it was not incorporated until about 1840, it was the county seat of Union County, which had been formed in 1820 from parts of Delaware, Franklin, Madison, and Logan counties as well as a part of "old Indian territory." By 1843 Marysville's population consisted of only 360 inhabitants, yet it contained three churches—one Methodist and two Presbyterian.[5]

Such a small community had two Presbyterian churches because of a split in the Presbyterian church in the late 1830s, but the roots of this schism originated in centuries-old differences between Presbyterians and Congregationalists. While both groups historically shared a common religious heritage and maintained similar doctrinal beliefs, administrative differences divided them.[6] Congregationalist ministers had jurisdiction only over their own churches. Presbyterians had an administrative superstructure that governed church bodies. In the United States their common heritage contributed to an 1801 plan of union adopted by the General Assembly of the Presbyterian Church and the General Association of Congregational Churches in Connecticut that provided for the interchange of ministers in new settlements.[7] Based on this agreement, hundreds of churches were formed cooperatively in western New York and Ohio.

The Presbyterian church in America split into two major branches in 1837. One, known as the New School, was generally more progressive and urged a liberal interpretation of religious doctrine. It supported union with the Congregationalists and favored voluntary societies for missions and education. The New School comprised slightly more than 40 percent of the Presbyterians at the time. Since its faithful mainly lived in New England and New York, it generally opposed slavery. The other branch, known as the Old School, was generally more conservative and maintained a strict interpretation of church doctrine and polity. It favored church boards for missions and educational endeavors. As a large component of the Old School was based in the South, it took no stand against slavery.[8]

In Marysville the First Presbyterian Church was incorporated in 1831. Reflecting the national division, the Old School maintained control of the First Presbyterian Church, while the New School advocates founded the Second Presbyterian Church in 1840.[9] The Second Presbyterian Church reached out to Congregationalists, many of whom joined.[10] During the Civil War the Southern Presbyterians broke off from the Northern Presbyterians, and the differences separating the Old School and New School in the North decreased. In Marysville, however, unity was unreachable. Rather than re-merge with the First Presbyterian Church, in 1864 members of the Second Presbyterian Church decided "with the utmost harmony" to change their creed and become the First Congregational Church of Marysville.[11] Seven years later the First Congregational Church was strong enough to commence construction of a new church building at the northeast corner of West and South streets. The basement lecture room was quickly finished, but then work ground to a halt owing to lack of funds.[12] Sometime before 1876 the churchwomen decided to compile and sell a cookbook to raise funds to support their "weak and struggling church."

THE CONTEXT.

The *Centennial Buckeye Cook Book* was in many ways a reflection of both previously published cookery works and oral culinary traditions. While cookbooks had been published in America since 1742, early works were reprints of British cookbooks. One popular British work was Susannah Carter's *The Frugal Housewife*, first published in London in 1772, which saw six American editions before 1803. Carter's and other British cookbooks influenced subsequent American cookery writers. Amelia Simmons's *American Cookery* (Hartford, 1796), the first cookbook authored by an American, was deeply influenced by British cookery traditions. Specifically, many of her recipes had been borrowed without attribution from Susannah Carter's *The Frugal Housewife*. However, Simmons's book also presented American recipes, such as "Indian Slapjack" (which had maize as a major ingredient). The American publishers of Carter's *The Frugal Housewife* responded in kind. The 1803 edition featured an appendix containing "several new receipts adapted to the American mode of cooking." These American recipes had been inspired by those published by Simmons.

During the early nineteenth century, cookery to a large extent was an art passed down from mother to daughter. Daughters copied family cookery manuscripts when they married. When white settlers arrived in Ohio, they brought cookery manuscripts.[13] In addition to manuscripts, the settlers also brought cookbooks, such as those of Susannah Carter and Amelia Simmons. The first cookbook published in Ohio was Colin Mackenzie's *Five Thousand Receipts in All the Useful and Domestic Arts, Adapted to the Western States* (Hamilton, 1830). Mackenzie was a British author whose previous claim to fame was his voluminous *One Thousand Experiments in Manufacturing and Chemistry*. For his cookbook he had reviewed agricultural journals and available cookbooks, collecting and simplifying the recipes that he found. His encyclopedic *Five Thousand Recipes* was first published in England in 1822 and three years later in the United States. The anonymous American editor claimed to have employed only those practical recipes from the British work that would be of use in America. He also claimed to have supplemented the work with additional recipes borrowed from American sources. However, the American edition differed little from the original British work. Whatever the source or quality of the recipes, the work obviously struck a positive note in America, where it went through at least twenty-five editions and printings by 1868.[14]

Ohio was peopled not only by settlers from within the United States but also by immigrants from many countries and cultures. One immigrant, George Girardey, produced a most unusual cookbook, *Manual of Domestic Economy, or House-Keeper's Guide* (Dayton, 1841). Girardey is thought to have been of Swiss or Alsatian extraction, but may have been trained as a chef in Philadelphia. In 1842 he translated his cookbook into German, making it the first German-language cookbook published in America.[15] He had planned to publish it in French as well, but, if he did, copies have not been located.

Another interesting Ohio cookbook published in the 1840s was Philomelia Hardin's *Every Body's Cook and Receipt Book: But More Particularly Designed for Buckeyes, Hoosiers, Wolverines, Corncrackers, Suckers and All Epicures Who Wish to Live in Present Times* (Cleveland, 1842). Reflecting Midwestern cookery in the mid-nineteenth century, it was the first cookbook to employ the term *buckeye* in its title. The word originally referred to a tree of the genus *Aesculus,* also called the chestnut or horse chestnut. During the 1820s, it was used throughout the Ohio valley to mean "an indigenous backwoodsman as opposed to recent immigrants from the east coast." By 1833 it was specifically associated with Ohio. Some observers claimed that this association derived from the buckeye tree on the seal of Arthur St. Clair, the first governor of the Northwest Territory.[16]

According to the *History of Union County,* the word *buckeye* transmuted into the national sobriquet for Ohioans during the election campaign of 1840, in which William Henry Harrison, then a resident of Ohio, was the Whig candidate for president. A scurrilous newspaper article described Harrison "as living in a log cabin, drinking hard cider, and without ambition or ability to fill the highest office in the land." Ohioans were not upset with the hard-drinking appellation or the low assessment of Harrison's ambition and abilities, but they were incensed with the comment disparaging his log-cabin origins. Harrison supporters fabricated a log cabin and transported it to the Ohio Whig convention. Songs were written glorifying Harrison and his vice-presidential running mate John Tyler. Two became famous: "Tippecanoe and Tyler Too," by A. C. Ross of Zanesville, and the "Log Cabin Song," by Otway Curry of Marysville. The "Log Cabin Song" commences with the question "Oh, where, tell me where, was your Buckeye Cabin made?" Ross attended the national Whig convention in New York and was asked to sing his song. When he introduced himself, he announced that he was a Buckeye from the Buckeye State, and the word *buckeye* entered into the national consciousness.[17] To the extent that Ross's song contributed to Harrison's election to the presidency, it also hastened his death. Harrison took ill at the inauguration ceremonies and died of pneumonia one month later. And "Tyler too" became president.

Sixteen cookbooks were published in Ohio during the 1850s, but the pace slacked off during the Civil War. After the war, Ann Howe's *The American Kitchen* (Cincinnati, 1868) added another dimension to Ohio cookbooks. It was sold by Howe's Subscription Book Concern. Before the cookbook was published, Howe collected a list of subscribers who agreed to purchase it upon publication. Subscribers did not have to pay for the book until they received it. This system permitted publishers an efficient calculation of the appropriate number of copies to print.

During the early 1870s, cookbook publication in Ohio exploded, with the major growth sector being charity cookery books. The first known charity cookbook had been authored by Alexis Soyer. A Frenchman by birth, Soyer had lived much of his adult life in England and was particularly famous as the chef of London's Reform Club. In 1845 a bad grain harvest in England caused the price of wheat and bread to escalate. When the potato crop was decimated the following year, English soup kitchens averted starvation. But the Irish were more dependent on the potato and suffered grievously. When famine broke out in Ireland, Soyer raised funds to support soup kitchens. He also developed plans for larger and more efficient soup kitchens. The British government asked Soyer to put his ideas into service, and he did so in Dublin.[18] At the height of the famine, his kitchen fed twenty-six thousand people daily. Based on his experiences, Soyer published the *Poor Man's Regenerator, or Charitable Cookery,* which sold for sixpence, but he donated one pence to charity.[19] Soyer's charitable work was well known, as was his work assisting the British military in overcoming cookery challenges posed by the Crimean War.

Soyer's recipes were lifted verbatim and republished in American cookbooks during the Civil War. Some Civil War cookbooks were compiled and sold at Sanitary Fairs. According to Margaret Cook, author of *America's Charitable Cooks: A Bibliography of Fund-Raising Cook Books Published in the United States (1861–1915),* these were the origin of American charity cookbooks.[20] The first post–Civil War fund-raising cookbook located by Margaret Cook was *Nantucket Receipts* (Boston,

1870), which was intended for sale at "the fair for the New England Hospital for Women and Children." The following year three charity cookbooks were published in Massachusetts communities and one in Grand Rapids by the Congregational church, which was the first known work published by a religious group. It was about fifty pages in length and possessed some blank pages on which purchasers could add their own favorite recipes. In 1872 a sixty-six-page charity cookbook was published for the benefit of a Christ Church Fair in Connecticut and a 128-page one was published by the Congregational church in Fort Wayne, Indiana. These early works, like most subsequent charity cookbooks, were printed in small quantities and sold locally to those attending fairs or other events.[21] Their success encouraged other groups to compile and publish charity cookbooks of their own.

Ohio charitable groups quickly adopted and adapted the cookbook art form as a fund-raising tool. The first known Ohio charity cookbook, the *Presbyterian Cook Book,* was compiled by the women of Dayton's First Presbyterian Church in March 1873. This work had many characteristics that came to symbolize subsequent works. Its profits supported unspecified church activities. Many recipes were signed or initialed, and most were supplied by members of the church. However, some recipes were borrowed from other sources. For instance, nine recipes were ascribed to a "Mrs. H. B. Sherman," who was not otherwise identified, but was later the proprietress of the Plankinton House in Milwaukee.[22] Also, several recipes were borrowed from *Common Sense in the Kitchen* (New York, 1871), a very popular work written by Mary Virginia Terhune, who employed the pseudonym of Marion Harland. Only five hundred copies of the first edition were printed, and they possessed a paper cover. By July 1873 these copies had been sold, so a second printing was commissioned. This, too, sold out quickly, and the *Presbyterian Cook Book* was again reprinted, this time in a hardback version. By 1875 five thousand copies had been sold and still more were ordered. Eventually it was reprinted ten times, the last dated 1889.

Four Ohio charity cookbooks were published in 1874. In Toledo, *Tried and True: The Home Cook Book* was published "for the joint benefit of the Home for Friendless Women and the Orphans' Home." It embraced a format similar to that of the *Presbyterian Cook Book,* with the exception of numerous paid advertisements that promoted local merchants. *Practical Receipts of Experienced Housekeepers* was published by the women of the Seventh Presbyterian Church in Cincinnati. The *Portsmouth Monumental Cook Book* generated funds for the Soldiers' Aid Society in Portsmouth, Ohio. The fourth work, *Congregational Cook-Book,* was released by the First Congregational Church in Columbus, which was closely associated with the First Congregational Church in Marysville.[23]

In just a few years, the new genre of charity cookbooks had come into its own. The Ohio versions contained common elements. As Anne Bower writes in *Recipes for Reading: Community Cookbooks, Stories, Histories* (Amherst, 1997), community cookbooks commonly featured: prefaces explaining the group's philanthropic intent and/or how the cookbook was compiled; illustrations; chapters divided by food categories; sometimes paid advertisements; and recipes often signed by the donors' names or initials.[24] To Bower's list should also be added another common characteristic: many, if not most, recipes in charity cookbooks were mundane and simplistic. And many recipes were lifted from published sources. Plagiarism was not a new phenomenon—it was a common practice among those writing and publishing commercial cookbooks. With the latter plagiarism was often a blatant process; in charity cookbooks it may have occurred quite innocently. Women copied good recipes from a variety of sources and passed them on to others. Those contributing recipes to a community cookbook may not even have been aware of the original source.

Whatever the origins of their recipes, contributors associated their names or initials with them, which suggests that they were proud of their donation. Contributors may have liked them because they used them frequently or just for special occasions, or perhaps the recipes were supplied to impress the neighbors. Whatever the reasons, cookbooks compiled locally by committees often offer a picture of a community frozen in time. By deciphering these works, we can better understand the community in which the works were prepared. By contrasting what was included and excluded from the work we gain insight into donors' values. By reviewing food products contained in recipes, we can infer trade and marketing patterns. By uncovering the sources of recipes, we can map communication networks. Community cookbooks are snapshots of the communities in which they were spawned.

The *Centennial Buckeye Cook Book* is no exception. It reflects life in Marysville in 1876. Moreover, it also mirrors broader issues in Ohio and America, such as the hoopla surrounding the celebration of the nation's one hundredth birthday, the presidential election then underway, the roles of men and women, and the temperance movement. An additional advantage of this work is that it went through nine major revisions in the ensuing twenty-nine years. While subsequent editions were based on the work originally published in Marysville, they also reflected other traditions and patterns. If *Centennial Buckeye Cook Book* is a snapshot, then comparing this work's later versions provides us with time-lapse photography of culinary America during the late nineteenth century.

THE ORIGIN.

The charity cookbooks published by Ohio communities and those of other Congregational churches in the Midwest likely inspired the women of the First Congregational Church in Marysville to compile a cookbook of their own. The *Centennial Buckeye Cook Book* was structured similarly to other community cookbooks. It was divided into several sections, of which by far the largest was a cookery section grouped alphabetically into thirty-two general categories. Categories commenced with an introductory note brimming with practical advice. At the end of the cookery section was a mishmash compilation of an additional twenty-six recipes from "Centennial Governors," tables of weights, measures, and cooking times, and bills of fare. Following this was a chaotic series of sections, three of which ("Fragments," "Hints for the Sick Room," and "Hit and Miss") incorporated more recipes. Other sections contained generalized advice on "How to Cut and Cure Meats," "Carving," "Housekeeping," "The Laundry," "Floral," "Farm and Garden," "Medical," and "Miscellaneous." The book was capped with twenty-two pages of advertisements. Interspersed among the printed pages were ruled blank pages inserted so that readers could add additional recipes.

The chaos that exists at the end of the first edition was likely rooted in the tension between the compilers' desire to be thorough and their desire to publish the book before the centennial was celebrated. Unable to meet this deadline, the committee rescheduled publication for September 1, but on August 30 the *Marysville Tribune* reported that, while the writing had been completed, only a few pages had "passed through the press."[25] Had the printing press been in Marysville, it might have been released sooner. Although J. H. Shearer and Son in Marysville was the publisher, the book was printed by the Tribune Engravers and Binders in Minneapolis, Minnesota.

Several possible explanations account for the decision to print the book in Minneapolis. The cookbook had probably become too large for Shearer's presses, while the *Minneapolis Tribune* had large presses that could handle the binding. Still there were presses in Ohio that could have handled the large job, as demonstrated by the fact that some subsequent editions were published in Ohio. The *Minneapolis Tribune* bindery claimed they had "lower prices than any other establishment west of New York City or Chicago," so there may have been a cost savings for printing it out of state.[26] However, the most important reasons were that Estelle and Alfred G. Wilcox, who assembled the manuscript and prepared it for publication, lived in Minneapolis and that Alfred just happened to be the manager of the *Minneapolis Tribune*. More than other contributors, the Wilcoxes were the driving force behind this cookbook.

THE FAMILIES.

Estelle Hemans Woods and Alfred Gould Wilcox were wed on his thirty-fourth birthday in 1874. Estelle had been born in Marysville in 1849. She graduated from Marysville's high school in 1868 and attended Ohio Wesleyan Female College in nearby Delaware, Ohio. She received her Bachelor of Literature degree four years later. Her graduation speech focused on women's suffrage. She intended to become a teacher, but instead worked as an assistant cashier at her father's Bank of Marysville.[27]

Alfred Wilcox had been born in Madison, Ohio.[28] When he graduated from college, the Civil War had just commenced. He received an appointment as a first lieutenant in the 105th Ohio Volunteers and served with distinction throughout the war. He was promoted to captain and finally breveted to major. His regiment served under General Tecumseh Sherman and was part of the Union Army that captured Atlanta and marched through Georgia to the sea in 1864. After the war Alfred took up journalism. He served his apprenticeship as city editor of the *Cleveland Leader* and sequentially owned the Fremont *Journal,* the Richmond *Telegram,* and the New Castle *Courier.* He moved to Minnesota in 1872 and became manager first of the *Daily News* and afterward the *Minneapolis Tribune.*[29] How Estelle and Alfred met remains unclear. Perhaps they met in Minneapolis, since Estelle's older sister, Florence Woods Hush, lived there with her family, and Estelle and Florence's father, Judge William W. Woods, owned extensive property in Minnesota.

For Estelle and Alfred's wedding, more than four hundred guests were invited to the home of Judge Woods. He had been born in 1814 in what would become Union County and was the youngest child of Samuel Woods, the first pastor of a Presbyterian church in a small community not far from Marysville. In 1839 William Woods married Martha Jane Thompson, who taught school in the basement of the Presbyterian church before her marriage. Woods had served on the school committee along with Philander B. Cole.[30] One year after their marriage, Woods's business failed and his debts piled up. Rather than declare bankruptcy, Woods worked harder and eventually paid off his debts. He engaged in a variety of businesses in Marysville, most of which were financially successful. For instance, the "Marysville Pearlash Factory" that he launched with Darius Buxton was reported to be the largest in the nation by 1874. Along with two others, Woods founded the Bank of Marysville in 1854. During the Civil War they sold "United States Government Twenty-five dollar Bonds." The bank became the largest private banking business in Ohio outside large cities. He also invested in land in Minnesota, owning several stock and wheat farms, one of which consisted of 2,400 acres. Woods was elected judge in 1849.[31] By the time Estelle and Alfred were married, Judge Woods was reputed to be the wealthiest man in Marysville and was the owner of one of the town's larger houses.

However, when 350 guests accepted the invitation to the wedding of his youngest daughter, Estelle, even Judge Woods's house was taxed "to its utmost, the guests finding it all they could do to stand packed 'rank and file' thus necessitating the ignoring of seats altogether." At 8:30 P.M. a bell chimed and the moving crowd stood still. The ushers, R. M. Henderson and Hattie Mendenhall entered first, followed by the attendants H. W. Morey with Dora Woods, W. M. Leggett with Abbie Curtis, L. L. Woodburn with Ella Southard, R. W. Thompson with Josie Buxton, and A. Howard with Jennie Fullington. The bride and groom passed through the files and took their appropriate places. The wedding ceremony was performed by the Reverend W. E. Lincoln of the First Congregational Church. By midnight the guests started to disperse, and at 1 A.M. the newlyweds started for the train depot, where they departed for a two-week honeymoon in the East. According to the *Marysville Tribune,* Estelle "bid her friends farewell" and took the arm of one whom she loved, "to share in the future his joys and his sorrows."[32] One unpredictable joy that they both shared was the *Centennial Buckeye Cook Book*.

While the Wilcoxes played a pivotal role in the assembling of the *Centennial Buckeye Cook Book,* their names did not appear on the title page. Neither did their names appear on the title pages of subsequent editions. All existing evidence suggests that the first edition was genuinely a collective effort by a committee of women at the First Congregational Church in Marysville, Ohio. The first edition so credited them. Two years after the cookbook's publication, the *Marysville Tribune* similarly attributed the work "to the enterprise and toil of a committee" of the Congregational church, who completed their work only "after months and months of patient endeavor."[33] Estelle Wilcox was a member of the committee, but it is unlikely that she took the commanding lead in the first edition. At twenty-seven years of age, she had limited experience in cookery or housekeeping compared with the other women serving on the committee. Her name was noted as the author of only one cookery recipe, for "Pyramid of Coconut Drops," hardly one of the important cookery recipes in the work; and also for a one-line medical recipe "For Sore Throat."[34] At the time the cookbook was published, the Wilcoxes were living in Minneapolis; however, they frequently returned to Marysville to visit her family. Three years after their marriage and their move to Minneapolis, Estelle was still listed as a member of Marysville's First Congregational Church.[35]

Of the signed cookery recipes, the majority were identified only by initials. However, most of these initials correspond with names of women who were members of the First Congregational Church. For some recipes, subsequent editions identified the full name of the contributor. More than half of the probable authors are easily identified. These fall into four categories. In the largest category are church-women from Marysville. At the date of publication, the church counted fifty-four women members. Almost all supplied something to the cookbook. As one might expect, a major contribution was made by "Mrs. W. A. J.," who likely was Mary James, the wife of William A. James, minister of the First Congregational Church. She furnished eleven recipes.[36]

Another major contributor was "Mrs. J. H. S.," who was probably Josie Shearer, the wife of John H. Shearer, publisher of the first edition. The Shearers were members of the Congregational church, and John Shearer had at one time served as the church's deacon. Josie offered thirteen recipes.[37] The wives of the deacons of the church also furnished recipes: Hattie Scott, wife of Orlando M. Scott; Sarah M. Wood, wife of Franklin Wood; and Eliza Starr, wife of John W. Starr.[38] Likewise, the wives of the church trustees contributed: Tillie Long, wife of Nathan S. Long; Abby Morey, wife of Abraham B. Morey; and Harriet Lee, wife of William Lee.[39] Other churchwomen who offered recipes were Clara Morey, Sabina A. Morey, Elizabeth Robinson, and Mrs. M. K. Pasco, wife of the future pastor of the First Congregational Church.[40]

The second largest category of contributors is comprised of women who were outside Ohio. Women supplied recipes from many Midwestern states: Illinois, Indiana, Minnesota, Iowa, and Michigan. Others hailed from Eastern states: New York, Pennsylvania, New Jersey, and Massachusetts; and one from a Southern state, North Carolina. The single largest contributor in the cookbook was Mrs. H. B. Sherman, who, it may be recalled, furnished recipes to the *Presbyterian Cook Book*. In 1875 the Shermans had taken control of Milwaukee's Plankinton House, which was considered "the *ne plus ultra* of American hotels," with 320 guest rooms and two major dining rooms.[41] In the *Centennial Buckeye Cook Book*, Sherman provided fourteen recipes.[42]

Outside Ohio, the largest donation of recipes by state was from Minnesota. The major reason for the large number of recipes from Minnesota can only be attributed to the Wilcoxes, who then lived in that state, the contributions of which overlap the third category of contributors: the relations and friends of the Woods and Wilcox families. Almost all of the women in Estelle and Alfred's wedding party donated recipes, as did the wives of the male attendants. For instance, Abbie Curtis, a cousin of Alfred's living in St. Louis, supplied a recipe for "Canned Peaches." Estelle's sister, Florence Hush, furnished recipes for "Canellons" and "Fig Pudding." One of Florence's in-laws offered a recipe for "Baked Spring Chicken." Several recipes were contributed by members of the Wilcox family then living in Madison, Ohio, such as M. E. Wilcox and R. S. Wilcox.[43] The Woods family friends counted the wife of T. J. Buxton, who served as cashier at the Bank of Marysville until 1869. At the time of publication of the *Centennial Buckeye Cook Book* the Buxtons lived in Minneapolis, where T. J. served as the president of the City Bank. A relative of T. J. who remained in Marysville was Dora Buxton, who brought forth at least ten recipes, among them "Graham Gems," "Potato Yeast," "Orange Cake," "Lemon Cake," "Frizzled Ham and Eggs," and "Sliced Apple Pie."[44] When T. J. Buxton moved to Minneapolis, R. M. Henderson became the cashier at Judge Woods's Marysville bank. Henderson's wife, Sarah A. Henderson, presented recipes for "Hard Times Cake" and "Ginger Cakes."[45]

Another contributor was Dolly B. Cole, the wife of Judge Philander B. Cole, who served as prosecuting attorney for Union County. Judge Cole launched the Marysville *Argus* in 1844, but sold out to Cornelius Hamilton in 1849. Cole served in the Ohio legislature. He subsequently became a Republican and was a strong supporter of Abraham Lincoln and the war effort. He was a delegate to the 1864 Republican Convention and was elected judge in 1871. He married Dolly B. Whitter in 1839. Dolly furnished several recipes to *Centennial Buckeye Cook Book*, one of which was for "Stewed Tomatoes."[46] Their daughter, Cornelia Cole, was Estelle's friend. Like Estelle, Cornelia attended the local

Marysville high school and Ohio Wesleyan Female Seminary. Like Estelle, Cornelia married in 1874. At the time of publication of the *Centennial Buckeye Cook Book*, she and her husband, Charles W. Fairbanks, lived in Indianapolis, Indiana. Cornelia supplied a recipe for "Corn Starch Morange." Her husband had attended Ohio Wesleyan Male Seminary. Upon graduation he studied in law and became politically active. In 1904 he ran for and was elected to the office of vice president of the United States on a ticket with Theodore Roosevelt.[47]

A final category were those recipes associated with celebrities. As previously mentioned, the households of twenty-six state and territorial governors added their own recipes. Among the more interesting was one for enchiladas offered by the territorial governor of Arizona, Anson Safford. It is the first known published recipe reflecting America's Mexican culinary heritage. Safford chimed in at the end of his recipe: "Any one who has ever been in a Spanish speaking country will recognize this as one of the national dishes, as much as the pumpkin pie is a New England speciality."[48]

Two other recipes furnished by governors' households were "Veal Loaf" from Samuel Tilden of New York and "French Pickle" from the wife of Rutherford B. Hayes of Ohio.[49] At the time the book was published, Hayes and Tilden were candidates for the presidency of the United States. Recipes for "Tilden Cake" and "Hayes Cake" in *Centennial Buckeye Cook Book* likely reflected the hoopla surrounding the presidential election. (The "Hayes Cake" has additional interest in that it was submitted by Flora D. Ziegler, a nine-year-old from Columbus.)[50] In November 1876, shortly after the cookbook was published, Tilden received a quarter of a million more popular votes and twenty-one more uncontested electoral votes than did Hayes. However, when the smoke-filled room cleared, Tilden lost the election in the Electoral College by one vote owing to manipulation of the contested returns in four states—all of which were cast for Hayes. In subsequent editions of *Centennial Buckeye Cook Book* the "French Pickle" recipe was cited as coming from "Mrs. President R. B. Hayes, Washington, D. C."[51]

Two important national cookery figures also supplied recipes— Mary Virginia Terhune and Maria Parloa. Terhune, writing under the name of Marion Harland, was born in rural Virginia in 1830. At the age of twenty-four she published her first novel, *Alone*. Her *Common Sense in the Household* (New York, 1871) was an instant success, as was her *Breakfast, Luncheon and Tea* (New York, 1875). For the *Centennial Buckeye Cook Book* Terhune's recipe was "Coffee with Whipped Cream." Her directions for making "self-freezing ice cream," originally published in *Common Sense in the Household*, were also incorporated in the *Centennial Buckeye Cook Book*. Maria Parloa was born in 1843 in Massachusetts. She worked as a cook in private families and as a pastry chef in several hotels, principally at summer resorts, such as the famous Appledore House on the Isles of Shoals. Based on these experiences, she published *The Appledore Cook Book* (Boston, 1872). She taught school in Mandarin, Florida, where Harriet Beecher Stowe then lived. During the summer of 1876 she gave her first lecture on cooking in New London, Connecticut. In March 1879, Parloa helped launch the Boston Cooking School. She was invited to take charge but declined (Mary Johnson Lincoln became its first principal). To the *Centennial Buckeye Cook Book* Parloa furnished three recipes: "Charlotte Russe," "Canned Blackberries," and "Soda Biscuits." Like Terhune, Parloa went on to produce many more books on cookery and household management.[52] Parloa later published the recipe for "Charlotte Russe" in the second edition of her *Appledore Cook Book*.[53]

Other celebrities counted the sister of General Philip Sheridan, the Union Civil War commander, and W. A. Croffut, editor of the New York *Daily Graphic*, who submitted two poetic recipes, "Sidney Smith's Winter Salad" and, a poem written especially for the *Centennial Buckeye Cook Book*, "Clam Soup." Croffut was one of the few male contributors identified in the cookbook. His wife submitted three more recipes, for "Sweet Pickle," "Stuffed Cabbage," and "Peas Stewed in Cream."[54]

For those unfamiliar with nineteenth-century cookery, some recipes and techniques employed in the *Centennial Buckeye Cook Book* may come as a surprise. Cookery was an art that required extensive knowledge about many things we take for granted today. The cooking equipment was, of course, quite different. There were no gas oven ranges, electric refrigerators, or electrical equipment of any kind. Stoves and ranges were fueled by wood and coal. Electric refrigerators were not commonly used until the 1920s, but ice houses, ice boxes, and underground cold storage rooms were common. Ice boxes, ice houses, and cold rooms clearly had their limitations, so it may come as a surprise to find so many recipes for ices and ice cream flavored with chocolate, vanilla, oranges, lemons, pineapples, coffee, coconut, strawberries, raspberries, arrowroot, apples, pears, peaches, and quinces. Extensive directions for freezing them were supplied.[55]

Ice boxes and cold storage were supplemented by many traditional food preserving techniques, such as salting, sugaring, drying, and home canning—all commonly employed in homes since the late eighteenth century. Home canning was particularly important and was made easier by John L. Mason's invention of the self-sealing zinc lid and glass jar in 1859. As the Mason jar was easy to use and comparatively inexpensive to produce, it revolutionized the preservation of fruits and vegetables in the home. By 1860 it was shipped throughout the United States. Although no specific mention of the Mason jar is made in *Centennial Buckeye Cook Book,* there is a discussion of self-sealing glass containers and "grooved jars," as Mason jars were sometimes called.[56]

THE FEATURES.

While the *Centennial Buckeye Cook Book* shared many elements with other charity cookbooks, the differences were extremely significant. Most charity cookbooks were not very thick. Charity cookbooks usually supplemented other more comprehensive cookbooks, and their small size reduced publication costs. The previously mentioned *Congregational Cook-Book* published in Columbus was a mere forty-seven pages, while *Tried and True: The Home Cook Book* came at 124 pages. By comparison, *Centennial Buckeye Cook Book* was a hefty 406 pages including the advertising section. The compilers offered an explanation for its unusual size. They reported in the preface that they had had little "expectation that it would reach its present proportions," but that they had "met a most kind and generous response from friends in every part of the country, and soon found themselves in possession of material for a book fuller, more complete and practical, and better adapted to the wants of the average American housewife than any previous work."[57]

The preface to the *Centennial Buckeye Cook Book* proudly proclaimed that all recipes were "new to print," a boast inaccurately made by many other cookbooks.[58] However, unlike in other cookbooks, only a handful of the recipes in this work were plagiarized directly from other published sources. The cranberry recipes were borrowed directly from a circular published by C. G. and E. W. Crane of Caldwell, New Jersey.[59] As previously noted, the directions for making ice cream were borrowed from *Common Sense in the Household*.[60] But these were exceptions. From a broader perspective, many recipes published in *Centennial Buckeye Cook Book* paralleled those in Maria Parloa's *Appledore Cook Book* and Terhune's *Common Sense in the Household*. The contents of the recipes were revised, however. The originality in *Centennial Buckeye Cook Book* was a remarkable feat.

The *Centennial Buckeye Cook Book* yielded a collection of commonly used recipes that had been uncommonly published. Many recipes reveal a cookbook on the cutting edge of culinary life in America. Previous cookbooks had recipes for mushroom, walnut, and tomato ketchup, but *Centennial Buckeye Cook Book* additionally featured ones for cucumber, cherry, gooseberry, and currant ketchup. The latter recipe was one of the first published recipes for ketchup based on currants.[61] Mirroring the inclusion of popcorn at the Centennial Exposition in Philadelphia, the *Centennial Buckeye Cook Book* offered recipes for "Popcorn Pudding" and "Pop Corn Balls." Evidently a third recipe for "Sugared Popcorn" was also intended for publication, since it was listed in the table of contents, but in the text a recipe for "Vanity Puffs" was substituted.[62] The cookbook possessed fourteen tomato recipes. While tomatoes had appeared in American cookbooks for decades, it was only after the Civil War that tomato cookery blossomed. The *Centennial Buckeye Cook Book* had many more recipes than was typical at the time, with especially unusual ones for "Tomato Batter Cakes," and "Tomato Toast."[63] Also unusual was the recipe for "Saratoga Potatoes." Better known today as potato chips, Saratoga potatoes reportedly had been created during the decade before the Civil War by an African-American chef at Morris Lake Hotel in Saratoga, New York.[64]

Several other recipes in the *Centennial Buckeye Cook Book* were from historical sources. Four were identified as one hundred years old: "Rhode Island Sprat Outs," "Salem Election Cake," "Old Hartford Election Cake," and "Grandma Thompson's White Pudding."[65] These recipes were indeed old. "Rhode Island Sprat Outs" were a variation of the "Indian Slapjack" recipe published in the first edition of Amelia Simmons's *American Cookery*. The recipes for Salem and Hartford election cake were slightly revised versions of the "Election Cake" recipe published in Simmons's second edition. As culinary historian Karen Hess points out, Election Cake was "simply one of the 'Great Cakes' of English culinary tradition, to be made for festival occasions, huge loaves of highly enriched yeasted bread, flavored with sugar, spices, and lovely rosewater or spirits of some kind, as well as raisins."[66] The "Grandma Thompson's White Pudding" recipe is also a traditional British recipe, for "Boiled Suet Pudding," a version of which appears in the American edition of Susannah Carter's *The Frugal Housewife* (Philadelphia, 1796). From Carter's work, four additional recipes were borrowed verbatim: roast venison, steak pudding, pigeons, and roasted fowl with chestnuts.[67] These recipes were supplied by Elizabeth Thompson, the wife of Dr. M. Thompson, a lifelong resident of Union County whose grandmother was likely the "Grandma Thompson" noted in the title of the white-pudding recipe. The Thompsons were closely connected with the First Presbyterian Church in Marysville.[68]

The *Centennial Buckeye Cook Book* is also interesting for what was *not* included. Typical of other charity cookbooks, few recipes were identified as originating with men. While this was a work compiled by a women's committee, it is unlikely that they would have intentionally excluded recipes from men. Men could and did publish cookbooks, as exemplified by Mackenzie's and Girardey's works, but these reflected the efforts of professional writers and chefs. In the nineteenth century men were appropriately engaged in cooking as a profession, but home cooking was predominantly conducted by women. As presented in *Centennial Buckeye Cook Book*, the major roles of women were to cook and to housekeep. This is paradoxical. Estelle Wilcox, while clearly a successful cook and housekeeper, spent much of her time engaged in activities outside the home—running a business with her husband, campaigning for social causes, and editing a magazine called *The Housekeeper*, to name but a few.

If there are few recipes identified as coming from men, no recipes are identified as originating with African Americans, some of whom lived in Marysville at the time. Although the First Congregational Church championed the antislavery cause, it is not likely that African Americans were members of that church in 1876. Similarly, few recipes were associated with what we would consider "ethnic" dishes today. Particularly absent are those recipes representing Southern or Eastern European or Jewish cooking traditions. Few ethnic names appear on the Congregational-church roll, and it is not likely that the women in Marysville in 1876 were greatly influenced by Italian, Spanish, Greek, Jewish, Polish, or Russian cooking. It is interesting to note how these recipes creep into subsequent editions of this work as immigration dramatically expands during the latter part of the nineteenth century and migration patterns increase the ethnic diversity of many regions within the United States.

Also absent from the *Centennial Buckeye Cook Book* are recipes representing the upper and lower classes of America. While economy is promoted as a virtue, the cookbook is not a reflection of what less affluent Americans ate. The recipes contain a variety of ingredients that would have been unaffordable by poorer Americans. Alternately, few recipes reflected high cuisine currently under development in the United States. For instance, French cookery, long the rage of the American upper classes, makes no appearance. This cookbook is the work of white middle- and upper-middle-class women and it reflects what these women did in their own kitchens.

Finally, intentionally excluded from the cookbook were alcoholic beverages. Unlike most other cookbooks published in America at the time, directions for making or serving wine, beer, hard cider, and spirits were completely absent. A few recipes mentioned alcoholic beverages as cooking ingredients. For instance, one for "Jelly Wine" contained sherry, one for "Boiled Indian Pudding" made a sauce with wine, and the "Old Hartford Election Cake" featured gills of wine and brandy. In the introduction to a fruit-cake recipe the author wrote, "Most ladies think fruit cake quite incomplete without wine or brandy; but it can be made equally as good on strictly temperance principles," but the author did recommend wrapping the fruit cake "in a cloth wet in whisky or brandy to keep it moist."[69] Finally, at the end of the work is an intriguing recipe for making unfermented wine for communion.[70]

The lack of alcoholic beverages can be attributed to the temperance movement that was growing in America at the time. This movement had been gaining in strength since the 1830s, and temperance cookbooks had been published in America since the early 1840s. In 1876 a prohibition amendment was introduced into the U.S. House of Representatives. The bill failed, but the temperance movement marched on. The First Congregational Church was a supporter of the temperance movement, and Estelle Wilcox was a card-carrying member of the Women's Christian Temperance Union (W.C.T.U.).

To help defray the costs of printing, other charity cookbooks incorporated advertisements, some of which promoted products that were distributed nationally. The *Centennial Buckeye Cook Book*'s advertisements were different. The advertisements were not solely from merchants in and around Marysville, Ohio. Some advertisers lived in Columbus and Cleveland. Others were based outside of Ohio, such as "Duryea's Improved Corn Starch" in New York; Ezra F. Landis's "Clothes Horse or Drier" in Lancaster, Pennsylvania; "The Christian Union" in New York; D. F. Townsend's "Oxygenated Air" in Rhode Island; Robinson Brothers and Company's "Indexical Silver Soap" in Boston; the Missouri Valley Novelty Works' "Combination Kitchen Safe" in Saint Joseph, Missouri; and C. G. and E. W. Crane's "First Premium 'Star Brand' Cranberries" in Caldwell, New Jersey. The extent and geographic dispersion of the advertisers suggest that the compilers intended this to be distributed nationally.

THE GROWTH.

The *Centennial Buckeye Cook Book* and its successor editions differed dramatically from other contemporary cookbooks in several ways. One significant difference was the magnitude of the promotional campaign waged on its behalf. This campaign was launched even before the cookbook was published. Although it was not printed until months later, the compilers sold subscriptions at the Marysville Centennial celebrations on July 4, 1876. John Shearer, editor of the *Marysville Tribune* and the publisher of the *Centennial Buckeye Cook Book,* encouraged everyone to "subscribe so as to have something useful and substantial by which to remember the Centennial 4th of July." Shearer also suggested that "persons wishing to give a valuable present to a friend, can not for the money, give any thing more useful." Less useful was another promotional gimmick: at the subscription stand there were scales, where subscribers were weighed and received a card "bearing their name, weight and date—July 4th, 1876." There was no charge for the cards, which were considered an "interesting relic for your next Centennial fourth."[71]

Newspapers in Ohio received and published promotions on behalf of the *Centennial Buckeye Cook Book*. According to the *Cincinnati Gazette*, although the publishers had not seen the cookbook, it promised "to be the best of its kind yet compiled." The *Marysville Tribune* was even more effusive: the cookbook promised "to be the most complete work of the kind that has ever emanated from the American press." It was "designed to be *practical* in all its features, and to this end nothing is to be admitted that has not been amply demonstrated to be correct by the best housekeepers of the country." The purpose of the cookbook, said the *Marysville Tribune*, was to realize "enough means from the sale of the book to complete their church edifice."[72] When the book finally came out, canvassers spread throughout Marysville to fulfill the subscriptions and sell additional copies.

The first edition of *Centennial Buckeye Cook Book* sold for a dollar, and it was a tremendous success. Within a few months of its publication, second and third editions were published under the title *Buckeye Cookery and Practical Housekeeping*, selling for $1.75 per copy. The reasons for changing the title were severalfold. On the inside cover of the first edition was a note reporting that it had been licensed by "H. E. Newton, Trade Mark No. 3875, issued from the United States Patent Office, July 25th, 1876." At the time, the process of establishing trademark was new and the U.S. Patent Office approved almost every application. Henry Newton had trademarked the word symbol "Centennial," and technically everyone who used the term in the title of a book or on a product was required to pay him a licensing fee. Subsequent editions of this book did not include "centennial" in the title, probably because it was passé by then, but perhaps also to avoid paying Newton additional fees.

THE RISE.

The *Centennial Buckeye Cook Book* was the only known major cookbook to convert from charitable to commercial use. The first edition was the only one copyrighted by the First Congregational Church. The second and third editions were copyrighted by the Buckeye Publishing Company in Marysville, which had been formed by Estelle and Alfred Wilcox. The following year Alfred and Estelle Wilcox purchased the copyright.[73] No evidence has surfaced indicating the specific arrangements for the transfer of rights to the Wilcoxes, although the minutes of the First Congregational Church report that the women "realized a very considerable sum of profits." A joint committee of women and church trustees was established and "agreed upon the general plan of work to complete the church-building, which plan has been submitted to, and approved in the main, at a meeting of the members of the church."[74]

The formal dedication of the Congregational church took place on March 14, 1878. According to an article in the *Marysville Tribune*, its completion was due mainly to the financial assistance generated by the sale of the cookbook. The amount realized from sales was by that date $1,630. But money kept pouring in. After completing the church building, the women decided to construct a parsonage. According to *The History of Union County*, the parsonage was completed in 1881 at a cost of more than $1,500, which was completely paid for by the proceeds from the sale of the cookbook.[75] Hence, the known profits from cookbook sales amounted to more than $3,130—a tidy sum in the 1870s.

At least two more editions of *Buckeye Cookery* were published during 1877: one in Minneapolis and the other in Marysville. These were identical except that the former announced that it was the "twenty-fifth thousandth" and the latter claimed to be the "twenty-seventh thousandth." If these sales figures were correct, this represents a phenomenal accomplishment. The *Marysville Tribune* attributed this success to the labor of the women of the First Congregational Church and to Alfred and Estelle Wilcox, whose "invaluable services have been cheerfully given to aid the committee of ladies in this work. Capt. W. with his large business ability and skill aided greatly in pushing forward and perfecting the enterprise. Few of the church realize the debt of obligation which is due them."[76]

The Wilcoxes went all out to promote and sell the cookbook. Arrangements with other churches were made to sell copies and generate revenue for those churches. An article in the *Springfield Republic* reported that everyone should purchase a copy, "especially as the proceeds of its sale in this city are to go into the Parsonage fund of the First Presbyterian Church."[77] Another successful promotional technique was the development of a network of women agents who sold subscriptions as well as the cookbooks themselves. A card inserted in the second edition, titled "Paying Work for Women," stated: "This book was compiled and published by women, and, as a rule, women are employed as agents. We believe every one who obtains it will find it an indispensable help. And, for this reason, will feel an interest in giving it a wide circulation. The Publishers will consider it a great favor, if ladies who have the book and value it, will put them in correspondence with *bright, wide-awake women, who need work that will pay liberally, no matter in what part of the country they may live.* Such friends as want a copy of the book, may get it direct from us by remitting $1.75."

The establishment of a network of sales agents seems like a relatively serious endeavor just for the sale of a single cookbook. However, the vision of Alfred and Estelle was not limited to selling a single book. In August 1878 they launched *The Housekeeper* magazine in Minneapolis.[78] The agents recruited for *Buckeye Cookery* were also employed to sell subscriptions to the magazine. The publishers also continued to expand the agent network: they wanted "competent, wide-awake agents in every county in the United States, for this and other publications." They reported that women who had served as agents for two years made one hundred dollars per month selling subscriptions and the cookbook.[79] This network paid off. By 1884 the circulation for *The Housekeeper* had reached fifty thousand.[80] Subscriptions jumped to one hundred thousand by 1887.[81]

In addition to subscriptions to *The Housekeeper,* the Buckeye Publishing Company's network of agents sold other books, such as *The World's Cyclopedia or Library of Universal Knowledge; The Children's Hour; The Home: How to Make and Keep It* (by Mrs. H. W. Beecher);

Webster's Unabridged Dictionary; Huckleberry Finn; What Everyone Should Know; and *How to Get Well, Keep Well and Live Long.*[82] The *Housekeeper* advertised these books simultaneously with new editions of *Buckeye Cookery*. For instance, an 1879 advertisement reported that *Buckeye Cookery* was "The Queen of the Cook-Books." The advertisement reported that the cookbook had "blessed thousands of homes and will bless thousands more." It was "clear, full, common-sense, practical, suited to purses of plain people as well as the rich, and in every way a treasure to the housewife."[83] This reinforcing promotion and sales network greatly enhanced the success of the enterprise.

Another promotional technique used for *Buckeye Cookery* involved announcements sent out regularly to newspapers and magazines. These promotions were then published as news articles. For instance, in an article titled "What Cook Book Shall I Get?" the editors of *The Central Baptist* reported that *Buckeye Cookery* was a household treasure with nearly five hundred pages, containing over nine hundred cookery recipes originating with "scores of different practical housekeepers from all parts of the country." *The Central Baptist* went even further, with an endorsement: *Buckeye Cookery* was "indeed a *multum in parvo,* and all good wheat. Thus we have answered the question regarding cook books in a gratuitous puff, without fee or reward, but simply because we honestly think that we cannot better benefit our housekeeping readers than by drawing their attention to this labor and pocket saving work."[84] Of course, the Wilcoxes promptly reprinted this article in *The Housekeeper.*

Many other techniques were employed to sell *Buckeye Cookery*. To attract the German-speaking immigrants who were flooding into the Midwest, *Buckeye Cookery* was translated into German in 1880, successfully enough to warrant the publication of a second German-language edition in 1887. By this date, several American cookbooks had been translated to reach this audience, but this work was the first known German-language cookbook published in Minnesota.

The term *buckeye* disappeared from the fourth edition of the cookbook, titled *Practical Housekeeping: A Careful Compilation of Tried and Approved Recipes.* Reflecting the changing audience, the Wilcoxes noted at the beginning of this 1883 edition that "the first edition was published for a benevolent object, and necessarily had many purely local features. Since then this book has been four times revised and enlarged, and all its local features dropped, and with them now disappears that part of the title which identified the book with the state where it originated."[85]

Connected with this name change was the establishment of offices in Atlanta with L. A. Clarkson and Company, in Denver with Perry and Baldy, and in Chicago with H. J. Smith and Company. The Home Publishing Company maintained offices in Dayton and Minneapolis. In Chicago, Dayton, and Denver, the cookbook was published under its new title. In Atlanta, it was released under the title *The Dixie Cook-Book*. Since this was a "revised edition," there may well have been an earlier edition of this work that has not been located. According to the subtitle it was "largely supplemented by tested recipes of the more modern southern dishes, contributed by well-known ladies of the South," but, in reality, the work was an almost verbatim copy of *Practical Housekeeping*. The *Dixie Cook-Book* title was successful, for it was reprinted in 1885. A revised and expanded version, now titled the *New Dixie Cook-Book*, was published four years later, but the culinary content was virtually the same as in the earlier edition. This revised work was also successful and it was reprinted again in 1893.[86]

At least thirty-seven different printings of *Buckeye Cookery* are known to have been issued from 1876 to 1905.[87] Subsequent editions added and replaced recipes. Over the years, the "Centennial Governors" recipes were incorporated into the main section on cookery and an index was added. Old recipes were removed and new ones inserted. Some originated in published sources, such as Elizabeth Miller's *In the Kitchen* (Boston, 1875).[88] Subsequent editions contained recipes for bananas and for soda, both of which had been popularized at the Centennial Exposition in Philadelphia. As previously stated, banana recipes routinely appeared in cookbooks only after the beginning of the twentieth century.[89] Even more banana recipes graced later editions: baked bananas, bananas and cream, and banana pie. Finally, bananas were proclaimed as "the most nutritious of all fruits," which were "becoming more popular every year."[90] Likewise, subsequent editions featured recipes for making "Effervescing Soda" in the home. This was accomplished by combining powdered bicarbonate of soda with powdered tartaric acid. This soda had to be consumed immediately or stored in a bottle that was quickly corked.[91] *The Housekeeper* magazine generated new recipes as well. As Virginia M. Westbrook, author of the introduction to a later reprint of *Buckeye Cookery,* has pointed out, recipes "sent in by subscribers from all over the country, helped update revisions of the cookbook."[92]

New editions also added considerable material on noncookery matters. These added to an already voluminous work. The *Centennial Buckeye Cook Book* was 384 pages plus advertising. The second edition published in 1877 expanded to 464 pages. Most editions published after 1880 averaged between 536 pages and 688 pages. Some editions eventually counted a hefty 1,288 pages.

These revisions enhanced sales. By 1886 250,000 copies had been sold. By 1892 sales had jumped to 750,000. The 1894 edition, retitled *The Housekeeper Cook Book,* introduced a new concept in selling cookbooks. Copies were sold to businesses, which in turn sold them or gave them away to their customers. For instance, the New England Furniture and Carpet Company, "The One-Price House Furnishers" in Minneapolis, purchased copies of the cookbook and printed their name on the outside cover. Other companies did the same. Two years later another edition was released, this time with the title *The Original Buckeye Cook Book.* By 1900 more than a million copies had been distributed.[93] Still more copies were sold in 1904 and 1905. No other American cookbook came close to selling a million copies in the nineteenth century. As few other American books of any kind had sold more copies, the *Centennial Buckeye Cook Book* and its successor editions was one of the most widely distributed books in America.

THE FALL.

Despite his outward commercial success, Alfred Wilcox suffered business reverses and relinquished control of *The Housekeeper* during the early 1890s. What caused this commercial decline remains a mystery. According to his obituary, readers were assured that these reverses "never reflected upon his business ability or integrity" and that he was never "familiar with commercial dishonor in any form." Despite his loss of control of *The Housekeeper,* he remained active. From 1892 to 1895

Wilcox served as a department editor of *The Northwestern Agriculturist.* In the following year he served as editor of the St. Paul *Farmer.* He subsequently became the secretary of the State Live Stock Breeders' Association. In 1895 the Wilcoxes had moved to Clovercrest—a 360-acre farm three miles from Hugo, Minnesota. Alfred died peacefully in his sleep at Clovercrest on June 6, 1900, leaving Estelle and six children.[94]

After her husband's death, Estelle Wilcox continued to lead an active life. She managed Clovercrest, served as assistant editor for *The Housekeeper,* and produced the ninth edition of *Buckeye Cookery* in 1904. It highlighted two testimonials. One was from the aforementioned Cornelia Cole Fairbanks, whose husband was running for vice president. Cornelia announced that she had used the *Buckeye Cook Book* for years. In addition to the host of reliable cookery recipes, Cornelia also assured readers, there were "many suggestions in regard to sanitary matters and antidotes for accidental poisoning most valuable." She believed that "every new housekeeper should choose some good cook-book to aid her in doing well her work" and she cheerfully recommended "the famous Buckeye Cook Book." Cornelia signed the letter, addressed to Estelle, "Ever Your Friend." The other testimonial in the 1904 edition was from Julia B. Foraker, then living in Cincinnati. Julia was the wife of Joseph Benson Foraker, who had served as governor of Ohio from 1885 to 1889 and became a U.S. Senator in 1897. In her testimonial Julia Foraker affirmed that the *Buckeye Cook Book* deserved "a high place in the estimation of all housekeepers" and she heartily commended it.[95]

The 1905 edition, ironically titled *The Original Buckeye Cook Book,* contained few recipes published in the original *Centennial Buckeye Cook Book.* No contributor was identified for the recipes. The original work had been dedicated to those plucky women of 1876: this edition was dedicated "To those American Housewives who cannot afford to employ a French Cook." Times had changed, and this final edition of *Buckeye Cookery* partially reflected those changes. In the preface Estelle wrote: "Such wonderful progress has been made in invention and scientific discovery, that the day laborer now has at his command more of the conveniences and comforts of life than the Kings themselves possessed fifty years ago." She observed that "the luxuries of one decade became the necessities of the next. As living conditions improved, there were ever more demands upon time and simpler approaches were needed by housewives who needed to keep abreast of the latest and best information in her department of the family work." However, while Estelle understood that revolutionary changes were underway in American cookery, neither she nor *Buckeye Cookery* were a part of that revolution.[96]

The beginning of this culinary revolution can be traced to the same year in which the *Centennial Buckeye Cook Book* was published. In 1876 Ellen Richards offered unpaid lectures in chemistry at the Massachusetts Institute of Technology. Richards strongly advocated a scientific approach to cookery. Two individuals who shared her views were Mary Johnson Lincoln and Fannie Merritt Farmer. Lincoln, who had no professional experience in cooking or teaching, became—as already mentioned—principal of the Boston Cooking School after Maria Parloa declined the position. Lincoln was an able administrator and in time became a solid professional chef. Her cookery expertise was demonstrated in her book *Mrs. Lincoln's Boston Cook Book* (Boston, 1883). In keeping with the traditions set forth by Ellen Richards, Lincoln wrote in the preface that her book contained "all the chemical and physiological knowledge that is necessary for a clear understanding of the laws of health."[97] Lincoln left the Boston Cooking School to pursue lecturing and writing in 1884.

Carrie Dearborn succeeded Lincoln. One of Dearborn's students was Fannie Merritt Farmer. Upon completion of her two-year course of study, Farmer was appointed assistant principal of the Boston Cooking School. When Dearborn resigned owing to illness in 1893, Fannie Farmer became principal and commenced rewriting the school text originally developed by Mary Lincoln. She published several of her revisions in a cooking pamphlet *The Horsford Cook Book,* paid for by the Rumford Chemical Works in Providence, Rhode Island.[98] This experience perhaps convinced her to seek a publisher for her complete revised work. A publisher, Little, Brown, agreed to print the book provided that Farmer financially underwrite its expenses. It was a good investment. The book quickly exhausted its initial print run and was reprinted. When Fannie Farmer died in 1915, over 360,000 copies of this work and its subsequent editions had been printed. It was not until the 1930s that Farmer's *Boston Cooking School Cook Book* outsold the *Centennial Buckeye Cook Book*'s million copies. Ingrained in Farmer's work were the same "scientific principles" espoused by Ellen Richards and Mary Lincoln, except that Farmer went a few steps further. Like the chemist in the laboratory, Farmer emphasized exact measurements and she tried to eliminate imprecise language that had frequently accompanied recipes in other cookbooks.

While Farmer is properly credited with popularizing this approach, other writers preceded her in incorporating them into their cookbooks. For instance, the 1894 edition of *Buckeye Cookery*, retitled *The Housekeeper Cook Book*, defined heaping and level teaspoons, and other inexact measurements. Likewise, most recipes featured a list of ingredients at the beginning. This edition was published two years before Fannie Farmer's *The Boston Cooking School Cook Book*.[99] It is interesting to note that Estelle abandoned this approach in the 1896 edition, titled *The New Buckeye Cook Book*, and reverted to the original recipe structure.[100]

Unlike Estelle Wilcox, Fannie Merritt Farmer simplified her recipes and kept information to a bare minimum. As Laura Shapiro observed, "Miss Farmer's reliable instructions made it possible for even the least sophisticated housekeeper to serve *Bombe de Fillets de Fish à la Richelieu* if she could afford the ingredients." Using Fannie Farmer's cookbook, proponents proclaimed, anyone who could read could cook.[101] The success of such simplicity spelled the downfall of more complicated works, such as *Buckeye Cookery*, which, even when updated and revised, forever remained a part of the previous culinary epoch.

Despite the downfall of *Buckeye Cookery*, Estelle Wilcox survived and thrived. She lived to see the success of two of her important endeavors. The first was women's suffrage. As will be recalled, her graduation speech in 1872 had focused on women's suffrage. As ferment increased to give women the right to vote, Estelle secured the largest list of suffrage signatures in one Minnesota district. In 1920 the Nineteenth Amendment to the Constitution was ratified and women gained the right to vote. Estelle's second reformist success ultimately ended in failure. As previously mentioned, Estelle Wilcox supported the temperance movement. In 1910 she organized the Langford Park Women's Christian

Temperance Union office. The temperance movement reached its peak when Congress overrode President Woodrow Wilson's veto of the Volstead Act in 1919, which provided for the enforcement of the Eighteenth Amendment to the Constitution. The prohibition era spawned an unexpected crime wave throughout the United States. As a result, prohibition was repealed in 1933 with the passage of the Twenty-first Amendment to the Constitution.

Throughout this period Estelle Woods was active in Minnesota politics, and she campaigned for her son in his bid to win election to the Minnesota state legislature. Even as late as 1922, at the age of seventy-two, she was still very active and taught school on her own farm. She died in 1943 at the age of ninety-four.[102]

THE REINCARNATION.

Although *Buckeye Cookery* went out of print in 1905, it was not forgotten. Its excellence has been recognized by culinary historians, cookbook collectors, publishers, and people who like good food. Numerous copies survived. A copy of the second edition found its way to Texas, where Dorman H. Winfrey, the director of the Texas State Library, located it and encouraged its reprinting in 1970. According to Winfrey, *Buckeye Cookery* had a special fascination: it gave hours of pleasant browsing and brought forth "the memory of when and where one first tasted a special treat." The book also offered "the historian much useful commentary of the culture of the American past." Specifically, she pointed to the rural nature of America in the late nineteenth century, and to the state of the medical profession, agriculture, and trade. *Buckeye Cookery* offered the reader a document in social history, and for "the modern cook with a yen to produce authentic period dishes and a willingness to experiment," it offered "a guide to good cooking."[103] The reprint was so well received that it went through a second printing the following year.

Almost simultaneously, the 1879 edition was reprinted by the Willson Publishing Company of Lawndale, California. According to the publisher of this reprint, King Willson, *Buckeye Cookery* was "much more than a good and still useful cookbook"; it was "a glimpse into the past which helps us to see more clearly what we have become by showing us what we were." The compiler, said Willson, reflected "the most common facts of every day life" and expressed "the views and the values of her time." Willson believed that there was nothing "more striking about the book than this attitude toward life as compared to our own; especially the taking for granted of values which now, less than one hundred years later, are honored principally in rhetoric." Just what were these values? Willson reports that the compiler demonstrated "a cheerful, self assured, matter of fact accommodation to life evident throughout the book: a determined, self confident assumption that whatever comes can be handled by the means at hand." Willson identified these values as "consideration for others, thrift, self sufficiency, pride in ones [sic] work, resourcefulness, moderation."[104]

In 1975 Dover Publications came forth with an unabridged republication of the cookery sections of the 1883 edition under the title *The Buckeye Cookbook; Traditional American Recipes as Published by the Buckeye Publishing Company in 1883*. According to the publishers, *Buckeye Cookery* was "not just a historical document," but a "very rich book which achieved its success by imparting a gourmet flavor to many traditional American dishes." These recipes were "much superior to the versions found in general books either of its own period or today." There were hundreds, claimed Dover, "of recipes that can offer novelty from the past." The Dover edition excluded the preface, some illustrations, and much material not concerned with cooking. According to Dover the 1883 edition was the best edition of *Buckeye Cookery*, "which had the virtue of maintaining traditional recipes, yet offering them in very carefully stated versions that were modern in preparation." The Dover edition remains in print twenty-five years after its initial printing.[105]

As many editions were published in Minneapolis, *Buckeye Cookery* also reflected life in Minnesota during the late nineteenth century. Recognizing this significance, the Minnesota Historical Society reprinted the 1880 edition of *Buckeye Cookery* in 1988. This edition featured an excellent introduction by Virginia M. Westbrook. Her introduction was the first to place *Buckeye Cookery* within a historical context and accurately reflect the significance of the work. According to Westbrook, *Buckeye Cookery* started as a local fund-raising effort and ended as "one of the most popular publications in nineteenth-century America."[106]

The First Congregational Church of Marysville still stands. Its members still remember with pride the cookbook that paid for the church's completion and the building of the parsonage. The story of the *Centennial Buckeye Cook Book* survives in magazines and newspapers. Mark Shelton retold the story in a 1990 article in the *Ohio Magazine.* Shelton believed that *Buckeye Cookery* was "arguably the first Buckeye best seller." The book made for "marvelously diverting reading, equal parts surprise and dismay, with a dash of fascination, charm and amusement."[107]

Neither was the *Centennial Buckeye Cook Book* forgotten by the academic community. In 1996 Anne Bower, associate professor at Ohio State University at Marion, organized a series on cookbooks and an exhibit on cookery at the Ohio Historical Center. On April 13 a lecture in the series was held on "Buckeye Cooking: The Marysville Connection" at the First Congregational Church. Following the session, the participants car-pooled to the Ohio Historical Center in Columbus, where Anne Bower conducted a special tour of the exhibit, with a specific focus on the important influence that the *Centennial Buckeye Cook Book* has had on other community cookbooks in Ohio.[108] The session held at the First Congregational Church was led by Charles Thompson, whose father had been a supply minister of the First Congregational Church when he was born. Thompson had a particularly soft spot for the *Centennial Buckeye Cook Book:* he came into the world in the parsonage that the women of the church had constructed with proceeds from the sale of the cookbook.

The spirit of the *Centennial Buckeye Cook Book* lives on in this first reprint of the original edition. Long may the spirit of those plucky women of 1876 thrive!

NOTES.

Thanks to Charles Thompson, historian, First Congregational Church, Marysville, Ohio, for archival material and research for this introduction; Barbara Kuck, curator, Culinary Archives and Museum, Johnson and Wales University, Providence, Rhode Island, for extensive photocopying of Ohio cookbooks and permission to use their copy of *Centennial Buckeye Cook Book* for this reprint; Geoffrey Smith, head of

Ohio State University's Rare Book Division, Columbus; Barbara K. Wheaton, culinary historian, Cambridge, Massachusetts; and David Schoonover, curator of rare books, University of Iowa, Iowa City, for researching Ohio cookbooks. Further thanks to Anne L. Bower, associate professor, Ohio State University at Marion; Karen Hess, culinary historian, New York; and Virginia Westbrook, author of the introduction to the Minnesota Historical Society's reprint of *Buckeye Cookery*, for their willingness to review and comment on this introduction.

1. *Visitor's Guide to the Centennial Exhibition and Philadelphia 1876* (Philadelphia: J. B. Lippincott and Company, 1875), 16; *Frank Leslie's Illustrated Historical Register of the Exposition 1876* (New York: Frank Leslie, 1877), 219; Richard J. Hooker, *Food and Drink in America: A History* (Indianapolis/New York: Bobbs-Merrill Company, Inc., 1981), 232; Virginia Scott Jenkins, *The Fruit with A-Peel: The Impact of the Importation of Bananas on American Culture* (Washington, D.C.: Smithsonian Institution Press, forthcoming).

2. J. S. Ingram, *Centennial Exposition* (Philadelphia: Hubbard Bros., 1876), 758; *Frank Leslie's Illustrated Newspaper* 153 (November 18, 1876): 179, 186; *Frank Leslie's Illustrated Historical Register of the Exposition 1876*, 56, 210, 306. For more information about popcorn, see Andrew F. Smith, *Popped Culture: A Social History of Popcorn in America* (Columbia: University of South Carolina Press, 1999).

3. "Druggist Circular," as in *Confectioner's Gazette* 34 (August 10, 1913): 34, 36–37; John J. Riley, *A History of the American Soft Drink Industry. Bottled Carbonated Beverages 1807–1957* (Washington, D.C.: American Bottlers of Carbonated Beverages, 1958), 60–61; Hooker, *Food and Drink in America*, 273–74.

4. *National Cookery Book* (Philadelphia: Women's Centennial Committee, 1876); Ella Meyer's *The Centennial Cook Book and General Guide. Practical Receipts: Cookery, Remedies, Farm Hints, Events of the Last Century* (Philadelphia: J. B. Meyers, 1876); *The Centennial Buckeye Cook Book* (Marysville, Ohio: Congregational Church, 1876); "The Late Major A. G. Wilcox," *The Northwestern Agriculturist* 15 (June 15, 1900): 178.

5. Henry Howe, *Historical Collections of Ohio* (Cincinnati: Published for the Author, 1847), 495; *The History of Union County, Ohio*, 2 vols. (Chicago: W. H. Beers and Company, 1883), vol. 2: 3, 48.

6. The differences among the Church of England, the Presbyterians, and the Congregationalists originated in late sixteenth-century England. The Church of England had been established and supported by Henry VIII and Elizabeth I. During this period, many British Protestants were influenced by John Calvin's teachings. Out of this cauldron of religious ferment emerged the Puritans, who had a separate identity by 1565. Generally, the Puritans believed that scriptures were the only guide in all matters of faith and that individuals had the right to judge what the scriptures taught. Within the Puritan movement were the Separatists. Their congregations selected their pastors, whose responsibilities were limited to the jurisdiction of a single church. The

English Parliament passed acts aimed at banishing all those who refused to join in common prayer. In 1604 a group of Separatists were exiled to Holland and they formed a church in Leyden. The Separatists did not thrive in Holland, and many decided to move to Virginia. The group set sail from Holland, but due to problems, the vessels called at Plymouth, England. After overcoming several more difficulties, one vessel sailed for Virginia in 1620. By accident they established Plimouth Plantation in Massachusetts. Other Puritans followed the Separatists and settled in Massachusetts. In Great Britain, the principles advocated by the Puritans continued to percolate. They were particularly strong in Scotland and in northern Ireland. The differences in views between the Puritans and those who supported the monarchy resulted in armed conflict and the rise to power of Oliver Cromwell. In 1649 Parliament established Presbyterianism as the state religion. With the death of Cromwell this decree was revoked. This religious ferment encouraged many to leave Great Britain and settle in America.

7. E. W. Andrews, "Congregationalists," in I. Daniel Rupp, *An Original History of the Religious Denominations at Present Existing in the United States* (Philadelphia: J. Y. Humphreys, 1844), 184–205; John M. Krebs, "Presbyterian Church," in I. Daniel Rupp, *An Original History of the Religious Denominations at Present Existing in the United States* (Philadelphia: J. Y. Humphreys, 1844), 573–90.

8. Vergilius Ferm, ed., *An Encyclopedia of Religion* (New York: The Philosophical Library, 1945), 529, 541–52.

9. *Yearbook of the Congregational Church* (Marysville: n.p., 1901), 15–16.

10. *Yearbook of the Congregational Church*, 1901, 15–16.

11. *Manual of the Congregational Church of Marysville, Ohio* (Marysville, Ohio: Tribune Steam Press, 1877), 1, 19.

12. *The History of Union County*, vol. 2: 41.

13. Bertha E. Josephson, ed., "Ohio Recipe Book of the 1820s," *Mississippi Valley Historical Review* 36 (June 1949): 97–107.

14. Arnold Whitaker Oxford, *English Cookery Books to the Year 1850* (Oxford: Oxford University Press, 1913), 152; Eleanor Lowenstein, *Bibliography of American Cookery Books, 1742–1860* (Worcester: American Antiquarian Society, 1972), 22, 23, 25–26, 28, 30, 63, 70, 81, 86, 95, 100, 118, 122–23; Katherine Bitting, *Gastronomic Bibliography*, reprint (London: Holland Press, 1981), 299.

15. G[eorge] Girardey, *Höchst nützliches Handbuch über Kochkunst* (Cincinnati: F. U. James, 1842).

16. William A. Craigie and James R. Hulbert, eds., *A Dictionary of American English on Historical Principles*, 4 vols. (Chicago, Ill.: University of Chicago Press, 1938–44), vol. 1: 334; Frederic G. Cassidy, ed., *Dictionary of American Regional English*, 3 vols. (Cambridge, Mass.: Belknap Press of Harvard University Press, 1985), vol. 1: 416–17; J. E. Lighter, ed., *Random House Historical Dictionary of American Slang*, 3 vols. (New York: Random House, 1994), vol 1: 285.

17. *The History of Union County*, vol. 2: 101–2; Henry Howe, *Historical Collections of Ohio*, vol. 2: 707–8.

18. Elizabeth Ray, *Alexis Soyer Cook Extraordinary* (Lewes, South Sussex: Southover Press, 1990), 43–49.

19. In the same year that Alexis Soyer printed the *Poor Man's Regenerator,* the "New York Associates for improving the condition of the poor" published *The Economist; or Plain Directions about Food and Drink with the Best Modes of Preparation.* It contained instructions "to the poor on living on limited incomes," but it was apparently not a book sold to generate money for them or other charitable causes. See Margaret Cook, *America's Charitable Cooks: A Bibliography of Fund-Raising Cook Books Published in the United States (1861–1915)* (Kent, Ohio: n.p., 1971), 173; Lowenstein, *Bibliography of American Cookery Books,* 66.

20. Margaret Cook noted only four cookbooks published during the Civil War. No evidence was presented by Cook to indicate that the *Confederate Receipt Book* was published to raise funds for war relief. The second work, *Camp Cookery and Hospital Diet,* consisted of recipes borrowed almost verbatim from *Soyer's Culinary Campaign* (London, 1857). *Camp Cookery* was "inscribed to the Union Defence Committee of New York," but no evidence was offered indicating that it was sold for the benefit of charity. The third work, Annie Wittenmyer's *A Collection of Recipes for the Use of Special Diet Kitchens,* was dedicated to James G. Yeatman, president of the Western Sanitary Commission, but the aim of the author was to write "a manual, adapted to the circumstances, necessities, and peculiarities of diet kitchen cookery." No evidence is present in the booklet indicating that it was sold for the financial benefit of a charitable cause. The fourth work cited by Cook was Maria J. Moss's *A Poetical Cook-Book,* whose dedication reads: "When I wrote the following pages, some years back at Oak Lodge, as a pastime, I did not think it would be of service to my fellow-creatures, for our suffering soldiers, the sick, wounded, and needy, who have so nobly fought our country's cause, to maintain the flag of our great Republic, and to prove among Nations that a Free republic is not a myth. With these few words I dedicate this book to the Sanitary Fair to be held in Philadelphia, June, 1864." Cook concluded that this dedication meant that the cookbook was sold for the financial benefit of the Sanitary Fairs. Her conclusion is arguable. A dedication to a sanitary fair or to someone engaged in charitable work does not necessarily mean that the revenues from the sale of the works were given to charity. A fifth Civil War cookbook not cited by Cook was Joseph H. Riley's *The Volunteer's Cook-book: for the Camp and March* (Columbus, 1862), similar to those cookery pamphlets issued in Iowa and New York. What is clear is that Civil War cookbooks differed dramatically from the charitable works that emerged around 1870—five years after the end of the Civil War. See Cook, *America's Charitable Cooks,* 7, 77–78, 173, 222, 258; Maria J. Moss, *A Poetical Cook-Book* (Philadelphia: Caxton Press of C. Sherman, Son and Company, 1864), and reprint (New York: Arno Press of the New York Times Company, 1972), preface; Mrs. Annie Wittenmyer, *A Collection of Recipes for the Special Diet Kitchens in Military Hospitals,* reprint (New York: J. M. Carrol and Company, 1983), introduction; *Confederate Receipt Book* (Richmond: West and Johnson, 1863) and reprint (Athens: University of Georgia Press, 1989).

21. Cook, *America's Charitable Cooks*, 40, 71, 106, 131.

22. [Fannie D. Jermain, comp.], *Tried and True Recipes: The Home Cookbook* (Toledo: Toledo Commercial Company, 1874), 33, 34, 40, 47, 74, 75, 77, 90, 107.

23. Several members of the First Congregational Church in Columbus submitted recipes for the *Centennial Buckeye Cook Book*. What the relationship, if any, between the two cookbooks is unknown, since the *Congregational Cook Book* published in Columbus has not been located.

24. Anne Bower, *Recipes for Reading: Community Cookbooks, Stories, Histories* (Amherst: University of Massachusetts, 1997), 1–2.

25. *Marysville Tribune*, July 5, 1876, p. 1; *Marysville Tribune*, August 30, 1876, p. 3.

26. *Minneapolis Tribune*, June 20, 1876, p. 1.

27. Estelle Woods Student Card, Ohio Wesleyan University Historical Collections; Mary Dillon Foster, comp., *Who's Who among Minnesota Women: A History of Woman's Work in Minnesota from Pioneer Days to Date, Told in Biographies, Memorials and Records of Organizations* (N.p.: The Author, 1924), 344.

28. Reynold Webb Wilcox, *Wilcoxson-Wilcox, Webb and Meigs Families* (New York: National Historical Society, 1938), 89.

29. "The Late Major A. G. Wilcox," 178.

30. *The History of Union County*, vol. 2: 43–44.

31. *Ohio Wesleyan Magazine* 21 (October 1943): 27.

32. *Marysville Tribune*, April 8, 1874, p. 1.

33. *Marysville Tribune*, March 20, 1878, p. 1.

34. *Centennial Buckeye Cook Book*, 139, 379.

35. *Manual of the Congregational Church of Marysville, Ohio*, 22; Foster, *Who's Who among Minnesota Women*, 344.

36. *Centennial Buckeye Cook Book*, 28, 30, 31, 37, 39, 42, 48, 49, 51, 60, 107.

37. *Centennial Buckeye Cook Book*, 33, 35, 39, 50, 81, 94, 97, 130, 177, 182, 194, 266, 168.

38. *Centennial Buckeye Cook Book*, 46, 136, 145.

39. *Centennial Buckeye Cook Book*, 41, 73, 79, 82, 200, 221, 224.

40. *Centennial Buckeye Cook Book*, 24, 25, 27, 45, 53.

41. Frank Fowler, ed., *History of Milwaukee* (Chicago: Western Historical Society, 1881), 1425–26.

42. *Centennial Buckeye Cook Book*, 32, 34, 41, 51, 52, 53, 97, 127, 168, 169, 173, 221, 253, 281.

43. *Centennial Buckeye Cook Book*, 34, 84, 134–35, 147–48, 231, 300.

44. *Centennial Buckeye Cook Book*, 26, 29, 49, 60, 87, 101, 168, 219, 223, 253.

45. *Marysville Tribune*, April 8, 1874, p. 3; *The History of Union County*, vol. 2: 57, 116, 138; *Centennial Buckeye Cook Book*, 100, 114.

46. *Centennial Buckeye Cook Book*, 300; *The History of Union County*, vol. 2: 16–18.

47. *Centennial Buckeye Cook Book*, 230; *The History of Union County*, vol. 2: 19; Bessie Beal, ed., *Ohio Wesleyan University Alumni Directory 1846–1927* (Columbus, Ohio: Stoneman Press, 1928), 351.

48. *Centennial Buckeye Cook Book,* 311.

49. *Centennial Buckeye Cook Book,* 304, 305.

50. *Centennial Buckeye Cook Book,* 83, 92.

51. *Buckeye Cookery,* 1877, 229.

52. *Centennial Buckeye Cook Book,* 126, 145, 161, 186; Edward T. James, ed., *Notable American Women 1607–1950,* 3 vols. (Cambridge, Mass.: The Belknap Press of Harvard University Press, 1971), vol. 3: 16–17; Mary Anna DuSablon, *America's Collectible Cookbooks: The History, the Politics, the Recipes* (Athens: Ohio University Press, 1994), 62.

53. M[aria] Parloa, *The Appledore Cook Book,* 2nd ed. (Boston: Graves, Locke, and Company, 1878), 77.

54. *Centennial Buckeye Cook Book,* 90, 256, 272, 278, 291, 297.

55. *Centennial Buckeye Cook Book,* 184–88.

56. *Centennial Buckeye Cook Book,* 141.

57. *Centennial Buckeye Cook Book,* v.

58. *Centennial Buckeye Cook Book,* vi.

59. *Centennial Buckeye Cook Book,* 381.

60. *Centennial Buckeye Cook Book,* 186–87; Marion Harland [Pseud. for Mary Virginia Terhune] , *Common Sense in the Household: A Manual of Practical Housewifery* (New York: Charles Scribner's Sons, 1871), 444–46.

61. For more information about ketchup, see Andrew F. Smith, *Pure Ketchup: The History of America's National Condiment* (Columbia: The University of South Carolina Press, 1996).

62. *Centennial Buckeye Cook Book,* 139, 140, 234.

63. For more information about tomatoes, see Andrew F. Smith, *The Tomato in America: Early History, Culture and Cookery* (Columbia: University of South Carolina Press, 1994). For more information about tomatoes in Ohio, see Alexander Livingston, *Livingston and the Tomato with a Preface and Appendix by Andrew F. Smith,* facsimile (Columbus: Ohio State University Press, 1998).

64. The earliest recipe for "Saratoga Potatoes" I've found appears in Ladies of the Congregational Church, *Grand Rapids Receipt Book,* New Edition (Grand Rapids, Mich.: H. M. Hinsdill, 1873), 29; Artemas Ward, *The Grocer's Encyclopedia* (New York: James Kempster Company, 1911), 503.

65. *Centennial Buckeye Cook Book,* 49, 77–78, 236–37.

66. Amelia Simmons, *American Cookery,* A Facsimile of the First Edition with an Essay by Mary Tolford Wilson (New York: Oxford University Press, 1958), 54; Amelia Simmons, *American Cookery,* 2nd ed. (Albany: Charles and George Webster, 1796) and facsimile with an introduction by Karen Hess (Bedford, Massachusetts: Applewood Books, 1996), xiii–xiv, 43.

67. *Centennial Buckeye Cook Book,* 383–84; Susannah Carter, *The Frugal Housewife* (Philadelphia: James Carey, 1796), 23, 25, 58, 101.

68. *The History of Union County,* vol. 2: 146.

69. *Centennial Buckeye Cook Book,* 68–69, 78, 193, 231.

70. *Centennial Buckeye Cook Book,* 379–80.

71. *Marysville Tribune,* July 5, 1876, p. 1.

72. *Cincinnati Gazette,* as in the *Marysville Tribune,* August 30, 1876, p. 3.

73. Foster, *Who's Who among Minnesota Women,* 344.

74. Minutes of the First Congregational Church, Marysville, Ohio, dated July 6, 1877.

75. *The History of Union County,* vol. 2: 41.

76. *Marysville Tribune,* March 20, 1878, p. 1.

77. *Springfield Republic,* as quoted in the *Marysville Tribune,* March 20, 1878, p. 3.

78. The early issues of *The Housekeeper* have not been located, and may not have survived. Several secondary sources claim that it was launched in 1877. While it is possible that a specimen edition was published at this time, no copies have been located. All evidence indicates initial publication during the following year. Foster, *Who's Who among Minnesota Women,* 344.

79. *The Housekeeper* 2 (September 1, 1879): 16.

80. *The Housekeeper* 5 (January 1884): 14.

81. "Death of Major Wilcox," *Farm, Stock and Home* 16 (June 15, 1900): 243.

82. *The Housekeeper* 8 (February 1885): 16.

83. *The Housekeeper* 2 (September 1, 1879): 16.

84. *The Central Baptist,* as quoted in *The Housekeeper* 1 (April 1, 1879): 14.

85. [Estelle Woods Wilcox, comp.], *Practical Housekeeping: A Careful Compilation of Tried and Approved Recipes* (Minneapolis: Buckeye Publishing Company, 1883), publisher's note.

86. [Estelle Woods Wilcox, comp.], *The Dixie Cook-Book; Carefully Compiled from the Treasured Family Collections of Many Generations of Noted Housekeepers; Largely Supplemented by Tested Recipes of the More Modern Southern Dishes, Contributed by Well-known Ladies of the South,* rev. ed. (Atlanta: L. A. Clarkson and Company, 1883); [Wilcox], *The Dixie Cook-Book,* rev. ed. (Atlanta: L. A. Clarkson and Company, 1885); [Wilcox], *The New Dixie Cook-book and Practical Housekeeper, Carefully Comp. From the Treasured Family Collections of Many Generations of Noted Housekeepers,* rev. and enl. ed. (Atlanta: L. A. Clarkson and Company, 1889); [Wilcox], *The New Dixie Cook-book and Practical Housekeeper,* rev. and enl. ed. (Atlanta: Dixie CB Pub. Company, 1893).

87. For complete bibliographical information, see appendix II.

88. *Buckeye Cookery and Practical Housekeeping,* 1880, 28, 35; Elizabeth S. Miller, *In the Kitchen* (Boston: Lee and Shepard; New York: Lee, Shepard, and Dillingson, 1875), 292–93.

89. *Buckeye Cookery and Practical Housekeeping,* 1877, 136, 280; Jenkins, *The Fruit with A-Peel.*

90. [Estelle Woods Wilcox, comp.], *The Original Buckeye Cookery and Practical Housekeeping* (Chicago: Trade Supplied by Reilly and Britton Company, St. Paul, Minn.: Webb Publishing Company, 1905), 279, 293, 294.

91. [Wilcox], *The Original Buckeye Cookery and Practical Housekeeping*, 190, 196.

92. Virginia M. Westbrook, "Introduction to the Reprint Edition," in Estelle Woods Wilcox, ed., *Buckeye Cookery and Practical Housekeeping: A Nineteenth-Century Best Seller* (St. Paul: Minnesota Historical Society Press, 1988), xi.

93. "The Late Major A. G. Wilcox," 178.

94. "The Late Major A. G. Wilcox," 178; "Death of Major Wilcox," 243; *Ohio Wesleyan Magazine* 21 (October 1943): 27.

95. Estelle Woods Wilcox, comp., *The New Buckeye Cook Book. A Revised and Enlarged Edition of Practical Housekeeping. A Careful Compilation of Tried and Approved Recipes for All Departments of the Household*, 9th ed. (St. Paul, Minn.: Webb Publishing Company, 1904), n.p.

96. [Estelle Woods Wilcox, comp.], *The Original Buckeye Cookery and Practical Housekeeping*, 1905, 5.

97. Mary J. Lincoln, *Boston Cooking School Cook Book* (Boston: Roberts Brothers, 1887); reprint with introduction by Janice Longone (Mineola, New York: Dover Publications, Inc., 1996), xv.

98. Fannie Merritt Farmer, *The Horsford Cook Book* (Providence, R.I.: Rumford Chemical Works, 1895).

99. [Estelle Woods Wilcox, comp.], *The Housekeeper Cook Book* (Minneapolis: Housekeeper Publishing Company, 1894), 11.

100. One possible explanation for this shift is that Estelle Wilcox did not compile the 1894 edition. Her husband did have financial losses during this period and he was obligated to give up control of *The Housekeeper* magazine. Perhaps others revised *Buckeye Cookery*, incorporating these changes without Estelle's involvement. Subsequent editions are copyrighted by Estelle Wilcox, but not this 1894 edition.

101. Laura Shapiro, *Perfection Salad: Women and Cooking at the Turn of the Century* (New York: Henry Holt and Company, 1987), 37–43, 106–26.

102. Foster, *Who's Who among Minnesota Women*, 344; *Ohio Wesleyan Magazine* 21 (October 1943): 27.

103. Estelle Woods Wilcox, comp., *Buckeye Cookery and Practical Housekeeping*, facsimile reproduction of the 1877 edition with introduction by Dorman H. Winfrey (Austin, Texas: Steck-Warlick Company, 1970), n.p.

104. [Estelle Woods Wilcox, comp.], *Buckeye Cookery and Practical Housekeeping, Compiled from Original Recipes* with a publisher's introduction by King Willson (Lawndale, California: Willson Publishing Company, 1971), n.p.

105. Estelle Woods Wilcox, comp., *The Buckeye Cookbook; Traditional American Recipes as Published by the Buckeye Publishing Co, 1883* (New York: Dover Publications, Inc., 1975), n.p.

106. Virginia M. Westbrook, "Introduction to the Reprint Edition," in Wilcox, ed., *Buckeye Cookery and Practical Housekeeping*, 1988, vii–xxiii.

107. Mark Shelton, "Buckeye Cookery," *Ohio Magazine* 13 (August 1990): 45–47.

108. Press release dated March 5, 1996, Ohio State University at Marion.

CENTENNIAL

BUCKEYE

COOK BOOK,

COMPILED BY

THE WOMEN

OF THE

First Congregational Church,

MARYSVILLE, OHIO.

———————— ◆ ————————

"Bad dinners go hand in hand with total depravity, while a properly fed man is already half saved."

———————— ◆ ————————

MARYSVILLE :
J. H. SHEARER & SON.
1876.

TO THE

PLUCKY HOUSEWIVES

OF 1876,

*WHO MASTER THEIR WORK INSTEAD OF ALLOWING
IT TO MASTER THEM,*

THIS BOOK IS DEDICATED.

PREFACE.

The compilation of this new candidate for the favor of housekeepers, was begun as a labor of love in the interest of a weak and struggling church, with little expectation that it would reach its present proportions, but the women of the church, who had the work in hand, met a most kind and generous response from friends in every part of the country, and soon found themselves in possession of material for a book, fuller, more complete and practical, and better adapted to the wants of the average American housewife than any previous work. This material, made up as it was of choice bits of the best experience of hundreds who have long traveled the daily round of household duties, they found to be of the greatest interest to themselves as practical housekeepers, and believing it would equally interest and benefit all who came into possession of it, they determined to arrange, classify and publish it in a more convenient and substantial form than was at first intended, primarily, of course, in the interest of their beloved church, but scarcely less, they believe, in the interest of their sister housewives.

The work of compiling has been done in time snatched from other duties, and the one aim has been to express ideas as clearly and concisely as possible, and to arrange all with especial reference to convenience, following so far as possible the simple order of the alphabet. The instructions which precede the recipes of each department, have been carefully made up and are entirely trustworthy, and the recipes themselves are new to print, well endorsed, and, it is believed, invaluable to young or old housekeepers. Several new features have been introduced, which though not belonging strictly to cookery, bear such close relations to it that the fitness of their appearance in the connection is evident. The very full tables of time and measures, and the articles

3

on Housekeeping, Marketing, Carving, The Sick Room, The Laundry, Hints to the Well, and the Medical and Floral departments will be found quite as suggestive as the pages which precede them.

There has been no attempt at display or effect, the only purpose being to make a thoroughly simple and practical work. In the effort to avoid the mistakes of others, greater errors may have been committed, but the work is submitted just as it is to the generous judgment of those who consult it, with the hope that it may lessen their perplexities, and stimulate that just pride without which work is drudgery and great excellence impossible.

CONTENTS.

BREAD.

Instructions—Sponge—Bread—Coffee Bread—Light Yeast Bread —Milk Yeast Bread—Poor Man's Bread—Salt Rising Bread— Yeast Bread—Buckeye Brown Bread—Brown Bread—Eastern Brown Bread—Graham Bread—Steamed Corn Bread—Boston Corn Bread—Mrs. B.'s Corn Bread—Corn Cake—Corn Bread   15–27

BREAKFAST AND TEA CAKES.

Instructions—Breakfast Cake—Buns—North Carolina Buns—Buttered Toast—Breakfast Toast—Minnonite Toast—Milk Toast— Mrs. Gould's Drop Cakes—Lucy's Pop Overs—Pocket Books— Rusk—South Carolina Biscuit—Soda Biscuit—Superior Biscuit— Spoon Biscuit—Sally Lunn—American House Rolls—Cream of Tartar Rolls—Common Rolls—French Rolls—Nice Rolls—Philadelphia Rolls—Rolls—Wedding Sandwich Rolls—Crumpets— Muffins—Quick Waffles—Waffles—Egg Crackers—Buckwheat Short Cake—Centennial Biscuit—Corn Rolls—Cushman Cake— Corn Mush—Johnny Cake—Rhode Island "Spat Outs"—Graham Biscuit—Mrs. Buxton's Graham Gems—Graham Gems—Gems without sour milk—Muffins—Rye or Graham Drop Cakes—Biscuit for Dyspeptics—Graham Mush—Graham Muffins   27–40

FRITTERS.

Instructions—Apple Fritters—Clam Fritters—Corn Oysters— Cream Fritters—Cucumber Fritters—Fritters—Snow Fritters— Vanities   40–42

GRIDDLE CAKES.

Instructions—Buckwheat—Bread—Breakfast—Batter—Crumb— Flannel—Indian—Rice—Soft Short—Tomato Batter   42–44

YEAST.

Instructions—Dry—Hop—Potato—To Hasten Milk Yeast   45–47

CAKE.

Instructions—Centennial—Buckeye—Almond—Black—Breakfast
—Bread—Cream—Cider—Corn Starch—Coffee—Cup—Car-
amel—Cincinnati—Delicate—Salem Election—Old Hartford
Election—Apple Fruit—Fruit Loaf—Farmer's Fruit—Poor Man's
Fruit—Scotch Fruit—Thanksgiving Fruit—Feather—Fig—
Grove—Hard Money—Hayes—Hoosier—Hickory Nut—Impe-
rial—Lady—Yellow Lady—Lemon—Raised Loaf—Loaf—Aunt
Hettie's Loaf—Minister's—Marble—Marbled Chocolate—One
Egg—Orange—Peach—Plain—Citron Pound—Measured Pound
—Pyramid Pound—White Pound—Queen Vic—Sponge—Sheri-
dan—Spice—Snow—Tea—Ten Minute—Tilden—Watermelon
—Wedding—White   48–69

LAYER CAKES.

Instructions—Almond—Almond Cream—Boston Cream—French
Cream—Ice Cream—Tip-Top Cream—Cocoanut—Caramel—
Cooper—Chocolate—Just Splendid Custard—Hard Times—
Lady Fingers—Lemon—Minnehaha—Neapolitan—Orange—
Rolled—Ribbon—Snow—Velvet Sponge—Vanity—Washington
—White Mountain   69–76

FROSTING.

Instructions—Almond Frosting—Boiled Frosting—Frosting—Frosting with Gelatine—Frosting without Egg—Hickory Nut Frosting
—Ornamental Frosting—Yellow Frosting   77–79

CRULLERS AND DOUGHNUTS.

Instructions—Crullers—Fried Cakes—Albert's Favorite Doughnuts
—Raised Doughnuts—Sponge Doughnuts   79–81

COOKIES AND JUMBLES.

Instructions—Ada's Sugar Cakes—Cookies—Lemon Snaps—Molasses Cookies—Nutmeg Cookies—Peppernuts—Sand Tarts—
Cocoanut Jumbles—Rich Jumbles   81–82

GINGER BREAD.

Instructions—Aunt Molly's Ginger Bread—Ginger Bread—Excellent Soft Ginger Bread—Sponge Ginger Bread—Ginger Cookies— Ginger Crackers—Ginger Cakes—Best Ginger Drops—Ginger Puffs—Ginger Snaps—Hotel Ginger Snaps   82–85

CREAMS AND CUSTARDS.

Instructions—Charlotte Russe—Hamburg Cream—Italian Cream— Rock Cream—Tapioca Cream—Velvet Cream—Whipped Cream —Blanc Mange—Raspberry Blanc Mange Mont Blanc—Apple Custard—Apple Snow—Chocolate Custard—Corn Meal Custard —Floating Island—Flummery—Good Baked Custard—Lemon Custard—Rice Custard—Spiced Chocolate—Snow Flake   86–92

CONFECTIONERY.

Instructions—Centennial Drops—Buckeye Kisses—Almond Maca- roons—Buckeye Butter Scotch—Canellons—Chocolate Caramels —Chocolate Drops—Cocoanut Caramels—Cocoanut Drops— Everton Ice Cream Candy—Graham Cakes—Hickory Nut Taffy —Hickory Nut Macaroons—Lemon Candy—Molasses Candy— Pyramid of Cocoanut Drops—Pop Corn Balls—Peanut Candy— Sugared Calamus, or Sweet Flag—Sugared Pop Corn   93–98

CANNING FRUITS.

Instructions—Blackberries—Green Gooseberries—Peaches or Pears—Peaches—Pine Apples—Peaches—Strawberries—Corn —Sweet Corn—Tomatoes in Stone Jugs—Tomatoes— Watermelon   99–105

CATSUP AND SAUCES.

Instructions—Cucumber—Currant—Cherry—Gooseberry—To- mato—Bread Sauce—Cranberry—Celery—Curry Powder— Chili Sauce—Drawn Butter—Holland Sauce—Oyster Sauce— Onion Sauce—Parsley Sauce—Roman Sauce—Salad Sauce—To Prepare Mustard   106–111

DRINKS.

Instructions—Coffee and Tea—Coffee with Whipped Cream—Co- coa—Chocolate—Cider—Grandmother's Harvest Drink—Lem- onade—Lemon Syrup—Apple Tea—Iced Tea   112–116

EGGS.

Instructions—Boiled Eggs—Baked Eggs—Eggs on Toast—Egg Gems—Frizzled Ham and Eggs—Omelet—Corn Omelet—Omelet Souffle—Puff Omelet—Poached Eggs—Rumbled Eggs 117–121

FISH.

Instructions—Fried, Baked and Boiled—Brook Trout—Fish Balls —Croquettes of Fish—Fish Chowder—Katy's Codfish—Baked Herring 122–125

FRUITS.

Instructions—Ambrosia—Iced Currants—Mock Strawberries— Peach Pyramid 126–128

GAME.

Instructions—Broiled Pheasant, Squirrels and Prairie Chickens— Partridge Pie—Prairie Chickens—Roast Quails—Roast Haunch of Venison 129–132

ICES AND ICE CREAM.

Instructions—Chocolate Ice Cream—Ice Cream—Lemon and Orange Ice Cream—Pine Apple Ice Cream—Mrs. Watson's Ice Cream —Apple Ice 133–136

JELLIES AND JAMS.

Instructions—Apple and Blackberry—Currant—Cranberry—Grape —Lemon—Quince—Crabapple—Wild Crabapple—Wine— Blackberry Jam—Currant—Gooseberry—Raspberry—Strawberry 137–141

MEATS.

Instructions—Broiled Beefsteak—Fried Beefsteak—Beefsteak Toast —Beefsteak Smothered in Onions—Boiled Corn Beef—Beef a la Mode—Boiled Fresh and Salt Beef Tongue—Ragout Beef—Roast Meat with Pudding—Frizzled Beef—Fried Liver—Toad-in-the-Hole—Mutton Chops—Boiled Leg of Mutton—Roast Leg of Mutton—Fricatelli—Boiled Ham—Broiled Ham—Delicious Fried Ham—Mixed Sandwiches—Spare Rib Pot-Pie—Pig's Feet Sauce —Pork Head-Cheese—Fried Salt Pork—Yankee Pork and Beans

—Sausage—Canned Sausage or Tenderloin—Fried Veal Cutlets—
Pate de Veau—Roast Loin of Veal—Veal Stew—Veal Sweetbread   142–153

OYSTERS.

Instructions—Escaloped Oysters—Fried Oysters—Oyster Fritters
—Oyster Patties—Oyster Short Cake—Oyster Pie   154–156

PASTRY.

Instructions—Aunty Phelps' Pie Crust—Apple Pie—Apple Meringue—Dried Apple—Sliced Apple—Cream—Crumb—Cocoanut—Combination—Custard—Lemon—Mince Meat—Mock
Mince—Pie-Plant—Dried Peach—Potato—Pumpkin—Bina's
Strawberry Short Cake—Orange Short Cake—Cream Tarts   157–164

PUDDINGS AND SAUCES.

Instructions—Apple Roley Poley—Boiled Apple Dumplings—
Birdnest—Bread—Batter—Cottage—Corn Starch Morange—
Fannie's Pudding—Fruit—Fig—Green Corn—Boiled Indian—
Jelly—Kiss—Lemon—March—Orange   Souffle—Plum—Pop
Corn—Quick Puff—Rice—Sago and Apple—Suet—Transparent
—Apple Tapioca—Grandma Thompson's White Pudding—Bread
Pudding Sauce—Cream—Every Day—Lemon   165–173

PRESERVES.

Instructions—Cherry—Pear—Peach—Quince—Tomato—Watermelon Rind—Apple Butter—Lemon Butter—Peach Marmalade
—Mrs. Cooper's Marmalade—Dried Apple Sauce   174–178

PICKLES.

Instructions—Chow Chow Pickles—Chow Chow—Cauliflower
Pickle—Cucumber Pickles—Chopped and Sliced Pickles—Man-
goes, Nasturtions and Peppers—Pickled Chicken—Pickled Oysters
—Pickled Onions—Piccalilli—Pyfer Pickles—Spanish Pickles—
Pickled Cucumbers—Spiced Currants—Pickled Grapes—Spiced
Grapes—Spiced Gooseberries—Muskmelon Pickles—Peach Pick-
les—Pear and Apple Pickles—Euchered Plums—Pickled Raisins
—Sweet Tomato Pickles—Pickled Walnuts or Butternuts—Water-
melon Pickles   179–188

POULTRY.

Instructions—Baked Chickens—Boned Chicken—Chicken or Beef Croquettes—Broiled Chicken or Quails—Chickens for Lunch—Chicken Pot-Pie—Chicken Pie—Chicken Pie with Oysters—Dressing for Chicken—Fried Spring Chicken—Fried Gumbo—Jellied Chicken—Roast Turkey—Roast Turkey with Oyster Dressing—English Roast Turkey   189–197

SALADS.

Instructions—Sidney Smith's Winter Salad—Cabbage Salad—Chicken Salad—Cucumber Salad—Ham Salad—Herring Salad—Tomato Salad—Salad Dressing—Cream Dressing for Cold Slaw—Dressing for Lettuce—Cream Slaw   198–201

SOUPS.

Instructions—Clam—Beef and Noodle—Grandmothers' Bean—Green Corn—Green Pea—Mock Turtle—Oyster—Pot au Feu—Tomato—Turkey—Veal—Vermicelli   202–208

VEGETABLES.

Instructions—Asparagus—A Good Boiled Dinner—Beets and Young Beet Greens—Baked Beets—String and Shelled Beans—Bina's Stewed Corn—Dried Corn—Drying Corn—Preserving Corn—Boiled Cauliflower—Stuffed Cabbage—Stewed Cabbage with Egg and Fried Cabbage—Egg Plant—Italian Macaroni—Macaroni—Boiled and Fried Onions—Boiled and Baked Potatoes, Baked and Steamed Sweet Potatoes—Fricassee of Old Potatoes and Fried Potatoes—Fried Raw Potatoes—Mashed Potatoes—New Potatoes—Potato Cakes—Saratoga Potatoes—Baked Parsnips—Green Peas—Peas Stewed in Cream—How to boil Rice—Salsify—Summer Squash—Winter Squash—Succotash—Baked Tomatoes—Mother's Sliced Tomatoes—Stewed Tomatoes—Tomatoes in Brine—Tomato Toast—Turnips   209–220

CENTENNIAL GOVERNORS.

Lemon Custard—Soda Biscuit—Potato Pudding—Rice Cake—Buford Cake—Salad Dressing—To keep Cut Roses Fresh—Veal Loaf—Isinglass Jelly—Silver Cake—French Pickle—Cup Cake—Maine Sponge Cake—Good Bread—Orange Pie—Christmas Plum Pudding—Black Cake—White Sponge Cake—Delicious

Pumpkin Pie—Orange Cake—Iced Plum Pudding—Charlotte Russe—Lemon Ice—Enchilidas—Spice Cake—Snow Custard   221–228

TABLE OF WEIGHTS AND MEASURES.

Cooks' Table—Liquids Avoirdupois—Liquid Measure   229

COOKS' TIME TABLE.

Mode of Preparation—Time of Cooking—Time of Digestion   230–231

BILLS OF FARE.

Spring Breakfast, Dinner and Supper—Summer Breakfast, Dinner and Supper—Autumn Breakfast, Dinner and Supper—Winter Breakfast, Dinner and Supper—Lunch No. 1 and 2—Tea for Company —Economical Breakfast No. 1 and 2—Economical Dinner No. 1, 2, 3, 4, 5, 6 and 7   232–233

FRAGMENTS.

How Mother makes Hash—After Thanksgiving Dinner—Always Save—Sweet Pickles—A Crumb of Bread—Stuffed Beefsteak— How to make nice Gravy—The care of Fat and Drippings   234–237

HINTS FOR THE SICK ROOM.

Instructions—Arrow Root Custard—Alum Whey—Beef Tea—Barley Water—Chicken Broth for Sick—Egg Gruel—Fever Drink— Graham Gems for Invalids—Jellies—Mulled Buttermilk—Milk Porridge—Oat Meal for the Sick—Panada—Raspberry Vinegar— Raspberry Relish—Currant Shrub—Sassafras Drink—Toast Tea —Tamarind Whey—Vegetable Soup—Wine Whey—Wheat Gruel—Excelsior Blackberry Wine   238–243

HINTS FOR THE WELL.

Instructions—A Dyspeptic's Fight for Life   244–246

HINTS ABOUT MARKETING.

Beef—Veal—Mutton—Lamb—Pork—Turkey—Geese—Ducks— Fowls—Pheasants—Quails—Pigeons—Prairie Chickens—Plover—Woodcock—Snipe—Venison—Fresh Fish—Salt Fish— Smoked Fish—Wood   247–251

HOW TO CUT AND CURE MEATS.

The Divisions of the Hind and Fore Quarters of Beef, Veal, Pork and Mutton—Brine for Beef, Tongue, Hams and Pickled Pork—To Cure Hams—To Keep Hams   252–254

CARVING.

Turkey—Chickens—Partridges—Sirloin of Beef—Shoulder of Mutton—Ham—Leg of Mutton—Tongue—Haunch of Venison—Loin and Fillet of Veal—Breast of Veal—Fish   255–257

HOUSEKEEPING.

As an Accomplishment—The Model House and the care of it—The Parlor—The Sitting Room—The Dining Room—The Bed Room —The Guest Chamber—The Kitchen—House Cleaning—General Suggestions—Housekeeper's Alphabet   258–269

THE LAUNDRY.

Instructions—Prof. Liebig's Washing Fluid—Soap for Family use—Bluing—Flour Starch—To make Fine Starch—Enamel for Shirt Bosoms—How to do up Shirt Bosoms—To Wash Flannels—To Wash Blankets—To Wash Lace Curtains—To Wash Thread Lace —To Wash a Silk Dress—Gall Soap—To Prevent Blue from Fading—To Bleach Muslin—Brown Linen—To clean articles made of White Zephyr   270–276

FLORAL.

My Morning Glories—House Plants—To keep Plants without a fire at night—Window Gardening—Sure Shot for Rose Slugs—Another—To Prepare Autumn Leaves and Ferns—To Prepare Skeleton Leaves—Drying Flowers—To Crystalize Grasses—To make a Rustic Flower Stand—To Protect Dahlias from Earwigs—To Clear Rose Trees from Blight—To Free Bedding Plants from Leaf Lice—An excellent Shading for a Green House   277–282

FARM AND GARDEN.

Apples—The Cherry—Pears—The Quince—To Raise Plants of Currants and Gooseberries—To Prevent Mildew on Gooseberry Bushes—The Raspberry—Remedy for the Plum Curculio—To Prevent Rabbits from Eating the Bark of young Fruit Trees—Protecting Cabbage from Worms—To Raise Celery—How to Raise

Indian Corn—Remedy for Smut in Wheat—The Horse—Good
Feed for Horses—For Colic in Horses—For Wounds in Horses, for
Botts in Horses, Loss of Appetite in Horses—Cure for Bloat in
Calves and Horses—If Cows give Bloody Milk—Choked Cattle—
Lice on Cattle—Hog Cholera—To Kill Ticks on Sheep—To Cure
Grub in Sheep—To Cure Foot Rot in Sheep—Chicken Cholera—
Gapes in Chickens—To Remove Lice on Fowls—Chicken Feed—
To Prevent Cats Killing Chickens   283–291

MEDICAL.

Antidotes to Poison—Diphtheria—Scarlet Fever—Cholera Mixture
—Pig's Feet Oil—Cure for Corns—Good Croup Remedies—
Constipation—Sure Cure for Cholera Infantum—Blackberry Cor-
dial—Eye Wash—For Sore Mouth in Nursing Babies—Golden
Ointment for Salt Rheum, Scald Head and Catarrh—Healing Salve
—Itch Ointment—Salve for Cuts and Burns—Liniment—Salt
Rheum—Tetter Ointment—Teas—For Sore Throat—To Prevent
a Child Coughing at Night—To Prevent Taking Cold—To Cure a
Felon—To Stop Bleeding at the Nose—To Stop Bleeding—
Whooping Cough—To Remove Warts—Cure for Wounds from
Rusty Nails—To Remove Cinder from the Eye   292–299

MISCELLANEOUS.

Canary Birds—Teeth—Cutting Teeth—Queen Bess Complexion
Wash—Cologne Water—Clean Hair Brushes—Boston Bernett
Powder—For Chapped Hands, Face or Lips—Indelible Ink—
Magic Furniture Polish—To Clean Silverware Easily—To Make
Rag Rugs—To Destroy Weeds in Walks—To Keep away Moths—
To Preserve Books—Black for Woolens—Unfermented Wine for
Communion—To Press Satin—To Press and Clean Black Silk—
To take out Mildew—Cement for Mending Stone Jars, etc., Cement
for attaching Metal to Glass, Cement for China, To Paste Paper on
Tin, Cement for Horn, Pearl, Shell and Bone—Lightning Cream
for Clothes or Paint—Cochineal Coloring   300–305

HIT AND MISS.

Baking   Powder—Bread—Soda   Biscuit—Cranberries—Japanese
Paperware—Maryland Biscuit—Lebanon Rusk—Sauer Kraut—
To Keep Butter Fresh—Clover Vinegar   306–307

THE FRUGAL HOUSEWIFE.

Title Page—To Roast Venison—A Fowl or Turkey Roasted with Chestnuts—To Jug Pigeons—A Steak Pudding   308–310

ILLUSTRATIONS.

Hind and Fore Quarter of Beef—Veal—Pork—Mutton—Sirloin of Beef—Shoulder of Mutton—Ham—Leg of Mutton—Tongue—Haunch of Venison   252–257

ADVERTISEMENTS.

Duryea's Starch—Delaware Fence Co.—The Independent—Way's Clothes Wringer—Landis' Clothes Horse—The Christian Union —Dr. E. F. Townsend—Domestic Steam Engine—St. John's Sewing Machine—W. H. Robinson—Hitt, White & Mitchell—Robinson Bros. & Co.—Housekeeper's Companion—Union County Journal—Harrison Kitchen Safe—John H. Gause & Co.— Whiteley, Fassler & Kelly—Smith & Curtis—The Congregationalist—Mrs. A. H. Sells—Freemans, Staley & Morton—Woods, Weeks & Co.—C. G. & E. W. Crane—Gillet's Cream Yeast— Prof. Wm. B. Tarr—W. Z. Evans—Halm, Bellows, & Butler—Buchan's Carbolic Soap—Jas. C. Dunn—Pocket Cook Stove—L. M. Baker—J. Landon—J. H. Shearer & Son—Mrs. C. S. Ogden— F. O. Pierson—R. Brandriff—C. M. Ingman—W. E. Baxter—Leroy Decker—Morey & Son—N. S. Long—O. M. Scott—B. Newlove—H. W. Morey, D. D. S.—McCloud & Bro.—Mahncke, Muchlenbruch & Co.—S. L. Irwin—Robinson & Robinson— S. McCampbell & Son—Marysville Butter Tub and Spoke Co— Morse Bros.—Lever Spring Bed Co.   311–333

THE BUCKEYE COOK BOOK.

BREAD MAKING.

"All that a man hath will he give for his life;" and yet thousands are daily robbed of half life's worth because its *staff* is so unsuitably prepared. There is no one thing upon which the health and comfort of a family so much depend as light, sweet, tender bread; and the only kind that is good for the health, and at the same time acceptable to the palate, is the well-raised, home-made loaf. The coarsest fare is acceptable and appetizing with good bread, but the most luxurious table is not even tolerable without it. If for breakfast you have light crisp rolls, for dinner, spongy, sweet bread, and for supper, flaky raised biscuit, the bill of fare will be excellent the year round. Although bread making seems a simple process, it requires delicate care and watchfulness, and a thorough knowledge of all the contingencies of the process, dependent upon the different qualities of flour, the varying kinds and conditions of yeast, and the change of seasons—(as the process of raising bread in winter makes it sour in summer.) There are many little things in bread making which require accurate observation, and though you may have valuable recipes and well defined methods in detail, nothing but experience will secure the name merited by so few, though earnestly coveted by every practical, sensible housekeeper,—"an excellent bread-maker." Three things are indispensable to success,—good flour, good yeast, and watchful care. Good flour adheres to the hand, and, if pressed, shows the impress of the lines of the skin. Its tint is cream white; never buy that which has a blue-white tinge. Poor flour is not adhesive, can be blown about easily, and sometimes has a dingy look, as though mixed with ashes. Never use flour without sifting, and you will find a large tin or wooden pail with a tight fitting cover, kept full of sifted flour, a great convenience. All kinds of flour and meal, except buckwheat and Graham, need sifting, and all except wheat flour should be bought in small quantities as they become damp and musty by long standing.

THE SPONGE.

This is made from warm water or milk, yeast and flour, (some add mashed potatoes,) mixed together in proper proportions. In summer, care must be taken not to set sponge too early, at least not before nine or ten o'clock in the evening. Make up a rather thick batter of flour and tepid water or milk; scald the latter to prevent souring, and cool before using; add yeast, cover closely, and place to rise on the kitchen table. In very hot weather, sponge can be made with cold water. In winter, mix the batter with very warm water or milk, (blood warmth, 98°, testing it with the finger, and making it as warm as you can bear); stir in the flour, and this will cool it sufficiently for the yeast. Cover closely and place in a warm and even temperature. A good plan is to fold a clean blanket several times and cover over, providing the sponge is set in a very large crock or jar, so that there is no danger of its rising and running over. As a general rule, one small teacup of yeast and three pints of "wetting" will make sponge enough for four ordinary loaves. A very excellent sponge, (especially for winter use), is made with mashed potatoes, as follows: peel and boil four or five medium sized potatoes in two quarts of water; (it will boil down to one quart); when done, take out, press through a colander, or mash very fine in the crock in which you make your sponge; make a well in the center, into which put one cup of flour, and pour over it the boiling water from the potatoes; stir thoroughly, and when cool, add a pint of tepid water, flour enough to make a *thin* batter, and a cup of yeast. This sponge makes very moist bread. In all sponges, add the yeast last, being sure that it will not scald; when placed to rise, always cover closely. Many think it an improvement to beat the sponge thoroughly, like batter for a cake. All the various sponges are very nice baked on a griddle for breakfast cakes, or, better still, in muffin rings. When used in this way, add a little salt and make your sponge rather thick.

TO MAKE YOUR BREAD.

Always be

"Up in the morning early, just at the peep of day,"

in summer time to prevent the sponge becoming sour by too long standing, and in winter to be getting materials warmed and in readiness for use. A large, seamless tin dish pan with handles and a tight-fitting cover, kept for this purpose alone, is better than a wooden bowl for bread. It should be thoroughly washed and scalded every time it is used. Measure and sift the flour. It is convenient to keep two quart cups, one for dry and the other for liquid measuring. In winter, always warm the flour and also the sponge. Put the flour in bread pan, make a large well in the center, into which pour your sponge, adding a small handful or two level teaspoons salt, (this is the quantity for four loaves of bread); mix well, being careful not to get the dough too stiff; turn out on your bread board; rub your pan clean, and add the "rubbings" to the bread. Knead for fully twenty minutes, or until your dough ceases to stick to either bread or pan. The process of kneading is very important. Some good bread makers knead with the palm of the hands until the dough is a flat cake, then fold once, repeating this operation until the dough is perfectly smooth and elastic; others close the hands and press hard and quickly into the dough with the fists, dipping them into the flour when the dough sticks; or, after kneading, chop with the chopping knife and then knead again; others still knead with a potato masher, thinking it a great saving of strength. No exact directions can be given, but experience and practice will secure the desired results. After the bread is thoroughly kneaded, form into a round mass or large loaf; sprinkle the bread pan well with flour, and having placed the loaf in it, sprinkle flour lightly on the top, cover, and set to rise in a warm temperature; let it rise well this time, say from one to two hours, owing to the season of the year. Place again on the bread board, knead lightly,—that is, with elastic movements, five minutes, and again form into one large loaf, return to pan, and let rise, not so long this time. Then knead down in the pan, cut into equal parts, place one at a time on the board, mould each into a smooth, oblong loaf, and put one after another into a well greased baking pan, and set to rise. In moulding, do not leave any lumps or loose flour adhering to the outside, but mould until the loaves are perfectly smooth. No particular directions can be given in regard to the time bread should stand after it is moulded and placed in the pans, because here is the point where observation and discretion are so indispensable. In hot weather when the yeast is very good and the bread very light, it must not stand over fifteen minutes before placing to bake. If it is cold weather and the yeast is less active, or the bread not perfectly raised, it may sometimes stand an hour in the pans without injury. When it is risen in the pans so as to seam or crack, it is ready for the oven; if it stands after this it becomes sour, and even if it does not sour it loses its freshness and sweetness, and becomes dry sooner by long standing. Bread, like cider, undergoes three fermentations: the saccharine or sweet fermentation; the vinous, when it smells something like foaming beer; and if you would have good, sweet bread, you must never let it pass this change, because if you do, the third or acetous fermentation takes place. This last can be remedied by adding soda in the proportion of one teaspoon to each quart of wetting; or, which is the same thing, a teaspoon to four quarts flour; but your bread will not be nearly so nutritious and healthful, and you have lost some of the best elements of the flour. Always add salt to all breads, biscuits, griddle cakes, etc.; *never* salt your sponge. A small quantity of white sugar is also an improvement to all bread dough. Bread should always be mixed as *soft as it can be handled.*

TO BAKE YOUR BREAD.

And here is an important point, for the bread may be perfect thus far, and then spoiled in baking. No definite rules can be given that will apply equally well to every stove, but one general rule must be observed, which is to have a steady, moderate heat, such as you will find more minutely described in the directions for baking large cakes. The oven must be just hot enough; if too hot, a firm crust is formed before the bread has expanded enough, and it will be heavy. Many test the oven by sprinkling a little flour on the bottom; if it browns very quickly it is too hot, but if it browns gradually it is just right. An oven in which you cannot hold your hand longer than to count twenty moderately, is hot enough for bread. When loaves are done, (to test which, break apart, press the bread gently with the finger, if it is elastic it is done, if clammy, not done, and must be returned to the oven,) wrap in a coarse towel or bread cloth, and stand on the edge of the loaf until cool; if by accident or neglect the bread is baked too hard, rub the loaves over with butter, wet the towel in which they are wrapped, and cover with another dry towel. In the winter, bread dough may be kept sweet several days either by placing it where it will be cold without freezing, or by putting it down deep into the flour barrel, so that it may be entirely excluded from the air, (beef suet will also keep in this way.) When wanted for use make into bread, or by adding the proper ingredients, make into cake, rusks, biscuit, apple dumplings, chicken pie, etc.

GRAHAM AND CORN BREAD.

It is very desirable that every family should have a constant supply of bread made of unbolted flour, or rye and Indian corn. Most persons find it palatable, and it promotes health. For these coarse breads, always add a little brown sugar or molasses. Thus made, they rise quicker and in a less warm atmosphere than without this sweetening. A little lard or butter always improves bread or cakes made of Indian meal, rendering them light and tender. Graham bread bakes slower than wheat, and corn requires more time to bake than either. In cutting the latter while warm, hold the knife perpendicularly. Rye is said to absorb more moisture from the air than any other grain; hence, all bread from this meal needs a longer application of heat, and keeps moister after being baked than that made from other grain. Corn bread requires a hot oven.

BREAD SPONGE.
S. A. M.

Five pints of warm water, five quarts of sifted flour, one coffee-cup yeast; mix in a two gallon stone jar, cover over tight and set in a large tin pan, so that if sponge rises over the top of jar the drippings may fall in the pan. Set to rise the evening before baking. In winter be careful to set in a warm place.

BREAD.

Sift six quarts flour in a pail; pour your sponge into your bread-pan or bowl, add two tablespoons salt, then the flour gradually, mix and knead well. This first kneading is the most important, and should occupy at least twenty minutes, (nearly all the flour will be used in mixing up and first kneading.) Make the bread in one large loaf and set away in a warm place to rise, cover with a cloth, and it ought to rise in half an hour; knead thoroughly again for ten minutes, take enough dough for three good sized loaves, (a pint bowl of dough to each loaf); give five minutes kneading to each loaf, and place to rise in a dripping-pan well greased with lard. The loaves will be light in five or ten minutes, and will bake in a properly heated oven in half an hour. Take the remaining dough, make a well in the centre into which put one-half teacup white sugar, one teacup lard, and two eggs, mix thoroughly with the dough, and knead into one large loaf; set in a warm place about fifteen minutes to rise. When light knead five minutes and let rise again, (this time it ought to be light in ten minutes.) Take out of bread-pan and knead on bread-board, and roll about an inch in thickness; cut out with a biscuit cutter and place in dripping-pan; let rise five minutes and bake twenty minutes. This makes ninety biscuits.

BREAD.
M. C. M.

The evening before baking, bring to a boil as much buttermilk as will wet the bread you wish to make. Have ready a large spoonful of flour in a crock, to which add the buttermilk. Let it stand till sufficiently cool, then add half a cup of yeast, and flour to make a thick batter; the better and longer you stir the sponge, the whiter will be your bread. In the morning sift your flour in bread pan, pour the sponge in the centre, stir in some of the flour, and let stand until after breakfast; then mix, kneading for about half an hour, the longer the better; when light, mould into loaves, this time kneading as little as possible. The secret of good bread is having good yeast, and not baking too hard.

BREAD.
Mrs. Clara Morey.

Pare and boil four or five potatoes, and mash fine, then add one pint of flour, pour on this boiling water enough to moisten well, then about one quart of cold water, after which add flour enough to make a stiff batter. When sufficiently cold or "scarcely milk warm," put in one-half pint (or more will do no harm) of yeast, and let it stand in a warm place over night; in the morning add to this sponge one cup of lard, then stir in flour and knead well; the more kneading the finer and whiter the bread will be; pounding also with a potato masher improves the bread greatly, and is rather easier than so much kneading. When quite stiff, well worked and pounded, let it rise again, and when light, make into loaves or biscuit, adding no more flour except to flour the hands and board—merely enough to prevent the bread from sticking. Let it rise again, then bake, and immediately after taking from the oven wrap in a wet towel until partly cold, in order to soften the crust. If *yeast* and *flour* are good (*essentials* in all cases) the above process will make good bread.

BREAD, (IN SUMMER.)
Mrs. D. Buxton.

Take three pints cold or tepid water, four tablespoons yeast, one teaspoon salt; stir in flour enough to make a thick sponge, (rather thicker than griddle cakes.) Let stand until morning, then add more flour, mix stiff, and knead ten minutes; place in pan, let rise until light, knead for another ten minutes; mould into four loaves, and set to rise, (don't let it get too light); bake in moderate oven one hour. If you mix your bread at six o'clock in the morning, ought to be through baking at ten o'clock.

BREAD, (IN WINTER.)

Take one pint buttermilk (or clabbered milk) let it scald, (not boil); make a well in the centre of your flour into which turn the hot milk, add one teaspoon salt, and enough flour and water to make sufficient sponge; let stand until morning, then prepare your bread as above. This is more convenient to make in winter, since you need a hot fire to heat the milk.

COFFEE BREAD.
S. A. M.

When doing up your Saturday's baking, take some of your biscuit dough, roll it very thin, put in a baking pan, and let it rise until light; then roll a few crackers fine, (bread crumbs or stale cookies are nice to roll up and mix with the cracker,) rub some butter and sugar together, mix with the cracker, and spread or sprinkle on top of the dough,—let it rise until light, then pour over the top about one-half teacup sweet milk or cream, and sprinkle cinnamon over the whole,—put in the oven at once, and bake about twenty minutes. Nice to have warm for your Saturday's dinner.

LIGHT YEAST BREAD.

Take good sized potatoes, peel, boil and mash, pour on to them one quart of boiling water, strain the whole through a sieve; when this is milk-warm add one cup of yeast, one tablespoon of white sugar, one tablespoon of salt, and three quarts and a half of flour; beat well with a spoon and set in a warm place to rise, when well risen, take pint of flour, put part of it on kneading board, then turn the dough upon the board; add one tablespoon of lard; knead twenty minutes using the pint of flour. Let this dough rise one hour, then form into loaves; do not have more than one pint of dough in a loaf; let the loaves rise forty minutes, and bake forty-five minutes. Bread made this way cannot be excelled.

MILK YEAST BREAD.
Mrs. W. A. James.

Put into a pail holding two quarts and a half, one pint of new milk, one pint of boiling water, mix with this one tablespoon of sugar, one of salt, and three pints of flour; beat this well together, and cover tightly. Set this pail into another pail or kettle, with water enough to come nearly to the top of it; to have the water of the right temperature, let half of it be boiling and half cold. Set it where it will keep about the same temperature until risen. You must be particular about this. Beat the batter as often as once in every half hour until the last hour, when it must not be disturbed: it will rise in about five hours. When it is risen enough the pail will be full; put two quarts of flour into a pan, and make a well in the middle of it: dissolve a teaspoon of soda in a little hot water, and when the batter is risen just enough, turn it into the middle of the flour, and pour the dissolved soda in with it; knead well and make into loaves. Set them where they will be warm and let them rise forty-five minutes; bake in a quick oven. It will take nearly a pint of flour to knead the bread on the board. This bread makes the nicest dry toast and sandwiches. It is the most difficult to make of all kinds, but is the best of all.

POOR MAN'S BREAD.
Mrs. D. B.

One pint butter milk or sour milk, one level teaspoon soda, a pinch of salt, and flour enough to make as stiff as soda biscuit dough; cut into three pieces; handle as little as possible; roll an inch thick; place in your dripping pan, and bake twenty or thirty minutes—when done, wrap in a bread cloth; eat while warm, breaking open just as you would a biscuit; bake in a hot oven. Each cake will be about the size of a pie.

SALT RISING BREAD.
Mrs. Col. Moore, Hamilton.

Take two quarts new sweet milk, warm, add flour and mix into a batter; set in warm water, (to get the right temperature take half boiling and half cold water,) in a warm place to rise; keep an even heat, (pretty warm); when light the first time, (usually in about three or four hours), thicken by stirring in flour until you have a stiff batter; let rise again; when light, take flour enough for six or seven loaves, mix with warm milk, (sweet,) or water, add one good tablespoonful of salt, one each of lard and white sugar, and a little soda; mould into loaves as rapidly as possible or it will become too cool; bake well, keep in a pure atmosphere, and you have a good bread which never sours.

YEAST BREAD.
Mrs. W. A. J.

Make a well in the middle of four quarts flour, into which turn one tablespoon sugar, one of salt, and one cup of yeast; then mix with one pint of milk which has been warmed with one pint of boiling water; add one tablespoon lard; knead well and let it rise over night; in the morning knead again, and make into loaves. Let them rise one hour, and bake fifty minutes. Water can be used instead of the pint of milk, in which case, use twice as much lard.

BUCKEYE BROWN BREAD.
Mrs. W. W. Woods.

One cup each of corn, rye and Graham meal. The rye meal should be as fine as the Graham. Use a coffee cup for measuring. Heap the cup before sifting, then sift all together, (the three kinds), as closely as possible. Two cups Porto Rico molasses, two cups sweet milk, one cup sour milk, one dessert spoon soda, one teaspoon salt; beat all together thoroughly, pour into a tin form and place in a kettle of boiling water, and steam four hours. Boil as soon as mixed. It may appear to be too thin, but it is not, as this recipe has never been known to fail. Serve warm, with your Thanksgiving turkey. The bread should not quite fill the form, (or a tin pail with cover will answer,) as it must have room to swell. See that the water does not boil up to the top of the form; also take care it does not boil entirely away or stop boiling. To serve it, remove the lid and set it a few moments into the open oven, so as to dry the top of the loaf; then it will turn out in perfect shape. This bread can be used as a pudding, and served with a sauce made of thick *sour* cream, well sweetened and seasoned with nutmeg; or, it is good toasted the next day.

BROWN BREAD.
Mrs. W. A. James.

One pint of rye or Graham meal; one pint of Indian meal; one cup of molasses; three-fourths cup of sour milk; one-half teaspoon soda; one and one-half pints of cold water. Steam this four hours and then brown it over in the oven.

BROWN BREAD.
Mrs. F. W.

One quart warm water, teacup of yeast; stir in Graham flour to make sponge; when risen, add a tea cup of molasses, with one-half teaspoon soda. Make as stiff as soft gingerbread, and put right in the pans.

BROWN BREAD.
Mrs. D. Bassett, Minneapolis, Minn.

Two and one-half cups sour milk and one-half cup molasses; into these put one heaping teaspoon soda, two cups corn meal, one cup Graham flour and one teaspoon salt. Use coffee cups. Steam three hours,— better steamed longer.

EASTERN BROWN BREAD.
Mrs. C. F.

One quart of rye meal, two quarts of Indian meal; scald the Indian meal; one-half teacup molasses, two teaspoons salt, one teaspoon soda, one teacup of yeast; make it as stiff as can be stirred with a spoon, mixing with warm water; let it rise all night; then put it all in a large pan and smooth the top with the hand dipped in cold water; let it stand a short time; bake five or six hours; if put in the oven late in the day let it remain in all night.

GRAHAM BREAD.
Mrs. Clara Woods Morey.

Take one and a half pints of tepid water, add one heaping teaspoon of salt and one-half cup of sugar; stir in one half pint or more of the sponge made of white flour, as in my rule for white bread; then add Graham flour until almost *too stiff to stir;* put it in the baking pan; let it rise well, which will take about two hours; then bake in a moderate oven; when done, wrap in a wet towel until cool.

GRAHAM BREAD.
Mrs. H. B. Sherman, Plankinton House, Milwaukee, Wis.

Take a little over a quart of warm water, one-half cup brown sugar or molasses, one-fourth cup hop yeast, and one and a half teaspoons salt. Thicken the water with unbolted flour to a thin batter; then add sugar, salt and yeast; then stir in more flour until quite stiff. In the morning add a small teaspoon soda, and flour enough to make the batter stiff as can be stirred with a spoon; put it into pans; let it rise again; then bake in even oven, not too hot at first; keep warm while rising; smooth over the loaves with a spoon or knife dipped in water.

GRAHAM BREAD.
Mrs. J. H. S.

Make the sponge up in the evening as late as you can conveniently, in the following proportions: three pints Graham flour, one cup molasses, one quart warm water; pour the molasses on the flour, rinse the cup with the water, and pour it in gradually, beating well; then add a small cup good yeast—well stirred in, and in Winter set in warm place to rise; in Summer this does not matter. In the morning add a dessertspoon of salt, and stir in Graham flour until the spoon will stand alone; pour in pans and set to rise in a warm place, but do not get it too light, as brown bread does not require to rise as long as white. Have fire enough when put in the oven to complete the baking; a fresh blaze will burn the crust while a steady fire will sweeten it.

STEAMED CORN OR GRAHAM BREAD.
Mrs. Jennie Guthrie Cherry, Newark.

Two cups corn meal, two cups Graham flour, two cups sour milk, two-thirds cup molasses, one teaspoon soda; steam two hours and a half.

BOSTON CORN BREAD.
Mrs. Canby, Bellefontaine.

One cup sweet milk, two cups sour milk, two-thirds cup of molasses, one cup flour, four cups corn meal, two teaspoons soda; steam three hours, then brown a few minutes in the oven.

MRS. B.'S CORN BREAD.

One quart sour milk, three eggs, two tablespoons lard or butter (or half and half), one tablespoon sugar, a pinch of salt, handful of wheat flour, and enough corn meal, (sifted,) to make a good batter, (not too stiff—not nearly so stiff as for Graham gems;) then add one level teaspoon soda, stir thoroughly, and bake in long dripping pan.

CORN CAKE.
M. E. Wilcox, Madison.

Three cups buttermilk, one-half cup cream, two-thirds cup sugar, two eggs, one-half cup flour, one-half teaspoon salt, three and a half teaspoons soda, corn meal enough to make a batter as thick as ordinary cake. Bake in round tins or gem-irons. Corn meal requires a hotter oven than flour.

CORN CAKE.
Mrs. H. B. Sherman.

One pint corn meal sifted, one pint flour, one pint sour milk, two eggs beaten light, one-half cup sugar, piece of butter size of an egg; add, the last thing, one teaspoon soda in a little milk; add to the beaten egg the milk and meal alternately, then the butter and sugar. If sweet milk is used, add one teaspoon cream-tartar; bake twenty minutes in a hot oven.

CORN BREAD.
Mrs. J. H. S.

Take one pint buttermilk, and one quart corn meal, one teaspoon soda, one teaspoon salt, one tablespoon sugar and three eggs; have the stove very hot, and don't bake in too deep a pan. We use the dripping pan; and we think, of all the corn bread we ever tasted, this is the best.

BREAKFAST AND TEA CAKES.

To make biscuits take a part of the dough left from bread making, when it is ready to mould into loaves, work in the lard, and any other ingredients desired, such as butter, eggs, sugar, spice, etc., also using a little more flour; let rise once, then mix down and let rise again; turn out on the bread board; knead a few minutes, roll, and cut out with a biscuit cutter or mould with the hand. Place in a well-greased dripping-pan, and when light, bake in a quick oven from fifteen to twenty minutes. To make them a nice color, wet them over the top with warm water just before placing in the oven. To glaze them, brush lightly with milk and sugar, or the well beaten yolk of an egg sweetened, with a little milk added.

Biscuits may be baked in eight minutes by making the oven as hot as can be without burning them and allowing it to cool off before they are taken out; this makes them very light—but one has to watch them to keep them from being scorched. Any kind of bread or pastry mixed with water requires a hotter fire than if mixed with milk.

If you wish biscuit for tea at six, begin to mould two hours before, which will give ample time for rising and baking. If you want American House rolls for breakfast at eight, you must be up at five to get them ready. Many persons think it unnecessary to knead down either bread or biscuit, as often as we have directed, but if attention is given to the dough at the right time, and it is not suffered to become *too light,* it will be much nicer, whiter and of a finer texture if these directions are followed.

Soda biscuit must be handled as little and made as rapidly as possible; mix soda and cream tartar or baking powder in the flour, so that the effervescence takes place in the mixture; one teaspoon soda and two of cream tartar, or three teaspoons baking powder, to every three pints of flour, is about the right proportion; bake in a quick oven as soon as made. Gems of all kinds require a hot oven, but the fire should be built sometime before they are put into the oven and allowed to go down by the time they are light, as the heat necessary to raise them will burn them in baking if kept up.

Soda and raised biscuit, bread or cake when stale can be made almost as nice as when fresh by plunging for an instant into cold water, then placing in a pan in the oven ten or fifteen minutes; but thus treated they should be used immediately.

Waffle irons should be heated, then buttered or greased with lard, and one side filled with batter, then closed and laid on the fire or placed on the stove, and after a few minutes turned on the other side; they take about twice as long to bake as griddle cakes. Muffins are baked in muffin rings. In eating them, do not cut but break them open.

BREAKFAST CAKE.
Miss M. E. W.

When yeast bread is ready to knead from the sponge, knead and roll out three-fourths of an inch thick, put thin slices of butter on the top, sprinkle with cinnamon, then with sugar; let rise well and bake.

BREAKFAST CAKE.

Two cups sweet milk; four even cups of flour; two eggs; half cup sugar; two teaspoons melted butter; three teaspoons cream tartar and two teaspoons soda.

BUNS.
Mrs. James.

Break one egg into a cup and fill with sweet milk; half cup yeast, half cup butter, one cup sugar, enough flour to make a soft dough; flavor with nutmeg. Let it rise till it is very light, then mould into biscuit with a few currants. Let them rise a second time in the pan; bake, and when nearly done, glaze with a little molasses and milk. Use the same cup for each measure. The size is immaterial.

NORTH CAROLINA BUNS.
Mrs. Hattie Clemmens, Ashville, N. C.

One cup butter, four cups flour, one cup sour milk, three cups sugar, one teaspoon soda dissolved in the milk, four eggs, one tablespoon wine or brandy, raisins, citron and nutmeg to your taste; bake in long tin pans and cut in slices.

BUTTERED TOAST.

Although this toast is so commonly used, few know how to prepare it nicely. Beat one cup of butter, and three tablespoons flour to a *cream,* pour over this one and a half pints *boiling* water; place over a kettle of *boiling* water, for ten minutes; cut bread in thin slices, toast *brown,* and dip into the butter, etc. Serve hot.

Or, dip each slice of toast in boiling hot water, (slightly salted,) spread with butter, cover and keep hot.

BREAKFAST TOAST.
Mrs. Dr. M.

Add to one-half pint of sweet milk, two tablespoons of sugar, a little salt and a well-beaten egg; dip in this slices of bread, (if dry, let it soak a minute,) and fry on a buttered griddle until it is a light brown on each side. This is a good way to use dry bread.

MENNONITE TOAST.
Mrs. J. P. R.

Three eggs well beaten and stirred in half pint of milk with a little salt; dip into it thin slices of stale bread, and fry in hot lard like doughnuts.

MILK TOAST.
Mollie E. Fisher.

Cut some bread in thin slices, and toast nicely on each side; take one quart of sweet milk, and a half teaspoon of salt; place in a vessel and let it come to a boil; then add a large tablespoon of flour dissolved in some milk, and one tablespoon butter; dip the toast in this until it is saturated; place in a dish, and pour over it the remaining gravy.

MRS. GOULD'S DROP CAKES.

Two eggs, three teacups of milk, three and a half teacups flour, one tablespoon melted butter, two tablespoons maple sugar, little salt; mix all together except the last cup of milk, which add last of all. Do not beat the eggs separately.

LUCY'S POP OVERS.
W. A. J.

Two teacups sweet milk, two teacups flour heaped a little, butter size of a walnut, two eggs, one tablespoon sugar, a little salt.

POCKET BOOKS.
Mrs. J. H. S.

Warm one quart of new milk, to which add one cup butter or lard, four tablespoons of sugar, and two well-beaten eggs; stir in flour enough to make a moderately stiff sponge, and set in a warm place to rise, which will take three or four hours; then mix in flour enough to make a soft dough and let rise again. When well risen, dissolve a lump of soda, size of a bean, in a spoon of milk, work in the dough and roll into sheets one-half inch in thickness; spread with thin layer of butter, cut into squares, and fold over, pocket book shape; put on tins or in pans to rise once more, which will only take a little while, till they are fit for the oven. In the summer the sponge can be made up in the morning, and rise in time to make for tea. In cool weather it is best to set over night.

RUSK.

One pint milk, three eggs, one cup butter, one cup sugar, and one coffee cup potato yeast; thicken with flour, and sponge over night; in the morning stir down, let rise, and stir down again; when it rises again make into a loaf, and let rise again; then roll out like soda biscuit, cut and put in pans, and when light, bake carefully.

SOUTH CAROLINA BISCUIT.
Mrs. Col. Moore, Hamilton.

One quart sweet cream or milk, one and a half cups butter or fresh lard, two tablespoons white sugar, one good teaspoon salt; add flour sufficient to make a stiff dough, knead *well* and mould into neat, small biscuit with the hands, as our grandmothers used to do; add one good teaspoon cream tartar if preferred; bake well and you have good sweet biscuit that will keep for weeks in a dry place, and are very nice for traveling lunch. They are such as we used to send to the army, and the "boys" relished them "hugely."

SODA BISCUIT.
Mrs. J. P. R.

Two quarts of flour, four teaspoons cream tartar, two teaspoons soda, one pint of sweet milk, one-half teacup lard.

SUPERIOR BISCUIT.
Mrs. B. T. Skinner.

Three and a half cups sweet milk, one cup butter and lard mixed; add yeast and flour and let rise over night. In the morning add one beaten egg, knead thoroughly and let rise again, then form into biscuit; when light, bake delicately.

SPOON BISCUIT.
Mrs. A. B. M.

Take one quart sour milk or buttermilk, one teaspoon soda, a little salt, two tablespoons melted lard, and flour enough for a stiff batter; drop in a hot gem pan and bake in a quick oven.

SALLY LUNN.
Mrs. Wm. Lee.

One pint milk, one cup yeast, one tablespoon each of butter and sugar, three eggs, and flour enough to make a stiff batter; put by the stove to rise, and when light bake.

SALLY LUNN, OR SWEET GEM.
Mrs. E. M. Skinner, Battle Creek, Mich.

One-half cup sugar, three tablespoons melted butter, one egg, one pint flour, one cup sweet milk, three teaspoons baking powder; bake in a quick oven.

SALLY LUNN.
Mrs. H. B. S.

One quart flour, two eggs, one pint sweet milk, two tablespoons sugar; piece of butter size of two eggs, (large size,) one-half teaspoon salt, two teaspoons cream tartar, one teaspoon soda; beat butter and sugar together; add eggs well beaten. Mix soda with milk, and cream tartar with flour.

AMERICAN HOUSE ROLLS.
Mrs. V. G. H.

Rub one half tablespoon of butter, and one-half tablespoon lard into two quarts sifted flour; into a well in the middle pour one pint of cold boiled milk; one-half cup yeast, one-half cup sugar, and a little salt. If you wish them for tea, the night before you must rub the flour and butter, boil the milk and cool it; then add sugar, yeast and salt, and turn it into your flour, but do not stir it. Let this stand over night; in the morning stir it up, knead it and let it rise till near tea time; mould and let it rise again; bake quickly. To mould them, cut with cake-cutter; put a little melted butter on one-half and lap it on the other half, nearly over. Place them in the pan about three-quarters of an inch apart.

CREAM OF TARTAR ROLLS.
Mrs. W. A. J.

Take one pint of flour, one teaspoon cream tartar, one half teaspoon soda, one-half teaspoon salt, one teaspoon sugar, mix all these and run them through the sieve; wet with half pint of milk; heat and grease the French roll pan; bake fifteen minutes.

COMMON ROLLS.
J. S. H.

A convenient way to make rolls is to take a piece of your bread dough on baking day, when you mould it out the last time—about enough for a small loaf; spread it out a little, and add to it one egg, two tablespoons sugar, and three-fourths cup lard; you will have to add a little flour and a small teaspoon soda if it is the least bit sour; mix well, let rise, and mould into rolls or biscuit. Set to rise again, and they will be ready for the oven in twenty or thirty minutes.

FRENCH ROLLS.
Mrs. J. W. R.

Peel six common sized, mealy potatoes, boil in two quarts of water, press and drain both potatoes and water through a colander; when cool enough, so as not to scald, add flour to make a thick batter, beat well, and when luke warm, add one-half cup potato yeast. Make this sponge early in the morning, and when light turn into a bread pan, add a teaspoon salt, half cup lard, and flour enough for a soft dough; mix up, and set in a warm, even temperature; when risen knead down and place again to rise, repeating this process five or six times; cut in small pieces and mould on the bread board in rolls about one inch thick by five long;

roll in melted butter or sweet lard, and place in well-greased baking pans, (nine inches long by five wide and two and a half in depth make a convenient sized pan, into which you can put fifteen of these rolls, or if twice the width, put in two rows); press your rolls closely together, so that they will only be about half an inch in width. Let rise a short time and bake twenty minutes in a hot oven; if the top browns too rapidly, cover with paper. These rolls, if properly made, are very white, light and tender.

Or make your rolls larger, and just before putting them in the oven, cut deeply across each one with a sharp knife. This will make the cleft roll, so famous among French cooks.

NICE ROLLS.
Mrs. Wm. Brown, Massillon.

To one quart of bread sponge take two eggs, one cup of sugar, and one cup shortening; mix with flour enough to make a soft dough, let rise well and make into rolls or biscuit; put in a pan and set to rise again; when ready for the oven, take the yolk of an egg, beat and add one tablespoon sugar, and a teaspoon of sweet milk; brush the cakes over with this and bake.

PHILADELPHIA ROLLS.
Mrs. A. S. Chapman.

One and a half quarts of flour, one egg, and yeast enough to raise; when risen make into a loaf; let it stand till light, then roll out thin, spread with butter, then fold and cut out; when very light, bake.

ROLLS.
Mrs. Judge West, Bellefontaine.

Rub one-half tablespoon lard into one quart of flour; make a well in the middle, put in one-half cup of baker's yeast—or one cup of home-made—two teaspoons sugar, one-half pint cold boiled milk; do not stir it, and let it stand over night; in the morning knead well; after dinner knead again, cut out, put in pans and let rise until tea time; bake in a quick oven.

WEDDING SANDWICH ROLLS.
Mrs. James W. Robinson.

Late in the evening make a rather stiff potato sponge, (see directions under "Bread Making,") and in the morning mix in as much flour as will make a soft dough, knead well, and place to rise; when sufficiently light, knead down again, repeating the operation two or three times, remembering not to let the dough become sour by rising too light; mould into common sized loaves, place in your dripping pan to rise and bake very carefully, so as to secure the very lightest brown crust possible; on taking out of oven roll in a cloth tightly wrung out of water, with a large bread blanket folded and wrapped around all. Let cool three or four hours, cut lengthwise of the loaf, (not using the outside piece), first spreading lightly with good sweet butter, then cutting in slices not more than a quarter of an inch, or just as thin as possible, using for this purpose a very thin, sharp knife; lay on cold boiled ham cut in very thin shavings, (no matter if in small pieces;) roll up very slowly and carefully and place where it will not unroll. Treat each sandwich in the same manner, always spreading the bread with butter before cutting. If by chance, the bread is baked with too hard a crust, cut off a thin shaving of the brownest part very smoothly before making into sandwiches. These sandwiches are truly delicious if properly made, but they require great care, experience and good judgment. Served on an oblong platter, piled in pyramid style, row upon row, they will resemble nicely rolled dinner napkins. They must be made and served the same day.

CRUMPETS.
Miss Mary Gallagher.

One quart of milk with two tablespoons yeast, and flour enough to make a stiff batter; let rise over night, and in the morning add four eggs, two tablespoons sugar, one-half cup butter; put them in muffin rings and let them rise nearly half an hour; bake quickly.

MUFFINS.
Mrs. J. S. R.

One pint bread sponge, one pint sweet milk, two eggs, one-half cup butter, a pinch of salt; let rise three hours and bake in muffin rings.

QUICK WAFFLES.
C. W. M.

Two pints sweet milk, one cup butter melted, sifted flour to make a soft batter, add the well beaten yolks of six eggs, then the beaten whites, and lastly (just before baking) four teaspoons baking powder, beating very hard and fast for a few minutes. These are very good with four or five eggs, but much better with more.

WAFFLES.
Mrs. O. M. S.

Four eggs, one quart milk, one-fourth pound butter, a little salt, flour to make a batter—not very thick, beating the eggs separately; heat and butter the irons well and bake very quickly. If for tea, grate on a little sugar and nutmeg; if for breakfast, only butter.

WAFFLES.
Mrs. S. C. Lee, Baltimore, Maryland.

Boil half a pint of rice and let it get cold; mix with it one-fourth pound butter and a little salt. Sift in it one and a half pints flour; beat five eggs separately; stir the yolks in together with one quart milk; add whites beaten to a stiff froth; beat hard and bake at once in waffle iron.

EGG CRACKERS.
Mrs. J. S. R.

Six eggs, twelve tablespoons sweet milk, six tablespoons butter, and one-half teaspoon soda; mould with flour half an hour and roll thin.

BUCKWHEAT SHORT CAKE.
Mrs. V. W.

Take two or three cups sour milk and enough soda to sweeten; stir in buckwheat flour enough to make quite a stiff batter and bake; no shortening. This takes the place of griddle cakes, and is very nice to eat with meat, butter, honey or molasses.

CENTENNIAL BISCUIT.

Make good corn mush, just as if you were going to eat it with milk. Add half cup lard or butter, half cup yeast, and a tablespoon of sugar.

When it is lukewarm take a quart of it, work in flour enough to make a stiff dough; make into biscuits, put in your bake pan and set in a warm place over night; bake in a very hot oven, and you have the best and sweetest biscuits you ever ate. Eat while hot, for breakfast.

CORN ROLLS.
Mrs. Capt. Rea, Minneapolis, Minn.

Eight heaping tablespoons of corn meal, two tablespoons sugar, one teaspoon salt, one quart boiling milk; stir all together and let stand till cool. Add six eggs well beaten, and bake in gem-pans or well buttered cups.

CUSHMAN CAKE.
Mrs. W. A. J.

Two cups flour, one cup Indian meal, four tablespoons sugar, two teaspoons cream tartar; mix and add one egg, two teacups sweet milk, one tablespoon melted butter, one teaspoon soda; then bake.

CORN MUSH.
Mrs. W. A. J.

Put fresh water in a kettle to boil, salt to suit the taste; when it begins to boil stir in the meal, letting it sift through the fingers slowly to prevent lumps; at the last it may be added a little faster; keep adding until it is as thick as can be conveniently stirred with one hand; set it in the oven, in the kettle, let it bake an hour, and it will be thoroughly cooked. It takes corn meal so long to cook thoroughly that it is very tedious to boil until done without letting it burn. If you wish to fry it cold for a delicious breakfast relish, add while making it about a pint of flour to three quarts of mush.

JOHNNY CAKE.
Mrs. W. A. J.

Two-thirds teaspoon soda, three tablespoons sugar, one teaspoon cream tartar, one egg, one cup sweet milk, six tablespoons Indian meal, three tablespoons flour and a little salt. Excellent.

RHODE ISLAND "SPAT OUTS."
One Hundred Years Old.

One pint sweet milk, four tablespoons wheat flour, two eggs well beaten, Indian meal to make a stiff batter, and a little salt; spat into round cakes half an inch thick, fry in lard like doughnuts, and split and eat warm with butter.

GRAHAM BISCUIT.

One cup white flour, three of Graham, three of sweet milk, two tablespoons lard, one of sugar, a pinch of salt, two teaspoons cream tartar and one of soda; mix and bake like white flour biscuit.

MRS. BUXTON'S GRAHAM GEMS.

Take one egg and beat well, add pinch of salt, one quart butter or sour milk, and flour enough to make a stiff batter; add one teaspoon soda and stir thoroughly with a spoon; heat and grease gem-irons, and after dipping the spoon in cold water, drop a spoonful of batter in each pan, repeating until all are filled; bake in a quick oven half an hour. This measure will make a dozen.

GRAHAM GEMS.
Mrs. R. L. Partridge.

Beat one egg well, add pint of new milk, a little salt, and Graham flour until it will drop off the spoon nicely; heat and butter the gem-pans before dropping in the dough; bake in a hot oven twenty minutes.

GOOD GRAHAM GEMS.
J. H. S.

Three cups sour milk, one teaspoon soda, one of salt, one tablespoon brown sugar, one of melted lard, one beaten egg; to the egg add the milk, then the sugar and salt, then the Graham flour, (with the soda mixed in,) together with the lard; make a stiff batter, so that it will drop, not pour, from the spoon. Have gem pans very hot, grease, fill, and bake fifteen minutes in a hot oven.

GRAHAM GEMS.
E. M. S.

One cup sour milk, one-half cup sugar, one egg, one teaspoon soda, three tablespoons melted butter, and Graham flour to thicken; have the irons well greased and hot when mixture is put in, and bake with quick oven.

GEMS WITHOUT SOUR MILK.
Aunt Betsy.

Mix with Graham flour enough sweet milk to make a rather thin batter, add a little salt and beat well; have gem pans hot, fill, and bake in a very hot oven until they are a light even brown. Batter should be thin enough to pour into the pans.

MUFFINS OR GEMS.
Mrs. O. M. S.

With very cold or ice water and Graham flour, make a rather stiff batter; heat and grease the irons, and bake twenty minutes in a hot oven.

RYE OR GRAHAM DROP CAKES.
W. A. J.

Two cups rye or Graham meal, one and one-half teacups flour, two eggs, one half cup sugar, one full teaspoon soda, sour milk enough to make a thick batter.

BISCUIT FOR DYSPEPTICS.
Ola W.

One quart Graham flour, one pint corn meal, three tablespoons butter, half cup molasses, sour milk to wet it up, and soda; roll out, bake, and when cold it is excellent for dyspeptics.

GRAHAM MUSH.

Make the same as corn mush, except that it will cook sufficiently without baking; it is just as good for frying as corn mush.

GRAHAM MUFFINS.
Mrs. H. B. S.

Two cups sour milk, two tablespoons brown sugar, a little salt, one teaspoon soda, sufficient Graham flour to make moderately stiff. If not convenient to use sour milk, use sweet, adding cream tartar.

FRITTERS.

Make fritters quickly and beat thoroughly. Have the lard in which you cook them nice and sweet and boiling hot; test the heat by dropping in a teaspoon of the batter,—if the temperature is right it will quickly rise in a light ball with a splutter, and soon brown; take up carefully *the moment* they are done, with a wire spoon. Drain in a hot colander and sift powdered sugar over them; serve hot.

APPLE FRITTERS.

Three large sour apples sliced thin, one pint sour milk, one-half teaspoon soda, one tablespoon sugar, pinch of salt, flour to stiffen; fry and serve hot with brandy sauce or molasses.

CLAM FRITTERS.
Mrs. H. B. S.

Take raw clams chopped fine and make a batter with juice and an equal quantity of sweet milk, with four eggs to each pint of liquid, and flour sufficient to stiffen; fry like other fritters.

CORN OYSTERS.

To one quart grated corn add three eggs and three or four grated crackers; beat well and season with pepper and salt; have ready in skillet butter and lard or beef drippings in equal proportions, hot but not scorching; drop in little cakes about the size of an oyster, and for this purpose use a teaspoon; when brown, turn and fry on the other side, watching constantly for fear of burning. If the fat is just the right heat, the oysters will be light and delicious, but if not, heavy and "soggy." Serve hot and keep dish well covered. It is better to beat whites of eggs to a stiff froth and add just before frying.

CORN OYSTERS.
Mrs. H. B. S.

Mix well together one quart of grated sweet corn, two teacups sweet milk, one teacup flour, one teaspoon butter, two eggs well beaten; season with pepper and salt and fry in butter like pan cakes.

CREAM FRITTERS.
Mrs. M. K. Pasco.

One and a half pints flour, one pint milk, six well beaten eggs, one-half nutmeg, two teaspoons salt, one pint cream; stir the whole enough to mix the cream; fry in small cakes.

CUCUMBER FRITTERS.
Mrs. A. H. T.

Peel four large cucumbers, cut and cook in a sauce pan with just a little water; mash and season well with salt and pepper; add two beaten eggs and flour to make a thick batter; put a table spoon of lard in a skillet, make hot and fry in little cakes.

FRITTERS.
Mrs. J. S. R.

Make like batter cakes, only stiffer, and fry in skillet one-fourth full of lard; serve hot with molasses and butter.

SNOW FRITTERS.
Mrs. H. A. Stimson.

Stir together milk, flour and a little salt and make a rather thick batter; add new fallen snow in the proportion of a teacup to a pint of milk; have the fat hot when you stir in the snow, and drop the batter into it with a spoon; or bake as pan-cakes on a hot griddle.

VANITIES.

Mrs. D.C. Harrington, Westfield, N.Y.

Beat two eggs, stir in a pinch of salt and half a teaspoon of rose water; add sifted flour till just thick enough to roll out; cut out with a cake cutter and fry quickly in hot lard. Sift powdered sugar on them while hot, and when cool put a teaspoon of jelly in the centre of each one, and they will be nice for tea or dessert.

GRIDDLE CAKES.

Griddle cakes should be well beaten, when first made, and they are much lighter if the eggs are separated, whipping the yolks to a thick cream, and adding the whites beaten to a stiff froth just before baking. Some persons never stir buckwheat cakes after they have risen, but take them out carefully with a large spoon, placing the spoon when emptied, in a saucer, and not back again into the batter. In baking griddle cakes have the griddle clean, and instead of greasing it, tie some salt in a rag and rub the griddle with it. If the griddle is not allowed to burn, the cakes will not stick, and there will be no smoke or unpleasant odor in the room; or better still, provide a soapstone griddle which needs no greasing. Griddle cakes may be made with new fallen snow, in the proportion of a teacup of snow to a pint of milk. Fresh fallen snow contains a large proportion of ammonia which renders the cakes light, but which soon evaporates, rendering old snow useless for this purpose.

BUCKWHEAT CAKES.

A pint warm water, half cup good yeast, one teaspoon salt, two tablespoons molasses, buckwheat flour enough to make a thin batter; set in a warm place and let rise over night; if you have them every morning, save a little of the batter to start with instead of yeast. They will be nicer in a week than when first started. Never add more flour in the morning. If the batter is sour, add a teaspoon soda, stir in and fry at once.

BREAD CAKES.

Take stale bread and soak over night in sour milk; in the morning rub through a colander, and to one quart, add two eggs, one teaspoon salt, two tablespoons sugar, and flour enough to make a batter a little thicker than for buckwheat cakes. These cakes are nice and not unwholesome.

BREAKFAST CAKES.
Mrs. E. B. W.

To each pint buttermilk add one even teaspoon soda and one of salt; stir in sifted wheat flour until the batter will not pour off the spoon when lifted; fry on griddle like buckwheat cakes.

BATTER CAKES.
Mrs. J. S. R.

One quart buttermilk, one teaspoon soda, three eggs, one-half teaspoon salt, and flour to thicken; bake on griddle.

CRUMB GRIDDLE CAKES.
Mrs. W. E. Scobey, Kankakee, Ill.

The night before using put some bread crumbs to soak in one quart of sour milk; in the morning rub through a sieve and add four well beaten eggs, two teaspoons soda dissolved in a little water, one tablespoon melted butter, and enough corn meal to make them the consistency of ordinary griddle cakes. It is better to beat yolks and whites separately, stirring the whites lightly in just before baking.

FLANNEL CAKES.
A. J.

Make hot a pint of sweet milk in which put two ounces of butter, let melt, then add a pint of cold milk, the well beaten yolks of four eggs—placing the whites in a cold place—a teaspoon of salt, two tablespoons of potato yeast, and sufficient flour to make a stiff batter; set in a warm place to rise, let stand three hours or over night; before baking add the beaten whites, fry as any other griddle cakes. Be sure to make your batter just stiff enough, for you must not add flour in the morning unless you can let it rise again.

INDIAN PANCAKES.
W. C. A.

One pint Indian meal, one teaspoon salt, small teaspoon soda; pour on boiling water until a little thinner than mush; let stand until cool, add the yolks of four eggs, half a cup of flour in which is mixed two teaspoons cream tartar; stir in as much sweet milk or water as will make the batter suitable to bake; beat the whites well and add just before baking.

RICE GRIDDLE CAKES.
Mrs. Walter Mitchell, Gallipolis.

Boil half a cup of rice; when cold, take one quart milk, the yolks of four eggs, and flour sufficient to make a stiff batter; beat the whites to a froth, stir in one teaspoon soda, and two cream tartar; add a little salt, and lastly the whites of the eggs; bake on a griddle.

SOFT SHORT CAKE.
Harriet O. Backus, West Killingly, Conn.

One cup sour cream, one teaspoon saleratus; stir in flour enough to make a batter a little stiffer than for griddle cakes; bake on a griddle. Split open each cake, putting on milk and butter, and place them in layers.

TOMATO BATTER CAKES.
Mrs. G. W. Collins, Urbana.

Make an egg batter as for batter cakes; take and slice large, solid ripe tomatoes, cover with batter and fry on a griddle like any griddle cakes; season with pepper and salt while frying. Tomatoes so prepared make a nice breakfast dish.

YEAST.

There are various ways of making, but the three best kinds are dry, soft hop, and potato yeast. The dry should be made in May or June for summer use, and in October for winter use. In hot and damp weather, dry yeast sometimes loses its vitality; however, many use it on account of its convenience, since there is no danger of its souring in summer or freezing in winter. Soft hop or potato yeast will keep in a cool place one or two weeks in warm weather, and in cold weather five or six weeks, care being taken that it does not freeze. Never add soda to yeast; if it becomes sour it will do to start fresh yeast, but will *never* make good bread. Potato yeast is made either by boiling and mashing the potatoes, or by grating them while raw, and adding them to the boiling hop water *immediately*, for if allowed to stand they darken, and the yeast will not be as white. A stone jar with a close-fitting cover is best to keep yeast in, and should be scalded as often as emptied. In taking out for use, stir up well from the bottom.

DRY YEAST.
Mrs. E. T. C.

Boil two large potatoes and a handful of hops, (the latter in a bag), in three pints water; when done, take out the potatoes, mash well, add one pint flour, and pour the boiling hop water over all; beat well together, adding one tablespoon salt, one of ginger, and one half cup sugar; when luke warm add one cup good yeast and let stand two days, (or only one day, if very warm weather), stirring down frequently; add good white corn meal until thick enough to make into cakes about a half inch in thickness; place to dry in the shade where the air will pass freely so as to dry them as soon as possible; turn the cakes frequently, breaking them up somewhat so they will dry out evenly; when thoroughly dried put in a paper sack, and keep in a dry place. A small cup will make sponge sufficient to bake five or six ordinary sized loaves.

HOP YEAST.
Mrs. J. S. R.

Two tablespoons hops boiled in half pint water; boil to half the quantity, strain and pour over three tablespoons flour, stirring until there are no lumps; add three tablespoons sugar and one of salt; put in a quart bottle and fill up with cold water. Use one teacup for common baking.

HOP YEAST.
Mrs. M. C. Moore, Granville.

Take eight to ten large pared potatoes, and a pint good hops in a bag; put these in two quarts of water, boil till potatoes are done; then mash and strain through a colander, add one teacup sugar and half cup salt; when cool enough add a teacup good yeast, stir frequently, till it is risen enough to bottle. Keep in a dry, cool place.

POTATO YEAST.
Mrs. W. A. J.

Pare and boil six good sized potatoes; when done mash and pour on them three pints of boiling water; run through the colander and stir into it two tablespoons sugar and one of salt; when milk warm, stir in half a cup of yeast. In summer this will rise in three or four hours.

POTATO YEAST.
Mrs. D. Buxton.

Take four small Irish potatoes or three large ones, peel and grate raw, and place in a porcelain kettle with two quarts water; put one cup hops in a bag, drop in the kettle and boil until the water tastes bitter; take out hops and add one cup white sugar and one tablespoon salt; keep constantly boiling, and stir continually; cook from five to ten minutes, and when done it will boil up thick like starch; turn into a jar, and when just tepid, in summer, or quite warm in winter, add one-half pint good yeast, (always save some to start with.) Set jar in a large tin pan, and as often as it rises stir down until fermentation ceases; (it will then be quite thin;) tie up, and set away in a cool place and it will keep two weeks. When yeast smells sour but does not taste sour it is good; if it has no smell it is dead. One cup will make six good sized loaves, and if properly made you need never have sour bread. I have used it four years, and always with success.

TO HASTEN MILK YEAST.

Take one teacup of wheat "shorts," one teaspoon salt, one of soda, one of ginger; add boiling water enough to make a thin batter; add two tablespoons or less to common milk yeast and it will rise in an hour or two. If kept in a cool place it will be good for two weeks in winter.

YEAST.
Mrs. C. M.

Pare and boil four ordinary sized potatoes, boiling at the same time in a separate vessel a good handful of hops. When the potatoes are done mash fine and add, after straining, the water in which the hops were boiled; put into this one cup white sugar and one-half cup salt, and add sufficient water to make one gallon; when cold add one cup of good yeast, let stand in a warm place for a few hours until it will "sing" on being stirred. When it is ready for use, sprinkle a little flour on top, and keep covered in a cellar or cool place.

CAKE MAKING.

"Let all things be done decently and in order," and the first to put in order when you are going to bake is yourself. Secure the hair in a net or other covering, to prevent any from falling, and brush the shoulders and back to be sure none are lodged there that might blow off; make the hands and finger nails clean, roll the sleeves up above the elbows, and put on a large clean apron. Clean your kitchen table of utensils and everything not needed, and provide yourself with everything you will need until the cake is baked, not forgetting even the broom splints which you had picked off the new broom and laid away carefully in a little box. If it is warm weather place your eggs in cold water, and let stand a few minutes, as they will then make a finer froth, and be sure they are fresh, as they will not make a stiff froth with any amount of beating if too old. Grease the pans with fresh lard, which is much better than butter; line the bottom with paper—six or eight thicknesses, greasing the top one well, if the cake is to be large,—the papers can all be cut and put in at once; sift flour and sugar, (if not pulverized,) and measure or weigh. Firkin or very salt butter should be cut in bits and washed to freshen a little; if very hard, warm it carefully, but in no case allow any of it to melt. Beat the yolks of eggs thoroughly, and strain; set the whites away in a cool place until the cake is ready for them, then beat them vigorously in a cool room, till they will remain in the dish when turned upside down. Take the measured flour, and mix thoroughly in it the baking powder or soda and cream tartar. In using new flour for either bread or cake making, it can be "ripened" for use by placing the quantity intended for baking in the hot sun for a few hours, or before the kitchen fire. In using milk, note this, that sour milk makes a spongy light cake, sweet milk, one that cuts like pound cake.

Having thus gathered your material, beat the butter to a cream and add the sugar gradually, then the milk in small quantities, (never use fresh and stale milk in same cake,) next the yolks of eggs, then a part of the flour, then a part of the whites, and so on until all is used; lastly add the flavoring. There is a great "knack" in beating cake; don't *stir* but *beat* thoroughly, bringing the batter up from the bottom of the dish at every stroke; in this way you drive the air into the cells of the batter, instead of out of them, but the cells will be finer to beat more slowly at the last, remembering that the motion should always be upward. In the winter it is easier to beat with the hand, but in summer a wooden spoon is better; never beat a cake in tin, but use earthen or stone ware. All cakes not made with yeast should be baked as soon as possible after they are mixed. Unskillful mixing, too rapid or unequal baking, or a sudden decrease in heat before it is quite done, will cause streaks in the cake.

FRUIT CAKE.

Most ladies think fruit cake quite incomplete without wine or brandy; but it can be made equally as good on strictly temperance principles, by substituting one-third of a cup of molasses for a wine glass of brandy. To facilitate the operation of seeding raisins, pour boiling water on a few at a time (it will not injure the fruit or cake.) To seed, clip with the scissors, or cut with a sharp knife. Do not chop too fine; if for light fruit cake, seeding is all that is necessary. Slice the citron thin and do not have the pieces too large or they will cause the cake to break apart in cutting. Currants should be kept prepared for use as follows: wash in warm water rubbing well, pour off water, and repeat until the water is clear; drain them in a sieve, spread on a cloth and rub dry; pick out the bad ones, dry carefully in a cool oven, and set away for use. When the fruit is all mixed, cream the butter and sugar, (this is very important, in all cakes,) add the spices, molasses or liquors, then the milk (if any is used,) next the eggs well beaten, then the flour; (when making a "black" fruit cake brown the flour,) prepared with baking powder or soda and cream tartar, then the flavoring, half and half of lemon and vanilla, and lastly the fruit, dredged with a *very little* flour. Some prefer to *mix* the fruit with all of the flour. When eggs are beaten separately, which is the better plan for all cakes, observe the directions already given. It is well to test your dough by baking a small sample cake. When the cake is cold wrap in a cloth wet in whiskey or brandy to keep it moist.

In making very large cakes that require three or four hours to bake, an excellent way for lining the pan is the following: fit three papers carefully and grease thoroughly; make a paste of equal parts Graham and white flour, wet with water just stiff enough to spread easily with a spoon; place the first paper in the pan with the greased side down; spread the paste evenly over the paper about as thick as piecrust. In covering the sides of the pan, use a little paste to stick a portion of the paper to the top of the pan to keep it from slipping out of place; press the second paper carefully into its place with the greased side up, and next put in the third paper as you would into any baking pan, and pour in the cake.

All except layer cakes, should be covered with a paper cap, when first put into the oven. Take a square of brown paper large enough to cover well the cake pan, cut off the corners, and lay a plait on four sides, fastening each with a pin, so as to fit nicely over your pan; this will throw it up in the centre, so that the cover will not touch the cake. Save the cap as it can be used several times.

THE OVEN.

Too much care cannot be given to the preparation of the oven, which is oftener too hot than too cool; however, an oven too cold at first will ruin any cake. Cakes should rise and begin to bake before browning much, large cakes requiring a good steady solid heat, about such as for baking bread; layer cakes a brisk hot fire, as they must be baked quickly. A good plan is to fill the stove with hard wood, let it burn until there is a good body of heat, and turn damper so as to throw the heat to the bottom of oven for fully ten minutes before the cake is put in. In this way a steady heat to start with is secured. Generally it is better to close the hearth when the cake is put in, as this stops the draft and makes a more regular heat. Keep adding wood in small quantities, for if the heat becomes slack, the cake will be heavy. Great care must be taken, for some stoves need to have the dampers changed every now and then, but as a rule, more heat is needed in the bottom of the oven than in the top. Many test their ovens in this way: if the hand can be held in from twenty to thirty-five seconds (or while counting twenty or thirty-five) it is a quick oven, from thirty-five to forty-five seconds is "moderate," and from forty-five to sixty seconds is "slow;" thirty-five seconds is a good oven for large fruit cakes. All systematic housekeepers will hail the day when some enterprising Yankee or Buckeye girl shall invent a stove or range with a thermometer attached to the oven, so that the heat may be regulated accurately and intelligently. If necessary to move the cake while baking, do it very gently, and be careful not to remove from the oven until done; do not leave oven door open; allow about thirty minutes for each inch of thickness in a quick oven, and more time in a slow one. Test with a broom splint, if the dough does not adhere it is done. When the cake settles a little away from the pan it is done, and when it stops "singing," is another indication that it is ready to leave the oven. Cake should remain in the pan at least fifteen minutes after taking from the oven, and it is better to leave the "cap" on; remove carefully from the pan and never leave upside down. A tin chest or stone jar is best to keep it in. Coffee cake should be put away before it is cold, and closely wrapped in a large napkin, so that the aroma will not be lost.

SPONGE CAKE.

The good quality of all delicate cake, and especially of sponge, depends very much upon its being made with fresh eggs. It must be quickly put together, beaten with rapidity, and baked in a rather quick oven. It is made "sticky" and less light by being stirred long. There is no other cake so dependent upon care and good judgment in baking as sponge cake. In making white cake, if not convenient to use the yolks that are left, they will keep until the next day, by being *thoroughly* beaten and set in a cool place.

CENTENNIAL CAKE.
Mrs. A. S. Chapman.

Two cups pulverized sugar, one cup butter rubbed to a light cream with the sugar, one cup sweet milk, three cups flour, one-half cup corn starch, four eggs, one-half pound chopped raisins, one-half a grated nutmeg and two teaspoons baking powder.

BUCKEYE CAKE.
Mrs. W. W. W.

One cup butter, two cups white sugar, four cups sifted flour, five eggs beaten separately, one cup sour milk, one teaspoon soda, one pound seeded raisins chopped a little; beat the butter and sugar to a cream, add the milk and stir in the flour with soda and raisins well mixed through it; then add the whites of the eggs well beaten; bake one and one-half hours; use coffee cups to measure; this will make a cake for a six quart pan.

ALMOND CAKE.
Mrs. H. W. Morey.

Two coffee cups sugar, one of butter, half cup of sweet milk, eight eggs beaten separately, one teaspoon cream tartar, one-half teaspoon soda, one and a half pounds almonds, which should first be put in hot water until the skin will peel off, and then sliced thin.

BLACK CAKE.
Mrs. M. M. Munsell, Delaware.

One pound powdered white sugar, three quarters pound butter, one pound sifted flour, three teaspoons baking powder, twelve eggs, two pounds raisins stoned and part of them chopped, two pounds currants carefully cleaned, half pound citron cut in strips, a quarter ounce each of cinnamon, nutmeg, and cloves mixed, one wine glass wine, and one of brandy; rub butter and sugar together, add yolks of eggs, part of flour, the spice, and whites of eggs well beaten, then add remainder of flour, and wine and brandy; mix all thoroughly together; cover bottom and sides of a milk pan with buttered white paper, put in a layer of the mixture, then a layer of the fruit, (first dredging the fruit with flour,) until pan is filled up three or four inches, and then bake four hours: A small cup of Orleans molasses makes the cake blacker and more moist. When the cake is cold, wrap in a cloth wet in brandy or whiskey, and keep the cloth moistened from one to four weeks.

BLACK CAKE.
Miss Mary Sealts, Mt. Vernon.

One pound butter, one of brown sugar, one of flour, one of raisins, one of currants, one-half pound citron, one tablespoon each cinnamon, allspice and cloves, ten eggs the whites and yolks beaten separately, three teaspoons baking powder; add just before baking a wine glass brandy, or one-third cup good molasses; seed raisins, chop citron fine, and wash and dry the currants; mix butter and sugar, add the eggs, and lastly the flour in which the fruit, spices and baking powder have been well mixed; bake in a six quart pan four hours.

BLACK CAKE.
Mrs. Col. James Woods, Greensburg, Pa.

One pint molasses, one of sugar, two of flour, one of butter, three teaspoons ginger, one ounce cinnamon, and three eggs.

BLACK CAKE.
Mrs. A. B. Morey.

Two cups brown sugar, one and a half of butter, six eggs beaten separately, three cups flour, (brown the flour) two tablespoons molasses, one of cinnamon, one teaspoon mace, one of cloves, two cups sweet milk, two pounds raisins, two of currants, a half pound citron, one teaspoon soda, two of cream tartar—bake three hours.

BREAKFAST CAKE.
Mrs. A. F. Ziegler, Columbus.

One cup Orleans molasses, one cup brown sugar, four cups flour, one cup cold coffee, one cup shortening (butter and lard mixed), one teaspoon soda in the coffee, one each of cloves, cinnamon and allspice, and one nutmeg—add fruit if you desire.

BREAD CAKE.
Mrs. C. F.

Three coffee cups yeast dough light enough to bake for bread, two and two-thirds cups sugar, one cup butter, three eggs, one nutmeg; put all together and work with the hands until smooth as pound cake. It is very important that all should be mixed thoroughly with the light dough; add raisins and as much fruit as you desire; let it rise half an hour in the pans in which you bake. The oven should be about right for bread; easily made and quite as nice as common loaf cake.

CREAM CAKE.
Miss Sarah Cryder.

Put two cups flour in a crock and mix with two level teaspoons cream tartar and one of soda; make well in the center into which put one cup sugar, one cup sweet cream, one egg and small teaspoon salt; mix all quickly together, flavor with one teaspoon lemon; put in pan to bake; add one cup raisins or currants, if you like, and it makes a nice cake pudding to eat hot with sauce; sour cream can be used instead of sweet by omitting the cream tartar and using two eggs instead of one.

CIDER CAKE.
Miss Mary A. Dugan.

Six cups flour, three cups sugar, one cup butter, one cup sour cider, one teaspoon soda, four eggs; beat the eggs, butter and sugar to a cream, stir in the flour, then add the cider in which the soda has first been dissolved.

CORN STARCH CAKE.
Mrs. J. S. R.

Two cups white sugar, one of butter, one-half cup sweet milk, one cup corn starch, one cup flour, whites of six eggs and three teaspoons baking powder; flavor to taste.

COFFEE CAKE.
Mrs. Wm. Skinner, Battle Creek, Mich.

Two cups brown sugar, one cup butter, one cup molasses, one cup strong coffee as prepared for the table, four eggs, one teaspoon salera-tus, two teaspoons cinnamon, two teaspoons cloves, one teaspoon grated nutmeg, one pound raisins, one pound currants, four cups flour.

COFFEE CAKE.
Mrs. H. W. M.

One and one-half cups brown sugar, one cup molasses, one cup butter, one egg, five cups flour, one pound raisins, one grated nutmeg, one tablespoon cinnamon, one of cloves, one of allspice, one teaspoon saleratus, one-half teaspoon cream tartar, one cup strong coffee, one teaspoon lemon and one of vanilla essence.

CUP CAKE.
Mrs. Dr. Thompson.

Three cups sugar, one cup butter, six cups flour, two-thirds pint sour cream, seven eggs, (leaving out the whites of two for icing,) one even teaspoon soda in the cream, one teaspoon soda in the flour, one of cream tartar, and one of lemon or vanilla.

CARAMEL CAKE.
Mrs. George Bever.

One cup butter, two of sugar, a scant cup milk, one and a half cups flour, one cup corn starch, whites of seven eggs, three teaspoons baking powder in the flour; bake in a long pan. Take one-half pound brown sugar, scant quarter pound chocolate, one-half cup milk, butter size of an egg, two teaspoons vanilla; mix thoroughly and cook as syrup until stiff enough to spread; spread on the cake and set in the oven to dry.

CINCINNATI CAKE.
Mrs. G. E. Kinney.

One pound fat pork chopped fine, over which pour one pint boiling water, two cups brown sugar, one of molasses, one tablespoon each of cloves and nutmeg, and two of cinnamon, two pounds raisins, one-fourth pound citron, one-half glass brandy, one teaspoon salt, three of baking powder, and seven cups of sifted flour; bake slowly two and one-half hours.

DELICATE CAKE.
Miss Mary E. Miller.

Three cups flour, two of sugar, three-fourths cup of sweet milk, whites of six eggs, one-half cup butter, one teaspoon cream tartar, one-half teaspoon of soda; flavor with lemon.

DELICATE CAKE.
Mrs. Hyde, Mt. Vernon.

One cup sugar, small half cup butter, one-half cup sweet milk, whites of four eggs beaten to a froth, one and a half cups flour, one teaspoon baking powder, two of lemon, one cup seeded raisins; bake slowly.

DELICATE CAKE.
Miss Mary S. Moore, Granville.

Four cups fine white sugar, five of sifted flour, one of butter, one and a half of sweet milk, one teaspoon soda dissolved in the milk, two of cream tartar, whites of sixteen eggs; stir sugar and butter to a cream, then add whites of eggs beaten to a stiff froth, next add the flour, then the milk and soda; stir several minutes, then add cream tartar and flavoring. This makes a large cake.

SALEM ELECTION CAKE.
(One hundred years old.)

Four pounds flour, one and a half pounds sugar, half pound butter, four eggs, one pint yeast, and spice.

OLD HARTFORD ELECTION CAKE.
(*Over one hundred years old.)

Five pounds flour, two pounds butter, two pounds sugar, one quart milk, three gills distillery yeast or twice the quantity of home brewed, four eggs, one gill of wine, one gill of brandy, half an ounce of nutmeg, two pounds raisins, one pound citron; rub the butter and flour together very fine, add half the sugar, then the yeast and half the milk, (hot in

---

* This old and valuable recipe was a favorite with the late Mrs. Eliza Burnham, Milford Center, and was contributed by her daughter, Mrs. Charles Fullington.

winter, blood warm in summer,) then add the eggs, then remainder of the milk, and the wine; beat well and let rise in a warm place all night; in the morning beat a long time, adding the brandy, sugar and spice, and allow to rise again very light. Add fruit, well floured, and put in cake pans and let rise ten or fifteen minutes; have the oven about as hot as for bread. This cake will keep any length of time. For raised cakes use the yeast made from Mrs. Buxton's recipe; if fresh made it is always a perfect success for cake.

APPLE FRUIT CAKE.
Mrs. C. M. Ingman.

One cup butter, two of sugar, one of milk, two eggs, one teaspoon soda, three and a half cups flour, two of raisins, three of dried apples soaked over night and then chopped fine and stewed two hours in two cups molasses; beat butter and sugar to a cream, add milk in which dissolve soda, then the beaten eggs and flour, and lastly the raisins and apples well stirred in; pour in pan and bake an hour and a half.

FRUIT CAKE.
Mrs. M. E. Nicely.

One cup butter, one of brown sugar, one-half pint molasses, two eggs, one cup sour milk, one teaspoon soda, one pound flour, one of currants, one and one-half pound raisins; flavor to taste.

FRUIT LOAF CAKE.
Mrs. N. S. Long.

One cup butter, two of brown sugar, one of New Orleans molasses, one of sweet milk, three eggs, five cups sifted flour, two teaspoons cream tartar in the flour, one teaspoon soda in the milk, one tablespoon cinnamon, one nutmeg, one pound raisins, one of currants, one-quarter pound citron, (citron may be omitted, and half the quantity of raisins and currants will do.) Put flour in a large crock, mix well with cream tartar, make a well in the center, put in other ingredients, having warmed the butter and molasses a little; mix well together with the hands, putting in the fruit last after it has been floured; bake two hours in a moderate oven. This will make two common sized loaves.

FRUIT CAKE.
Mrs. H. E. Roberts, Upper Alton, Ill.

Five cups flour, five eggs, one cup butter, one of lard, two of sugar, one of molasses, one pound raisins, one of currants, one-half pound citron, half teaspoon soda, and half teaspoon cream tartar.

FRUIT CAKE.
Miss Emma Skinner, Somerset.

One pound brown sugar, one of butter, one of eggs, one of flour, two of raisins, two of currants, half pound citron, a nutmeg, tablespoon cloves, one of allspice, half pint brandy, and two teaspoons baking powder; after baking, while yet warm, pour over cake a half pint wine. This makes the cake delicious.

FARMER'S FRUIT CAKE.
Mrs. W. G. March.

Two cups dried apples, one of molasses, two and a half of flour, one-half cup butter, two eggs, one and a half teaspoon soda, one of cloves, one tablespoon cinnamon; wash and soak the apples over night in water to cover; in the morning chop fine and add with the spices to the molasses and water in which apples were soaked; cream the butter, add to it the beaten eggs and the apple and molasses mixture, and then the soda mixed with the flour; pour in pan and bake one hour in moderate oven.

POOR MAN'S FRUIT CAKE.

One and a half teacups brown sugar, one of butter, one of chopped raisins, half cup blackberry jam, three eggs, three tablespoons sour milk, half teaspoon soda, and flour to your judgment.

SCOTCH FRUIT CAKE.
Mrs. J. H. Shearer.

A cup butter, two white sugar, four of sifted flour, three-fourths cup sour milk, half teaspoon soda, nine eggs beaten separately, one pound raisins, half pound currants, a fourth pound citron; cream the butter and sugar, add milk gradually, then beaten yolks of eggs, and lastly, while stirring in flour, the whites well whipped; flavor with one teaspoon lemon and one of vanilla extract; have raisins chopped a little, or, better still, seeded, and citron sliced thin. Wash and dry currants before using, and flour all fruit slightly. In putting cake in pan, place first a thin layer of cake, then sprinkle in some of the three kinds of fruit, then a layer of cake and so on, always finishing off with a thin layer of cake; bake in a moderate oven for two hours.

THANKSGIVING FRUIT CAKE.
Mrs. Woodworth, Springfield, Mass.

Six pounds flour, three of butter, three and a half of sugar, an ounce mace, two glasses wine, two glasses brandy, four pounds raisins, half pound citron, six eggs, one pint yeast, small teaspoon soda put in at last moment. After tea, take all the flour, (except one plate for dredging raisins), a small piece butter, and a quart or more of milk, and mix like biscuit; then mix butter and sugar, and, at nine o'clock in the evening, if sufficiently light, put one-third of butter and sugar into dough; at twelve add another third, and very early in the morning the remainder; about eleven o'clock, if light enough, begin kneading, and continue for an hour, adding meanwhile all the other ingredients. This will make seven loaves.

FEATHER CAKE.
Mrs. E. L. C., Springfield.

Half cup butter, three of flour, two of sugar, one of milk, three eggs, a little grated lemon, two teaspoons baking powder.

FIG CAKE.
Mrs. A. B. Morey.

A large cup butter, two and a half of sugar, one of sweet milk, three pints flour with three teaspoons baking powder, whites of sixteen eggs, a pound and a quarter of figs well floured and cut in strips like citron; no flavoring. Splendid.

GROVE CAKE.
Mrs. W. F. W.

Two and a half cups sugar, one of butter, one of sweet milk, four and a half of flour, eight eggs, omitting the yolks of four, two teaspoons baking powder.

HARD MONEY CAKE.
Miss Emma Fisher.

GOLD PART—Yolks of eight eggs, one cup butter, two of sugar, four of flour, one of milk, one teaspoon soda, two of cream tartar; flavor with lemon and vanilla.

SILVER PART—Two cups sugar, one of butter, four of flour, one of milk, one teaspoon soda, two of cream tartar, whites of eight eggs; flavor with almond or peach. Put in pan alternately one spoonful of gold and one of silver.

HAYES CAKE.
Miss Flora D. Ziegler, (Nine years old,) Columbus.

One cup sugar, one-half cup butter, three eggs beaten well together, one level teaspoon soda stirred in one-half cup sour milk, two small cups flour; flavor with lemon, and pour in small dripping pan; bake half an hour and cut in squares.

HOOSIER CAKES.
M. E. W.

Mix crust for biscuit, roll to twice the thickness of pie-crust, spread with butter and sugar, cut in strips, roll up and bake.

HICKORY NUT CAKE.
Mrs. Judge West, Bellefontaine.

Two cups sugar, one of milk, two-thirds cup butter, three of flour, three eggs, two teaspoons baking powder, one cup nut kernels cut fine.

IMPERIAL CAKE.
Mrs. E. R. May, Minneapolis, Minn.

One pound butter beaten to a cream, one pound sugar, one pound flour, the grated rind and juice of a lemon, nine eggs, one and a quarter pounds almonds before they are cracked, half pound citron, half pound raisins; beat the yolks light, add sugar and butter, then the whites beaten to a stiff froth, and lastly the nuts blanched, cut fine and mixed with fruit, and part of the flour. This is very delicious and will keep for months.

LADY CAKE.
Miss M. E. W., Madison.

One-half cup butter, one and a half of sugar, two of flour, nearly one of sweet milk, one-half teaspoon soda, one of cream tartar, whites of four eggs well beaten; flavor with peach or almond.

YELLOW LADY CAKE.
O. S. H., Battle Creek, Mich.

One and a half cups flour, one of sugar, one-half cup butter, one-half cup sweet milk, one teaspoon soda, two teaspoons cream tartar, yolks of four eggs.

LEMON CAKE.
Mrs. Franklin Woods.

Three cups white sugar, one of butter, one of milk, four of flour, five eggs, one teaspoon soda in milk, juice of one lemon; and grated rind if desired.

RAISED LOAF CAKE.
Mrs. C. F.

Six pounds flour, three of sugar, two and one-half of butter, four eggs, four nutmegs, half pint wine, half pint brandy; in the afternoon mix butter and sugar together and rub the flour into half of it; take a quart of sweet milk and one quart yeast, and wet the above; when very light mix all, and set to rise all night; add spices, brandy and wine, in the morning; bake in an oven about hot enough for bread. This makes several cakes and will keep any length of time.

LOAF CAKE.

One pint of lukewarm sweet milk, half teacup butter, one of yeast, one of sugar; add flour to stiffen until you can mould in a pan, and put to rise; when light mix in three cups sugar, one of butter, six eggs, one-half teaspoon soda; put in baking pans and let rise till very light. This is enough for a large family.

AUNT HETTIE'S LOAF CAKE.

Two cups sugar, and one of butter beaten to a cream, three eggs the whites beaten separately, three cups flour with one teaspoon cream tartar stirred in, yolks of the eggs, sugar and butter stirred well; now add three cups more flour with one teaspoon cream tartar, and one cup sweet milk and the whites of the eggs, and then stir again; add one nutmeg, one pound raisins or currants dredged with flour, one teaspoon soda dissolved in four tablespoons water. This makes two nice loaves, and is excellent.

LOAF CAKE.
Mrs. J. L. Porter.

One cup butter, two of sugar, three eggs, one cup molasses, one of milk, five of flour, two teaspoons cream tartar, one teaspoon soda, one pound raisins, one pound currants, and one-quarter pound citron; spices to taste.

MINISTER'S CAKE.
Mrs. O. M. Scott.

One and a half cups sugar, one of butter, three eggs, one cup sweet milk, three of flour, and two teaspoons baking powder.

MARBLE CAKE.
Mrs. M. E. Smith, Cleveland.

White Part.—Seven eggs, (whites), three cups white sugar, one of butter, one of sour milk, four of flour, sifted and heaping, one teaspoon soda; flavor to taste.

DARK PART.—Seven eggs, (yolks), three cups brown sugar, one of butter, one of sour milk, four of flour, sifted and heaping, one table-spoon each of cinnamon, allspice and cloves, one teaspoon soda; put in pans a spoonful of white part, then a spoonful of dark, and so on; bake an hour and a quarter. Use coffee cups to measure. This will make one large and one medium sized cake.

MARBLE CAKE.
Miss Mary Sealts, Mt. Vernon.

WHITE PART—One and a half cups white sugar, one-half cup butter, one-half cup milk, two and a half cups flour, two teaspoons baking pow-der, whites of four eggs beaten to a stiff froth; flavor to taste.

DARK PART—Yolks of four eggs, one and a half cups brown sugar, one-half cup butter, one-half cup milk, two and a half cups flour, two teaspoons baking powder, one teaspoon cinnamon, one teaspoon all-spice, one-quarter teaspoon black pepper, one-half a nutmeg; stir butter and sugar, add the milk, then the eggs, and lastly the flour in which the spices and baking powder have been well mixed; bake one hour. Of course the white and dark part are alternated, either by putting in a spoonful of white, then of dark, or a layer of white, and then of dark part, being careful that the cake may be nicely "marbleized."

MARBLED CHOCOLATE CAKE.
Mrs. Sarah Phelps, Springfield.

Make a batter as you would for white cake, take out one teacup, and to it add five tablespoons grated chocolate; moisten with milk, and fla-vor with vanilla; pour a layer of the white batter into your baking pan, then drop the chocolate batter with a spoon in spots, and spread the remainder of the white batter over it.

ONE EGG CAKE.
Mrs. A. S. C.

One cup butter, one and a half cups sugar, three of flour, one of sweet milk, one egg, one teaspoon soda, and one cup raisins chopped fine.

ORANGE CAKE.
Mrs. D. Buxton.

Two cups sugar, four eggs, leaving out the whites of two, one-half cup butter, one of water, two teaspoons baking powder, three cups flour, and juice and grated rind and pulp of one orange; use the remaining whites for frosting the top.

PEACH CAKE.
Mrs Woodworth, Springfield, Mass.

Bake three sheets of sponge cake as for jelly cake; cut peaches in thin slices; prepare cream by whipping and sweetening, adding flavor of vanilla if desired; put layers of peaches between the sheets of cake, and pour the cream over each layer, and over the top. This may also be made with ripe strawberries.

PLAIN CAKE.
Miss Hannah Snell.

Three eggs, one and one-half cups sugar, three-fourths cup butter, or butter and lard mixed, one teaspoon soda dissolved in a cup of sour milk, one teaspoon lemon, flour enough to make it pretty stiff; bake in quick oven.

CITRON POUND CAKE.
Mrs. J. M. Southard.

Three-fourths pound butter, one of sugar, one of flour, eight eggs; beat yolks and sugar together; beat flour and butter to a cream; add one pound citron sliced thin, then the whites well beaten; flavor with lemon.

MEASURED POUND CAKE.
Mrs. S. W. Dolbear.

One coffee cup sugar, one-half cup butter, one of flour, five eggs beaten separately; citron and currants.

PYRAMID POUND CAKE.
Miss L. Southwick.

One pound sugar, one of flour, ten eggs; bake in a dripping pan so that it will not be more than one inch in thickness when done; cut when cold in squares of four inches, and frost top and sides; form on the cake stand in pyramid before the icing is quite dry; in serving, the squares are the slices.

WHITE POUND CAKE.
Mrs. Ada Estelle Bever, Cedar Rapids, Iowa.

One pound sugar, one of flour, half pound butter, whites of sixteen eggs, one teaspoon baking powder sifted thoroughly with the flour, put in cool oven with gradual increase of heat; for boiled icing for the cake, take three cups sugar boiled in one of water until clear; beat whites of three eggs to very stiff froth and pour over them the boiling liquid, beating all the time for ten minutes; frost while both cake and icing are warm. Good.

QUEEN VIC. CAKE.
Miss M. B. F.

One pound flour, one of sugar, one-half pound butter, four eggs, one nutmeg, lemon if desired, gill of wine, one of brandy, one of cream, one pound raisins; rub the butter, sugar and yolks of eggs to a perfect cream, beating a long time; put in flour and fruit the last thing; bake an hour and a half; this makes two three pint pans full.

SPONGE CAKE.
Mrs. S. M. Guy, Darby Plains.

Six eggs, two teacups pulverized sugar; beat yolks and sugar to a cream, then add one and a half cups of flour with two small teaspoons baking powder in it; then add the whites beaten to stiff froth, stir all slowly till top is covered with bubbles; bake in moderately quick oven.

SPONGE CAKE.
Mrs. Eliza J. Starr.

Three eggs, one and a half cups powdered sugar, two of sifted flour, two teaspoons cream tartar, one-half cup cold water, one teaspoon soda, and grated rind and half of juice of one lemon; bake in dripping pan.

SPONGE CAKE.
Miss S. Alice Melching.

Twelve eggs, one pint pulverized sugar, one of flour, *not* sifted, one small teaspoon salt, one heaping teaspoon baking powder, essence of lemon for flavor; beat the whites to a very stiff froth, and add sugar; beat the yolks, strain and add them to the whites and sugar, beat the whole thoroughly; mix baking powder and salt in the flour and add last, stirring in small quantities at a time; bake in a six quart pan in a moderate oven. This makes one very large sized cake.

SPONGE CAKE.
Mrs. Mary Reynolds, Hamilton.

One pound sugar, one of flour, ten eggs; stir yolks of eggs and sugar until perfectly light; beat whites of eggs and add them with the flour, beating together lightly; flavor with lemon; three teaspoons baking powder in the flour will add to the lightness, but it never fails without. Bake in a moderate oven.

SHERIDAN CAKE.
By Gen. Phil Sheridan's Sister.

Four cups sugar, one and a half cups butter, whites of sixteen eggs, five cups flour, two teaspoons cream tartar with the flour, one teaspoon soda with one cup sweet milk; flavor to taste.

SPICE CAKE.
Mrs. E. L. Coles, Springfield.

One cup butter, one of Orleans molasses, two of sugar, four of flour, one of sweet milk, five eggs, one pound raisins, one-half nutmeg, one tablespoon each of cloves, allspice, ginger, and one teaspoon soda.

SNOW CAKE.
Mrs. Wm. Patrick, Midland, Mich.

One-half teacup butter, one of sugar, one and a half of flour, one-half cup sweet milk, whites of four eggs, one teaspoon baking powder; flavor with lemon.

SNOW CAKE.
Mrs. Dr. Koogler, Connersville, Ind.

Whites of ten eggs beaten to a stiff froth, sift lightly on this one and one-half cups fine white or pulverized sugar, stir well, and add one cup flour mixed with one teaspoon baking powder; flavor with lemon or vanilla.

TEA CAKE.
Mrs. Canby, Bellefontaine.

One quart flour, one cup sour milk, one teaspoon soda, one-half pound lard, one-half pound chopped raisins or currants; roll two inches thick and bake in a quick oven; split open, butter, and eat while hot.

TEN MINUTE CAKES.
Mrs. S. C. Lee, Baltimore, Md.

One-fourth pound butter, a little less than a pound flour, the same of sugar, six eggs beaten separately; flavor with mace; bake in muffin rings.

TILDEN CAKE.
Mrs. T. B.

One cup butter, two of pulverized sugar, one of sweet milk, three of flour, one-half cup corn starch, four eggs, two teaspoons baking powder, two of lemon extract.

WATERMELON CAKE.
Mrs. Baxter.

WHITE PART—Two cups white sugar, one of butter, one of sweet milk, three and one-half of flour, whites of eight eggs, two teaspoons cream tartar, one of soda dissolved in a little warm water.

RED PART—One cup red sugar, one-half cup butter, one-third cup sweet milk, two cups flour, whites of four eggs, teaspoon cream tartar, one-half teaspoon soda, one teacup raisins; be careful to keep the red part around the tube of the pan and the white around the edge. It requires two persons to fill the pan.

WEDDING CAKE.
Mrs. M. L. France.

One pound white sugar, one of flour, three-fourths pound butter, a dozen eggs, two pounds raisins, two of currants, one-half pound citron, fourth ounce nutmeg, fourth ounce cloves, half ounce cinnamon, a cup of molasses, and a little soda.

WEDDING CAKE.
Mrs. C. H. D., Northampton, Mass.

Fifty eggs, five pounds sugar, five of flour, five of butter, fifteen of raisins, three of citron, ten of currants, one pint brandy, one-fourth ounce cloves, one ounce cinnamon, four of mace, four of nutmeg. This makes forty-three and a half pounds, and keeps twenty years.

WHITE CAKE.
Mrs. Daniel Miller.

One cup butter, two of sugar, one of sweet milk, three of flour, whites of five eggs, two teaspoons baking powder.

WHITE CAKE.
Mrs. Clara G. Phellis, Darby Plains.

Whites of ten eggs, two cups sugar, one of butter, one of milk, three and a half of flour, three and a half teaspoons baking powder; flavor to taste.

WHITE CAKE.
Mrs. Harvey Clark, Piqua.

Whites of twelve eggs, three cups sugar, small cup butter, a cup milk, four small cups flour, half cup corn starch, two teaspoons baking powder, lemon to taste. By adding a cup citron sliced thin and dusted with flour, you have a beautiful citron cake.

WHITE CAKE.
Mrs. L. E. Bellus.

Whites of fourteen eggs, (some use whites of sixteen eggs,) one pound sugar, one of flour, three-fourths pound butter, two teaspoons baking powder; this cake keeps well.

By measure; one coffeecup (not quite full) butter, two of sugar, three of flour, (not sifted,) eggs and baking powder as above.

LAYER CAKES.

In baking this kind of cake, it is important to thoroughly grease the tins,—to make it emphatic, we will say thoroughly grease and then grease again; after using them, rub them off with a coarse towel, taking care that they are perfectly free from all small particles of cake, then grease and fill again, thus obviating the necessity of washing them every time they are filled. If jelly is used to spread between the layers, it is a good plan to beat it up smoothly and spread before the cakes are quite cold. When cold, set away on a plate, wrap a cloth around, and put away in a tin cake box.

To blanch almonds, pour boiling water over them, let stand a moment, then drain and throw into cold water, slip off the skins and pound.

ALMOND CAKE.
Mrs. J. H. Shearer.

Two cups sugar, three-fourths cup butter, one of sweet milk, two of flour and one of corn starch well mixed, whites of six eggs, two teaspoons cream tartar in the flour, one teaspoon soda in the milk; cream the butter and sugar; add milk gradually, then the whites of eggs together with the flour, and bake in jelly tins. To put between layers, take two pounds almonds, blanch and pound fine in a mortar, (or a cloth will do), beat whites and yolks of two eggs together lightly, add a cup and a half sugar, then the almonds with one tablespoon vanilla.

ALMOND CREAM CAKE.
Mrs. Paris Gibson, Minneapolis, Minn.

On beaten whites of ten eggs sift one and a half goblets pulverized sugar, and one goblet flour through which has been stirred one heaping teaspoon cream tartar; stir very gently and do not heat it; bake in jelly pans. For cream, take a half pint sweet cream, yolks of three eggs, tablespoon pulverized sugar, teaspoon corn starch; dissolve starch smoothly with a little milk, beat yolks and sugar together with this, boil the cream and stir these ingredients in as for any cream cake filling, only make a little thicker; blanch and chop fine a half pound almonds and stir into the cream. Put together like jelly cake while icing is soft, and stick in a half pound of almonds split in two.

BOSTON CREAM CAKE.
Mrs. M. B. Fullington.

One pint butter rubbed into a quart of flour, one quart hot water with the butter and flour stirred in; cool, break in ten eggs and, if needed, add flour till thick enough to drop on buttered tins in round cakes the size of a small teacup; when baked open and fill with mock cream made as follows: beat three eggs well, add three teaspoons flour or one tablespoon butter, and stir into a pint and a half boiling milk; add saltspoon of salt, sugar to taste, and flavor with lemon or vanilla.

FRENCH CREAM CAKE.
Mrs. Charles Morey.

Three eggs, one teacup granulated sugar, one and a half cups flour, two tablespoons cold water, one teaspoon baking powder. This is enough for two cakes baked in pie pans, to be split while warm, spreading the hot custard between them, or for four cakes baked in jelly pans, with the hot custard spread between them; the latter is the preferable plan. For custard boil nearly one pint sweet milk, mix two tablespoons corn starch with a little sweet milk, add two well beaten eggs; stir in slowly when milk has boiled; let this boil, put in nearly a teacup sugar, and add one-half cup butter stirred until dissolved, flavor with one teaspoon vanilla, and spread between cakes while hot. This cake can be used as a pudding by pouring over each piece a spoonful of the custard that is left.

ICE CREAM CAKE.
Miss Mattie Fullington.

Make good sponge cake, bake half an inch thick in jelly pans, and let them get perfectly cold; take a pint thickest sweet cream, beat until it looks like ice cream, then make very sweet and flavor with vanilla; blanch and chop a pound almonds, stir into cream, and put very thick between each layer. This is the queen of all cakes.

ICE CREAM CAKE.
Mrs. H. B. Sherman.

One cup butter, two of sugar, one of milk, two of flour, one of corn starch; extract salt from butter, cream the butter and sugar, add one teaspoon baking powder, white of eight eggs beaten to a stiff froth; this makes five layers. For filling, take four cups sugar, one of water, cook until it drops thick, cool a little, add whites of four eggs beaten to a stiff froth, and one teaspoon citric acid; flavor with vanilla.

TIP-TOP CREAM CAKE.
Miss Alice Trimble, Mt. Gilead.

One cup water, one-half teaspoon baking powder, one-half cup of butter, three eggs, one cup flour; let the water and butter boil, then stir in the flour, when cool add the eggs one at a time. Heat the tins before putting them in the oven. Inside cream for above cake; one cup milk, half cup sugar, one egg, one-half cup flour, beat the sugar, flour and eggs together and add the milk when boiling.

COCOANUT CAKE.
Miss Nettie Miller, Columbus.

To the well beaten yolks of six eggs, add two cups powdered white sugar, three-fourths cup butter, one of sweet milk, three and a half of flour, one level teaspoon soda and two of cream tartar, whites of four eggs well beaten; bake in jelly cake pans. For icing, grate one cocoanut, beat whites of two eggs, one teacup powdered sugar, mix thoroughly with the grated cocoanut and spread evenly on the layers of cake when they are cold.

COCOANUT CAKE.
Mrs. Mary S. Moore, Granville.

One cup butter, two of sugar, three of flour, four eggs, one cup sweet milk, one of corn starch, (not filling cups of butter and flour very full if eggs are small,) two teaspoons cream tartar, one of soda. Make custard as follows: one cup thick sour cream stirred thin, one cup sugar, one grated cocoanut, one egg beaten separately; spread between layers like jelly cake.

CARAMEL CAKE.
Mrs. Ella Snider, Minneapolis, Minn.

One and a half cup sugar, three-fourths cup butter, one-half cup milk, two and a fourth cups flour, three eggs, one and a half heaping tea-spoons baking powder, or a small teaspoon soda and two teaspoons cream tartar; bake in jelly tins. Make caramel as follows: butter size of an egg, one pint brown sugar, one-half cup milk or water, one-half cake chocolate; boil twenty minutes (or until thick enough) and pour over cakes while warm, piling the layers one upon the other. For frosting for top of cake, take whites of three eggs, one and one-half cups sugar, a teaspoon vanilla, three heaping teaspoons grated chocolate.

COOPER CAKE.
Mrs. C. Fullington.

One cup butter, two of sugar, one of sweet milk, three of flour, whites of five eggs, two teaspoons cream tartar, one teaspoon soda; take one cup of above batter, stir into it a large tablespoon sweet chocolate, wet it with a tablespoon of milk, and alternate the layers, dark and white. It is an addition to put spices in the dark part. For filling, take half cake chocolate grated, a half cup sweet milk, a half cup sugar, yolk of one egg and one tablespoon vanilla; scald until thick like jelly and allow to cool.

CHOCOLATE CAKE.
Mrs. J. H. S.

One cup butter, two of sugar, one of milk, five eggs, leaving out the whites of three, four cups sifted flour, two teaspoons baking powder, or one small teaspoon soda and two cream tartar, in the flour. For icing, take whites of two eggs, beaten stiff, one and a half cups powdered sugar, six tablespoons grated chocolate, two teaspoons vanilla; buy the German or French chocolate that comes in little cakes, and two of the small sections will generally do for a cake.

JUST SPLENDID CUSTARD CAKE.
Mrs. C. Hawks, Goshen, Ind.

Two cups sugar, two and a half cups flour, one-half cup milk, butter size of an egg, whites of ten eggs, two teaspoons cream tartar, one of soda dissolved in milk. For custard take three-fourths pint rich sour cream, yolks of four eggs beaten well with two tablespoons white sugar, whites of two of the eggs beaten with the same quantity of sugar, two pounds almonds blanched and chopped very fine; add the beaten yolks to the cream and beat until as thick as sponge cake, then add the whites and almonds; flavor with vanilla. Spread thick between the cakes.

HARD TIMES CAKE.
Mrs. R. M. Henderson.

One-half cup butter, two of sugar, one of sour cream, three of flour, three eggs, one-half teaspoon soda; bake in layers and spread with jelly.

LADY FINGERS.
Chas. W. Cyphers, Minneapolis, Minn.

Three-fourths pound butter, one of sugar, ten eggs; beat eggs and sugar as light as for sponge cake; sift in with flour one teaspoon baking powder and stir slowly. Make a funnel-shaped bag of heavy ticking or strong brown paper; through the hole in the small end, push a funnel shaped tin tube, one-third inch in diameter at small end and provided with a flange at the other to prevent it from slipping quite through; tie the small end of bag firmly around the tube, and you have a funnel shaped sack with a firm nozzle projecting slightly from the small end. Into this bag pour the batter, over which gather up the bag tightly so that none will run out, press and run the dough out quickly through the tube into a pan lined with light brown paper, (not buttered), making each about a finger long, and about as thick as a lead pencil. Care is required not to get them too wide; sprinkle with granulated sugar, bake in a quick oven, and, when cool, wet the underside of the paper with a brush, remove and stick the fingers together back to back. The bag, when made of ticking, will be useful in making macaroons and other small cakes.

LEMON CAKE.
Mrs. D. Buxton.

One-half cup butter, one of sugar, one of flour, four eggs, three teaspoons milk. For jelly, take one cup sugar, two eggs, juice and rind of lemon; boil in a teacup of water until the consistency of jelly.

MINNEHAHA CAKE
Mrs. E. W. Herrick, Minneapolis, Minn.

One and a half cups granulated sugar, half cup butter stirred to a cream, whites of six eggs, two teaspoons cream tartar stirred in two cups flour, one of soda in half cup sweet milk; bake in three layers. For filling, take a teacup sugar and a little water boiled together until it is brittle when dropped in cold water, remove from stove and stir quickly into the well-beaten white of one egg, add to this a cup of stoned raisins chopped fine, and place between layers and over the top.

NEAPOLITAN CAKE.
Mrs. Calista Hawks Gortner, Goshen, Ind.

Black Part—One cup brown sugar, two eggs, one-half cup butter, one half cup molasses, one-half cup strong coffee, two and a half cups flour, one of raisins, one of currants, a teaspoon each of soda, cinnamon, and cloves, and one-half teaspoon mace.

White Part—Two cups sugar, one-half cup butter, one of milk, two and a quarter of flour, one of corn starch, whites four eggs, small teaspoon cream tartar; make frosting of whites of two eggs to put between the layers. This is excellent.

ORANGE CAKE.
Mrs. W. B. Brown, Washington, D.C.

One cup butter, one of water, two of sugar, four of flour, three eggs, three teaspoons baking powder; bake in layers; take the juice of two large or three small oranges, one coffee cup pulverized sugar, one egg; mix yolk of egg, sugar and juice together; beat whites to a stiff froth, stir in and spread between the layers.

ORANGE CAKE.
Mrs. Sarah Phelps, Springfield

Four and half teacups sifted flour, three teaspoons baking powder stirred into the flour, five eggs, with the yolks of two left out, two cups sugar, one of butter and one of milk; bake in thin layers. For custard, take juice and grated rind of one large orange, add the two yolks that were left out, sweeten to taste, and place on stove and stir until thick enough to spread.

ROLLED CAKE.
Mrs. Major Hall, Minneapolis, Minn.

Five eggs, one and a half cups sugar, one cup flour, one tablespoon cold water, one teaspoon baking powder; bake in a long tin, spread jelly on and roll while warm. Good.

RIBBON CAKE.
Miss A. T.

Two and half cups sugar, one of butter, one of sweet milk, teaspoon cream tartar, half teaspoon soda, four cups flour, four eggs; reserve a third of this mixture, and bake the rest in two loaves of the same size. Add to third reserved, one cup raisins, fourth pound citron, a cup currants, two tablespoons molasses, teaspoon each of all kinds of spice; bake in a tin the same size as other loaves; put the three loaves together with a little icing, or currant jelly, placing the fruit loaf in the middle; frost the top and sides.

SNOW CAKE.
Walter Moore's Favorite.

Beat one cup butter to a cream, add one and a half cups flour, and stir very thoroughly together; then add one cup corn starch, and one cup sweet milk, in which three teaspoons baking powder have been dissolved; last add the whites of eight eggs and two cups sugar well beaten together; flavor to taste, bake in sheets and put together with icing.

VELVET SPONGE CAKE.
Mrs. Wm. Brown, Massillon.

Two cups sugar, six eggs leaving out the whites of three, one cup boiling hot water, two and one half cups flour, one tablespoon baking powder in the flour; beat the yolks a little, add the sugar and beat fifteen minutes, add the three beaten whites, and the cup of boiling water just before the flour; flavor with a teaspoon lemon extract and bake in three layers, putting icing between, made by adding to the three whites of eggs beaten to a stiff froth, six dessert spoons of pulverized sugar to each egg, with lemon to flavor.

VANITY CAKE.
Olivia S. Hinman, Battle Creek, Mich.

One and a half cups sugar, half cup butter, half cup sweet milk, one and a half cups flour, half cup cornstarch, teaspoon baking powder, whites of six eggs; bake in two cakes, putting frosting between and on top.

WASHINGTON CAKE.
Mrs. A. S. C.

Two cups sugar, one of butter, one of sweet milk, four eggs whites and yolks beaten separately, three cups flour, one teaspoon cream tartar, one half teaspoon of soda; bake in jelly pans. For filling, peel and grate two large apples and the rind of one lemon or orange with the juice, one large cup sugar, one egg; boil in a stew-pan and when cold spread over the cakes, placing one on the other, icing the top one with common icing.

WHITE MOUNTAIN CAKE.
Mrs. Skinner, Somerset.

Half cup butter, two of sugar, three and a half of flour, one of sweet milk, two eggs, two teaspoons cream tartar, one of soda; bake in jelly pans and spread with jelly or icing.

DIRECTIONS FOR FROSTING.

Beat whites of the eggs to a stiff froth, add powdered sugar gradually, *beating well all the time*, lastly add flavoring, rose, pineapple or almond for white or delicate cake, and lemon or vanilla for dark or fruit cake. If the cake is rough or brown when baked, dust with a little flour, rub off all loose particles with a cloth, and put on frosting, pouring it around the center of the cake; smooth off as quickly as possible with a knife. If the frosting is rather stiff, dip the knife in cold water. It is better to frost while the cake is still warm. A good general rule for frosting is ten heaping teaspoons powdered sugar to each white of an egg, and some add to this a teaspoon of corn starch. As eggs vary in size, the measurement must also vary, and practice only will teach when the frosting is just stiff enough. If the flavor is lemon juice, allow more sugar for the additional liquid. It is nice when your frosting is almost cold, to take a knife and mark your cake in slices.

ALMOND FROSTING.

Half pint sweet almonds, blanched by putting them in boiling water, stripping off the skins and spreading upon a dry cloth until cold; pound a few of them at a time in a mortar till well pulverized; prepare the frosting, mixing carefully whites of three eggs and three-quarters pint powdered sugar; flavor with a teaspoon vanilla or lemon, and dry in a cool oven or in the open air when weather is pleasant.

BOILED FROSTING.
Mrs. A. S. C.

Whites of three eggs beaten to a stiff froth, one large cup granulated sugar moistened with four tablespoons hot water; boil sugar briskly for five minutes or until it "ropes" from the end of the spoon; turn while hot upon the beaten eggs and stir until cold. If you choose, add half pound sweet almonds, blanched and pounded to a paste, and it will be perfectly delicious. This amount will frost the top of two large cakes.

FROSTING.
Mrs. W. W. W.

Beat whites of two eggs to a stiff froth, add gradually half pound best pulverized sugar, beat well for at least half an hour, flavor with lemon juice (and some add tartaric acid, as both whiten the icing). To color a delicate pink, use strawberry, currant or cranberry; or the grated peeling of an orange or lemon moistened with the juice and squeezed through a thin cloth will color a handsome yellow. This amount will frost one large cake.

FROSTING.
F. M. W.

Break the whites into a broad platter, and *at once* begin adding powdered and sifted sugar, keep adding gradually, beating well all the while until the icing is perfectly smooth; thirty minutes beating ought to be sufficient. A golden color can be given by adding a part of the yolk of an egg; use a quarter of a pound of sugar for each egg.

FROSTING WITH GELATINE.
Mrs. W. A. J.

Dissolve large pinch gelatine in six tablespoons boiling water; strain and thicken with sugar and flavor with lemon. This is enough to frost two cakes.

FROSTING WITHOUT EGG.
Ola Kellogg Wilcox.

Take two even teaspoons Poland starch, add just enough cold water to dissolve, cook until transparent, partially cool and *thicken* with pulverized sugar; flavor to taste. This takes longer to dry than frosting made of eggs, but never becomes brittle so as to snap in pieces when cutting. The above amount will cover a large cake.

HICKORY NUT FROSTING.
Mrs. A. S. C.

Take one or two eggs according to size of cake, with a teacup of sugar to an egg, grind or pound the meats very fine, sprinkle the top of cake as thickly as you choose, and then spread with the frosting.

ORNAMENTAL FROSTING.
Mrs. M. J. W.

Draw a small syringe full of the icing and work it in any design you fancy; wheels, Grecian borders, flowers, or borders of beading look well.

YELLOW FROSTING.
Mrs. J. S. W.

The yolk of one egg to one teacup pulverized sugar, or enough sugar to make it stiff as white frosting.

CRULLERS AND DOUGHNUTS.

To make these good the fat should be of the right heat. When hot enough, it will cease to bubble and be perfectly still; try with a bit of the batter, and if the heat is right the dough will rise in a few seconds to the top and occasion a bubbling in the fat, the cake will swell, and the under side quickly become brown; clarified drippings of roast meat are more healthful to fry them in than lard. If the dough is cut about half an inch thick, five to eight minutes will be time enough to cook, but it is better to break one open as a test. When done, drain well in a skimmer, and place in a colander. The use of eggs prevents the dough from absorbing the fat. Doughnuts should be watched carefully while frying, and the fire must be regulated just right. When you have finished frying, cut a potato in slices and put in the fat to clarify it, place the kettle away until the fat "settles," strain into an earthen pot kept on purpose for this, and set in a cool place. The sediment remaining in the bottom of the kettle can be used for soap grease. Fry in an iron kettle, the common skillet being too shallow for the purpose. Do not eat doughnuts between April and November. Crullers are better the day after they are made.

CRULLERS.
Miss R. J. S.

Two coffee cups sugar, one of sweet milk, three eggs, a tablespoon butter, tablespoon quick yeast, mixed with flour enough to roll, a half nutmeg, teaspoon cinnamon; cut in rings; cook like doughnuts.

CRULLERS.
Mrs. Helen M. Stevenson.

One pint sweet milk, two cups sugar, two tablespoons melted butter, a little salt, four teaspoons cream of tartar, two of soda mixed in the flour, one egg, flour sufficient to make tolerably stiff; roll out in thin sheets; cut in squares, making three or four long incisions in each square; pick each cruller up by one or two of the "straps" thus formed, and drop into boiling fat, and a variety of fanciful shapes may easily be secured.

FRIED CAKES.
Mrs. S. Watson, Upper Sandusky.

One coffee cup sour cream, not too thick, or one of sour milk and one tablespoon of butter, two eggs, a little nutmeg and salt, one teacup sugar, one small teaspoon soda dissolved; mix soft.

ALBERT'S FAVORITE DOUGHNUTS.
Mrs. A. F. Ziegler.

One pint sour milk, one cup sugar, two eggs, one teaspoon soda, half cup lard, nutmeg to flavor; mix to a moderately stiff dough, roll to half inch in thickness, cut in rings or twists, drop into boiling lard and fry to a light brown.

RAISED DOUGHNUTS.

Warm together one pint milk and one cup lard, add one cup yeast; stir in flour to make a batter, let rise over night, then add four eggs, two and a half cups sugar, two teaspoons cassia and half teaspoon soda, a teaspoon salt; knead and let rise again; roll, cut out and let rise fifteen minutes before frying.

SPONGE DOUGHNUTS.

Two cups white sugar, one of sweet milk, three eggs, two teaspoons baking powder, flour enough to roll; cut in rings and fry in hot lard.

COOKIES AND JUMBLES.

These require a quick oven. A nice "finishing touch" can be given by sprinkling them with granulated sugar and rolling over lightly with the rollingpin, then cutting out and pressing a whole raisin in the centre of each; or when done a very light brown, brush over while still hot with a soft bit of rag dipped in a thick syrup of sugar and water; sprinkle with currants and return to the oven a moment.

ADA'S SUGAR CAKES.

Three cups sugar, two of butter, three eggs well beaten, one teaspoon soda, flour sufficient to roll out.

COOKIES.
Mrs. Mary F. Orr.

One cup butter, two of sugar, one of cold water, half teaspoon soda, two eggs, and just flour enough to roll.

LEMON SNAPS.
Mrs. E. L. C., Springfield.

A large cup sugar, two-thirds cup butter, half teaspoon soda dissolved in two teaspoons hot water, flour enough to roll thin; flavor with lemon.

MOLASSES COOKIES.
Miss J. O. De Forest, Norwalk.

Two and a half cups of sugar, half cup molasses, a cup butter, half cup sweet milk, two eggs well beaten, a teaspoon soda and flour enough to roll out.

NUTMEG COOKIES.
Miss M. S., Mt. Vernon.

Two cups white sugar, three-fourths cup butter, two-thirds cup sour milk, half teaspoon soda, two eggs; flavor with nutmeg; cut thin and bake in quick oven.

PEPPERNUTS.
Mrs. Emma G. Rea.

One pound sugar, five eggs, half pound butter, half teacup milk, two teaspoons baking powder, flour enough to roll.

SAND TARTS.
Mrs. Clara G. Phellis.

Two cups sugar, one of butter, three of flour, two eggs leaving out the white of one; roll out thin and cut in square cakes with a knife; spread the white of egg on top, sprinkle with cinnamon and sugar, and press a blanched almond or raisin in the centre.

COCOANUT JUMBLES.
Miss M. E. C.

Two cups sugar, one of butter, two of cocoanut, two eggs, small teaspoon soda mixed with flour; drop heaping teaspoons on buttered paper in pans.

RICH JUMBLES.

One pound sugar, one pound butter, two pounds flour, four eggs, five tablespoons wine or grated peel and juice of lemon; flavor with vanilla or rose water; roll in fine white sugar and cut in rings.

GINGER BREAD.

If in making ginger bread the dough becomes too stiff before you roll it out, set it before the fire. Snaps will not be crisp if made on a rainy day. Ginger bread and cakes require a moderate oven, snaps a quick one. If cookies or snaps become moist in keeping, put them in the oven and heat them for a few moments.

AUNT MOLLY'S GINGER BREAD.
Mrs. Woodworth, Springfield, Mass.

Three and a half pounds flour, one of butter, one quart molasses, half a pint milk, one teaspoon soda; mix the milk, molasses and flour together, melt and add the butter; bake in sheets. This recipe is one hundred years old.

GINGER BREAD.
For General Muster days. Over fifty years old.

One gallon molasses or strained honey, one and a quarter pounds butter, quarter pound soda stirred in a half teacup sweet milk, teaspoon alum dissolved in just enough water to cover it, flour to make it stiff enough to roll out; put the molasses in a very large dish, add the soda and butter melted, then all the other ingredients; mix in the evening and set in a warm place to rise over night; in the morning knead it a long time like bread, roll into squares half an inch thick and bake in bread pans in an oven heated about right for bread. To make it glossy, rub over the top just before putting it into the oven the following: one well beaten egg, the same amount or a little more sweet cream stirring cream and egg well together. This ginger bread will keep an unlimited time.

EXCELLENT
SOFT GINGER BREAD.
Mrs. S. Watson.

One and a half cups Orleans molasses, half cup brown sugar, half cup butter, half cup sweet milk, teaspoon soda, teaspoon allspice, half teaspoon ginger, mix all together thoroughly, add three cups sifted flour and bake in shallow pans.

SPONGE GINGER BREAD.
Mrs. M. M. M.

One cup sour milk, one of Orleans molasses, a half cup butter, two eggs, one teaspoon soda, one tablespoon ginger, flour to make thick as pound cake; put butter, molasses and ginger together, make them quite warm, add the milk, flour, eggs and soda, and bake as soon as possible.

GINGER COOKIES.
Miss Tina Lay, Clyde.

Two cups molasses, one of lard, one of sugar, two-thirds cup sour milk, tablespoon ginger, four teaspoons soda, three stirred in the flour and one in the milk; two eggs.

GINGER CRACKERS.
Mrs. Emeline McChord, Springfield.

One cup brown sugar, two of molasses, two of lard, two teaspoons soda dissolved in a half cup hot water, two even tablespoons ginger.

GINGER CAKES.
Mrs. R. M. Henderson.

One quart Orleans molasses, pint lard or butter, pint buttermilk, two tablespoons soda, two tablespoons ginger, flour enough to make a stiff batter; pour the molasses and milk boiling hot into a large tin breadpan in which have been placed the ginger and soda, (the pan must be large enough to prevent running over,) stir in all the flour possible, after which stir in the lard or butter; when cold mould with flour and cut in cakes. Care must be taken to follow these directions implicitly or the cakes will not be good; remember to add the lard or butter last, and *buttermilk*, not sour milk must be used; boil the molasses in a skillet, and after pouring it into the pan, put the buttermilk in the same skillet, boil and pour it over the molasses, ginger and soda.

GINGER COOKIES.
Mrs. B. T. Skinner, Battle Creek, Mich.

One and a half cups molasses, one of lard, two eggs, one teaspoon salt, one of ginger, one of cinnamon, one tablespoon soda; mix all thoroughly together with only enough flour to roll.

BEST GINGER DROPS.
Mrs. C. Hawks, Goshen, Ind.

Half cup sugar, a cup molasses, half cup butter, one teaspoon each cinnamon, ginger and cloves, two teaspoons soda in a cup *boiling* water, two and a half cups flour; add two well beaten eggs the last thing before baking. Bake in gem tins or as a common ginger bread, and eaten warm with a sauce it makes a nice dessert.

GINGER PUFFS.

Half pound flour, four eggs, teaspoon ginger, a little grated nutmeg, tablespoon loaf sugar, half glass wine, beat well together, bake in cups in a quick oven and serve with wine sauce.

GINGER SNAPS.
Miss Mary Gallagher.

Two cups molasses, one of lard, one tablespoon soda, one of ginger, flour to roll stiff.

HOTEL GINGER SNAPS.
Mrs. Hattie Clemmons.

One gallon molasses, two pounds brown sugar, one quart melted butter, half teacup ground cloves, one-half teacup of mace, half teacup cinnamon, half teacup ginger, two of soda. Very excellent.

GINGER SNAPS.
Mrs. W. P. Anderson.

One pint Orleans molasses, half pint melted lard, half pint boiling water, one and a half tablespoons soda dissolved in water, tablespoon ginger and a little salt; stir in flour to make as soft a dough as possible to roll; take a small quantity at a time, roll thin, and bake in a hot oven.

CREAMS AND CUSTARDS.

For creams and custards, eggs should never be beaten in tin, but always in stone or earthen ware, as there is some chemical influence about tin which prevents their attaining that creamy lightness so desirable in custards. Beat quickly and sharply right through the eggs, beating whites and yolks separately. Allow four eggs, one cup sugar, and one small half teaspoon salt to each quart of milk. Bake in a baking dish until firm in the centre, taking care that the heat is moderate or the custard will turn in part to whey. It is much nicer to strain the yolks after they are beaten, through a small wire strainer, kept for this purpose by every good housekeeper. For boiled custards or floats, always place the milk to boil in a pan or pail set within a kettle of *boiling* water: when the milk reaches the boiling point, which is shown by a slight foam rising on top, add the sugar which cools it so that the eggs will not curdle when added. Let remain a few moments, stirring constantly until it thickens a little, but not long enough to curdle, then either set the pail immediately in cold water, or turn out into a cold dish, (allow ten or fifteen minutes boiling to a quart of custard;) add flavoring after removing from the stove. Peach leaves give a fine flavor, but must be boiled in the milk and then taken out before the other ingredients are added. Boiled custards are very difficult to make, and must have the closest attention until they are finished.

CHARLOTTE RUSSE.
M. Parloa.

Cut stale sponge cake into slices about half an inch thick and line three moulds with it, leaving a space of half an inch between each slice; set the moulds where they will not be disturbed until the filling is ready; take a deep tin pan and fill about one-third full of either snow or pounded ice, and into this set another pan that will hold at least four quarts. Into a deep bowl or pail (a whip churn is better,) put one and a half pints of cream, (if the cream is thick take one pint of cream and a half pint of milk,) whip to a froth, and when the bowl is full, skim the froth into the pan which is setting on the ice, and repeat this until the cream is all froth; then with the spoon draw the froth to one side, and you will find that some of the cream has gone back to milk; turn this into the bowl again, and whip as before; when the cream is all whipped, stir into it two thirds cup powdered sugar, one teaspoon vanilla, and half a box of gelatine which has been soaked in cold water enough to cover it, for one hour, and then dissolved in boiling water enough to dissolve it, (about half a cup full;) stir from the bottom of the pan until it begins to grow stiff; fill the moulds and set them on the ice in the pan for one hour, or until they are sent to the table. When ready to dish them, loosen lightly at the sides and turn out on a flat dish; have the cream ice cold when you begin to whip it; it is a good plan to put a lump of ice into the cream while whipping it.

CHARLOTTE RUSSE.
Mrs. H. B. Sherman.

One quart milk, six ounces sugar, two ounces isinglass; put all into a sauce-pan and on the stove; when dissolved, take off, strain through a seive and put on ice until it begins to set, then add one cup of wine and flavor to taste; when it begins to set, take one quart cream, beat to a stiff froth, and stir all together. Then take charlotte russe moulds, line them with sponge cake with a layer of jelly at the bottom; fill with the custard and set on ice for two hours.

HAMBURG CREAM.
Mrs. C. Fullington.

The rind of one and juice of two large lemons, eight eggs, one cup sugar; put all in a bucket, set in a pan of boiling water, stir for a few minutes, take from the fire, add the whites of eggs beaten and eat when cold.

ITALIAN CREAM.
Mrs. N. P. Wiles, Ripley.

Soak one-third box gelatine half an hour in cold milk, put a quart milk on to boil and when boiling, stir in yolks of eight eggs well beaten, add one cup and a half of sugar and the gelatine; when the custard begins to thicken, take it off and pour into a deep dish in which the eight whites have been beaten to a stiff froth; mix well together and flavor to taste; put in moulds and allow four hours to cool. This cream is much more easily made in winter than in summer.

ROCK CREAM.
Miss Libbie S. Wilcox, Madison.

Boil one cup rice in sweet milk until soft, add two tablespoons loaf sugar, pour into a dish and place on it lumps of jelly; beat the whites of five eggs and three tablespoons pulverized sugar to a stiff froth; flavor to taste, add one tablespoon rich cream and drop the mixture on the rice.

TAPIOCA CREAM.
Mrs. R. M. Henderson.

Soak over night two tablespoons tapioca in one-half teacup milk, (or enough to cover); bring one quart milk to boiling point; beat well together the yolks of three eggs, one-half teacup sugar, and one teaspoon lemon or vanilla for flavoring; add the tapioca, and stir the whole into the boiling milk, let boil once, turn into the dish, and immediately spread on the whites. Serve when *cold*.

VELVET CREAM.
Mrs. J. A. Rea, Minneapolis, Minn.

One and a half quarts of cream, one pint wine, one pound sugar, one ounce gelatine; dissolve gelatine in wine over the fire; dissolve the sugar in the cream and whip; add the wine when cold and whip; pour into moulds.

WHIPPED CREAM.

Baked apples are delicious with it, also all kinds of fresh or preserved berries. Fill your jelly glasses one-third full of jelly, and fill up with whipped cream, and you will have a healthful and delicious dessert. By all means procure a "whip-churn."

BLANC MANGE.
Mrs. E. M. R.

Dissolve three heaping tablespoons corn starch and three of sugar in one pint of milk; add to this three eggs well beaten, and pour this mixture into one pint of boiling milk, stirring constantly until it boils again; just before taking from the stove, flavor to suit the taste and pour into moulds.

RASPBERRY BLANC MANGE.
Mrs. E. M. R.

Stew nice fresh raspberries, strain off the juice and sweeten it to taste, place over the fire and when it boils stir in corn starch wet in cold water, allowing two tablespoons of corn starch for each pint of juice; continue stirring until sufficiently cooked, pour into moulds wet in cold water and set away to cool; eat with cream and sugar. Other fruit can be used instead of raspberries.

MONT BLANC.
Miss Lou Brown, Washington City.

One-half box gelatine soaked half an hour in half pint cold water; add half pint boiling water and, when cool, whites of three eggs well beaten, two cups of sugar, juice of two lemons; beat the whole thoroughly half an hour or more, and put away to cool in a mould or in a dozen egg glasses, (the latter make a handsome dish and easier to serve.) Make a boiled custard of the yolks and one and one-half pints of milk; sweeten to taste. Put the dozen snow balls in the glass fruit dish, and pour over them the cold custard.

APPLE CUSTARD.
Mrs. G. W. Hensel, Quarryville, Pa.

One pint of mashed stewed apples, one pint sweet milk, four eggs, one cup sugar and a little nutmeg; bake slowly.

APPLE SNOW.
Mrs. W. H. E.

Add to the pulp of eight baked apples half pound powdered sugar, the juice of one lemon and the whites of three eggs; beat well together for one hour; make custard of yolks, sugar, and milk, place in a dish, and drop the froth on it in large flakes.

CHOCOLATE CUSTARD.
Mrs. J. H. Shearer.

Two sections chocolate dissolved in one quart of milk, one cup sugar, yolks of six eggs, a heaping tablespoon corn starch; beat the yolks, add the sugar and corn starch, stir all slowly in the boiling milk in which the chocolate is dissolved, add a pinch of salt, and let cook a few minutes stirring constantly; eat cold with white cake.

CORN MEAL CUSTARD.
E. M. R.

One-fourth pound corn meal, one pint milk, boil together fifteen minutes, add one-fourth pound butter, six eggs, rose water, brandy, salt, and sugar to suit the taste; very fine.

FLOATING ISLAND.
Mrs. W. W. W.

Make a custard of the yolks of six eggs, one quart milk, a small pinch of salt, sugar to taste; beat and strain yolks before adding to the milk;

place custard in a large tin pan, and set on stove, stirring *constantly* until it boils, then remove, flavor with lemon or rose, and pour into a dish, (a shallow wide one is best,) spread smoothly over the boiling hot custard the well beaten whites, grating some loaf sugar and cocoanut on the top. Set your dish in a pan of ice water and serve cold.

FLUMMERY.
Mrs. C. F.

Cut sponge cake into thin slices and line a deep dish with it and make it moist with white wine; pour over it a rich custard with the whites on the top.

GOOD BAKED CUSTARD.
M. G.

Eight well beaten eggs, leaving out two whites for the top, three pints milk, sweeten and flavor to taste; bake two hours. Beat whites stiff for the top with a little powdered sugar.

LEMON CUSTARD.

One and a half pints sweet milk, four eggs, juice and rind of one lemon, one cracker rolled and sifted, one cup sugar.

RICE CUSTARD.

One cup cooked rice, one quart sweet milk, three eggs, one cup sugar, one-fourth teaspoon salt, one tablespoon butter, one cup raisins.

SPICED CHOCOLATE.

One quart milk, two squares chocolate, one stick cinnamon, a little grated nutmeg; grate chocolate, boil the milk, reserving a little cold to moisten chocolate which must be mixed perfectly smooth to a paste; when the milk boils put in and boil cinnamon; stir in the chocolate and let boil quickly; pour in a pitcher, and grate in nutmeg. It is nice to add rich cream.

SNOW FLAKE.
Mrs. Col. Woods, Greensburg, Pa.

One package gelatine, pint cold water, quart boiling water, pint wine, three lemons, three pounds sugar, half bottle vanilla; put this away until cold; take the whites of six eggs, beat stiff, then beat up with the jelly and place in moulds. This is a favorite.

CONFECTIONERY.

The first step in candy making is the reduction of sugar to a simple syrup, which is done by dissolving four pounds white sugar in one quart water; place this in a porcelain kettle over a slow fire for half an hour, pour into it a small quantity of gelatine and gum arabic dissolved together; all the impurities will rise to the surface and should be at once skimmed off. Instead of gelatine and gum arabic, the white of an egg may be used as a substitute with good results. To make the clarifying process still more perfect, strain through a flannel bag. When clarified, to make rock candy, boil a few moments, allow to cool, and crystalization takes place on the sides of the vessel. To make other candies, bring the syrup with great care and watchfulness, to such a degree of heat that the "threads," which drop from the spoon when raised into the colder air, will snap like glass. When this stage is reached, add a teaspoon of vinegar or cream tartar to prevent "graining," and pour into pans as directed in the recipes which follow. To make round stick candies, roll into shape with well floured hands as soon as cool enough to be handled. Colored candies are often injurious, and sometimes even poisonous, and should be avoided.

In baking macaroons and kisses use washed butter for greasing the tins, as lard or salt butter gives an unpleasant taste.

CENTENNIAL DROPS.
Miss Alice Trimble, Mt. Gilead.

White of one egg beaten to a stiff froth, one-quarter pound pulverized sugar, one-half teaspoon baking powder; flavor with lemon; butter

93

tins and drop with teaspoon about three inches apart; bake in a slow oven and serve with ice cream. This is also a very nice recipe for icing.

BUCKEYE KISSES.
Mrs. W. W. W.

Beat the whites of four small eggs to a high, firm froth, stir into it half a pound pulverized sugar, flavor with essence lemon or rose, continue to beat until very light; then drop half the size of an egg, and a little more than an inch apart, on well buttered letter paper; lay the paper on a half inch board and place in a hot oven; watch, and as soon as they begin to look yellowish take them out; or, beat to a stiff froth the whites of two eggs, stirring into them very gradually two teacups powdered sugar, and two tablespoons corn starch; bake on buttered tins fifteen minutes in a warm oven, or until slightly brown. Chocolate puffs are made by adding two ounces grated chocolate mixed with the corn starch.

ALMOND MACAROONS.
Miss L. S. W.

Pour boiling water on half a pound almonds, take skins off and throw into cold water for a few moments, then take out and pound, (adding a tablespoon essence lemon) to a smooth paste, add one pound of pulverized sugar and whites of three eggs, and work the paste well together with back of spoon; dip the hands in water and roll mixture into balls the size of a nutmeg, and lay on buttered paper an inch apart; when done, dip the hands in water and pass gently over the macaroons, making the surface smooth and shining; set in a cool oven three-quarters of an hour. If this recipe is strictly followed, the macaroons will be found equal to any made by professed confectioners.

BUCKEYE BUTTER SCOTCH.
Mrs. J. S. R.

Three pounds coffee "A" sugar, one-fourth pound butter, one-half teaspoon cream tartar, eight drops oil of lemon; add as much cold water as will dissolve the sugar; boil without stirring till it will easily break when dropped in cold water, and when *done,* add the oil of lemon; have a dripping pan well buttered and pour in one-fourth inch thick, and when partly cold, mark off in squares. If pulled when partly cold, till very white, will be like ice cream candy.

CANELLONS.
Mrs. V. G. Hush, Minneapolis, Minn.

Make a stiff paste with a quarter pound flour, half as much fine white sugar, half cup melted butter, and a tablespoon grated lemon peel or essence lemon; roll rather thin; make little tubes of stiff paper, about three inches long by one in diameter, butter well the outside and wrap each in some of the paste, close neatly on one side, and bake a few minutes in a quick oven; when done and cooled a little, take out the card and fill with a jelly or marmalade, smoothing over the open ends with a knife dipped in water.

CHOCOLATE CARAMELS.
Miss Emma Collins, Urbana.

One and a half cups grated chocolate, three of brown sugar, and one and a half cups water or milk; flavor with vanilla before taking off; pour into a well buttered and floured dripping-pan, and check off in squares while soft. Avoid stirring while cooking.

CHOCOLATE DROPS.
Mrs. O. M. Scott.

Two and a half cups pulverized or granulated sugar, one-half cup cold water; boil four minutes and stir till cold enough to make into little balls; take half a cake of Baker's chocolate, and cut off fine and set where it will melt; and when balls are cool enough, roll in the chocolate. This makes eighty.

COCOANUT CARAMELS.
Miss Nettie Brewster, Madison.

One pint milk, butter size of an egg, one cocoanut grated fine, three pounds white sugar, two teaspoons lemon, boil slowly until stiff; when partly cold cut in squares.

COCOANUT DROPS.
C. W. Cyphers, Minneapolis, Minn.

One pound cocoanut, half pound powdered sugar, and the white of one egg; work all together and roll into little balls in the hand; bake on buttered tins.

EVERTON ICE CREAM CANDY.
Mrs. J. S. R.

Take one and one-half pounds moist white sugar, two ounces of butter, one and one-half teacups water, one lemon; boil the sugar, butter, and water together with half the rind of the lemon, and when done, (which may be known by its becoming quite crisp when dropped into cold water), set aside till the boiling has ceased, and then stir in the juice of the lemon, butter a dish and pour in about an inch thick. The fire must be quick and the candy stirred all the time.

GERMAN CAKES.
Miss Flora Partridge.

One pound flour, one of white sugar, quarter pound almonds cut into small pieces, five eggs, grated rind of one lemon; drop this mixture into a large buttered pan, a teaspoonful in a place, and bake until tinged with brown. Eggs and sugar should be beaten fifteen minutes.

HICKORY NUT TAFFY.
Aunt Top's Recipe.

Two pints maple sugar, half pint water, or just enough to dissolve sugar, boil until it becomes brittle by dropping in cold water; just before pouring out add a tablespoon vinegar; having prepared the hickory nut meats, in halves if possible, butter well the pans, line with the meats, and pour the taffy over them.

HICKORY NUT MACAROONS.
Mrs. Walter Mitchell, Gallipolis.

Take meats of hickory nuts, pound fine and add ground spice; make frosting as for cakes, stir meats and spices in, putting in enough to make it convenient to handle; flour your hands and make the mixture into balls the size of marbles, lay them on buttered tins, giving room to spread, and bake in a quick oven.

LEMON CANDY.
Mrs. V. K. W.

Take a pound loaf sugar and a large cup water, and after cooking over a slow fire half an hour, clear it with a little hot vinegar, take off the scum as it rises, testing by raising with a spoon, and when the "threads" will snap like glass pour into a tin pan, and when nearly cold mark in narrow strips with a knife. Before pouring into the pans, chopped cocoanut, almonds, hickory nuts or Brazil nuts cut in slices, may be stirred into it.

MOLASSES CANDY.
Sterling Robinson.

Take equal quantities brown sugar and Orleans molasses, and when it begins to boil, skim well and strain, return to the kettle and continue boiling until it becomes brittle if dipped in cold water, then pour on a greased platter. As soon as cool enough, begin to throw up the edges and work by pulling on hook or by hand, until bright and glistening like gold; flour the hands occasionally, draw into stick size, rolling them to keep round, until all is pulled out and cold. Then with shears clip a little upon them at proper lengths for the sticks, and they will easily snap; flavor as you pour the candy out to cool.

PYRAMID OF COCOANUT DROPS.
Mrs. A. G. Wilcox, Minneapolis, Minn.

Boil some loaf sugar to the candy point, (see lemon candy,) rub butter over the outside of the tin or paper form, set firmly on a plate or table, and begin at the bottom by putting a row of "drops" around it, sticking them together with the prepared sugar, then adding another row, and so on until finished. When the cement is cold the pyramid may be taken from the form. Kisses or cocoanut drops, being lighter, are more difficult to make in this form than macaroons.

POP CORN BALLS.
Bert Robinson.

Pop the corn and reject all that is not nicely opened; place a half bushel on a table or dripping pan; put a little water in a suitable kettle, with one pound sugar, and boil until it becomes quite waxy in cold water; remove from fire and dip into it six or seven tablespoons of gum solution, (made by pouring boiling water on gum arabic and letting stand over night;) dip mixture over the corn, putting a stick or the hands under the corn, lifting it up and mixing until it is all saturated, then with the hands press quickly into balls; this amount will make one hundred pop corn balls such as the street peddlers sell, but for home eating, omit the gum solution, and use a half pint of stiff taffy made as above for one peck of popped corn. This will make twenty rich balls.

PEANUT CANDY.

To one pound of coffee sugar, add cold water to moisten, one tablespoon sharp vinegar, one of butter; boil till it will break in cold water; then take your peanut meats broken in bits, stir lightly through the taffy and pour in well buttered dripping pan to the thickness of half an inch, and when partly cold, cut in shapes to suit your fancy; when entirely cold it will easily break where desired.

SUGARED CALAMUS OR SWEET FLAG.
Mrs. R. S. Wilcox, Madison.

Dig the roots, wash and scrape carefully, cut crosswise in thin slices, put in a tin dish or porcelain kettle, cover with water, and boil till soft, (taking care to replace the water as it evaporates;) add its bulk of sugar, simmer slowly a few moments, (it burns easily now,) and pour out on a shallow plate; stir often while drying and the sugar will adhere better to the slices.

VANITY PUFFS.
Mrs. H. C. Mahncke.

Beat five or six whites of eggs very stiff, add a pound of sugar, flavor with lemon or cardamon, cut off about egg size with a tablespoon, put in thin paper, and let dry in a cool stove two hours.

CANNING FRUITS.

Cleanse the cans thoroughly and test to see if any leak or are cracked. If tin cans leak, send them to the tinner; if discolored inside they may be lined with writing paper just before using. If you buy stoneware for canning purposes, be sure that it is well glazed, as fruits canned in jars or jugs imperfectly glazed sometimes become poisonous. Never use defective glass cans, but keep them for storing things in the pantry; and in buying cans, take care that they are free from flaws and blisters, else the glass will crumble off in small particles when subjected to heat. "Self-sealers are very convenient, but the heat hardens the rubber rings, which it is difficult to replace, so that in a year or two they are unfit for use. For this reason, many prefer those with a groove around the top for sealing with wax or putty. The latter is very convenient for use, as jars sealed with it can be opened readily with a strong fork or knife, and are much more easily cleaned than when wax-sealed. Putty may be bought ready for use, and is soon made soft by moulding in the hand, when it should be worked out into a small roll, and pressed firmly into the groove with a knife, care being taken to keep it well pressed down as the can cools.

Fruit should be selected carefully, and all that is imperfect rejected. Large fruits, such as peaches, pears, etc., are in the best condition to can when not quite fully ripe, and should be canned as soon as possible after picking; small fruits, such as berries, should never stand over night. Use only the best sugar, in the proportion of half a pound of sugar to a pound of good fruit, varying the rule of course, with the sweetness of the fruit and your own taste. When ready to can, first place the jars (glass) in a large pan of warm water on the back of the stove, make ready the syrup in a nice clean porcelain kettle, add the fruit,—

it is better to prepare only enough fruit or syrup for two or three cans at a time,—and by the time it is done, the water in the pan will be hot and the cans ready for use. Take them out of the water and set on a hot platter, which answers the double purpose of preventing their contact with any cold surface, like the table, and saving any fruit that may be spilled. Fill as full as possible, and set aside where no current of air will strike them,—or, better, wring out a towel wet in hot water and set them on it,—let stand a moment or two, or until wiped off, when the fruit will have shrunk away a little; fill up again with hot syrup if you have any; if not, boiling water from the teakettle will do, and then seal.

There are several other ways of preparing glass cans for fruit, among them the following: Wring a towel from cold water, double and wrap closely about and under the can so as to exclude the air, put a cold silver spoon inside and fill; or, put a towel in a steamer, set in the cans, and place over a kettle of *cold* water, boil the water, and when ready to fill, remove the cans and wrap in a towel wrung from warm water, put a tablespoon rinsed in hot water inside and fill; or, wash the cans in tepid water, place an iron rod inside, and at once pour in the boiling fruit, but not too fast. In using glass cans with tops which screw on, be sure that the rubbers are firm and close fitting, and throw away all that are imperfect. When the can is filled to overflowing, put on the top at once and screw down tightly, and as the fruit and cans cool, causing contraction of the glass, turn down again and again, until perfectly air tight.

In canning berries, select those of which the skins have not been broken, or the juice will darken the syrup; fill cans compactly, set in a kettle of cold water with a cloth beneath them, over an even heat; when sufficiently heated, pour over the berries a syrup of white sugar dissolved in boiling water, (the richer the better for keeping, though not for preserving the flavor of the fruit,) cover the cans closely to retain heat on the top berries. To insure full cans when cold, have extra berries heated in like manner to supply the shrinkage. If the fruit swims, pour off surplus syrup and fill with hot fruit, and seal up as soon as the fruit at the top is thoroughly scalded.

Glass cans should be wrapped, as soon as cold, with brown wrapping paper, unless the fruit closet is very dark; light injures all fruit, but especially tomatoes, in which it causes the formation of citric acid, which no amount of sugar will sweeten. The place where canned fruits are kept should also be dry and cool. In canning, always use a porcelain lined kettle, silver fork and wire spoon or dipper.

Cans should be examined two or three days after filling, and if syrup leaks out from the rim, should be unsealed, the fruit thoroughly cooked, and kept for jam or jelly, as it will have lost the delicacy of color and flavor so desirable in canned fruits. Pint cans are better for berries than quart. Strawberries keep their color best in stone jars; if glass cans are used they should be buried in sand.

In using self-sealing cans, the rubber ring must show an even edge all round, for if it slips back out of sight at any point, air will be admitted.

On opening tin cans, remember to pour *all* the fruit out into an earthen or glass dish, never leaving it in tin.

Wines, cider, shrubs, etc., must be bottled, well corked, sealed, and the bottles placed on their sides in a box of sand or saw dust.

Plums pricked with a fork will not break when canned.

The fine display of canned fruits at the Centennial was prepared as follows: The fruit was selected with great care, of uniform size and shape, and *all perfect*. They were carefully peeled with a thin, sharp silver fruit knife, which did not discolor them, and immediately plunged into cold water in an earthen or wooden vessel to prevent the air from darkening them. As soon as enough for one can was prepared, it was put up by laying the fruit piece by piece in the can, and pouring syrup, clear as crystal, over it, and then, after subjecting the whole to the usual heat, sealing up.

CANNED BLACKBERRIES.
M. Parloa.

Put the berries in a bright tin pan and set over a boiler of boiling water, adding to a gallon of berries one cup boiling water; heat the berries to the boiling point; will heat much sooner if covered and stirred occasionally. Heat self-sealing jars by putting them in a pan of cold water, set on the stove and let the water boil; fill the jars to the top, put on the covers and set as tightly as possible, and as the glass shrinks in cooling set *very* tight. Always use the fruit as soon as opened. Any kind of fruit put up in this way will keep nice for years.

GREEN GOOSEBERRIES.
Mrs. O. M. S.

Cook the berries in water until white, but not enough, to break them; put into cans with as little water as possible, fill up the can with boiling water and seal; when opened pour off water and cook like fresh berries.

CANNED PEACHES OR PEARS.
Miss L. W. F.

Pare, halve and core, sweeten just as you would for palatable eating, (one or two pounds of sugar to ten or twelve quarts fruit,) let stand until sugar is dissolved, (use no water,) place on the stove in a porcelain kettle and keep at boiling point long enough to heat it through. The heating expels the air. Prepare all berries, cherries, plums, etc., in this manner. Follow the directions for canning in glass jars.

CANNED PEACHES.
Mrs. W. W. W.

Pare, halve and seed; make a syrup of one pint granulated sugar to one quart water, place on stove in a porcelain kettle; (enough for two one quart cans.) When syrup boils, drop in enough fruit for one can; watch closely, testing with a silver fork, so that the moment they are done they may be removed. When the peaches are tender, lift very gently with a wire spoon, and place in the can previously heated, according to instructions for preparing glass cans. When full of peaches, pour in the hot syrup, place the cover on and seal at once; then add more peaches to your hot syrup for next can and repeat the operation. If you have more peaches than will fill the can, place them in another can and *keep hot* until more are ready, and so on until all are canned. Skim the syrup before adding peaches, making only enough syrup at one time for two cans.

CANNED PEACHES.
Mrs. Frank Stahr, Lancaster, Pa.

Take one peck of large clingstone peaches, pour boiling water over them to remove the fuzz, make a syrup of three pounds of sugar and one pint of vinegar, using a little water if required to cover the peaches, cook until pretty soft, and can as usual.

CANNED PEACHES.
Mrs. R. A. Sharp, Kingston.

Have two porcelain kettles, one with boiling water, the other with a syrup made sweet enough with white sugar for your peaches; pare, halve, and drop them into the boiling water; let them remain until a silver fork will pierce them; lift them out with a wire spoon, and place in the can until full, then pour on enough of the boiling syrup to fill the can, and seal immediately; continue in this way, preparing and sealing only one can at a time, until done; boil down the water in your kettle with the syrup if any is left, if not add more sugar, and you will have quite a nice marmalade. This manner of canning peaches, has been thoroughly tested, and pronounced by the *experienced*, the *best* of all methods.

CANNED PINE APPLE.

Peel and slice, make syrup in proportion of two and a half pounds best white granulated sugar to nearly three pints of water; boil five minutes; skim or strain; add fruit and let it boil; have cans hot; fill and shut up as soon as possible.

CANNED PEACHES.
Miss Abbie Curtis, St. Louis, Mo.

To peel, place in a wire basket, such as is used for popping corn, dip into boiling water for a moment, then into cold water; strip off the skin; in this way save both fruit and labor. The fruit must be at a certain stage to be prepared in this way, for if too green, it will not peel, and if too ripe it will be too much softened by the hot water. After peeling, seed and place them in a steamer over a kettle of boiling water, first laying a cloth in bottom of steamer; fill about half full with fruit, cover tightly, make a syrup in a porcelain kettle kept for fruit alone, let the fruit steam until it can be easily pierced with a silver fork, drop gently for a moment into the hot syrup, place in the cans, fill, cover and seal. The above recipe is for canning a few at a time, and is equally as nice for pears.

CANNED STRAWBERRIES.

Fill glass jars with fresh whole strawberries sprinkled with sugar in the proportion of half pound sugar to a pound berries, lay covers on lightly, stand them in a wash boiler filled with water to within an inch of tops of cans; (the water must not be more than milk warm when the cans are placed in it.) When it has boiled for fifteen minutes, draw to back of stove, let the steam pass off, roll the hand in a towel, lift out the cans, and place on a table. If the berries are well covered with their own juice, take a tablespoon and fill up the first can to the very top of the rim from the second, wipe the neck, rub dry and screw the top down firmly, observing carefully the general directions for canning berries. Fill another from the second can, and so on until all are finished.

CANNED CORN.
Miss Lida Cartmell.

Dissolve one ounce tartaric acid in half teacup water, and of it take one tablespoon to every two quarts of sweet corn; cook it, and while boiling hot, fill the cans, which should be tin. When used, turn into a colander, rinse with cold water, add a little soda and sugar when you cook it, and season with butter, pepper and salt.

CANNED SWEET CORN.
Mrs. A. I. J.

Pick corn when milk-ripe, cut from the cob and scrape so as to get all the juice, place in tin cans and seal up air-tight; set them in boiling water from one to two hours according to size of can, and next day punch a small hole in the top of the can to allow the gases to escape, and immediately re-seal, after which place in boiling water and let remain as long or longer than at first.

CANNED TOMATOES IN STONE JUGS.
Mrs. W. A. C.

Wash, cut up, and put on to cook with a little salt; boil till perfectly soft, strain through a colander, turn back to cook again, and when they come to a boiling heat, pour into hot one or two-gallon stone jugs, cork and dip in hot cement, or pour the cement over the cork. When cool it is a good plan to dip again, so as to make perfectly air-tight.

CANNED TOMATOES.

Use glass or stone jars. Tin is nice for one year, but will not do any longer, and some save their oyster cans in the winter and use once for this purpose. To secure them take a cloth much larger than size of hole, cover it with sealing wax, place on the can sticking it down, cover again with sealing wax, and if you have succeeded in making the can air-tight, the cloth will be drawn considerably down into the hole. The tomatoes should be scalded so as to peel easily, cut up, all hard and decayed portions removed, drained in a sieve or colander, and allowed to boil a very few minutes, four or five at most if perfectly ripe; then canned and sealed tight. If they remain too long over the fire the seeds will impart a bitter taste. Never put salt in your tomatoes when you use tin cans, as it has a tendency to cause rust.

CANNED WATER MELON.
Mrs. C. T. C.

Cut the melons, and after taking out the cores peel all the green part off carefully, cut the rind into small pieces two or three inches long, and boil until tender enough to pierce with a fork; have a syrup made of white sugar, allowing one-half pound sugar to one pound fruit, skim out the melon and place in this syrup together with a few pieces of race ginger; let cook a few minutes, put in cans and seal hot.

CATSUPS AND SAUCES.

Always select perfect fruit; cook in porcelain, never in metal. Some, in making catsup, instead of boiling, sprinkle the tomatoes with salt and let them stand over night, then strain and add spices, etc., and a little sugar. Bottle in glass or stone, and never use tin cans for catsups; keep in a cool, dry, dark place. If, on opening, you find a leathery mould on top, carefully remove every particle of it, and the catsup will not be injured. To prevent this moulding of catsup some do not fill the bottles quite full, filling up with hot vinegar. If there are white specks of mould all through the catsup it is spoilt. If, on opening and using a part, you fear that the rest may sour, scald, and, if too thick, add vinegar. Sauces should always be made in a pan set in hot water, with great care, having your sauce pan *clean* if you want a delicate flavor, especially if the sauce is drawn butter.

CUCUMBER CATSUP.
Mrs. Hattie Clemmons, Asheville, N. C.

Three dozen cucumbers and eighteen onions peeled and chopped very fine; sprinkle over them three-fourths pint table salt, put the whole in a sieve and let drain well over night, add a teacup mustard seed, half teacup ground black pepper, mix well and cover with good cider vinegar.

CURRANT CATSUP.

Four pounds nice fully ripe currants, one and a half pounds sugar, tablespoon ground cinnamon, a teaspoon each of salt, ground cloves and pepper, pint vinegar; stew currants and sugar until quite thick, add other ingredients and bottle for use.

CHERRY CATSUP.
Miss M. Louise Southwick.

One pint cherry juice to half or three-fourths pound sugar, with cloves, cinnamon, and a very little cayenne pepper; boil to a thick syrup; bottle for use.

GOOSEBERRY CATSUP.
Mrs. Col. W. P. Reid, Delaware.

Nine pounds gooseberries, five pounds sugar, one quart vinegar, three tablespoons cinnamon, one and a half each allspice and cloves. The gooseberries should be nearly or quite ripe; take off blossom; wash them and put into a porcelain kettle, mash thoroughly, scald and put through the colander, add sugar and spices and boil fifteen minutes, and then add the vinegar cold; bottle immediately before it gets cold. Ripe grapes prepared by same rule, make an excellent catsup.

TOMATO CATSUP.
Mrs. H. C. Clarke, Kankakee, Ill.

Add to a bushel ripe tomatoes boiled until soft and squeezed through a wire sieve, half gallon best vinegar, half pint salt, two ounces cloves, quarter pound allspice, a half ounce cayenne pepper, three teaspoons black pepper, (spices whole,) five onions or garlics, skinned and separated in rings; mix all together and boil two hours; bottle without straining.

TOMATO CATSUP.
Mrs. Erastus Byers, Minneapolis, Minn.

One gallon skinned tomatoes, four tablespoons common salt, four of black pepper, two of allspice, three of ground mustard, one teaspoon cayenne; simmer slowly in one gallon cider vinegar to about five quarts and a half of tomatoes; strain through a sieve and bottle while hot; cork the bottle and dip into hot sealing wax.

BREAD SAUCE.
Mrs. H. C. E.

Half a pint grated bread crumbs, one pint sweet milk, and one onion; boil until the sauce is smooth, take out onion and stir in two spoonsful butter with salt and pepper; boil once and serve with roast duck or any kind of game.

CRANBERRY SAUCE.
C. G. & E. W. Crane, Caldwell, N.J.

To every pound of fruit add three-quarters of a pound of sugar and a half pint of water; stew together over a moderate but steady fire. Be careful *to cover* and *not to stir* the fruit, but occasionally shake the vessel, or apply a gentler heat if in danger of sticking or burning. If attention to these particulars be given, the berries will retain to a considerable extent, their shape, which is desirable, and adds greatly to their appearance on the table. Boil from five to seven minutes, when they should be removed from the fire, turn into a deep dish, and set aside to cool. If to keep, they can be put up at once in air-tight jars. Or, for strained sauce, one and a half pounds of fruit should be stewed in one pint of water for ten or twelve minutes, or until quite soft, then strain through a colander or fine wire sieve, and three-quarters of a pound of sugar thoroughly stirred into the pulp thus obtained—when after cooling, it is ready for use. Serve with roast turkey or game.

CELERY SAUCE.
Mrs. J. M.

Cut the heads of celery in pieces two or three inches long, boil till tender; add to half a pint of cream or milk, the well beaten yolks of two eggs, a little salt, a bit of butter and pepper, or a little grated nutmeg; bring just to the boiling point, pour over celery and serve with roast duck. Or, chop fine two bunches of celery, and boil an hour; when done have about one and a half pints of water in your kettle; stir in two spoonsful of flour mixed smooth in cold water, boil ten minutes, add two spoonsful butter and season with salt and pepper.

CURRY POWDER.
Mrs. C. Fullington.

An ounce of ginger, one of mustard, one of pepper, three of coriander seed, three of tumeric, one-half ounce cardamon, quarter ounce cayenne pepper, quarter ounce cumin seed; pound all fine, sift and cork tight. One teaspoonful of powder is sufficient to season anything. This is nice for boiled meats and stews.

CHILI SAUCE.
Mrs. E W. H., Minneapolis, Minn.

Twelve large ripe tomatoes, four ripe or green peppers, two onions, two tablespoons salt, two of sugar, one of cinnamon, three cups vinegar; peel tomatoes and onions, chop fine, and boil one and a half hours. This will keep any length of time.

DRAWN BUTTER.
Miss C. D.

Rub a small cup of butter into half a tablespoon flour, beating it to a cream, and, if needed, add a little salt; pour on it half a pint boiling water, stirring it fast, taking care not to let it *quite* boil, as boiling spoils it, making it *oily* and unfit for use. The boiling may be prevented by placing the saucepan containing it, in a larger one of boiling water, covering and shaking frequently until it reaches the boiling point. A great variety of sauces which are excellent to eat with fish, poultry or boiled meats, can be made by adding different herbs to sweet pleasant tasting butter melted. Make quickly, not suffering it to boil, and serve immediately. Two hard boiled eggs, chopped fine, added, make a nice sauce to serve with baked fish.

HOLLAND SAUCE.

Put into a saucepan a teaspoon flour, two ounces butter, two tablespoons each of vinegar and water, the beaten yolks of two eggs, and salt to taste; put over the fire and stir constantly until it thickens, but do not allow it to boil or it will curdle and require straining through a gravy strainer; add the juice of one-half lemon and serve with baked fish.

OYSTER SAUCE.
Mrs. H. C. M.

Set a basin on the fire with half a pint of oysters, from which all bits of shell have been picked, and one pint of boiling water; let them boil three minutes, skim well, and then stir in half a cup of butter beaten to a cream, with two spoons flour; let this come to a boil, and serve with roasted turkey.

ONION SAUCE.
E. H. W.

Boil three or four white onions till tender, mince fine, boil one-half pint milk, add butter half size of an egg, salt and pepper to taste, and stir in minced onion and a tablespoon of flour which has been moistened with milk.

PARSLEY SAUCE.
Mrs. W. E. H.

Tie a few sprigs together with a thread and throw them for a minute into boiling water, then cut fine, and add to drawn butter.

ROMAN SAUCE.
Miss E. T. E.

Take one teacup of water and one teacup milk, put on fire to scald, and when hot stir in a tablespoon flour previously mixed smooth with a very little cold water, add three eggs well beaten and strained, season with salt and pepper, two tablespoons butter and a little vinegar; boil four eggs hard, slice and lay over the dish; pour over sauce and serve with boiled fish.

SALAD SAUCE.
Mrs. A. E. Brand, Minneapolis, Minn.

Boil two eggs three minutes; mix with them a mustard spoon of prepared mustard, a little pepper and salt, six spoonsful drawn butter or salad oil, six of vinegar, one of catsup. This is excellent for cold meat, salad or fish.

TO PREPARE MUSTARD.
Mrs. Olivia S. Hinman, Battle Creek, Mich.

One pint vinegar, boil, stir in a quarter pound mustard while hot, add two tablespoons sugar, one teaspoon salt, and one of white pepper; let the mixture boil.

DRINKS.

Buy coffee in the grain to avoid adulteration, either raw, or in small quantities freshly roasted. The best kinds are the Mocha and Java, and some prefer to mix the two, having roasted them separately. West India coffee, though of a different flavor, is often very good.

Roast coffee with the greatest care—for here lies the secret of success in coffee-making—and in small quantities, as there is a peculiar freshness of flavor when newly roasted. Pick over carefully, wash and dry in a moderate oven, increase the heat and roast quickly either in the oven, or on top of the stove or range; in the latter case, stir *constantly,* and in the oven stir *often,* with a wooden spoon or ladle kept for this purpose. The coffee must be thoroughly and evenly roasted to a dark rich brown, not black, throughout, and free from any burnt grains, a few of which will ruin the flavor of a large quantity. It must be tender and brittle, to test which take a grain, place it on the table, press with the thumb and if it can be crushed, it is done; stir in a lump of butter while it is hot, or wait until about half cold, and then stir in a well beaten egg. This latter plan is very economical, since your coffee will not need any further clarifying. Keep in a closely covered tin or earthen vessel. Never attempt other work while roasting coffee, but give it the entire attention. Grind not too fine, as needed, for the flavor is dissipated if it is long unused after grinding even when under cover. If properly roasted, coffee will grind into distinct, hard, and gritty particles, and not into a powder. "One for the pot" and a heaping tablespoon of ground coffee for each person, is the usual allowance. Mix well either with a part or the whole of an egg and enough cold water to thoroughly moisten it, place in a *well scalded* "coffee boiler," and pour in half the quantity of boiling water needed, allowing one pint less of water than you have tablespoons of coffee. Boil rather fast five minutes, stirring down from the top and sides as it boils up, and place on back part of stove or range where it will just simmer for ten or fifteen minutes longer. When ready to serve add the remainder of the boiling water. Boiling coffee a great while makes it strong, but not so lively or agreeable.

The National Coffee Pot is considered by many the best, but the "gude wife" can improvise one equally as desirable and much more simple. Make a sack of canton flannel or muslin, *more* than long enough to reach the bottom of the coffee pot, whip a wire around the top, place the coffee, either mixed with or without an egg, in the sack, pour on boiling water, turn down the top of sack over the nose of the coffee pot, securing it well so that none of the aroma can escape, close the lid tightly, let simmer, (not boil,) half an hour, raise the sack off the nose, but not out of coffee pot, and pour for the table; or, a simpler way is to roll a cloth tightly and stop up the nose or spout, thus keeping in all the coffee flavor.

"Coffee for one hundred" can be made in no way so good as the following: Take five pounds roasted coffee, grind and mix with six eggs, make small muslin sacks, and into each place a pint of coffee leaving room to swell; put five gallons boiling water in a large coffee urn or boiler, having a faucet at the bottom; put in part of the sacks and boil two hours; five or ten minutes before serving raise the lid, and add one or two more sacks, and if you continue serving several times, add fresh sacks at regular intervals, taking out from time to time those first put in, and filling up with boiling water as needed. In this way the full strength of the coffee is secured, and the fresh supplies impart that delicious flavor consequent on a few moments boiling.

To make coffee for twenty persons, use one and a half pints ground coffee and one gallon of water.

MAKING TEA.

"Polly, put the kettle on, and we'll all take Tea."

For of all "cups that cheer" there is nothing like the smoking hot cup of tea, made with *boiling* water, in a *thoroughly scalded* tea-pot; and if it is the good old fashioned green tea of "ye ancient time," you must just put it to *draw* and not to boil; if it is genuine "English Breakfast" or *best* black tea, the water must not only be boiling hot, at the very moment of pouring it on, but the tea must actually boil for at least five or ten minutes. To insure "keeping hot" while serving, make the simple contrivance known as a "bonnet" which is warranted a "sure preventive" against that most insipid of all drinks—"a warmish cup of tea." It is merely a sack with a loose elastic in the bottom large enough to cover and encircle the entire tea-pot. Make it with odd pieces of silk, satin, or cashmere, lined, quilted and embroidered, if you like; draw this over the tea-pot as soon as the tea is poured into it, and it will remain piping hot for half an hour. One teaspoon of tea and one teacup of hot water is the usual allowance for each person. Freshly boiled soft water is the best for either tea or coffee. Always have a water-pot of hot water, on your waiter, with which to weaken each cup if desired. Serve with the best and richest cream, but, in the absence of this luxury, a good substitute may be found in boiled milk prepared as follows: place fresh new milk in a pan or pail, set where it will slowly simmer but *not boil* or reach the boiling point, stir frequently to keep the cream from separating and rising to the top, let simmer until it is rich, thick and creamy.

COFFEE WITH WHIPPED CREAM.
Marion Harland.

For six cups of coffee of fair size, one cup sweet cream, whipped light with a little sugar, will be needed; put into each cup the desired amount of sugar, and about a tablespoon boiling milk; pour the coffee over these, and lay upon the surface of the hot liquid a large spoonful of the frothed cream, giving a gentle stir to each cup before sending around. This is known to some as *meringued* coffee, and is an elegant French preparation of the popular drink.

COCOA.

Take three heaping tablespoons cocoa, mix with a little cold water, add one pint boiling water, boil ten minutes, add another pint of hot water and serve at once. This quantity is sufficient for three persons. Chocolate can be prepared in the same way.

CHOCOLATE.

Take six tablespoons scraped chocolate, or three of chocolate and three of cocoa, dissolve in a quart of boiling water, boil hard fifteen minutes, add one quart of rich milk, let scald and serve hot; this is enough for six persons. Cocoa can also be made after this recipe. Some boil either cocoa or chocolate only one minute and then serve, while others make it the day before using, and boil for one hour; when cool, skim off the oil, and when wanted for use, heat to the boiling point, and add the milk. In this way it is as good and much more wholesome.

CIDER.
C. T. Carson, Maple Grove Farm.

Take good grafted fruit, press and strain juice as it comes from the press through a woolen cloth into a barrel; let stand two or three days if cool, if warm not more than a day; rack once a week for four weeks, put in bottles and cork tightly. This will make perfect cider. Do not put anything in it to preserve it, as all so called preservatives are humbugs. Lay the bottles away on their sides in sawdust.

GRANDMOTHER'S HARVEST DRINK.

One quart of water, one tablespoon sifted ginger, three heaping tablespoons sugar, one half pint vinegar.

LEMONADE.
S. A. M.

Take six lemons, roll them well, slice thin in an earthen vessel, putting on them two teacups white sugar; let stand fifteen minutes, add one gallon water and lumps of ice, pour out into pitcher and serve. Some add soda and stir rapidly for "sparkling lemonade."

LEMON SYRUP.
Abby G. Backus, West Killingly, Conn.

Press the juice of lemons into a bowl, strain out all seeds, remove the pulp from the rind and boil in one pint of water for a few minutes.

Strain the water with the juice, add a pound of sugar to a pint of juice, boil ten minutes and bottle. Use one or two tablespoons of syrup to a glass of water.

APPLE TEA.

Take good sour apples, slice thin, pour on boiling water and let stand until cool; pour off water, sweeten a little, and flavor.

ICED TEA.

Prepare tea in the morning, making stronger and sweeter than usual; strain and pour into a nice clean stone jug or glass bottle, set aside in the ice chest until ready to use. Drink from goblets without cream. Serve ice broken in small pieces on a platter nicely garnished with well washed grape leaves. Iced tea may be prepared from either green or black alone, but it is considered an improvement to mix the two.

EGGS.

The fresher they are the better and more wholesome, though new laid eggs require to be cooked longer than others. Eggs over a week old, will do to fry but not to boil. In boiling they are less likely to crack if dropped in water not quite to the boiling point. Eggs will cook soft in three minutes, hard in five, *very hard* in ten to fifteen minutes, the last to serve with salads, or to slice thin, (seasoned well with pepper and salt,) and put between thin slices of bread and butter.

Put eggs in water to tell good from bad; those which lie on the side are good; reject those which stand on end as bad; the vessel should have a smooth level bottom; or, examine each egg separately and look through it at the sun, or toward a lamp in a darkened room; if the white looks clear, and the yolk can be easily distinguished, it is good; if a dark spot appears in either white or yolk, it is stale; if heavy and dark when you look through them, or they gurgle when shaken gently, they are "totally depraved." The best and safest plan is to break each egg in a saucer before using.

To keep eggs, pack closely in salt or bran, standing them on the small end, or place them in a stone jar, and pour over them a mixture made of half a gallon air-slacked lime, one tablespoon cream tartar, one ounce of salt, and half a gallon cold water. This quantity will keep four and a half dozen. If the water settles away, add enough to cover and turn a saucer over the top to keep the eggs down; or dip them in oil or a weak solution of gum; this renders the shell impervious to air and they will keep a long time. A nice way to keep those wanted for table use is to pour boiling water over them, repeating the operation several times, until the albumen is hardened; when cool, pack with the small end down in salt or bran. Always secure the freshest eggs for packing, cover closely, and keep in a cool place.

To make an omelet, beat the yolks until thick and creamy, then add the milk, the salt, pepper and flour if any is used, and lastly the whites beaten to a stiff froth. Have the skillet as hot as can be without scorching butter; put in a tablespoon of butter, pour in the omelet, which should at once begin to bubble and rise in flakes. Slip under it a thin, broad bladed knife, and every now and then raise it up to prevent burning. As soon as the underside is hard enough to hold well together, and the eggs begin to "set," fold over, shake the skillet so as to entirely free the omelet, then carefully slide it on a hot platter and serve at once. It should cook in from three to five minutes. To bake an omelet, place in the frying pan on top of stove until it begins to "set" in the middle, then place in a rather hot oven; when slightly browned, fold if you like, or turn a hot dish on top of the pan, upset the latter with a quick motion, and so dish the omelet with the underside uppermost. It should bake in from five to ten minutes. Where a large quantity of eggs are used, instead of making into one large omelet, divide and make several, sending each to the table as soon as done. Ham, chicken, and all kinds of meat omelets, are made by chopping the meat fine, and placing between the folds before dishing.

For a plain omelet, easily made, take three tablespoons milk and a pinch of salt for each egg; beat the eggs lightly for three or four minutes, pour them into a hot pan in which a piece of butter the size of a walnut has just been melted, cook three or four minutes, fold over and serve at once. Some scald a little parsley, pour off the water, chop it, and mix with the omelet just before pouring into the pan.

BOILED EGGS.
Miss L. S.

Put them into cold water, and when it has boiled, the eggs will be done, the whites being soft and digestible, as they are not when put into boiling water.

BOILED EGGS.
Mrs. A. R. Gould, Delaware.

Put the eggs in a dish without breaking the shells, pour boiling water over them and let them stand in it away from the fire for from five to eight minutes; this is better than boiling rapidly on the stove, as it cooks them through without hardening the whites too much.

BAKED EGGS.
Mrs. J. F. W.

Butter a dish and break into it as many eggs as will cover the bottom, set in the oven and bake till the whites are cooked; add a piece of butter, pepper and salt, stir in quickly and serve.

EGGS ON TOAST.
Mrs. L. E. Bellus.

Cut the bread three-quarters of an inch thick, warm through on each side, and brown nicely; from a dish of melted butter put some upon each slice with a spoon; place toast in a covered dish, and set in the oven or where it will keep warm; put a saucepan of boiling water on the stove, break in the eggs, let remain until whites are stiff, take up carefully with a spoon and lay one on each half slice of toast; put the toast thus crowned on a warm platter and send to table.

EGG GEMS.
Mrs. H. B. S.

Mix chopped meat, bread crumbs, salt, pepper, butter, and a little milk; fill some buttered gem-pans with the mixture, break an egg carefully upon the top of each gem, sprinkle a little salt, pepper and bread crumbs upon each egg, and bake eight minutes; serve hot.

FRIZZLED HAM AND EGGS.
Mrs. D. B.

Take bits of either boiled or fried ham, chop fine, and place in your skillet prepared with butter or beef drippings; take four to six well beaten eggs, pour over your ham, and when heated through, season well with pepper and salt; stir together, and cook until done brown, and turn over without stirring.

OMELET.
Mrs. H. B. S.

Seven eggs beaten separately, one teaspoon flour, one teaspoon salt, a pint of warm milk, (see directions for making an omelet;) this will make one large omelet or two small ones; bake twenty minutes.

CORN OMELET.
Mrs. Frank Stahr, Lancaster, Pa.

Take six ears corn, grate or cut the corn fine, add four eggs, a tablespoon of flour, a cup of milk, season with pepper and salt, and bake half an hour.

OMELET SOUFFLE.

Take eight eggs, beat whites to a stiff froth, and after beating the yolks add two tablespoons sugar, pour the yolks into the beaten whites, do not beat again, but pour all on a buttered tin plate and put in the oven. When it begins to rise take a spoon and pile in pyramid shape. The whole baking requires but three or four minutes.

PUFF OMELET.

The yolks of six eggs and the whites of three beaten very light, mix one tablespoon of flour into a teacup of cream or milk, stir into the beaten eggs, with salt and pepper to taste; melt a tablespoon butter in a pan; pour into the mixture and set the pan into a hot oven; when it thickens, pour over it the remaining whites of eggs well beaten, return it to the oven, and let it bake a delicate brown, slip off on a large plate and eat as soon as done.

POACHED EGGS.
Mrs. E. G. R.

Break the eggs in hot water and boil for two minutes, pour off the water, and beat the eggs until they are light; season with salt, pepper and butter; serve on toast, or simply in sauce dishes.

RUMBLED EGGS.
Mrs. C. C. Lyman, Harmar.

Beat up three eggs with two ounces fresh or washed butter, add a teaspoon of cream or fresh milk; put in a sauce pan and keep stirring over the fire for five minutes or till it rises; dish on toast.

FISH.

Before dressing fish, remove all scales, (these may be loosened by pouring on hot water,) and scrape out every particle of blood, entrails, etc., being careful not to crush the fish more than is absolutely necessary in cleaning. Wash thoroughly in cold water, (not allowing them to stand in it,) drain, wipe dry, and to remove earthy taste from fresh water fish, sprinkle with salt and let lie over night, or a few hours at least, before cooking; rinse off, wipe dry, and to completely absorb all the water, place in a folded napkin a short time. Soak salt fish in water from twelve to twenty-four hours. To fry fresh fish, clean as above, cut off the head; if a large fish, cut out the back bone, slice the body crosswise into five or six pieces according to the size; dip in Indian meal or wheat flour, or in a beaten egg and then in bread crumbs, fry rather slowly half or three-quarters of an hour, in boiling hot lard or beef drippings, (never in butter,) in a thick bottomed skillet, taking care to place the fish skin side uppermost, turning when a light brown. The flavor is improved by adding a few pieces of salt pork or bacon. The back bone, if previously removed, may be cut up and fried with other pieces, also the roe. In broiling fresh fish, prepare the same as for frying. Rub gridiron with lard or drippings, and to turn invert gridiron with one hand over an old platter or pan held in the other, then gently slip the fish back on the gridiron and broil the other side. All fish should have the skin side turned to the fire last, as it burns easily and the coals are less hot after using a few minutes. Salt fish may be broiled in the same manner after the soaking in cold water.

To bake fish, cleanse, rub the inside well with salt, and stuff with a delicate dressing such as is used for fowls. Chopped salt pork may be used instead of butter in dressing. Sew up, dredge with flour, lay on slices of pork or bits of butter, and place on a tin sheet that fits loosely into the baking pan; add half a pint hot water, and if it cooks away add more, taking care not to have too much water or the fish will boil instead of bake. When done, (a fish of four or five pounds will bake in an hour,) lift out the tin sheet, and slide the fish gently from it into the platter, and serve with a gravy made from the drippings. Instead of the tin sheet a wire rack may be used.

To boil fish, fill with a rich dressing of rolled crackers seasoned with butter, pepper, salt and sage, wrap it in a well-floured cloth, tie closely with twine or sew, and place in well salted boiling water. Allow ten minutes to the pound for boiling, or if large, six minutes will be sufficient. To try fish, pass a knife next to the bone, and if done the fish will separate easily, but if it adheres to the bone in the least, cook longer. Take out the moment it is done or it will become "woolly." If you have no fish kettle, lay the fish in a circle on a plate inside the cloth, to boil.

Salt fish, after freshening, should be wrapped in a cloth and boiled for five minutes; remove, lay on it two hard boiled eggs sliced, pour over it drawn butter, and trim with parsley leaves.

One of the most essential things in serving fish, is to have everything hot, and dish quickly so that all may go to the table at once. Serve fresh fish with squash and green peas; salt fish with beets and carrots; salt pork and potatoes go with either.

For hints on buying fish see "Marketing."

BROOK TROUT.

Split nearly to the tail and clean, wash and drain. For a dozen good sized trout, fry six slices of salt pork, take out when brown, put in trout, frying to a nice brown on all sides; serve the pork with them.

FISH BALLS.

Take equal quantities of cooked fish of any kind, chopped fine, and mashed potato; add a beaten egg and tablespoon melted butter; mix and mash well with a wooden spoon; roll the balls in flour, and fry them with salt pork and a little lard or beef fat. The whole surface of the balls should be gradually browned.

CROQUETTES OF FISH.
Mrs. H. B. S.

Take dressed fish of any kind, separate from the bones, mince with a little seasoning, one egg beaten with a teaspoon of flour and one of milk; make into balls; brush the outside with egg, dredge well with bread or cracker crumbs, and fry them to a nice brown. The bones, heads, tails, an onion, and an anchovy with a pint of water, will make the gravy.

FISH CHOWDER.
Mrs. Woodworth, Springfield, Mass.

The best fish for chowder are haddock and striped bass, although any kind of fresh fish may be used. Cut in pieces over an inch thick and two inches square; take eight good sized slices of salt pork put in the bottom of an iron pot and fry till crisp; remove the pork, leaving the fat; chop fine, put in the pot a layer of fish, a layer of split crackers and some of the chopped pork, black and red pepper and chopped onions, then another layer of fish, another of crackers and seasoning, and so on. Cover with water and stew slowly till the fish is perfectly done; remove from the pot and put in dish in which you serve it, keep hot, and thicken the gravy with rolled cracker or flour; boil the gravy up once and pour over the chowder. Some add to the gravy just before taking up, a little catsup, port wine and lemon juice, but I think it nicer without these.

KATY'S CODFISH.
Mrs. Helen M. Stevenson.

Soak pieces of codfish several hours in cold water, pick it fine, and place in skillet with water; boil a few minutes, pour off water and add fresh, boil again and drain off as before; then add plenty of sweet milk, a good sized piece of butter, and a thickening made of a little flour, (or corn starch,) mixed with cold milk until smooth like cream. Stir well, and when done, take from the fire and add the yolks of three well beaten eggs; stir quickly and serve.

BAKED HERRING.
Mrs. E. J. Starr.

Take salt herring, soak over night, roll in flour and butter, and place in a dripping pan with a very little water over them; season with pepper.

FRUITS.

Nothing is more tempting as a breakfast relish than fresh oranges, no dinner dessert is complete without its course of ripe fruits which are much more wholesome when eaten as a part of the regular meal, and no good housekeeper ever thinks of serving tea without peaches, pears, oranges, grapes, berries or other seasonable fruits, prepared so as best to bring out their luscious flavors. Fruit should be carefully selected. Havana and Florida oranges are the best, but do not keep well, and on the whole, the Messina are preferable. A rough yellow skin covers the sweetest oranges, the smooth being more juicy and acid; a greenish tinge indicates that they were picked unripe. The Messina lemons "November cut," are the best and come into market in the spring. Free-stone peaches with yellow meat are handsomest, but not always the sweetest. California pears take the lead for flavor, the Bartlett being the best. The best winter pear is the "Winter Nellis." The "Pound" pear is the largest, and is good only for cooking. Fine grained pears are best for eating. A pyramid of grapes made up of Malagas, Delawares and Concords makes a delicious dessert. The Malaga is the best foreign grape, and comes packed in cork dust, which is a non-conducter of heat and absorbs the moisture, and so is always in good condition. Of native grapes, the Delaware keeps best. In pine-apples the "Strawberry" is best, while the "Sugar Loaf" ranks next, but they are so perishable that to keep even for a few days they must be cooked. Buy cocoanut cautiously in summer, heat being likely to sour the milk. The "Princess" almonds are the best variety to buy in the shell; of the shelled the "Jordan" is the finest though the "Sicily" is good. For cake or confectionery, the shelled are less expensive. In melons every section has its favorite varieties, any of which make a wholesome and luscious dessert dish; they should be laid on ice for several hours before serving.

Sliced fruits or berries are more attractive and palatable sprinkled with pounded ice just before sending to the table.

AMBROSIA.
J. H. S.

Take one dozen sweet oranges, peel and slice crosswise, grate a fresh cocoanut; place in fruit dish a layer of oranges, then a layer of cocoanut, strewing plentifully with pulverized sugar; repeat until all are used, having cocoanut and sugar last; serve immediately.

ICED CURRANTS.

Take large bunches of ripe currants, wash and drain dry, dip into beaten white of eggs, put them on a sieve so they will not touch each other, sift powdered sugar thickly over them, and put in a warm place till dry.

MOCK STRAWBERRIES.
Miss C. B., Newburyport, Mass.

Take ripe peaches and choice well-flavored apples, three peaches to one apple, cut in squares about the size of a strawberry, place in alternate layers; sprinkle the top thickly with sugar, and add pounded ice; let stand about two hours, mix peaches and apples thoroughly, let stand an hour longer, and serve.

PEACH PYRAMID.
Miss E. Orissa Dolbear, Cincinnati.

Cut a dozen peaches in halves, peel and take out stones, crack half the seeds and blanch the kernels; make a clear boiling syrup of one pound of white sugar, and into it put the peaches and kernels; boil very gently for ten minutes, take out half the peaches and boil the rest for ten minutes longer, then take out all the peaches and kernels; mix with the syrup left in the kettle the strained juice of three lemons, and an ounce of isinglass dissolved in a little water and strained; boil up once, fill a mould half full of this syrup or jelly, let stand until "set," when add part of the peaches and a little more jelly, and when this is "set," add the rest of the peaches and fill up the mould with jelly. This makes an elegant ornament.

GAME.

Of game birds the woodcock out-ranks all in delicate tenderness and sweet flavor. The thigh is especially deemed a choice tidbit. The leg is the finest part of the snipe, but generally the breast is the most juicy and nutritious part of birds.

Birds should be carefully plucked or skinned, drawn, thoroughly washed, and all shot removed. The more plainly all kinds of game are cooked, the better they retain their fine flavor. They require a brisker fire than poultry, but take less time to cook. Their color, when done, should be a fine yellow brown; serve on toast.

Broiling is the favorite method of cooking game, though all birds are exceedingly nice roasted. To broil, split down the back, open and flatten the breast by covering with a cloth and pounding, season with pepper, and lay the inside first upon the gridiron, turn as soon as browned, and when almost done, take off, place on a platter, sprinkle with salt, and return to the gridiron. When done, place in a hot dish, butter both sides well, and serve at once. The time required is usually about twenty minutes.

To roast, season with salt and pepper, and place a lump of butter inside, truss, skewer, and place in oven. The flavor is best preserved without stuffing, but they are very nice with a plain bread dressing, with a piece of salt pork or ham skewered on the breast. A delicate way of dressing is to place inside each bird, an oyster dipped in the well-beaten yolk of an egg, or in melted butter, and then rolled in bread crumbs. Allow thirty minutes to roast; longer if stuffed.

To lard game, cut fat salt pork into thin narrow strips, thread a larding needle with one of the strips, run the needle under the skin of the bird and draw the pork half way through. The pieces should be about one inch apart.

Pigeons should be cooked a long time as they are usually quite lean and tough, and they are better to lie in salt water half an hour or to be parboiled in it for a few moments. They are nice roasted or made into a pie.

The larger birds, such as pheasants, prairie chickens, etc., lose a part of their wild flavor if soaked over night in salt water. The coarser kinds of game, such as geese, ducks, etc., should also lie in salt water for several hours, or be parboiled in it with an onion inside each to absorb the rank flavor, and afterwards thoroughly rinsed in clear water, stuffed and roasted. Some lay slices of onion over them while cooking, and remove before serving. In cooking wild turkeys, always allow plenty of butter, since the meat is neither very fat nor juicy.

Squirrels should be carefully skinned and laid in salt water a short time before cooking; if old, parboil. They are delicious broiled, and are excellent cooked with thin slices of bacon.

Venison, as in the days of good old Isaac, is still justly considered a "savoury dish;" the haunch, neck and shoulder should be roasted; roast or broil the breast, and fry or broil the steaks. Venison requires more time for cooking than beefsteak. The hams are excellent pickled, smoked and dried, but they will not keep so long as other smoked meats.

BOILED PHEASANT.
Mrs. W. W. W.

Scald and skin, cut up like common chicken, being careful to remove all the shot, put in hot water and boil until you can easily insert a fork, or until the meat seems about ready to separate from the bone; take out and broil over a good fire, put on a platter and set in the stove heater; have ready toasted bread, buttered and cut in pieces about two inches square, and put on the platter with the pheasants; place the kettle with liquor in which they were boiled on the fire, add a small lump of butter, season with salt and pepper, and thicken a little with flour; boil rapidly two or three minutes stirring well, pour over the toast and pheasant, and send at once to the table. Squirrels and prairie chickens are very nice when prepared in this way.

PARTRIDGE PIE.

Line a deep baking-dish with veal cutlets; over which place thin slices of ham and a seasoning of pepper and salt; pluck, draw, wipe and quarter four partridge; rub each part with a seasoning of pepper, salt, minced parsley and butter; put in a baking-dish, pour over them a pint of strong soup-stock, line the edges of the dish with a light puff paste, cover with the same, brush with the yolk of an egg, bake one hour. If the paste is in danger of becoming too brown, cover with a thick paper.

PRAIRIE CHICKENS.

Cut out all the shot, wash in several waters using some soda in the water, rinse and dry them, fill with dressing, sew up with cotton thread, and tie down the legs and wings. Place in a steamer over hot water and steam till done, remove to a dripping-pan, cover with butter, sprinkle with salt and pepper, dredge with flour and place in the oven, basting with the melted butter until a nice brown; serve with either apple sauce, cranberries or currant jelly.

ROAST QUAILS.
J. H. S.

Pluck and dress like chickens, wash well, and rub both inside and out with salt and pepper; stuff with any good dressing, and sew up with fine thread; spread with butter and place in an oven with a good steady heat, turning and basting often; bake an hour. When about half done add a little hot water to the pan, and it is well to insert a dripping pan over them to prevent browning too much; when done dish; add to the gravy, flour and butter rubbed together, also water if needed.

ROAST HAUNCH OF VENISON.

Wash it in warm water and dry well with a cloth; butter a sheet of white paper and put over the fat; lay the venison in a deep baking dish, with a very little boiling water, and cover with either a closely fitting lid or a coarse paste, one-half inch thick. If the latter is used, a thickness or two of coarse paper should be laid over the paste. Cook in a moderately hot oven for from three to four hours, according to the size of the haunch, and about twenty minutes before it is done, quicken the fire, remove the paste and paper, or the dish cover, dredge the joint with flour, and baste well with butter until it is nicely frothed and of a fine delicate brown color; garnish the knuckle bone with a frill of white paper, and serve with a gravy made from its own dripping, having removed the fat. Have the dishes on which the venison is served and the plates very hot. Always serve with currant jelly.

ICES AND ICE CREAM.

Ice cream intended for dinner or for tea should be prepared the evening before or early in the morning. A good general recipe for the custard is the following: take two quarts milk, put on three pints to boil, beat eight eggs, yolks and whites separately, mix the yolks with the remaining pint, and stir *slowly* into the boiling milk, boil two minutes, remove from stove, and *immediately* add one and a half pounds sugar, let it dissolve, strain while *hot* through a crash towel, cool, and add one quart rich cream and two tablespoons vanilla, (or season to taste, remembering that the strength of the flavoring and also the sweetness is very much diminished by the freezing.) Set the custard and also the whites (not beaten) in a cool place until needed; about three hours before serving, begin the preparations for freezing. Put the ice in a coarse coffee sack, pound with an ax or mallet until the lumps are no larger than a small hickory nut; see that the freezer is properly set in the tub, the beater in and the cover secure; place around it a layer of ice about three inches thick, then a layer of coarse salt, rock salt is best, then ice again, then salt, and so on until packed full, with a layer of ice last. The proportion should be about three-fourths ice and one-fourth salt. Pack very solid, pounding with a broom handle or stick, then remove the cover and pour into the freezer the custard, to which you have just added the well whipped whites, replace the cover and begin turning the freezer; after ten minutes pack the ice down again, drain off most of the water, add more ice and turn again, repeating this operation several times until the cream is well frozen, and you can no longer turn the beater. (The above quantity ought to freeze in half an hour; the more pure cream used the longer it takes to freeze). Brush the ice and salt from and remove the cover, take out the beater, scrape the cream down from the sides of freezer, beat well several minutes with a wooden paddle, replace the cover, fill the hole with a cork, pour off all the water, pack again with ice, using salt at the bottom but none at the top of tub, heap the ice on the cover, spread over it a piece of carpet or a thick woolen blanket, and set away in a cool place until needed; or if moulds are used, fill them when you remove the beater, packing the cream in very tightly, and place in ice and salt for two hours; on removing the cream, dip the moulds for an instant in warm water.

Coffee ice cream should be thickened with arrow root, and almond flavoring should be prepared by pounding the kennels to a paste with rose water, using arrow root for thickening. Grate cocoanut and add to the cream and sugar just before freezing. The milk should never be heated for pine-apple, strawberry or raspberry creams. Berry flavors are made best by allowing whole berries to stand for a while well sprinkled with sugar, mashing, straining the juice, adding sugar to it and stirring into the cream. For a quart of cream, allow a quart of fruit and a pound of sugar.

Freeze ice cream in a warm place, always being careful that no salt or water gets within the freezer. If while serving cream, it begins to melt, beat up well from the bottom with a long wooden paddle. Water ices are made from the juices of fruits, mixed with water, sweetened, and frozen as cream.

The following directions for making "self-freezing ice cream" are from "Common Sense in the Household." After preparing the freezer as above, remove the lid carefully, and with a long wooden ladle or flat stick beat the custard as you would batter, steadily for five or six minutes. Replace the lid, pack the ice and salt over it, covering it with about two inches of the mixture; spread above all several folds of blanket or carpet, and leave it untouched for an hour, at the end of that time remove the ice from above the freezer-lid, wipe off carefully and open the freezer. Its sides will be lined with a thick layer of frozen cream. Displace this with your ladle or a long knife, working every part of it loose; beat up the custard again firmly and vigorously, until it is all a smooth, half-congealed paste. The perfection of the ice cream depends upon the thoroughness of your beating at this point. Put on the cover again, pack in more ice and salt, turn off the brine, cover the freezer entirely with the ice and spread over all, the carpet. At the end of two or three hours more, again turn off brine and add fresh ice and salt, but do not open the freezer for two hours more. At that time you may take the freezer from the ice, open it, wrap a towel wet in hot water about the lower part, and turn out a solid column of ice cream, close grained, firm, delicious. Any of the recipes for custard ice cream may be frozen in this way.

CHOCOLATE ICE CREAM.
Mrs. G. H., Buffalo, N.Y.

Scald one pint new milk, add by degrees two cups sugar and two eggs, and five tablespoons of chocolate, rubbed smooth in a little milk. Beat well for a moment or two, place over the fire and heat until it thickens well, stirring constantly; set off, and when quite cold, stir in a quart of rich cream and put in freezer.

ICE CREAM.
Mrs. Cogswell, New York.

Three pints sweet cream, one quart new milk, one pint powdered sugar, the whites of two eggs beaten light, one tablespoon vanilla; put in freezer till thoroughly chilled through, then freeze.

ICE CREAM.
Mrs. S. W. D.

A small teacup flour to two quarts milk, boil three pints; mix flour with one pint until smooth, and stir it in the boiling milk; let boil from ten to fifteen minutes, strain, and, when cold, add one and one-half pounds powdered sugar; flavor with vanilla or lemon and strain through fine strainer.

LEMON ICE CREAM.

Squeeze a dozen lemons, make the juice quite thick with white sugar, stir in very slowly three quarts of cream and freeze. Orange ice cream is prepared in the same way, using less sugar.

PINE APPLE ICE CREAM.
Mrs. L. M. T., New York City.

Two quarts cream, two large ripe pine apples, two pounds powdered sugar; slice the pine apple thin, and scatter the sugar between the slices; cover and let the fruit steep three hours; cut or chop it up in the syrup, and strain through a hair sieve or double bag of coarse lace; beat gradually into the cream and freeze as rapidly as possible; reserve a few pieces of pine apple unsugared, cut into square bits, and stir through the cream when half frozen. Peach ice cream may be made in the same way.

MRS. WATSON'S ICE CREAM.

One-half pint arrow root mixed smooth with milk, two quarts milk; boil, and when cold add two quarts cream, whites of six eggs, tablespoon of flavoring and two pounds of sugar. Freeze.

APPLE ICE.

Take well flavored apples, pears, peaches or quinces, grate, sweeten and freeze; canned fruit may be mashed and prepared in the same way.

JELLIES AND JAMS.

Always make jellies in a porcelain kettle if possible, but brass may be used if scoured very bright and the fruit is removed immediately on taking from the fire. Use the best refined or granulated sugar, and do not have the fruit over ripe, especially currants and grapes.

To extract the juice place fruit in kettle, adding just enough water to keep from burning, stir often, and let remain on the fire until thoroughly scalded; or a better but rather slower method, is to place it in a stone jar, set within a kettle of tepid water, boil until the fruit is well softened, stirring frequently; then strain a small quantity at a time through a strong coarse flannel or cotton bag wrung out of hot water; let drain, and as it cools, squeeze with the hands, emptying and rinsing off the bag each time it is used. The larger fruits, such as apples and quinces, should be cut in pieces, cores removed if at all defective, water added to just cover them, and boiled gently until tender, then turned into bag and placed to drain for three or four hours, or over night. Make jelly in small quantities, not over two or three pints at a time; larger quantities require longer boiling. As a general rule, allow equal measures juice and sugar; boil juice rapidly ten minutes from the first moment of boiling, skim, add sugar, boil ten minutes longer; or spread the sugar in a large dripping pan, set in the oven, stir often to prevent burning, boil the juice just twenty minutes, add the hot sugar, let boil up once, and pour into jelly glasses; some strain through the bag into the glasses, but this involves waste, and if skimming is carefully done, is not necessary. If jelly is not very firm, let it stand in the sun a few days, covering with bits of window glass, or pieces of mosquito netting. To insure clearness and firmness, never attempt to make jellies in damp or cloudy weather. Currants and berries should be made up as soon as picked; never let them stand over night. When ready to put away, cover with pieces of tissue or writing paper, cut to fit and pressed closely upon the jelly, and before putting on the lid or covering of thick paper, brush over with the white of an egg.

APPLE JELLY.

Take nice tart juicy apples, prepare as in general directions. Prepare blackberry jelly according to general directions for berries.

CURRANT JELLY.
Mrs. A. B. M.

Carefully remove all leaves and imperfect fruit, but do not pick from the stem, place in a stone jar, and follow general directions; or, pick the currants off the stem, measure one pint currants and one pint sugar, put in the kettle on the stove, and scald well; skim out currants and dry on plates; or make into jam with one-third currants and two-thirds raspberries; strain juice already sweetened, and cook as above. After currants are dried put in stone jars and cover closely.

CRANBERRY JELLY.
C. G. & E. W. Crane, Caldwell, N.J.

Prepare juice as in general directions, add one pound sugar to every pint, boil and skim, test by dropping a little into cold water, and when it does not mingle with the water it is done; before pouring in the jelly, rinse glasses in cold water to prevent sticking. The pulp may be sweetened and used for sauce.

GRAPE JELLY.
M. E. W., Madison.

Prepare the fruit and rub through a sieve; to every pound of pulp add a pound of sugar, stir well together, boil slowly twenty minutes, then follow general directions; or, prepare the juice, boil twenty minutes, and add one pound of sugar to one pound of juice after it is reduced by boiling; then boil ten or fifteen minutes.

LEMON JELLY.
Miss Ella L. Starr.

Three good sized lemons sliced, half a pound white sugar, two ounces isinglass or gelatine dissolved in two quarts of cold water, a stick of cinnamon and a little grated nutmeg. Beat the whites of three or four eggs, and when the gelatine is all dissolved, stir them well with the other ingredients; boil five minutes, strain through a flannel jelly-bag into moulds and set on ice, or the eggs, cinnamon and nutmeg may be omitted.

QUINCE JELLY.
Mrs. M. J. W.

Rub the quinces with a cloth until perfectly smooth, cut in small pieces, pack tight in your kettle, pour on cold water until level with the fruit, boil until very soft; make a three cornered flannel bag, pour fruit in and hang up to drain, occasionally pressing on the top and sides to make the juice run more freely, taking care not to press hard enough to expel the pulp. There is not so much need of pressing a bag made in this shape, as the weight of the fruit in the larger part causes the juice to flow freely at the point. To a pint of juice add a pint of sugar and boil fifteen minutes, or until it is jelly; pour into tumblers, or bowls, and finish according to general directions. If quinces are scarce, the parings and cores of quinces with good tart apples, boiled and strained as above, make excellent jelly, and the quinces are saved for preserves.

CRABAPPLE JELLY.
Mrs. S. M. Guy.

Boil the apples, mash with potato-masher and strain; take one pint of sugar to a pint of juice, boil a pint at a time till it will drop from spoon in jelly. To make nice marmalade, add sugar to the pulp, pint for pint, boil half an hour stirring all the while; put into small jars and cover the top with writing paper.

WILD CRABAPPLE JELLY.
Mrs. Samuel Woods, Milford Center.

Cook the crab apples until the skins will peel off, after which remove, punch out core with a goose-quill, and to one gallon add a gallon of cold water, let them soak for three days, then add one-half as much water as there is liquid; to two pints of this add one and one-fourth pints of sugar, and boil until it is jelly.

WINE JELLY.
Mrs. J. A. Rea, Minneapolis.

Dissolve one box of Cox's gelatine in one pint of cold water, with the juice and rind of two lemons and one-half ounce of stick cinnamon if you wish; soak three-quarters of an hour; pour upon it three pints boiling water and one pint sherry wine; add four coffee cups sugar, and strain through flannel into moulds.

JAMS.

In making jams, the fruit should be carefully cleaned and *thoroughly* bruised, as mashing it before cooking prevents it from becoming hard; boil fifteen or twenty minutes before adding the sugar, as the flavor of the fruit is thus better preserved, (usually allowing three-quarters of a pound of sugar to a pound of fruit); then boil half an hour longer. Jams require almost constant stirring, and every housekeeper should be provided with a small paddle with handle at right angles with the blade (similar to an apple butter "stirrer," only on a smaller scale), to be used in making jams and marmalades.

To tell when any jam or marmalade is sufficiently cooked, take out some of it on a plate and let it cool. If no juice or moisture gathers about it, and it looks dry and glistening, it is done thoroughly. Put up in glass or small stone jars and secure like jellies. Keep jellies and jams in a cool, dry and dark place.

CURRANT JAM.
Mrs. J. H. S.

Prepare fruit as above; measure, and boil eight or ten minutes, add one coffee cup sugar to every pint of mashed fruit, and let boil ten minutes longer; pour in cans, let stand five minutes and seal; make blackberry jam in same way; or take two-thirds raspberries and one-third currants and prepare as above. Prepare gooseberries like blackberries, boiling one hour after putting in sugar.

STRAWBERRY JAM.

Sprinkle three pounds sugar over two quarts berries, let them stand an hour, mash and boil twenty minutes.

MEATS.

In boiling meats, inattention to the temperature of the water and too early application of salt, cause great waste. Fresh meat, to be rich and nutritious, should be placed in a kettle of boiling water—pure soft water is best—skimmed well as soon as it begins to boil again, and placed where it will slowly but constantly simmer. The meat should be occasionally turned and kept well under the water. Supply fresh hot water as it evaporates in boiling. The hot water hardens the fibrine on the outside, encasing and retaining the rich juices. No salt should be added until the meat is nearly done, as it will extract the juices of the meat if added too soon. Boil gently, as rapid boiling hardens the fibrine, and renders the meat hard, tasteless, and scarcely more nutritious than leather. Salt meat should be put on in cold water so that it may freshen in cooking. Allow twenty minutes to the pound for fresh, and thirty-five for salt meats, the time to be modified, of course, by the quality of the meat. A pod of red pepper in the water will prevent any unpleasant odor from boiling, in the house.

Dash over roasts with cold water, wash quickly and wipe dry. English cooks never wash beef, but wipe with a clean towel wrung out of cold water. Place in the dripping-pan with bony side up, flour well, put one pint hot water in pan, adding more when needed, and set in a rather brisk oven; afterward graduate to a moderate heat. Baste frequently, turning the pan often so that the parts may roast equally, and when about half done, flour again, salt, turn over and flour the other side, and about half an hour before serving, season with salt and pepper. Many roast meat on a grate placed in the dripping-pan, adding but little water at a time, (when there is too much the meat is steamed instead of roasting and the gravy will not become brown). In roasting all meats, success depends upon flouring thoroughly, basting frequently, turning often so as to prevent burning, and carefully regulating the heat of the oven. Allow fifteen to twenty-five minutes to the pound in roasting, according as it is to be rare or well done, and take into consideration the quality of the meat. Roasts prepared with dressing require more time. In roasting meats many think it nicer not to add any water until the meat has been in the oven about half an hour, or until it begins to brown.

Broiling is a far more wholesome method of cooking meats than frying. Tough steak is made more tender by pounding or hacking with a dull knife, but some of the juices are lost by the operation. Trim off all superfluous fat but never wash a freshly cut steak. Place the steak on a hot, well-greased gridiron, turn often so that the outside may be seared at once; when done, which will require from five to ten minutes, dish on a hot platter, season with salt and pepper and bits of butter, cover with a hot platter and serve at once. A small pair of tongs are best to turn steaks, as piercing with a fork frees the juices. If fat drips on the coals below, the blaze may be extinguished by sprinkling with salt, always withdrawing the gridiron to prevent the steak from acquiring a smoky flavor. Always have a brisk fire whether you cook in a patent broiler directly over the fire, or on a gridiron over a bed of live coals. Broiling steak is the very last thing to be done in getting breakfast or dinner; every other dish should be ready for the table, so that this may have the cook's undivided attention. A steel gridiron with slender bars is best, as the common broad flat iron bars fry and scorch the meat, imparting a disagreeable flavor. Never season with salt while cooking.

To thaw frozen meat, place in a warm room over night, or lay it early in the morning in cold water. If cooked before it is entirely thawed it will be tough.

Beef in boiling loses rather more than one-quarter; in roasting it loses one-third; legs of mutton lose one-fifth in boiling and one-third in roasting, and a loin of mutton in roasting loses rather more than one-third. It is more economical, then, to boil than to roast meat; and whether roasted or boiled, from one-fifth to one-third of its whole weight is lost.

BROILED BEEFSTEAK.
Mrs. W. W. W.

Lay a thick tender steak upon a gridiron well greased with butter or beef suet over hot coals; when done on one side have ready the platter warmed, with a little butter on it; lay the steak upon the platter with the cooked side down so that the juices which have gathered may run on the platter, but do not press the meat; lay the steak again on gridiron quickly and cook the other side; when done to your liking, put again on platter, spread lightly with butter, place where it will keep warm (over boiling steam is best) for a few moments, but do not let butter become oily. Serve on hot plates.

FRIED BEEFSTEAK.

If you have not the means to broil, the next best method is to heat the frying-pan very hot, put in steak previously hacked, turn quickly over and over several times so as to sear the outside and retain the juices; when done transfer to a hot platter, salt, pepper and put over bits of butter; pile the steaks one on top of another, and cover with a hot platter. This way of frying is both healthful and delicate. Or, heat the skillet, trim off the fat from the steak, cut in small bits, and place to fry; meanwhile pound steak, draw the bits of suet to one side and put in the steak, turn quickly over several times so as to sear the outside, take out on a hot platter previously prepared with salt and pepper, dredge well, return to skillet, repeating the operation until the steak is done; dish on a hot platter, covering with another platter, and place where it will keep hot while you make the gravy. Place a tablespoon dry flour in the skillet, being sure to have the fat boiling hot, stir until brown and free from lumps; the bits of suet may be left in, drawing them to one side until you brown the flour; pour in about half a pint boiling water (milk or cream is better), stir well, season with pepper and salt and serve in a gravy tureen. Spread bits of butter over your steak and send to table at once. This is more economical, but not so healthy as broiling.

BEEFSTEAK TOAST.
Mrs. John Gortner, Goshen, Ind.

Chop cold steak very fine, cook in a little water, put in cream or milk, thicken, season with butter, salt and pepper; pour over slices of toast which have been toasted slowly. Prepare boiled ham in the same way, adding the yolk of an egg.

BEEFSTEAK SMOTHERED IN ONIONS.
Mrs. Rettie Ziegler, Columbus.

Fry brown four slices of breakfast bacon, take out bacon and put in six onions sliced thin, fry about ten minutes stirring constantly, take out all except a thin layer and upon it lay a slice of steak, and then a layer of onions, then steak, covering thick with onions. Dredge each layer with pepper, salt and flour; pour over this one cup boiling water, cover tight and simmer half an hour. When you dish, place the steak in the centre of the dish, and heap the onions around it.

BOILED CORNED BEEF.
Mrs. S. H. J.

If very salty let soak over night, but if young beef and properly corned this is not necessary; pour cold water over it after washing off the salt, letting it be well covered. The rule is twenty-five minutes to a pound for boiling meats, but corned beef should be placed on a part of the stove or range where it will simmer, not boil, uninterruptedly from four to six hours, according to the size of the piece; if to be served cold, let the meat remain in the liquor until cold. It is a good plan to let tough beef remain in the liquor until the next day, and bring to the boiling point just before serving. Simmer a brisket or plate piece until the bones are easily removed, fold over, forming a square or oblong piece; place sufficient weight on top to press the parts closely together, and set where it will become cold. This gives a firm solid piece to cut in slices, and is a delightful relish. Boil liquor down, remove the fat and save to pour over finely minced scraps and pieces of beef; season with pepper or sweet herbs; press the meat firmly into a mold and pour over the liquor, lay over it a close cover, with a weight upon it. When turned from the mold, garnish with sprigs of parsley or celery, and serve with fancy pickles or French mustard.

BEEF A LA MODE.
Mrs. Wm. Lee.

Take about five or six pounds of the round of beef, gash it through at intervals of an inch to receive strips of salt pork half an inch wide, tie it securely by winding a string around and lengthwise; put it into a large pot with a plate in the bottom to prevent adhering, pour in a quart of water in which are salt, pepper, cloves, cinnamon and allspice; keep the pot closed, and when the beef is taken out, add a little water and flour to make a gravy.

BOILED BEEF TONGUE.
M. J. W.

Put pot on the fire with water to cover the tongue, wash clean, put in the pot with a pint of salt; if the water boils away, add more so as to keep the tongue nearly covered until done; boil until you can pierce easily with a fork, take out, and, if needed for present use, take off the skin and set away to cool; if to be kept some days, do not peel until wanted for table. The same amount of salt will do for three tongues if your pot is large enough to hold them, always remembering to keep sufficient water in the kettle to cover while boiling. Soak salt tongue over night and cook in same way—without salt.

RAGOUT BEEF.
Mrs. D. W. R., Washington City.

For six pounds of the round take half dozen ripe tomatoes, cut up with two or three onions in a vessel with a tight cover, add half a dozen cloves, a stick of cinnamon, and a little whole black pepper; cut gashes in the meat, and stuff them with half pound of fat salt pork, cut into square bits; place the meat on the other ingredients, and pour over half a cup of vinegar and a cup of water; cover tightly and bake in a moderate oven; cook slowly four or five hours, and when about half done salt to taste. When done, take out the meat, strain the gravy through a colander, and thicken with flour.

ROAST MEAT WITH PUDDING.
Mrs. C. T. Carson.

Never wash the meat, but if necessary wipe with a damp cloth, sprinkle with salt, pepper and flour; if not fat, put three or four small pieces of butter the size of a hickory nut on it; put in the dripping pan, letting it rest on a wire frame or some small sticks to keep it from the pan; no water is needed; baste and turn often, baking from fifteen to twenty minutes for every pound. Make a Yorkshire pudding to eat like vegetables with the roast as follows: For every pint of milk take three eggs, three cups of flour and a pinch of salt; stir to a smooth batter and pour into the dripping pan, under the meat, half an hour before it is done.

FRIZZLED BEEF.

Slice smoked beef, pour on boiling water to freshen, pour off the water and frizzle the beef in butter. A nice dressing can be made by adding milk and flour; stir well while cooking, and just before serving add the yolk of an egg; cold boiled or baked beef can be sliced and dressed in the same way, having been fried brown first.

FRIED LIVER.

Cut in thin slices and place on a platter, pour on boiling water and immediately pour it off, thus sealing the outside and taking away the unpleasant flavor, and making it much more palatable; have ready some crackers or dried bread crumbs rolled fine and nicely seasoned with pepper and salt; have ready in skillet on the stove some hot lard or beef drippings, or both together, dredge the liver with the rolled cracker, and put in the skillet, placing the tin cover on; fry slowly until both sides are dark brown, and the liver is thoroughly cooked, which will take about a quarter of an hour.

TOAD-IN-THE-HOLE.

One pint flour, one egg wet with milk, a little salt; grease dish well with butter, put in lamb chops, add a little water with pepper and salt, pour batter over it and bake one hour.

MUTTON CHOPS.

Season with salt and pepper, cover closely and fry for a few moments, dip each chop in cracker crumbs and eggs, and fry again; or put in oven in a dripping pan with a little water and melted butter, baste frequently and roast till they are brown.

BOILED LEG OF MUTTON.

Put mutton in boiling water with a small piece of pork, and boil, allowing from fifteen to twenty minutes for each pound of meat; make a sauce of drawn butter, putting in hard boiled eggs sliced, and capers.

ROAST LEG OF MUTTON.

Rub the mutton with a little butter, pepper, salt, and, if you choose, cloves and allspice; put it in the dripping pan in the oven, basting it frequently, allowing quarter of an hour for each pound of mutton; thicken the gravy with flour and water, season with spices and catsup, or with wine and currant jelly.

FRICATELLI.
Mrs. W. F. W.

Chop raw fresh pork very fine, add a little salt, plenty of pepper, and two small onions chopped fine, half as much bread as meat, soaked until soft, two eggs; mix well together, make into oblong patties, and fry like oysters. These are nice for breakfast; if used for tea serve with sliced lemon.

BOILED HAM.

Wash in quite warm water, scrape clean, (some have a coarse hair brush on purpose for cleaning hams,) put in a thoroughly cleansed boiler, in cold water enough to cover; boil steadily for five hours (if the ham weighs twelve pounds), take up and put into a baking-pan to skin; dip the hands in cold water, take the skin between the fingers and peel as you would an orange; set in a moderate oven—placing the lean side of the ham downwards, and if you like, sift over pounded or rolled crackers; bake one hour. The baking brings out a great quantity of fat and leaves the meat much more delicate. In warm weather it will keep in a dry cool place a long time; if there is a tendency to mould, set it a little while into the oven again; or, after the ham is boiled tender, cover with the white of a raw egg and sprinkle sugar or bread crumbs over it, place in the oven and brown; or it is delicious covered with a regular cake icing and browned. The nicest portion of a boiled ham may be served in slices, the ragged parts and odds and ends chopped fine for sandwiches, or by adding three eggs to one pint of chopped ham, a delicious omelet may be made. The bones should be put in a soup kettle; the rind and fat rendered and strained, and if not too strong, used for frying eggs or potatoes. If the ham is very salt, it should lie in water over night.

BROILED HAM.
Mrs. A. E. Brand, Minneapolis, Minn.

Cut the ham in slices of medium thickness, place on a hot gridiron, and broil until the fat readily flows out and the meat is slightly browned, take from the gridiron with a knife and fork, and drop into a pan of cold water, then return again to the gridiron, repeat several times and the ham is done; place in a hot platter, add a few lumps of butter and serve at once. If too fat trim off a part; it is almost impossible to broil the fat part without burning, but this does not impair the taste. Pickled pork and breakfast bacon are broiled in the same way.

DELICIOUS FRIED HAM.
Mrs. J. F. Woods, Milford Center.

Place the slices in boiling water and cook till tender, put in frying pan and brown, and dish on a platter, then fry some eggs and instead of turning, drip gravy over them till done, take up carefully and lay on slices of ham. This is a tempting dish, and if nicely prepared, quite ornamental.

MIXED SANDWICHES.
Mrs. E. Byers, Minneapolis, Minn.

Chop fine cold ham, tongue and chicken; mix with one pint of the meat half a cup melted butter, one tablespoon salad oil, one of mustard if desired, the yolk of a beaten egg, and a little pepper; spread on bread cut thin and buttered. Ham alone may be prepared in this way.

SPARE-RIB POTPIE.
Mrs. W. W. W.

Cut the spare-ribs once across and then in strips three or four inches wide, put on in kettle with hot water enough to cover, stew until tender, season with salt and pepper, turn out of kettle, replace a layer of spare-ribs in the bottom, season again and add a layer of peeled potatoes (quartered if large), and some bits of butter, some small squares of good baking powder dough rolled quite thin, then another layer of spare-ribs, and so on until the kettle is two-thirds full, leaving the squares of crust for the last layer; then add the liquor in which the spare-ribs were boiled, and hot water if needed, cover, boil half to three-quarters of an hour, being careful to add hot water so as not to let it boil dry. The above can be made of light biscuit dough, without egg or sugar. Roll thin, cut out, let rise, and use for pie, remembering to have plenty of water in the kettle, so that when the pie is made and the cover on, it need not be removed until dished. Always warm over all pot-pie in the dripping pan set in the oven.

PIGS FEET SAUCE.

Take off the horny parts of feet and toes, scrape, clean and wash thoroughly, and if needed, singe off the hairs, place in a kettle with plenty of water, boil, skim, pour off water and add fresh, and boil until the bones will pull out easily; do not bone, but pack in a stone jar with pepper and salt sprinkled between each layer; mix some good cider vinegar with the liquor in which feet were boiled, using two-thirds vinegar to one third liquor, and fill up jar. When wanted for the table, take out a sufficient quantity, put in a hot skillet, add more vinegar, salt and pepper if needed; boil until thoroughly heated, stir in a smooth thickening of flour and water, and boil until flour is cooked; serve hot as a nice breakfast dish; or, when the feet have boiled until perfectly tender, remove the bones and pack in stone jar as above. Slice down cold, when wanted for use.

PORK HEAD CHEESE.
Mrs. M. J. Gould, Delaware.

Take one head and boil until the bones can be taken out, chop fine, season to taste with salt, pepper and sage, pack in a crock and put a weight on it.

FRIED SALT PORK.

Cut in rather thin slices and freshen by letting lie an hour or two in cold water or milk and water, roll in flour and fry till crisp; if you are in a hurry, pour boiling water on the slices, let stand a few minutes, drain, roll in flour and fry as before; drain off most of the grease from the frying pan, stir in while hot one or two spoonsful of flour, about one-half pint of new milk, and a little pepper, and salt if not salt enough from the meat, let boil and pour into your gravy dish; this makes a nice white gravy when properly made.

YANKEE PORK AND BEANS.

Pick over carefully a quart of beans and let them soak over night; in the morning wash and drain in another water, put on to boil in cold water with half a teaspoon of soda, boil thirty minutes and then put them in an earthen pot with two tablespoons of molasses; when half the beans are in the pot, put in the dish half or three-fourths of a pound of well washed salt pork, with the rind cut in slices; cover all with hot water and bake six hours or longer—you cannot bake too long. Keep covered so that they will not burn on the top.

SAUSAGE.
Charles Phellis, Jr.

Forty pounds of meat, one pound salt, one-half pint of sage and three and one-half ounces pepper; scatter over the meat before grinding.

CANNED SAUSAGE OR TENDERLOIN.

Make the sausage in small cakes and fry until done, fill the can up with the cooked cakes, pour boiling lard over the top and seal the same as fruit; cut the tenderloin in squares, fry done and can the same way.

FRIED VEAL CUTLETS.

Take half pint of milk, a well beaten egg, and flour enough to make a batter; fry the veal brown in sweet lard or beef drippings, then dip it in the batter and fry again till brown, drop some spoonfuls of batter in the hot lard after the veal is taken up, and serve them on top of the meat; put a little flour paste in the gravy with salt and pepper, let it come to a boil and pour it over the whole; the veal should be cut thin and cooked nearly an hour. Cracker crumbs and egg may be used instead of batter, but the skillet should then be kept covered, and the veal cooked slowly for half an hour over a moderate fire.

PATE DE VEAU.
Mrs. Gen. Mitchell, Columbus.

Three and a half pounds leg of veal, fat and lean chopped fine, six or eight small crackers rolled fine, two eggs, piece of butter size of an egg, one table spoon salt, one of pepper, one nutmeg, a slice of salt pork chopped fine, or if preferred, a little more salt or butter; work all together in the form of a loaf, put bits of butter on top, grate bread crumbs over it, put into dripping pan and baste often; bake two hours and slice when cold.

ROAST LOIN OF VEAL.
Mrs. W. G. Hillock, New Castle, Ind.

Wash and rub thoroughly with salt and pepper, leaving in the kidney, around which put plenty of salt; roll up, let stand two hours; in the meantime make dressing of bread crumbs, salt and pepper, and chopped parsley or thyme moistened with a little hot water and butter,—some prefer chopped salt pork, also add an egg. Unroll the veal, put the dressing well around the kidney, fold, and secure well with several yards white cotton twine, covering the meat in all directions; place in the dripping-pan with the thick side down, put to bake in a rather hot oven, graduating it to moderate heat afterwards; in half an hour add a little hot water to the pan, baste often, in another half hour turn over the roast, and when nearly done, dredge lightly with flour, and baste with melted butter. A four pound roast thus prepared will bake thoroughly tender in about two hours; before serving, carefully remove the twine. To make the gravy, if there is too much fat in the drippings skim off, dredge some flour in the pan, stir until it browns, add some hot water if necessary, boil a few moments and serve in your gravy boat. This roast is very nice to slice down cold for Sunday dinners. Serve with green peas and lemon jelly.

VEAL STEW.
Kate Thompson, Millersburg, Ky.

Take two and a half pounds of the breast of veal, boil one hour in water enough to cover, add a dozen potatoes, and cook half an hour; before taking off the stove, add one pint of milk and flour enough to thicken; season to taste. If you like, you may make a crust as for chicken pie, bake in two pie-pans; place one of the crusts on the platter, pour over the stew, and place the other on top.

VEAL SWEETBREAD.

Slice, put in cold water, drain, and place in skillet prepared with hot drippings; when brown on under side then turn; make a stiff batter of two eggs, half pint milk, flour to thicken, and salt to taste, and into it dip each slice, return to the skillet and fry brown over a moderate fire.

OYSTERS.

The season for oysters is from August to May, and during that time they are a very nutritious and easily digested article of food. When fresh the shell is always firmly closed; if opened the oyster is dead and unfit for use. When in cans the dealer will have to be trusted as to freshness. Small-shelled oysters are finest in flavor. Oysters should always be kept in a cool place. When preparing them for cooking be careful to remove all bits of shell. Do not salt stewed oysters till just before they are removed from the fire, otherwise they will shrivel up and be hard. In frying, a little baking powder, put into the cracker dust, greatly improves them. They should always be served immediately after cooking. Oysters cooked in the shell retain their flavor best.

ESCALOPED OYSTERS.
Mrs. J. Gortner, Goshen, Ind.

Mix crushed cracker and dry bread crumbs in equal proportions, or use all crackers; drain the liquor from one quart of oysters; butter a deep dish or pan and cover the bottom with the bread crumbs and crackers, put in a layer of oysters seasoned with salt and pepper and bits of butter in plenty, then a layer of crumbs, then oysters, and so on until dish is full, finishing with the cracker and crumbs covered with bits of butter; pour over the whole the oyster liquor added to one pint of boiling water (and skimmed if necessary), place in a hot oven, bake half an hour, add another pint of hot water, or half pint of water and half pint of milk, in which a small lump of butter has been melted; bake another half hour, and to prevent browning too much, cover with a tin or sheet-iron lid.

FRIED OYSTERS.

Take two parts rolled crackers and one part corn meal, mix well, roll the oysters in it, and fry in equal parts butter and lard. Season with salt and pepper.

OYSTER FRITTERS.

Drain off liquor, boil, skim, and to a cupful add a cup of milk, two or three eggs, salt and pepper, and flour enough to make a rather thick batter. Have hot lard or beef drippings in a skillet ready, drop the batter into it with a large spoon, taking up one oyster for each spoonful. The oysters must be large and plump.

OYSTER PATTIES.

Drain dry, make a batter of sour milk, eggs and soda, stir pretty thick with flour; roll each oyster in the batter until well covered and fry in butter.

OYSTER PATTIES.

Pour oysters and liquor (free from all bits of shell) into a pan of rolled cracker; mix well and let stand fifteen minutes, season with salt and pepper, mould into small cakes with one or two oysters in each, roll in dry cracker until well incrusted. Fry to a nice brown in hot lard and butter or beef drippings. Serve hot and keep in a covered dish. This is a good way to use small oysters.

OYSTER SHORT CAKE.

One quart flour, three teaspoons baking powder, one tablespoon butter, a pinch of salt, and enough sweet milk to moisten well; roll about an inch thick and bake on tin pie plates quickly. While baking, take one quart of oysters and a half cup of water and put on the stove; then take half a cup milk and the same of butter, mixed with a tablespoon of flour, and a little salt and pepper; add all together, and boil at once. When the cakes are done, split open and spread the oysters between pieces and some on the top. Put the oysters that are left in a gravy dish, and replenish when needed.

OYSTER PIE.
Mrs. C. Beck.

Take a pie tin about an inch deep and line with ordinary pie-crust, spread on a layer of oysters, season with salt and pepper, cut some of the crust in small squares and lay around on the oysters, add another layer of oysters seasoning as before, pour on some of the oyster liquor, and cover with a crust having a good opening in the center to allow the steam to escape so that it will not boil out. One pint of oysters will make this pie.

PASTRY.

Use the best washed butter or lard; the proportions for a rich paste are a scant pound of butter or lard to a heaping quart of sifted flour and a teaspoon salt, and some add one tablespoon powdered sugar; mix in a cool temperature, handle as lightly and as little as possible, chop a large spoonful of the shortening into a fourth part of the flour, and with knife or wooden spoon, and cold or ice water, make as soft a dough as can easily be handled; dredge with flour, transfer dough to a marble slab or hard wood board, roll thin, cover the surface with thin slices of butter and lard, dredge over a layer of flour, double over, and with your bread-pin roll out again until as thin as before, repeating the process several times; after the last time, instead of rolling up, fold it once or twice, and cut the pieces for use from the edge to keep the layers of shortening as near horizontal as possible, and to prevent mixing them up as is done in moulding or rolling. This process makes flaky and delicious paste. Never fill pies until just before putting them in the oven. Always use tin pie-pans, since in earthen pans the under crust is not likely to be well baked. Just before putting on the upper crust, wet the rim of the lower with a thick paste of flour and water, and press the two crusts firmly together; this will prevent that bane of all pastry cooks— a bursted pie. Bake in a moderate oven, having as good a body of heat at the bottom as at the top of oven, or the lower crust will be clammy and raw.

It is proper to observe that very nice pastry for family use may be made, by reducing the quantity of shortening to even so little as a half pound to a quart of flour, especially when children or dyspeptics are to be considered.

In warm weather, when not ready to bake immediately after making up your pastry, keep it in the ice-chest until wanted, and in any event it is nicer to let it thus remain for one or two hours.

Say to your pastry, "keep cool," to your oven "do it brown."

To prevent the juice of pies from soaking into the under crust, beat an egg well, and with a bit of cloth dipped into the egg rub over the crust before filling the pies.

For a more wholesome pie-crust shortening, boil beans or potatoes until soft, make into a broth, work through a colander, mix as much into the flour as can be done and preserve sufficient tenacity in the dough. Knead moderately stiff and roll a little thicker than crust shortened with lard.

The virtues and vices of mince pies have served to point many a hygienic moral, but while it is quite true that the mince pie is not strictly hygienic, it is not an every-day dish. The mince pie is one of the few articles of food that have come down to us from a remote period, and still has the flavor of old associations and the solid respectability which belongs to centuries of history and tradition. It is less to be feared than many apparently simple forms of highly concentrated food, such as butter and sugar, and often a piece of common pound-cake will produce a bigger "nightmare" than a piece of the richest mince pie. Mince pie is not the real thing, if it is not rich, and it is the deterioration of mince pies, and the fact that they are left now-a-days, like almost everything else, to servants, who do not even know how to properly boil a piece of beef, that they have been brought into disrepute. Their preparation should therefore be confided to no careless or unworthy hands, but every ingredient should be thoughtfully provided and delicately prepared, and the whole put together and blended with the skill of an artist, and the precision of a mechanic. Tact, wisdom, judgment, knowledge and experience all go into the proper construction of a genuine mince pie, to say nothing of kindness of heart and liberality of disposition.

AUNTY PHELPS' PIE CRUST.

To one pint of sifted flour, add one even teaspoon baking powder, and sweet cream enough to wet the flour, leaving crust a little stiff. This is enough for two pies.

APPLE PIE.

Line your pan with crust made a little thicker than for custard pie; pare and quarter three or four nice tart apples and spread them around on your crust; mix one tablespoon flour, two teaspoons essence of lemon, and three or four tablespoons water together, and pour over the apple, and sugar to taste; serve warm with sweetened milk or cream; cinnamon is good in place of essence of lemon.

APPLE MERINGUE PIE.

Pare, slice, stew and sweeten ripe, tart and juicy apples, mash and season with nutmeg (if you like stew lemon peel with it for flavor), fill crust and bake till done; spread over the apple a thick meringue, made by whipping to froth whites of three eggs for each pie, sweetened with tablespoon powdered sugar for each egg; flavor with vanilla, beat until it will stand alone and cover pie three quarters inch thick; if too thin add a little corn starch. Set back in a quick oven till well "set," and eat cold. In their season, substitute peaches for apples, or to make it richer, after mashing add two eggs and one-fourth cup of butter for each pie, and finish as above.

DRIED APPLE PIE.

Put apples in warm water and soak over night; in the morning chop up, stew a few moments in a small amount of water, and while cooking add a sliced lemon, and sugar to taste; cook half an hour.

SLICED APPLE PIE.
Mrs. D. Buxton.

Line pie-pan with crust, sprinkle with sugar, fill with tart apples sliced very thin, sprinkle sugar and a very little cinnamon over them, add a few small bits of butter, and a tablespoon water; dredge in some flour, cover with the top crust, and bake one-half to three-quarters of an hour; allow four or five tablespoons sugar to one pie. Or, line pans with crust, fill with sliced apples, put on top crust and bake; take off top crust, put in sugar, bits of butter and seasoning, replace crust and serve warm. It is delicious with sweetened cream.

CREAM PIE.
Mrs. J. F. Woods, Milford Centre.

Take one pint sweet milk, three eggs, small teacup of sugar, (some only use one tablespoon,) two tablespoons corn starch; beat yolks, sugar and starch together, let the milk come to a boil, and stir in the mixture, adding a teaspoon of butter and a pinch of salt. Bake your crust, fill it with the custard, bake, then spread on your whites (previously beaten to a stiff froth with two tablespoons sugar) and brown in a quick oven.

CREAM PIE.
Mrs. Carrier.

Put on a pint of milk to boil, break two eggs into a bowl, add one cup white sugar, one-half cup flour, and after beating well stir into the milk just as it commences to boil, keep stirring one way till it thickens; flavor with lemon or anything you choose. Before making the cream, make a paste for three pies, roll out and cover the plates, roll out and cover a second time; when baked and quite warm, separate the edges with a knife, lift the upper crust and fill in the cream.

CRUMB PIE.
Miss Sylvia J. Courter.

Take one teacup bread crumbs, soak half an hour, make crust same as for other pies; when soaked add three tablespoons sugar, half a teaspoon butter, half a cup of water, a little vinegar, and nutmeg to suit the taste; bake with two crusts.

COCOANUT PIE.
Miss N. B. Brown, Washington City.

One pint milk, cocoanut, one teacup sugar, three eggs; grate cocoanut, mix with the yolks of the eggs and sugar, stir in the milk filling the pan even full, and bake. Beat the whites of the eggs to a froth, stirring in three tablespoons pulverized sugar, pour over the pie and bake to a light brown. If prepared cocoanut is used, one heaping teacup is required.

COMBINATION PIE.
Miss Mary Collins, Urbana.

Make a bottom crust, fill with ripe grapes or cranberries; sweeten well and dredge over a little flour; bake, and when done, pour over a sponge batter made as follows: Three eggs, one cup sugar, one cup flour, two tablespoons water, two teaspoons baking powder; return to oven and brown slightly. This is sufficient for two pies.

CUSTARD PIE.
Mrs. N. S. Long.

For a large pie, take three eggs, one pint of milk and half tablespoon of corn-starch; flavor to suit the taste.

LEMON PIE.
Mrs. W. E. Scobey.

One lemon grated, one cup sugar, the yolks of three eggs, small piece butter, three tablespoons milk, one teaspoon corn-starch; beat all together, and bake in a rich crust; beat the whites very light, with a little sugar, and place on the pie when done, then brown in the oven.

LEMON PIE.
Mrs. H. B. S.

One tablespoon corn-starch, one cup boiling water, into which stir a lump of butter the size of a walnut, let it cool, add one cup sugar, grate the rind and juice of one lemon and add one egg; cover with meringue paste, and brown in oven. For paste, whip to a stiff froth the whites of ten eggs and one pound powdered sugar; flavor with lemon, vanilla or rosewater; allow three eggs to a pie; spread over the top of the pies.

MINCE MEAT.

Take five or six pounds scraggy beef—a neck piece will do, and put to boil in water enough to cover it, take off the scum that rises when it comes to a boil; add hot water from time to time until it is tender, remove the lid from the pot, salt, let boil till almost dry turning the meat over occasionally in the liquor, take from the fire and let stand over night to get thoroughly cold; pick bones, gristle or stringy bits from the meat, chop very fine, mincing at the same time three pounds of nice beef suet; seed and cut four pounds raisins, wash and dry four of currants, slice thin one of citron, chop fine four quarts tart, good cooking apples; put into a large pan together, add two ounces cinnamon, one ounce cloves, one ounce ginger, four nutmegs, the juice and grated rinds of two lemons, one tablespoon salt, one teaspoon pepper, and two pounds sugar. Put in a porcelain kettle one quart boiled cider, or better still one quart currant or grape juice, (canned when grapes are turning from green to purple,) one quart nice molasses or syrup, and if you have any syrup left from sweet pickles, add some of that, also a good lump of butter; let it come to a boil and pour over the ingredients in the pan after first mixing well, then mix again thoroughly. Pack in jars and put in a cool place, and when cold, pour molasses over the top, cover tightly and it will keep two months. In baking take some out of a crock and if it is not moist enough add a little hot water, and strew a few whole raisins over each pie. Instead of boiled beef a beef's heart or roast meat may be used.

The above is a good formula to use, but, of course, may be varied to suit different tastes or the material at hand. If too rich, add more chopped apples; in lieu of cider, vinegar and water in equal proportions may be used; good preserves, marmalades, spiced pickles, currant or grape jelly, canned fruit, dried cherries, etc., may take the place of raisins, currants and citron. Wine or brandy is considered by many a great improvement, but if "it causeth thy brother to offend" do not use it. Lemon and vanilla extracts are often used, also preserved lemon or orange peel. It is better to stand over night, or several days, before baking into pies, as the materials will be more thoroughly incorporated. Many prefer to freeze their pies after baking, heating them as needed.

MOCK MINCE PIE.
Mrs. Annie E. Gillespie, Indianapolis, Ind.

Twelve crackers rolled fine, one cup hot water, one half cup vinegar, one cup molasses, one cup sugar, one cup currants, one cup raisins, spice to taste; measure with a teacup. Some use one cup dried bread crumbs. This is the correct quantity for four pies.

PIE-PLANT PIE.
Mrs. D. Buxton.

Mix one-half teacup white sugar and one heaping teaspoon flour together, and sprinkle over the bottom crust, then add the pie-plant cut up fine; sprinkle over this another half teacup sugar and heaping teaspoon flour; bake fully three-quarters of an hour in a slow oven; or stew the pie-plant, sweeten, add grated rind and juice of a lemon, yolks of two eggs, and bake and frost like lemon pie.

DRIED PEACH PIE.

Stew peaches until perfectly soft, mash fine, and add for two pies, one-half teacup sweet cream; bake with two crusts.

POTATO PIE.
Miss Sarah Thompson, Delaware.

One common size teacup of grated raw potato, one quart sweet milk; let the milk boil, stir in the grated potato; when cool add two or three eggs well beaten, sugar and nutmeg to taste; bake without upper crust; eat the day it is baked. This recipe is for two pies.

PUMPKIN PIE.
Mrs. A. B. Morey.

Stew pumpkin cut in small pieces in a half pint water, and when very soft, mash with potato masher very fine, let the water dry away, watching very closely to prevent burning or scorching; for each pie take one egg, half cup sugar, two tablespoons pumpkin, half pint of rich milk (a little cream will improve it), a little salt; stir well together and season with cinnamon or nutmeg; bake with one crust in a hot oven, taking care that it does not brown.

BINA'S STRAWBERRY SHORTCAKE.

Two heaping teaspoons baking powder sifted into two quarts of flour, scant half teacup butter, two tablespoons sugar, a little salt, enough sweet milk (or water) to make a soft dough; mix with a knife or spoon, roll out almost as thin as pie crust, place each layer in a baking pan, and spread with a very little butter, upon which sprinkle some flour. This will make four layers in a pan fourteen inches by seven. Bake about fifteen minutes in a quick oven, turn out upside down, take off the top layer, (the bottom when baking,) and place on a dish to send to the table; spread plentifully with strawberries (not mashed,) previously sweetened with pulverized sugar, place layer upon layer, treating each one in the same way, and when done you will have a handsome cake, to be served warm, with sugar and cream. The secret of having light dough is to handle it as little and mix it as quickly as possible. Short cake is delicious served with charlotte russe or whipped cream; raspberry and peach shortcakes may be made in the same way.

ORANGE SHORTCAKE.
Mrs. Canby, Bellefontaine.

One quart flour, two tablespoons butter, two teaspoons baking powder thoroughly mixed with the flour; mix with cold water, not very stiff; work as little as possible, bake, split open, and lay sliced oranges between; cut in squares and serve with pudding sauce.

CREAM TARTS.

One pound flour, one salt spoon salt, one quarter pound sugar, one quarter pound butter, one egg, one-half teaspoon soda or baking powder dissolved in a spoonful of water; mix, wet up with cold water, and line small patty pans; bake in a quick oven, fill with mock cream, as in recipe for Boston cream cakes, sprinkle over with sugar, and brown in the oven.

PUDDINGS AND SAUCES.

In making puddings always beat the eggs separately, straining the yolks and adding the whites the last thing. If boiled milk is used, let it cool somewhat before adding the eggs; when fruit is added, stir it in at the last; raisins are better to lie in hot water for one or two minutes until they are plumped. Puddings are either baked, boiled or stewed; rice, bread, custard and fruit require a moderate heat, batter and corn starch, a rather quick oven; always bake as soon as mixed.

For boiled puddings use either a tin mould, muslin bag, or bowl with cloth tied over; grease the former well on the inside with lard or butter, and in boiling do not let the water reach quite to the top. If a bag is used, make it of firm drilling, narrower at the bottom, rounded on the corners; stitch and fell the seams, which should be outside the bag when in use. Sew a tape to the seam about three inches from top of bag, wring out of hot water, flour the inside well, pour in pudding, tie securely, leaving room to swell (especially when made of Indian meal, bread, rice or crackers), place a saucer in the bottom of kettle to prevent burning; have enough boiling water to entirely cover the bag, which must be turned several times, keep water boiling constantly, and fill up from the tea-kettle when needed. If the pudding is boiled in a bowl, grease, fill and cover with a square of drilling wrung out of hot water, flour and tie on. To use a pan, tie the cloth tightly over the rim, lap the ends back and pin over the top of the pudding; the pudding may then be easily lifted out by a strong fork put through the ends or corners of the cloth. For plum puddings, invert the pan when put in the kettle, and the pudding will not become water-soaked. When the pudding is done, give whatever it is boiled in one sudden plunge into cold water, and turn out at once, serving immediately. As a general rule, boiled puddings require double the time required by baked. Steaming is safer than either boiling or baking, since your pudding will always be lighter and more wholesome.

In making sauces, do not boil after the butter is added. In place of wine or brandy, flavor with juice of the grape, or any other fruit, prepared for this purpose in its season by boiling, bottling and sealing while hot.

Pudding cloths, however coarse, should never be washed with soap; but should be dried as quickly as possible and kept dry and free from dust in a drawer or cupboard free from smell.

Dates are an excellent substitute for sugar in Graham or any other pudding.

APPLE ROLEY POLEY.
Mrs. T. B. J.

Peel, quarter and core sour apples, make good biscuit dough, roll to half an inch thick, slice the quarters and lay on the prepared paste or crust, roll up, tuck ends in, prick deeply with a fork, lay in a steamer and place over a kettle of boiling water, cook an hour and a quarter; or boil hard until cooked in bags; cut across, and eat with sweetened cream or butter and sugar. Cherries or any kind of berries can be used instead of apples.

BOILED APPLE DUMPLINGS.
Mrs. G. E. Kinney.

Two cups sour milk, two teaspoons soda, one of salt; with flour make a dough a little stiffer than for biscuit; quarter and core apples, put four pieces in each dumpling with a little sugar, (it is nice to tie a cloth around each one,) put into kettle of boiling water, slightly salted, boil half an hour; taking care that the water covers the dumplings. They are also very nice steamed. To bake, make in same way using a soft dough; place in a shallow pan, bake in a hot oven, and serve with cream and sugar.

BIRDNEST PUDDING.

Pare and core without quartering, enough tart, quick cooking apples to fill a pudding-pan, make a custard of one quart milk, the yolks of six eggs, sweeten and spice, pour over apples and bake; when done use the whites of eggs beaten stiff with six tablespoons white sugar; spread the custard on, brown lightly, and serve either hot or cold.

BREAD PUDDING.
Miss Mae Stokes, Milford Center.

One quart sweet milk, pint bread crumbs, four eggs, four tablespoons sugar; take half the milk, add the bread and soak until soft, mash fine, add the well beaten eggs and sugar, bake one hour, serve warm with warm sauce; or leave out the whites of three eggs, beat to a stiff froth with two tablespoons sugar, and when pudding is done, spread with a layer of jelly, canned fruit or berries, and over this spread the frosting, return to a quick oven and brown. Rolled cracker may be used instead of bread crumbs. Adding the grated rind of a lemon to the pudding, and the juice and more sugar to the frosting, makes a "Queen's pudding."

BATTER PUDDING.
Mrs. Dr. J. W. C. Ely, Providence, R. I.

Six eggs, seven tablespoons flour sifted into a dish, add a little milk at a time so as to make a small batter; add the yolks of the eggs well beaten, half teaspoon salt, the rest of the milk (one quart in all); pour over it the whites of the eggs whipped to a froth, and a tablespoon brandy; bake three-quarters of an hour in a quick oven.

COTTAGE PUDDING.
Mrs. Vosbury.

Three scant cups flour, one cup sugar, one cup sweet milk, half cup butter, two teaspoons cream-tartar, one egg; beat all together, add one teaspoon soda, flavor with lemon, bake half an hour and serve with this sauce; one tablespoon butter, one cup sugar, one teaspoon flour, half pint boiling water; let boil up once, add one teaspoon lemon or vanilla, and serve at once.

CORN STARCH MORANGE.
Mrs. Charles Fairbanks, Indianapolis, Ind.

Take six tablespoons corn starch, one and a half quarts milk, and a little salt; scald milk, having prepared starch in part of it cold, pour prepared starch into the scalded milk, let cool, add yolks of four eggs and three tablespoons sugar, pour in a buttered dish and bake half an hour or more. Make frosting of whites of four eggs and four tablespoons sugar, spread over the pudding, and place again in oven till brown; serve with plum or cream pudding sauce.

FANNIE'S PUDDING.
Mrs. W. E. Davidson, Boston, Mass.

One quart sweet milk, a little salt, two spoons corn starch, yolks of four eggs, half a cup sugar; scald milk, add corn starch and yolks, put into a dish, cover with whites of four eggs beaten to a froth, and one-half cup sugar, set into the oven and brown a little.

FRUIT PUDDING.
Mrs. S. W. Case, Minneapolis, Minn.

One cup molasses, one of sweet milk, one of suet chopped fine, one of raisins, one-half cup currants, two and a half cups flour, half teaspoon soda, mix with the molasses, salt and spice to taste; steam two hours.

FIG PUDDING.
Florence Woods Hush.

Half pound figs, quarter pound grated bread, two and a half ounces powdered sugar, three ounces butter, two eggs, one teacup milk; chop figs fine and mix with butter, and by degrees add the other ingredients; butter and sprinkle with bread crumbs a mould, cover closely and boil for three hours.

GREEN CORN PUDDING.
Mrs. J. R. Southwick.

Cut from cob two dozen full ears of corn, pound well, add about one pint milk, two eggs, one-fourth cup flour, one-fourth cup butter, one tablespoon salt; bake in a well greased dish in a hot oven one hour and a half, and serve for dinner with roast beef, mashed potatoes and stewed tomatoes.

BOILED INDIAN PUDDING.
Mrs. A. E. Brand, Minneapolis, Minn.

Warm a pint of molasses and pint of milk, stir well together, beat four eggs and stir gradually into molasses and milk a pound of beef suet chopped fine, and Indian meal sufficient to make a thick batter, add a teaspoon pulverized cinnamon, nutmeg and a little grated lemon peel, and stir all together thoroughly; dip cloth into boiling water, shake, flour a little, turn in the mixture, tie up leaving room for the pudding to swell, boil three hours; serve hot with sauce made of drawn butter, wine and nutmeg.

JELLY PUDDING.
Kate Thompson.

Four eggs beaten separately, two cups white sugar, one cup of butter, one of sweet cream, one of jelly, two tablespoons vanilla; stir together yolks and sugar, cream the butter, add the cream, the jelly, and last the white of eggs and vanilla.

KISS PUDDING.
Mrs. W. E. Baxter.

Stir well beaten and strained yolks of four eggs and four tablespoons sugar into one quart boiling milk, stirring constantly to prevent burning, dissolve four table spoons corn starch in a little cold water or milk, boil until it begins to thicken, pour into a dish ready for table. Have the whites of five eggs beaten to a stiff froth with teacup pulverized sugar and one teaspoon essence of vanilla, spread on top of pudding, set in a quick oven and brown. Take out, sprinkle with grated cocoanut and set dish away in a cool place; serve cold three or four hours after it is made. The sweet liquor which settles to the bottom in cooling serves as a sauce.

LEMON PUDDING.
Mrs. Walter Mitchell, Gallipolis.

Grate yellow rind from two lemons, squeeze out juice, stir yolks of six eggs into one cup of sugar and half a cup of water, soften in warm water six crackers, or some slices of cake, lay in bottom of a baking dish, pour custard over them, bake till firm; beat whites of the eggs to a froth, add four tablespoons sugar, beat well; when custard is done, pour frosting over it, return to the oven and brown; eat either warm or cold.

MARCH PUDDING.
Miss L. M.

One cup dried apples, cup molasses, one and one-fourths cup flour, fourth cup butter, one egg, one teaspoon each of soda and cinnamon, half teaspoon cloves; soak apples over night, cut fine and mix with water they were soaked in, and the molasses and spice; mix egg, butter and flour together, add apples and molasses, putting soda with the latter just before baking; serve hot with sauce made of one half cup butter, and one cup sugar, beaten smooth and flavored with nutmeg, lemon or vanilla.

ORANGE SOUFFLE.
Mrs. Mary A. Livermore, Melrose, Mass.

Peel and slice six oranges, put in a high glass dish a layer of oranges, then one of sugar and so on until all the orange is used, and let stand two hours; take yolks of three eggs, one pint of milk, and sugar to taste, flavor with grating of the orange peel, and make a soft boiled custard, and pour over the oranges when cool enough not to break the dish; beat the whites of the eggs to a stiff froth, stir in sugar, and put over the pudding, and it is done.

PLUM PUDDING.
Mrs. J. M. Southard.

Stew together a teacup raisins and half teacup citron; prepare dish with butter, put in a layer of cake, (any kind of cake will do, but sponge is best, or Boston crackers, sliced and buttered, may be used, or, if too rich, use stale Graham bread crumbs,) then a layer of fruit, and so on, with cake or bread for last layer; pour over it custard made of a quart of milk and yolks of four eggs, sweetened to taste; bake until you find, on inserting a knife, that the milk has become water. Make a frosting of the whites of four eggs and four tablespoons pulverized sugar, spread on pudding, place it in oven till brown, and serve with this sauce; one teacup white sugar, two-thirds pint water, one tablespoon butter, one teaspoon corn starch prepared with milk; let sugar and water boil, and add the rest, and allow to boil a few moments, then add the whites of one well beaten egg, with one teaspoon vanilla essence.

POP CORN PUDDING.

Crush popped corn in a coarse bag, grind in a coffee mill, mix two and a half pints of this meal with two pints sweet milk, keep warm and soak two hours, cool, add one egg, sugar, raisins and spice; boil a few minutes, stirring thoroughly to mix meal, which inclines to float, well with milk; bake from three-fourths to one hour, and serve hot.

QUICK PUFF PUDDING.
Mrs. B. T. Skinner, Battle Creek, Mich.

Stir one pint flour, two teaspoons baking powder and a little salt into milk until very soft; place in steamer well greased cups, put in each a spoon of batter, then one of berries, steamed apples, or any sauce convenient, cover with another spoon of batter and steam twenty minutes. This pudding is delicious made with fresh strawberries, and eaten with a sauce of two eggs, half cup butter, and cup of sugar beaten thoroughly, and one cup boiling milk and one cup strawberries stirred in.

RICE PUDDING.
Miss Mardie Dolbear, Cape Girardeau, Mo.

To a teacup of rice boiled in a pint of water until dry, add pint of milk and boil again, add the juice and grated rind of two lemons, the beaten yolks of four eggs, half teacup sugar; stir well together, adding when baked the well beaten whites of the eggs and cup of sugar; flavor with lemon or vanilla.

SAGO AND APPLE PUDDING.

Pare six apples and punch out the cores, fill holes in apples with cinnamon and sugar, using two teaspoons cinnamon to a cup of sugar; take one tablespoon sago to each apple, wash thoroughly and let soak an hour in water enough to cover the apples, pour water and sago over the apples, and bake hour and half.

SUET PUDDING.
Mrs. J. C. Ross.

One cup finely chopped suet, cup molasses, one of sour milk, one of raisins, four of flour, teaspoon soda; steam four hours and serve with pudding sauce.

TRANSPARENT PUDDING.
Mrs. Annie Gillespie, Indianapolis, Ind.

Take twelve eggs, a pound sugar, one of butter, wine glass wine; mix well, and spread on a rich pie crust and bake as for pies; when done beat the whites of eggs to a stiff froth, put on top and set in the oven to brown.

APPLE TAPIOCA PUDDING.
Mrs. S. C. Lee.

To half teacup of tapioca, add one and one-half pints cold water, let it stand on the fire till cooked clear, stirring to prevent burning, remove, sweeten and flavor with wine and nutmeg; pour the tapioca into a deep dish in which have been placed six or eight pared and cored apples, bake until apples are done, and serve cold with cream.

*GRANDMA THOMPSON'S WHITE PUDDING.
Over 100 years old.

Weigh equal quantities of best beef suet and sifted flour, shave down suet and rub into fine particles with the hands, removing all tough and stringy parts, mix well with the flour, season very highly with pepper,

---

* Contributed by Mrs. E. T. Carson, Mt. Pleasant Farm.

and salt to taste, stuff loosely in beef-skins (entrails cleansed as pork-skins for sausage) half a yard or less in length, secure the ends, prick every two or three inches with a darning needle, place to boil in a kettle of cold water hung on the crane; boil three hours, place on a table until cold, after which hang up in a cool place to dry; tie up in a clean cotton bag, and put away where it will be both dry and cool. When wanted for use cut off the quantity needed, boil in hot water until heated through, take out and place before the fire to dry off and "crisp." The above was considered an "extra dish" at all the "flax scutchings," "quilting frolics," and "log rollings" of a hundred years ago.

BREAD PUDDING SAUCE.

Two tablespoons butter, cup of sugar, tablespoon of flour, milk of one cocoanut, and a small piece grated.

CREAM SAUCE.

One teacup powdered white sugar, scant half teacup butter, half teacup rich cream; beat butter and sugar thoroughly, add cream, stir the whole into half teacup boiling water, place on stove for a few moments, stirring it constantly, take off and add flavoring.

EVERY-DAY SAUCE.

To one pint boiling water, add heaping teacup sugar, tablespoon butter, pinch of salt, and tablespoon Duryea's improved corn starch dissolved in cold water; season with nutmeg or vanilla, and boil half an hour, and if good and well cooked it will be very clear. Nearly all sauces are cooked too little.

LEMON SAUCE.

Two cups sugar, two eggs, juice of two lemons, and rind if you choose; beat all together, and just before serving add one pint boiling water; set on stove and let boil up once. Some add one-third cup butter and tablespoon corn starch.

PRESERVES.

Quinces, pears, citrons, watermelon rinds, and many of the smaller fruits such as cherries, currants, etc., harden when put, at first, into a syrup made of their weight of sugar. To prevent this they should be cooked till tender in water, or in a weak syrup made from a portion only of the sugar, adding the remainder of the sugar afterwards. Fruits which need hardening should be stewed over before cooking, with a part or the whole of the sugar; this extracts the juice, which may be boiled and poured hot over the fruit. Long protracted boiling destroys the pleasant natural flavor of the fruit, and darkens it.

Preserves should boil gently lest they burn, and in order that the sugar may thoroughly penetrate the fruit. Marmalades or the different butters will be smoother, better flavored, and will require less boiling if the fruit (peaches, quinces, oranges, and apples make the best) is well cooked and mashed before adding either sugar or cider. It is important to stir constantly.

In making either preserves or marmalades, follow the directions as regards kettle, sugar and putting up, already given for jellies and jams. Dried fruits are much nicer and require less boiling, if clean soft water is poured over them and allowed to stand over night. In the morning boil until tender in the water, sweetening five minutes before removing from the stove.

To dry corn or fruits nicely, spread in shallow boxes or box covers, and cover with mosquito netting to prevent flies reaching them. When dry put up in jars and cover closely, or in paper sacks. Dried peaches are better when halved and the cavities sprinkled with sugar in drying. The fruit must be good however, as poor fruit cannot be redeemed by any process. Another excellent way is to dry them in the oven, and when about half done, place in a crock a layer of peaches alternately with a layer of sugar. Cherries and all other kinds of fruit are excellent dried in this manner.

CHERRY PRESERVES.

Choose sour ones—the early Richmond is very nice,—seed nearly all, allow an amount of sugar equal to the fruit. Take half the sugar, sprinkle over the fruit, let stand about an hour, pour into a preserving kettle, boil slowly ten minutes, skim out the cherries, add rest of sugar to the syrup, boil, skim, and pour over the cherries; the next day drain off the syrup, boil, skim if necessary, add the cherries, boil twenty minutes, and seal up in small jars.

PEAR PRESERVES.
Miss Florence Williams.

Pare, cut in halves, core and weigh (if hard, boil in water until tender, and use the water for the syrup), allow three-quarters of a pound sugar for each pound fruit, boil a few moments, skim, and cool; when lukewarm add the pears, and boil gently until the syrup has penetrated them and they look clear; some of the pieces will cook before the rest, and must be removed; when done, take out, boil down the syrup a little and pour over them; a few cloves stuck here and there in the pears add a pleasant flavor. Put in small jars with glass or tin tops, and seal with putty.

PEACH PRESERVES.

Take nice cling-stone peaches, or any that do not mash readily in cooking, pare and cut out the seeds (adding the kernels of a few), weigh out fruit and an equal amount of sugar, take half of sugar and sprinkle over peaches in a deep earthen vessel, let stand over night, drain the juice in a preserving kettle, add the rest of the sugar, boil, skim, put in fruit, boil very slowly ten minutes, skim out fruit carefully and pour over it the boiling syrup; repeat for two or three days—till the fruit is quite clear; put in jars, cut a piece of writing paper to fit jar closely, lay it over the preserves, wet with a little brandy; seal with paper and egg like jelly.

QUINCE PRESERVES.

Take equal weights of quinces and sugar, pare, core, and leave whole or cut up, boil till tender in water enough to cover, carefully take out and put on a platter, add sugar to the water, replace fruit and boil slowly till clear, place in jars and pour syrup over them. To increase the quantity without adding sugar, take half or two-thirds in weight as many fair sweet apples as there are quinces, pare, quarter and core; after removing quinces, put apples into the syrup, and boil until they begin to look red and clear and are tender, place quinces and apples in jar in alternate layers, and cover with syrup.

TOMATO PRESERVES.

Take small perfectly formed tomatoes—the yellow, pear shaped are best. Scald and remove skins carefully, add equal amount of sugar by weight, let lie over night, then pour all the juice you can off them into a preserving kettle, and boil until it is a very thick syrup; add tomatoes and boil carefully until they look transparent; a piece or two of root ginger, and a few slices of lemon may be added.

WATERMELON RIND PRESERVES.
Miss Josie Smith.

Pare off outside green rind, cut in pieces two inches long, weigh, and throw into cold water, skim out and add a heaping teaspoon each of salt and pulverized alum to two gallons of rinds, let stand until salt and alum dissolve, fill the kettle with cold water, and place on top of stove where it will slowly come to a boil, covering with a large plate so as to keep rinds under; boil until they can be easily pierced with a fork; make and strain a strong ginger tea, take out rinds, put in tea, and let remain all night, then drain, add fresh strained ginger tea, add rind of four lemons cut thin, boil a few moments, skim out and make a syrup of the sugar (one pound to each pound of fruit) and a sufficient quantity of water, add the rinds with the four lemons sliced, and a few pieces of white race ginger, and boil gently one hour. When properly made they are transparent and beautiful.

APPLE BUTTER.

Boil one barrel of new cider down one-half, peel and core three bushels of good cooking apples; when the cider has boiled to one-half the quantity, add the apples, and when soft, stir constantly for from eight to ten hours. If done it will adhere to an inverted plate. Put away in stone jars (not potter's ware), covering first with writing paper cut to fit the jar, and pressed down closely upon the apple-butter; cover the whole with thick brown paper snugly tied down.

LEMON BUTTER.

One lemon, one teacup white sugar, the yolks of two eggs, butter the size of two eggs, grate the rind into the juice, and boil ten minutes.

PEACH MARMALADE.

Pare, seed and weigh soft peaches, boil slowly three-quarters of an hour in just enough water to keep from burning, stirring almost constantly; press through colander, put back in kettle, adding two and a half pounds sugar to every four pounds fruit, and a few of the blanched kernels; boil ten minutes stirring often; place in jars as elsewhere directed.

MRS. COOPER'S MARMALADE.

Pare, quarter and core quinces, cut in little squares, measure and allow an equal amount of sugar; place the fruit in a porcelain kettle with water enough to just cover, and boil till tender, skim out carefully and make a syrup of the sugar and the water in which the quinces were boiled; let come to a boil, skim well, and drop the quinces gently in; boil fifteen minutes and dip out carefully into jelly bowls or moulds. The syrup forms a jelly around the fruit so that it can be turned out on a dish, and is very palatable as well as ornamental. In this way quinces too defective for preserves may be used.

DRIED APPLE SAUCE.

Look over, wash thoroughly and soak in clean warm water half an hour; drain, cover with cold soft water, place on the stove, let boil slowly two to four hours, mash fine, sweeten and season with cinnamon very highly. Never add sugar until about five minutes before removing from the stove, otherwise the fruit will be toughened and hardened. Follow the same directions in preparing dried peaches, only do not mash nor season so highly. Cook in porcelain and do not stir while cooking.

PICKLES.

In making pickles use none but the best cider vinegar and boil in a porcelain kettle—avoid a metal one. A small lump of alum added when scalding pickles the first time renders them crisp and tender, but too much is injurious; keep in glass or stoneware, look at them frequently and remove all soft ones; if white specks appear in the vinegar, drain off and scald, adding a liberal handful of sugar to each gallon, and pour again over the pickles; bits of horse-radish and a few cloves assist in preserving the life of the vinegar. If put away in large stone jars, invert a saucer over the top of the pickles, so as to keep well under the vinegar. The nicest way to put up pickles is bottling, sealing while hot, and keeping in a cool dark place. Many think that mustard (the large white or yellow) improves pickles, especially chopped and bottled and mangoes. Never put up pickles in anything that has held any kind of grease, and never let them freeze; use an oaken tub or cask for pickles in brine, keep them well under, and have more salt than will dissolve, so that there will always be plenty at the bottom of the cask.

CHOW CHOW PICKLES.
Mrs. Ada Estelle Bever.

Let two hundred small cucumbers stand in salt and water closely covered for three days; boil fifteen minutes in half a gallon best cider vinegar the following: one ounce white mustard seed, one of black mustard seed, one of juniper berries, one of celery seed, one handful small green peppers, two pounds sugar, a few small onions and a small piece alum;

tie each ounce separately in swiss bags, pour the vinegar while hot over the cucumbers, let stand a day, repeating the operation three or four mornings. Mix one-fourth pound mustard with the vinegar, pour over cucumbers and seal up in bottles.

CHOW CHOW.
Miss Lou Browne, Washington City.

One peck of green tomatoes, half peck string beans, quarter peck of small white onions, quarter pint red and green peppers mixed, two large heads cabbage, four tablespoons white mustard seed, two tablespoons white or black cloves, two tablespoons celery seed, two tablespoons allspice, one small box yellow mustard, pound brown sugar, ounce of turmeric, some cauliflower; slice the tomatoes and let stand over night in brine that will bear an egg; then squeeze out brine, chop cabbage, onions and beans, chop tomatoes separately, mix with the spices, put in a porcelain kettle, cover with vinegar and boil three hours.

CAULIFLOWER PICKLE.
Mrs. Col W. P. Reid, Delaware.

Choose such as are fine and of full size, cut away all the leaves, and pull away the flowers by bunches; steep in brine two days, drain, put into bottles with whole black pepper, allspice and stick cinnamon; boil vinegar and with it mix mustard smoothly, a little at a time, and just thick enough to run into the jars; pour over the cold cauliflower and seal while hot.

CUCUMBER PICKLES.

Cover the bottom of cask with common salt; gather the cucumbers every other day early in the morning or late in the evening, as it does not injure the vines so much as in the heat of the day; cut the cucumbers with a short piece of the stem on, carefully laying them in a basket or pail so as not to bruise; pour cold water over and rinse, being careful not to rub off the little black briers, or in any way bruise them, as this is the secret of keeping them perfectly sound and good for any length of time. Lay them in the cask three or four inches in depth, cover with salt, and repeat the operation until all are in; (when the first are put in the barrel, pour in some water, after this the salt will make sufficient brine.) Now spread a cloth over them, then a board with stones on it; each additional pickling must be treated in like manner, except that the water must not be added. When ready to barrel the new supply of cucumbers, remove stone, board and cloth, wash them very clean, and wipe every particle of scum from the top of the pickles and sides of the cask; throw away any soft ones, as they will spoil the rest; now put in the fresh cucumbers, layer by layer, with salt to cover between them. When cask is nearly full, cover with salt, tuck cloth closely around the edges, placing the board and weight on top; cover cask closely, and the pickles will be perfect for two or three years. Cucumbers must always be put in the salt as soon as picked from the vines, for if they lie a day or two they will not keep. Do not be alarmed at the heavy scum that rises on them, but be careful to wash all off the board and cloth. When wanted for pickling, take off weight and board, carefully lift cloth with scum on it, wash stone, board and cloth clean, and wipe all scum off the cucumbers and sides of cask, take out as many as are wanted, return the cloth, board and weight, and cover closely. Place the cucumbers in a vessel large enough to hold two or three times as much water as there are pickles, cover with cold water (some use hot), change the water each day for three days, place the porcelain kettle on the fire, fill half full of vinegar (if your vinegar is very strong add half water), fill nearly full of cucumbers, the largest first and then the smaller ones, put in a lump of alum the size of a hulled hickory-nut, let come to a boil, stirring with a wire spoon so as not to cut the cucumbers; after boiling one minute, take out, place in stone jar, and continue until all are scalded, then pour over cold vinegar. In two or three days, if your pickles are too salt, turn off the vinegar and put on fresh, adding a pint of brown sugar to two gallons pickles, pod or two red pepper, a very few cloves, and some pieces of horse-radish. The horse-radish prevents a white scum rising.

CHOPPED PICKLES.

Take green tomatoes, wash clean, cut away a small piece from each end, slice and place in a large wooden bowl, chop quite fine, place in a crock and mix salt with them, (one pint to a peck,) let stand twenty-four hours and drain thoroughly; take twice or three times as much cabbage, chop fine, mix salt in same proportions, add enough water to make moist and let stand same time as tomatoes, drain, place again in separate jars, cover each with cold weak vinegar, after twenty-four hours drain well, pressing hard to extract all the juice; mix tomatoes and cabbage together, take a double handful at a time, squeeze as tightly as possible, and place in a dry crock; take the stone jar in which they are to be pickled, place in it a layer of tomatoes and cabbage, sprinkle with pepper, whole mustard seed, and horse radish, then another layer of tomatoes and cabbage, next spice, and so on until jar is almost full, occasionally sprinkling with cayenne pepper; cover with strong cider vinegar to each gallon of which a teacup sugar has been added. Place a saucer or pieces of broken china on pickles to keep them under vinegar. If a white scum rises, drain off vinegar, boil, skim, and pour hot over pickles. Prepare mustard, pepper and horse radish, as follows: take green garden peppers, cut in two, place in salt water over night; the next morning drain and chop quite fine; to a pint of mustard seed, add teaspoon salt, pour in boiling water, let stand fifteen minutes and drain; slice horse radish and chop fine. Tomatoes and onions are nice prepared in the same way. For sliced pickles, take cucumbers and onions, or tomatoes and onions; slice and prepare as above.

MANGOES.

Take green or half-grown muskmelons, cut a piece the length of the melon and an inch and a half wide in the middle, tapering to a point at each end, take out the seeds with a teaspoon, secure each piece to its own melon by taking a stitch with a needle and white thread. Make a strong brine of salt and cold water, pour it over them, and after twenty-four hours take them out. For filling, use chopped tomatoes, chopped cabbage, small cucumbers, small white onions, and nasturtion seed, each prepared in separate jars, by remaining in salt water twenty-four hours; add also green beans boiled in salt water until tender. For spice, use cinnamon bark, whole cloves, sliced and chopped horse radish, cayenne pepper, and mustard seed, the latter prepared as heretofore directed. Fill each mangoe with the cucumbers, onions, beans and nasturtion seed, then add the chopped cabbage and spice, sprinkling on the cayenne pepper last. Sew in the piece in its proper place with a strong white thread; when all are thus prepared, place in a stone crock, cover with weak cider vinegar, let remain over night; in the morning drain off this vinegar, place the mangoes in a porcelain kettle, add fresh vinegar enough to boil them in, and a pint of sugar to each gallon vinegar, boil half an hour; (as this vinegar cannot be used again, it may be weakened with water, or only a few mangoes may be boiled at a time, or when one side is boiled, turn them over on the other.) Place in a jar, cover with good cider vinegar, let stand all night, in the morning drain off vinegar and boil it, adding one pint of sugar to each gallon, and pour boiling hot over the mangoes, drain off and boil the vinegar three or four times and they are done. This is not the usual way of preparing mangoes, but it is much the best. To pickle nasturtions, soak as collected in salt and water for twenty-four hours, drain, and put into cold vinegar; when all the seed is thus prepared, drain, and cover with fresh boiling hot vinegar. To pickle peppers, take large green ones, make a small incision at the side; if you wish them very hot leave in the seeds, if not, take out all or the greatest part, being careful not to mangle the peppers; soak in salt water twenty-four hours, changing the water twice, stuff with chopped cabbage or tomatoes seasoned with spice as for mangoes, omitting the cayenne pepper; sew up the incision, place in a jar, and cover with cold vinegar.

PICKLED CHICKEN.
Emma Gould Rea.

Boil four chickens till tender, enough for meat to fall from bones; put meat in a stone jar, and pour over it three pints of cold vinegar, and a pint and a half of the water in which the chickens were boiled; add spice if you wish, and it will be ready for use in two days.

PICKLED OYSTERS.

Take fine large oysters, put over fire in their own liquor, add a bit of butter, let simmer until they are plump and white, take up with a skimmer, lay the oysters, each spread nicely out, on a large folded napkin; take equal parts of vinegar and the oyster liquor (must be warm and cover the oysters), and into a large stone jar put a layer of oysters, lay over it whole pepper, allspice, cloves and ground mace, add another layer of oysters, then more spice, and so on until all are in, then pour over the oyster liquor and vinegar, and let stand one night. Oysters prepared in this way are delicious.

PICKLED ONIONS.
S. E. W.

Remove the outer skin, boil the onions in salted water until you can penetrate them with a straw; drain and cover them while hot with cold spiced vinegar; small onions are best.

PICCALILLI.
Mrs. W. L.

One large white cabbage, fifty small cucumbers, five quarts small string beans, eight small carrots, one dozen sticks celery, five red peppers, three green peppers, two heads cauliflower; chop fine, soak over night in salt and water, wash well, drain thoroughly, and pour over them hot vinegar spiced with mace, cinnamon and allspice; turn off vinegar and scald until safe to leave like common pickles, or can while hot.

PYFER PICKLES.
Mrs. E. M. R.

Salt pickles down dry for ten days, soak in fresh water one day; pour off water, place in porcelain kettle, covering with water and vinegar, with alum enough to taste; stand over night on a stove which had fire in during the day; wash and put in a jar with cloves, allspice, pepper, horse radish and garlic; boil vinegar and pour over all; in two weeks they are ready for use. These pickles are always fresh and crisp and are made with much less trouble than by the old fashioned way of keeping in brine.

SPANISH PICKLES.
Mrs. Charles Morey.

One peck green tomatoes, one dozen onions; slice, sprinkle with salt, let stand over night, strain off juice; mix dry a pound sugar, fourth pound whole white mustard seed, ounce ground black pepper, ounce cloves, ounce ginger, ounce cinnamon; put a layer of tomatoes and on-ions in porcelain kettle, sprinkle with spice, lay in more tomatoes, and so on until all are used; cover with vinegar and boil slowly for two hours. Pack in small jars and set in cellar.

PICKLED CUCUMBERS.
Mrs. M. L. France.

Pare and quarter ripe cucumbers, take out seeds, clean, lay in strong brine nine days, stirring every day, take out and put in clear water one day, lay in alum water (a lump of alum size of a medium hulled hickory-nut to a gallon of water) over night, make syrup of a pint of good cider vinegar, pound brown sugar, two table spoons each broken cinnamon bark, mace and pepper grains; make syrup enough to cover the slices, lay them in and cook till tender.

SPICED CURRANTS.
Mrs. H. B. S.

Six pounds fruit, three of raisins, three of sugar, one pint vinegar, two tablespoons allspice, two of cinnamon, and one of cloves.

PICKLED GRAPES.
Mrs. C. T. Carson.

Fill a jar with alternate layers of sugar and bunches of nice grapes just ripe; fill one-third full of good cold vinegar and cover tightly.

SPICED GRAPES.
Miss Mae Stokes, Milford Centre.

Five pounds grapes, three of sugar, two teaspoons cinnamon and all-spice, one-half teaspoon cloves; pulp grapes, boil skins until tender, cook pulps and strain through a sieve, add it to the skins, put in sugar, spices and vinegar to taste; boil thoroughly and cool.

SPICED GOOSEBERRIES.
Mrs. D. Buxton.

Leave the stem and blossom on ripe gooseberries, wash clean; make a syrup of three pints sugar to one of vinegar, skim if necessary, add berries and boil down till thick, adding more sugar if needed; when almost done, spice with cinnamon and cloves; boil as thick as apple butter.

MUSKMELON PICKLES.
Mrs. J. Ross Southwick.

Pare unripe melons and cut into small pieces; cover in vinegar sweetened with a pound sugar to a quart sharp vinegar; spice with cinnamon and cloves, boil till transparent, or till they lose their raw taste, but not till they become soft.

PEACH PICKLES.
W. W. W.

Pare free-stone peaches, place in a stone jar, and pour over them boiling hot syrup made in the proportion of one quart good cider vinegar to three pints good sugar; boil and skim, and pour over the fruit boiling hot, repeating each day until the fruit is the same color to the centre, and the syrup like thin molasses. A few days before they are pickled, place the fruit, after draining, in the jar three or four inches thick, then sprinkle over bits of cinnamon bark and a few cloves, add another layer of fruit, then spice, and so on until the jar is full; scald the syrup each morning for three or four days after putting in the spice, and pour syrup boiling hot over them. To pickle clingstones, prepare syrup as for free-stones, pare fruit, put in the syrup, boil until they can be pierced through with a silver fork. As clings are apt to become hard when stewed in sweet syrup, it may often be necessary to add a pint of water the first time they are cooked, watching carefully until they are tender, or to use only part of the sugar at first, adding the rest as the syrup boils, skim out, place in jar, and pour boiling syrup over them; continue to drain and boil the syrup each morning until the fruit is the same color to the centre. A few days before they are done, spice like peaches. Use the large white Heath clings, if they are to be had. All that is necessary to keep sweet pickles is to have syrup enough to cover and to keep the fruit well under. Scald with boiling syrup until fruit is of same color throughout, and syrup as thick as molasses; watch every week, particularly if weather is warm, and if scum rises and syrup assumes a whitish appearance, boil and skim syrup, and pour over the fruit. If at any time syrup is lacking, prepare more as at first.

PEAR PICKLES.

Prepare syrup as for peaches, pare and cut fruit in halves, or quarters if very large, and if small leave whole, put syrup in porcelain kettle, and when it boils put in fruit, cook until a silver fork will easily pierce them; skim out fruit first and place in jar, and last pour over syrup boiling hot; spice like peach pickles, draining them each day, boiling and skimming the syrup, and pouring it boiling hot over the fruit until fully done. By cooking pears so much longer at first they do not need to be boiled so frequently, but they must be watched carefully until finished, and if perfectly done, will keep two or more years. Apple pickles may be made in the same way, taking care to select such as will not lose shape in boiling.

EUCHERED PLUMS.
Mrs. Capt. W. B. Brown, Washington City.

Nine pounds blue plums, six pounds sugar, two quarts vinegar, one ounce cinnamon; boil vinegar, sugar and spice together, pour over plums, draw off next morning and boil, pour back on plums, repeat the boiling five mornings, the last time boiling fruit about twenty minutes.

PICKLED RAISINS.
Mrs. H. C. H.

Two pounds raisins, leave on stem, one pint vinegar, one-half pound sugar; simmer over a slow fire half an hour.

SWEET PICKLE.
Mrs. W. A. Croffut, New York City.

Take eight pounds of green tomatoes and chop fine, add four pounds brown sugar and boil down three hours, add a quart of vinegar, a teaspoon each of mace, cinnamon and cloves, and boil about fifteen minutes; let it cool and put into jars or other vessel. Try this once and you will try it again.

PICKLED WALNUTS OR BUTTERNUTS.
Mrs. C. T. Carson.

Take well-grown nuts, but still tender enough to stick a pin through; put in water as salt as for fresh cucumber pickles, let stand two or three days, changing the water during that time, take out, rinse and lay in the sun a few hours, turning frequently until black; bring to a boil some good cider or white wine vinegar, with any spices you choose such as cinnamon, cloves, mace, race ginger, mustard seed, pepper and horse-radish, and if you like, about a pint of sugar to a gallon of vinegar. Put nuts into a jar and pour over hot; will be ready for use in a few days.

WATERMELON PICKLE.

Pare off very carefully the green part of the rind of a good ripe water-melon, trim off the red core, cut in pieces one or two inches in length, place in a porcelain-lined kettle, in the proportions of one gallon rind to two heaping teaspoons common salt and water to nearly cover, boil until tender enough to pierce with a silver fork, pour into a colander to drain, and dry by taking a few pieces at a time in the hand and pressing gently with a crash towel. Make syrup and treat rinds exactly as directed for pickled peaches. You may continue adding rinds as melons are used at table, preparing them at first by cooking in salt water as above; when you have prepared as many as you want, and they are nearly pickled, drain and finish as directed as in peach pickles, except when the syrup is boiled the last time, put in the melons, and boil fifteen or twenty minutes; set jar near stove, skim out melons and put in jar a few at a time, heating gradually so as not to break it, then pour in syrup boiling hot. A rind nearly an inch thick, crisp and tender, is best, although any may be used. If scum rises and the syrup assumes a whitish appearance, drain, boil and skim syrup, add melons and boil until syrup is as thick as molasses.

POULTRY.

Do not feed poultry the day before killing; cut off the head, hang up by the legs, as the meat will be more white and healthful if bled freely and quickly—in winter kill from three days to a week before cooking. Scald well by dipping in and out of a pail or tub of boiling water, being careful not to scald so much as to set the feathers and make them more difficult to pluck; place the fowl on a board with head towards you, pull the feathers away from you, which will be in the direction they naturally lie (if pulled in a contrary direction the skin is likely to be torn), be careful to remove all the pin-feathers with a knife or pair of tweezers; singe, but not smoke, over blazing paper, place on a meat board, and with a sharp knife cut off the legs at the joint above the feet and the oil bag above the tail; take out the crop, either by making a slit at the back of the neck or in front, (the last is better), taking care that everything pertaining to the crop or windpipe is removed, cut the neck bone off close to the body, leaving the skin a good length if you intend to stuff, cut a slit in the lower part of the fowl from the breast bone to the tail, being careful to cut only through the skin; put in your finger at the breast and detach all the intestines, taking care not to burst the gall bag (situated near the upper part of the breast bone, and attached to the liver; if broken, no washing can remove the bitter taint left on every spot it touches); squeeze the body of the fowl and force out the whole through the incision at the tail; if there is much fat, trim off a part; split the gizzard and take out the inside and inner lining (throw liver, heart and gizzard into water, wash well, and use for the gravy); wash thoroughly in several waters, hang up to drain, and the fowl is ready to be stuffed, skewered and placed to roast. Before stuffing, to make it look plump, flatten the breast bone by placing several thicknesses of cloth over it and pounding it, being careful not to break the skin; stuff the breast first, but not too full or it will burst in cooking; stuff the body rather fuller than the breast, sew up both openings with strong thread, and sew the skin of the neck over upon the back or down upon the breast, (these threads must be carefully removed before sending to the table). Lay the points of the wings under the back and fasten in that position with a skewer run through both wings and held in place with a twine; press the legs as closely towards the breast and side bones as possible, and fasten with a skewer run through the body and both thighs; push a short skewer through above the tail, and tie the ends of the legs down with a twine close upon the skewer; place to roast in an oven rather hot at first and then graduate the heat to moderate until done, to test which insert a fork between the thigh and body, if the juice is watery and not bloody it is done. If not served at once, the fowl may be kept hot without drying up, by placing on a skillet full of boiling water (set on top of stove or range), and inverting a dripping pan over it. Many persons roast fowls upon a wire rack or trivet placed inside the dripping pan. The pan should be three inches deep and measure at the bottom about sixteen by twenty inches with sides somewhat flaring. In roasting a turkey allow fifteen minutes time for every pound. Some steam turkey before roasting, and a turkey steamer may be easily improvised by placing the dripping pan, containing the turkey, on top of two or three pieces of wood (hickory or maple is the best) laid in the bottom of a wash boiler, with just enough water to cover the wood; place the lid, which should fit tightly on the boiler, and as the water boils away add more. Add the liquor in the dripping pan to the gravy.

Chickens are stuffed and roasted in the same way as turkeys, and are much better, whether broiled, fried, or roasted, for being first steamed, especially if over a year old. They roast in twenty or thirty minutes.

Some, in making chicken or meat pies, line the dish with the lower crust, and place in the oven until well "set," then fill, cover and bake; others, instead of lining the entire surface of the dish, use only strips of the dough.

BAKED CHICKENS.
Mrs. E. W. Herrick, Minneapolis, Minn.

Dress the chickens and cut them in two, soak for half an hour in cold water, wipe perfectly dry and put in a dripping pan, bone side down, without any water; have a hot oven, and, if the chickens are young, half an hour's cooking will be sufficient. Take out and season with butter, salt and pepper; pack one above another as closely as possible, and place in a pan over boiling water, covering them closely,—this keeps them moist until served,—boil the giblets in a little water, and after the chickens are taken from the dripping-pan, put into it the water in which giblets were boiled, thicken it and add the chopped giblets. This manner of baking chickens is fully equal to broiling them.

BAKED SPRING CHICKEN.
Mrs. Louisa Hush.

Cut each of four chickens into seven or nine pieces, wash thoroughly and quickly, and put in a colander to drain; put a half tablespoon each of lard and butter into a dripping-pan, set in the chickens and add half a pint hot water, at the side of the chickens; let steam and bake half an hour, turn, taking care that they get only to a light brown, and just before taking up add salt and pepper to taste; when done take out in a dish and keep hot. To make the gravy, add a half pint or more of water, set the dripping-pan on the stove, and add one tablespoon flour mixed with one-half cup of cream or milk, stirring slowly, adding a little of the mixture at a time. Let cook thoroughly, stirring constantly to prevent burning, and to make the gravy nice and smooth; season more if necessary.

BONED CHICKEN.

Take one or two chickens, boil in a small quantity of water with a little salt, and when thoroughly done, take all the meat from the bones, removing all the skin you can, and keeping the light meat separate from the dark; chop and season to taste with salt and pepper. If you have a meat presser, take it, or any other mould such as a crock or pan will do; put in a layer of light and a layer of dark meat till all is used, add the liquor it was boiled in, which should be about one teacupful, and put on a small weight; when cold cut in slices. Many chop all the meat together, add one pounded cracker to the liquor it was boiled in, and mix all thoroughly before putting in the mould; either way is nice.

CHICKEN OR BEEF CROQUETTES.

Take cold chicken, beef or veal, roast or boiled, mince it very fine, moisten with the cold gravy if you have it, or moisten well and add one egg, season with pepper, salt, and, if you like, an onion or sage; make into small cakes, cover with egg and bread crumbs, and fry in lard and butter.

BROILED CHICKENS OR QUAILS.
Mrs. A. S. Chapman.

Cut chicken open on the back, lay on the meat board and pound until it will lie flat, lay on gridiron, and place over a bed of coals, broil until a nice brown, but do not burn. It will take twenty or thirty minutes to cook thoroughly, and it will cook much better to cover with a pie-tin held down with a weight so that all parts of the chicken may lie closely to the gridiron. While the chicken is broiling, put the liver, gizzard and heart in a stew pan and boil in a pint of water until tender, chop fine and add flour, butter, pepper, salt, and if you have it, a cup of sweet cream, to the water in which they were boiled; when the chicken is done, dip it in this gravy while hot, lay it back on the gridiron a minute, then put it in the gravy and let it boil for a half minute and send to the table hot. Cook quails in the same way.

CHICKENS FOR LUNCH.
Mrs. W. W. W.

Split a young chicken down the back, wash, and wipe dry, season with salt and pepper. Put in a dripping-pan, and place in a moderate oven; bake three-quarters of an hour. This is much better for lunch than when seasoned with butter.

CHICKEN POT-PIE.
Mrs. B.

Put chicken on in cold water, and while boiling cut off a slice from your bread dough, add a small lump of lard, and mix up like light biscuit; cut out with cake-cutter and set by stove to rise; wash and pare potatoes of moderate size, and add them when chicken is almost done; when potatoes begin to boil, season with salt and pepper, and dredge with flour; add dumplings, season, and dredge again with flour. See that you have enough water to keep from burning, cover very tightly, and do not take cover off until dumplings are done. They will cook in half an hour, and you can then lift one edge of the lid, take out a dumpling, break it open, and see if it is done. Dish potatoes by themselves and chicken and dumplings together. Then make your gravy; if not enough add more water, butter and seasoning. Or make your dumplings with one pint sour milk, two well beaten eggs, half teaspoon soda mixed in the flour, salt, pepper, and flour enough to make as stiff as can be stirred with a spoon; or baking powder and sweet milk may be used. Drop in by spoonfuls, cover tightly, and boil as above. You can make a pot-pie from a good boiling piece of beef; if too much grease arises skim off.

CHICKEN PIE.
Mrs. W. W. W.

Cut up two young chickens, place in hot water enough to cover, boil until tender; line a four or five quart pan with a rich baking powder or soda biscuit dough quarter of an inch thick, put in part of chicken, season with salt, pepper and butter, lay in a few thin strips or squares of dough, add the rest of chicken and season as before; some add five or six fresh eggs or a few new potatoes in their season; season liquor in which the chickens were boiled with butter, salt and pepper, add a part of it to the pie, cover with crust a quarter of an inch thick, with a hole in the centre the size of a teacup. Bake one hour, keep adding the chicken liquor and hot water if needed, since the fault of most chicken pies is that they are too dry. You can scarcely have too much gravy.

CHICKEN PIE WITH OYSTERS.

Boil the chicken—a year old is best—until tender, line dish with a nice crust, put in chicken, season with salt, pepper and butter, add the liquor in which chicken was boiled, should not be more than one pint, cover loosely with a crust having a slit cut each way in the middle. Drain off liquor from a quart of oysters, boil, skim, season with butter, pepper, salt and a thickening of flour and water, boil up once and pour over oysters, and about twenty minutes before the pie is done, lift the crust and put them in.

DRESSING FOR CHICKEN OR BEEF.
Mrs. Carrie Beck.

Boil potatoes, mash as for the table except less moist, stuff the chicken or roast with this, and bake as ordinarily; for ducks add onions chopped fine; if you wish the bread dressing too, it may be laid in the corner of the pan.

FRIED SPRING CHICKEN.
Mrs. L. H.

Put skillet on the stove with about one-half tablespoon each of lard and butter, when hot lay in chicken, sprinkle over with flour, salt and pepper, place lid on skillet, and cook over a moderate fire; when a slight brown turn the chicken and sprinkle flour, salt and pepper over the top as at first, and if necessary add more lard and butter, cook slowly until done; make gravy just the same as for baked chicken. As a general rule half an hour is long enough to fry spring chicken. To make rich and nice gravy without cream, take the yolk of an egg, beat up light, strain and stir slowly into the gravy after the flour and milk have been stirred in and thoroughly cooked; as soon as it boils up the gravy is done, and should be removed from the stove. All gravies need to be stirred well and thoroughly cooked over a moderate fire.

FRIED GUMBO.
Mrs. J. H. S.

Take two young chickens, cut up and fry in skillet; when brown but not scorched, put in a pot with one quart of finely chopped okra, four large tomatoes, and two onions chopped fine; cover with boiling water, boil very slowly, and keep the kettle tightly closed; add boiling water as it wastes, and simmer slowly three hours; season with salt, pepper, and a little butter and flour rubbed together; serve with boiled rice.

JELLIED CHICKEN.
Mrs. E. M. R.

Cook six chickens in a small quantity of water, until the meat will part from the bone easily; season to your taste with salt and pepper; just as soon as cold enough to handle, remove bones and skin, place meat in a deep pan or mould, just as it comes from the bone, using gizzard, liver and heart, until the mould is nearly full. To the water left in the kettle, add three-fourths of a box of Cox's gelatine, dissolved in a little warm water, and boil until it is reduced to a little less than a quart, pour over the chicken in the mould, leave to cool, cut with a very sharp knife and serve. The slices will not easily break up if directions are followed.

ROAST TURKEY.
Mrs. J. L. Porter.

After picking and singeing the turkey, plump it by dipping three times into boiling water and once into cold holding it by the legs, place to drain, and dress as in general directions; prepare stuffing by taking pieces of dry, stale, not moldy, bread and crust (not too brown) cut off a loaf of bread fully three or four days old; place crust and pieces in a pan and pour on a very little boiling water, cover tightly with a cloth, let stand until soft, add a large lump of butter, pepper, salt, one or two fresh eggs, and the bread from which the crust was cut, so as not to have it too moist. Mix well with the hands, and season to suit taste; rub inside of turkey with pepper and salt, stuff it as already directed, and sew up each slit with a strong thread; tie the legs down firmly, and press the wings closely to the sides, securing them with a cord tied around the body (or use skewers if you have them), steam from one to three hours (or until you can easily pierce with a fork), according to the size, place in a dripping pan, skewer on the breast a piece of salt pork and the pieces of fat taken from the turkey before it was stuffed, dredge well with flour, put a quart of boiling water in the pan, and baste often. Cook until it is a nice brown and perfectly tender; remove to a hot platter and serve with cranberry sauce and giblet gravy. To make the gravy, after the turkey is dished, place the dripping pan on the top of range or stove, skim off the fat if there is too much, and add more water if necessary; chop the heart, gizzard and liver (previously boiled for two hours in two quarts of water) and add to the gravy with the water in which they were boiled, season with salt and pepper, add a smooth thickening of flour and water, stir constantly until thoroughly mixed with the gravy, and boil until the flour is well cooked, stirring often to prevent burning.

ROAST TURKEY WITH OYSTER DRESSING.
J. H. S.

Steam the turkey two hours, or until it begins to grow tender, lifting the cover occasionally and sprinkling lightly with salt. Then take out, loosen the legs, and rub the inside again with salt and pepper, and stuff with a dressing prepared as follows: Take a loaf of stale bread, cut off crust and soften by placing in a pan, pouring on boiling water, draining off immediately and covering tightly; crumble the bread fine, add half a pound melted butter, or more if you want it very rich; a teaspoonful each of salt and pepper, or enough to season rather highly; drain off liquor from a quart of oysters, bring to a boil, skim and pour over the bread crumbs, adding the soaked crusts, and one or two eggs; mix all thoroughly with the hands, and if rather dry, moisten with a little sweet milk; lastly add the oysters, being careful not to break them; or first put in a spoonful of stuffing, and then three or four oysters, and so on until the turkey is filled; stuff the breast first. Flour a cloth and place over the openings, tying it down with a twine; spread the turkey over with butter, salt and pepper, place in a dripping-pan in a well heated oven, add half a pint hot water, and roast two hours, basting often with a little water, butter, salt and pepper, kept in a tin for this purpose, and placed on the back of the stove. A swab, made of a stick with a cloth tied on the end, is better than a spoon to baste with. Turn until nicely browned on all sides, and about half an hour before it is done, baste with butter, and dredge with a little flour—this will give it a frothy appearance— when you dish the turkey if there is much fat in the pan, pour off most of it, and add the chopped giblets and the water they were cooked in, which should have been stewed down to about one pint; place one or two heaping tablespoons flour (nicer to have half of it browned) in a pint bowl, mix smooth with a little cream, fill up bowl with cream or rich milk and add to the gravy in the pan; boil several minutes, stirring constantly, and pour into the gravy tureen; serve with currant or apple jelly. A turkey steamed in this way does not look so well, but is very tender and palatable.

ENGLISH ROAST TURKEY.
Mrs. C. T. Carson.

Kill several days before cooking, prepare in the usual manner, stuff with bread crumbs (not using the crusts) rubbed fine, moistened with butter and two eggs, seasoned with salt, pepper, parsley, sage, thyme or sweet marjoram; sew up, skewer, and place to roast in a rack within the dripping pan; spread with bits of butter, turn and baste frequently, with butter, pepper, salt and water; a few minutes before it is done glaze with the raw white of an egg; dish the turkey, pour off most of the fat, add the chopped giblets and the water in which they were boiled, thicken with flour and butter rubbed together, stir in the dripping pan, let boil thoroughly and serve in a gravy boat. Garnish with fried oysters, and serve with celery sauce and stewed gooseberries. Choose a turkey weighing from eight to ten pounds. If it becomes too brown, cover with buttered paper.

SALADS.

In preparing the dressing, powder the hard boiled eggs, either in a mortar or by mashing with the back of a silver spoon, (if raw eggs are used beat well and strain) add the seasoning, then the oil, a few drops at a time, and, lastly and gradually, the vinegar. Always use the freshest olive salad oil, not the common sweet oil; if it cannot be obtained, melted butter is a good substitute, and by some considered even more palatable; or in making chicken salad use the oil from off the water in which the chickens were boiled. It is much nicer to cut the meat with a knife instead of chopping, always removing bits of gristle, fat and skin; the same is true as regards celery; if the latter cannot be procured, use crisp, white cabbage or nice head lettuce, well chopped. Pour the dressing over the chicken and celery, mixed and slightly salted; toss up lightly with a silver fork, turn on a platter, form into an oval mound, garnish the top with slices of cold boiled eggs, and around the bottom with sprigs of celery and set away in a cold place until needed. Many think turkey makes a nicer salad than chicken. Always make soup of the liquor in which turkey or chicken was boiled. Cabbage salad is very palatable, but few know how to prepare it properly. The milk and vinegar should be put on to heat in separate saucepans; when the vinegar boils, add butter, sugar, salt and pepper, and stir in the chopped cabbage; cover, and let scald and steam—not boil—for a moment, meanwhile, remove hot milk from stove, cool a little, and stir in the well beaten and strained yolks; return to stove, and boil a moment. Dish cabbage and pour custard over it, stir rapidly with a silver spoon until well mixed, and set immediately in a cold place. Serve all salads within a few hours after making.

SIDNEY SMITH'S WINTER SALAD.
W. A. Croffut—Daily Graphic.

Two large potatoes, passed through kitchen sieve,
Unwonted softness to the salad give;
Of mordant mustard add a single spoon—
Distrust the condiment which bites too soon;
But deem it not, though made of herbs, a fault
To add a double quantity of salt;
Three times the spoon with oil of Lucca crown,
And once with vinegar procured from town.
True flavor needs it, and your poet begs
The pounded yellow of two well boiled eggs.
Let onion atoms lurk within the bowl,
And, half suspected, animate the whole;
And lastly, on the favored compound toss
A magic tea-spoon of anchovy sauce.
Then, though green turtle fail, though venison's tough,
Though ham and turkey are not boiled enough,
Serenely full, the epicure shall say,
"Fate cannot harm me—I have dined to-day."

CABBAGE SALAD.
Mrs. Hawkins.

Two quarts finely chopped cabbage, two tablespoons salt, two of
white sugar, one of black pepper, and a heaping one of ground mustard;
rub yolks of four hard boiled eggs until smooth, add half cup butter,
slightly warmed; mix thoroughly with the cabbage and add teacup good
vinegar; serve with whites of the eggs sliced and placed on the salad.

CHICKEN SALAD.
Mrs. C. S. Ogden.

Chop fine one chicken cooked tender, and one head of cabbage, salt,
pepper, mustard, half teacup butter, pint vinegar, and five hard boiled
eggs chopped fine.

CHICKEN SALAD.
Mrs. C. E. Skinner, Battle Creek, Mich.

Boil three chickens until tender, cut into small pieces, add double the quantity of celery, four boiled eggs sliced and mixed. For dressing, put over fire a pint vinegar, butter size of an egg, tablespoon black pepper, two tablespoons sugar, two beaten eggs; stir all into vinegar until it thickens; slice lemon for the top.

CUCUMBER SALAD.
Mrs. H. C. Mahncke.

Peel and slice cucumbers, mix with salt and let stand half an hour; mix two spoons sweet oil of ham gravy with as much vinegar and a teaspoon sugar, add the cucumber, which should be pressed out a little; add a teaspoon pepper and stir well.

HAM SALAD.
Mrs. S. Watson, Upper Sandusky.

Cut up small bits of boiled ham, place in salad bowl with the hearts and inside leaves of a head of lettuce; pour over the dressing cold, and mix carefully. Make dressing as follows: Mix in a saucepan one pint sour cream as free from milk as possible, and half pint good vinegar, pepper, salt, a small piece of butter, sugar, and a small tablespoon of mustard mixed smooth; boil, add the well beaten yolks of two eggs, stirring carefully as for float until it thickens to the consistency of starch, then set in a cool place or on ice.

HERRING SALAD.
Mrs. H. C. Mahncke.

Soak three Holland herrings over night, cut in very small pieces, cook and peel eight medium potatoes and chop with two small cooked red beets, two onions, a few sour apples, some roasted veal, and three hard boiled eggs; mix with a sauce of sweet oil, vinegar, broth, pepper and mustard to taste. A spoonful of thick sour cream improves the sauce, which should stand over night in an earthen dish.

TOMATO SALAD.
Mrs. E. M. Rea, Minneapolis, Minn.

Take the skin, juice and seeds from nice, fresh tomatoes, chop what is left with celery, and add a good salad dressing.

SALAD DRESSING.
Mrs. Hazen.

Put on one teacup vinegar to boil, yolks of three eggs, desert spoon of flour, six mustard spoons of mixed mustard, pinch cayenne pepper, three table spoons white sugar, three of oil, two teaspoons salt; beat all together and cook until it thickens, stirring all the time. To prevent burning cook in a pan set in a pan of boiling water.

CREAM DRESSING FOR COLD SLAW.
Miss Laura Sharp, Kingston.

Two tablespoons whipped sweet cream, two of sugar, and four of vinegar; beat well and pour over cabbage previously cut very fine.

DRESSING FOR LETTUCE.

A teaspoon butter, one of ground mustard, yolk of one egg; beat all together till thoroughly mixed, add vinegar and two tablespoons sugar.

CREAM SLAW.
Mrs. Dr. Skinner, Somerset.

One gallon cabbage cut very fine, pint vinegar, pint sour cream, half cup sugar, teaspoon flour, two eggs and a piece of butter the size of a walnut; put vinegar, sugar and butter in a saucepan and let boil; stir eggs, cream and flour, previously well mixed, into the vinegar, boil thoroughly and throw over the cabbage, previously sprinkled with one teaspoon salt, one of black pepper and one of mustard.

SOUPS.

To make nutritious, healthful and palatable soup, with flavors properly commingled, is an art and requires study and practice; but it is surprising from what a scant allotment of material a delicate and appetizing soup may be produced. Pieces of gristle, odds and ends of meat, trimmings of steak and cutlets, bones (first thoroughly cracked), liquors left from boiling poultry, fresh or salt meats, (but not the smallest bit of fat) are good soup stock. Place in a large kettle with one quart water to each pound of meat, stir frequently, skim well and let simmer for six or eight hours, strain into a stone jar, and when cold remove the cake of fat from off the top, and the liquor may be used for almost any kind of soup.

A rich soup stock can be best made from a shank or shin of beef, (knuckle of veal is next best). Cut in several pieces, crack the bones, add four quarts of water and simmer until the liquor is reduced one-half; strain, cool and skim, and if properly boiled and long enough, you will have an excellent jelly. Stock made from any other beef than the shank or shin will not jelly, but will taste very like good beef tea. Never boil vegetables with it, as they will cause it to be sour.

To make the soup, put on as much stock as needed, (if in jelly, scrape the sediment from off the bottom), add seasoning, water and vegetables. The potatoes should be peeled, sliced and laid in salt and water for half an hour, the cabbage parboiled and drained, and all others either sliced or cut fine before adding them to the soup; boil until thoroughly dissolved, strain through a colander and serve at once, or omit the straining if you choose. Always use cold water for making soups, but if necessary to add more, add hot; skim well, especially during the first hour; some throw in a little salt, others add now and then a cup of cold water to cause the scum to rise. Keep kettle closely covered so that the flavor may not be lost.

Thickened soups require nearly double the seasoning used for thin; if wanted very clear and delicate, strain through a hair sieve.

Every kitchen should be provided with a soup kettle, made with a double bottom so as to prevent burning. In making oyster soups, add oysters to boiling water, and allow to stew about five minutes, or until the body is plump and the edges ruffled; too much cooking ruins the soup, and if underdone, they are wholly unpalatable.

CLAM SOUP.*

First catch your clams—along the ebbing edges
Of saline coves you'll find the precious wedges
With backs up lurking in the sandy bottom;
Pull in your iron rake, and lo! you've got 'em!
Take thirty large ones, put a basin under
And cleave, with knife, their stony jaws asunder;
Add water (three quarts) to the native liquor,
Bring to a boil (and, by the way, the quicker
It boils the better, if you'd do it cutely.)
Now add the clams, chopped up and minced minutely.
Allow a longer boil of just three minutes,
And while it bubbles, quickly stir within its
Tumultuous depths where still the molluscs mutter,
Four tablespoons of flour and four of butter,
A pint of milk, some pepper to your notion,
And clams need salting, although born of ocean.
Remove from fire; (if much boiled they will suffer—
You'll find that India-rubber isn't tougher.)
After 'tis off, add three fresh eggs, well beaten,
Stir once more, and it's ready to be eaten.

* This rhyme recipe was written for "The Buckeye Cook Book" by W. A. Croffut, Editor of Daily Graphic, New York.

Fruit of the wave! O, dainty and delicious!
Food for the gods! Ambrosia for Apicius!
Worthy to thrill the soul of sea-born Venus,
Or titillate the palate of Silenus!

BEEF SOUP.

Take cracked joints of beef, and after putting the meat in the pot and covering it well with water, let it come to a boil, when it should be well skimmed. Set the pot where the meat will simmer slowly until it is thoroughly done, keeping it closely covered all the time. The next day or when cold remove the fat which hardens on the top of the soup. Peel, wash and slice three good sized potatoes, and put them into the soup; cut up half a head of white cabbage in shreds, and add to this a pint of Shaker corn that has been soaked over night, two onions, one head of celery, and tomatoes as you like. When these are done, and they should simmer slowly—care being taken that they do not burn, strain the soup and serve. Noodle soup may be made by adding noodles to the soup after straining; these will cook in fifteen or twenty minutes, and are prepared in the following manner: To one egg add as much sifted flour as it will absorb, with a little salt; roll out as thin as a wafer, dredge very lightly with flour, roll over and over into a large roll, slice from the ends, shake out the strips loosely and drop into the soup. The different varieties of beef soup are formed by this method of seasoning and the different vegetables used in preparing it after the joints have been well boiled. Besides onions, celery, cabbages, tomatoes and potatoes, many use a few carrots, turnips, beets, and force meat-balls seasoned with spice; rice or barley will give the soup consistency, and are to be preferred to flour for the purpose. Parsley, thyme and sage are the favorite herbs for seasoning, but should be used sparingly. To make force meat-balls, add to one pound chopped beef, one egg, a small lump butter, a cup or less of bread crumbs; season with salt and pepper, and moisten with the water from stewed meat; make in balls and fry brown or make egg balls by boiling eggs, mashing the yolks with a silver spoon, and mixing with one raw yolk and one teaspoon flour; season with salt and pepper, make into balls, drop in soup just before serving.

GRANDMOTHER'S BEAN SOUP.

Take one pint beans, wash well, put on to cook in one quart of cold water; when water boils pour off and add quart cold water again; put in piece of pork the size of your hand, salt to your taste; as water boils away add so as to keep covered with water; cook till you can mash the beans easily; beat two eggs well, add two tablespoons water and a pinch of salt, stir in flour till as stiff as you can stir, then drop the batter with a spoon into the soup, (having previously taken two-thirds of the beans out into a pan, laid the piece of pork on the top, with a sprinkle of salt and pepper, and put all into the oven to brown) when the dumplings swell up, pepper slightly and the soup is done. If one does not like the pork taste, use butter instead of pork.

GREEN CORN SOUP.
Kate Thompson, Millersburg, Ky.

Simmer a fat chicken slowly for several hours; an hour before dinner add corn cut from a dozen ears, and just before taking from the fire, add one pint sweet milk and one egg beaten light with a teaspoon flour. This can be made in winter with dried corn, but the corn must be soaked over night, and requires longer cooking.

GREEN PEA SOUP.

Four pounds lean beef cut in small pieces, half peck green peas, gallon water, boil empty pods of peas in water one hour; strain out, add beef and boil slowly one and a half hours; half an hour before serving strain out meat, add peas, salt and pepper to taste, and if you like, add one teaspoon sugar and a little thickening.

MOCK TURTLE OR CALF'S HEAD SOUP.
Mrs. H. B. S.

One large calf's head well cleaned and washed, four pig's feet; lay head and feet in bottom of a large pot and cover with a gallon of water; boil three hours, or until flesh will slip from bones; take out head, leaving the feet to be boiled steadily while the meat is cut from the head;

select with care enough of the fatty portions in the top of the head and the cheeks to fill a teacup, and set aside to cool; remove brains to a saucer, and also set aside; chop the rest of the meat with the tongue very fine, season with salt, pepper, powdered marjoram and thyme, a teaspoon of cloves, one of mace, half as much allspice and a grated nutmeg. When the flesh falls from the bones of the feet, take out bones, leaving the gelatinous meat; boil all together slowly, without removing the cover, for two hours more, take the soup from the fire and set it away until the next day. An hour before dinner set the stock over the fire and when it boils strain carefully and drop in the meat you have reserved, which when cold, should be cut into small squares. Have these all ready as well as the force meat-balls; to prepare these rub the yolks of five hard boiled eggs to a paste in a wedgewood mortar, or in a bowl with the back of a silver spoon, adding gradually the brains to moisten them, also a little butter and salt. Mix with these two eggs beaten very light, flour the hands and make this paste into balls about the size of a pigeon's egg; throw them into the soup five minutes before taking it from the fire; stir in a large tablespoon browned flour rubbed smooth in a little cold water, and finish the seasoning by the addition of a glass and a half of sherry or madeira wine and the juice of a lemon. It should not boil more than half an hour on the second day. Serve with sliced lemons.

OYSTER SOUP.

Two quarts water, tablespoon salt, two of butter, half teaspoon pepper; heat together to boiling point, add pint oysters, six rolled crackers, half cup sweet cream. Remove as soon as at the boiling point. Serve immediately.

POT AU FEU.
Mrs. Col. Clifford Thompson, New York City.

Take a good sized beef bone with plenty of meat on it, extract the marrow and place in a pot on the back of the range, covering the beef with three or more quarts of cold water; cover tightly and allow to simmer slowly all day long. The next day, before heating, remove the cake of grease from the top, and add a large onion (previously stuck full of whole cloves, and then roasted in the oven till of a rich brown color), adding tomatoes or any other vegetables which one may fancy. A leek or a section of garlic adds much to the flavor. Rice may be added or vermicelli for a change. Just before serving burn a little brown sugar and stir through it. This gives a peculiar flavor and rich color to the soup.

TOMATO SOUP.
Mrs. Col. Reid, Delaware.

One gallon of stock made from nice fresh beef, skim and strain, take three quarts tomatoes, remove skin and cut out hard center, put through a fine sieve and add to the stock; make a paste of butter and flour and when the stock begins to boil, stir in half a teacup, taking care not to have it lumpy; boil twenty minutes, seasoning with salt and pepper to taste. When out of season, canned tomatoes will answer, two quarts being sufficient.

TOMATO SOUP.
Mrs. D.C. Conkey, Minneapolis, Minn.

One quart tomatoes, one of water; stew till soft; add teaspoon soda, allow to effervesce and add quart of milk, salt, butter and pepper to taste, with a little rolled cracker.

TURKEY SOUP.

Place the rack of a cold turkey and what remains of the dressing and gravy, in a pot, and cover with cold water; simmer gently for three or four hours, and let it stand till the next day; take off all the fat and skim off all the bits and bones; put the soup on to heat till it boils, then thicken slightly with flour wet up in water, and season to taste; pick off all the bits of turkey from the bones, put them in the soup, boil up and serve.

VEAL SOUP.
Mrs. R. M. Nixon, New Castle, Ind.

To about three pounds of a well broken joint of veal, add four quarts water, and set it over to boil; prepare one-fourth pound macaroni by boiling it in a dish by itself with enough water to cover it; add a little butter when the macaroni is tender, strain the soup and season to taste with salt and pepper, then add the macaroni with the water in which it was boiled.

VERMICELLI SOUP.
Mrs. H. C. Meredith, Cambridge City, Ind.

For vermicelli soup, take a knuckle of lamb, a small piece of veal, a small piece of ham and water to cover it all well; when cooked, season with salt, pepper and herbs to taste, and one small onion, to which may be added about one tablespoon of Halford or Worcestershire sauce. Have ready about one-fourth of a pound of vermicelli which has been boiled tender, strain the soup from the meat, add the vermicelli, let boil well and serve.

VEGETABLES.

All vegetables are better cooked in soft water, provided it is clean and pure. The fresher all vegetables are the more wholesome. After being well washed, they should lie in cold water half an hour before using, excepting green corn and peas, which should be husked or shelled, and cooked at once. Put all kinds into boiling water with a little salt in it, and cook until thoroughly done, draining well those that require it. Never split onions, turnips and carrots, but slice them in rings cut across the fibre, as they thus cook tender much quicker. Always add both salt and a little soda to the water in which greens are boiled. A little sugar added to turnips, beets, peas, corn, squash and pumpkin is an improvement, especially when the vegetables are poor in quality. Sweet potatoes require a longer time to cook than the common variety. In gathering asparagus, never cut it off, but snap or break it; in this way you do not get the white, woody part which no boiling can make tender.

A piece of red pepper the size of the finger nail dropped into meat or vegetables, when first beginning to cook, will aid greatly in killing the unpleasant odor. Remember this for boiled cabbage, green beans, onions, mutton and chicken.

ASPARAGUS.

Wash well, put on stove in boiling water, boil five minutes, pour off water and add more boiling hot; put in a lump of butter, salt and pepper, (some stir in a thickening made of one teaspoon flour mixed up with cold water), cut and toast two or three thin slices of bread, spread with butter and put in a dish, and over them turn asparagus and gravy. The asparagus must be boiled about a half hour in all, and the water must be boiled down until just enough for the gravy, which is made as above.

A GOOD BOILED DINNER.

Put meat on, after washing well, in enough boiling water to just cover the meat; as soon as it boils, set kettle on the stove where it will simmer or boil very slowly; boil until almost tender, put in vegetables in the following order: Cabbage cut up in quarters, turnips cut up in halves of medium size, and potatoes whole; peel potatoes and turnips and allow to lie in cold water for half an hour before using. The meat should be well skimmed before adding vegetables; boil together until thoroughly done (adding a little salt before taking out of kettle) when there should be left only just enough water to prevent from burning; take up vegetables in separate dishes, and lastly the meat; if there is any juice in the kettle, pour it over the cabbage. Boil cabbage three-quarters of an hour, turnips one-half hour, potatoes fifteen or twenty minutes. A soup plate or saucer turned upside down, or a few iron tablespoons are useful to place in bottom of kettle to keep meat from burning.

BEETS.

Remove leaves, wash clean, being careful not break off the little fibres and rootlets as the juices would thereby escape; boil in plenty of water, if young, two hours, if old four or five hours, trying with a fork to see when tender; take out, drop in a pan of cold water, and slip off the skin with the hands; slice those needed for immediate use, place in a dish, add pepper and cover with vinegar; put those which remain, into a stone jar whole, keep in a cool place, take out as wanted, slice, season, and send to table. A few pieces of horse radish put into the jar will prevent a white scum on the vinegar. To cook young beets for greens: Wash very clean, cut off tips of leaves, looking over carefully to see that no bugs or worms remain, but do not separate roots from leaves; fill dinner pot half full of boiling water, throw in a handful of salt, add beets, boil from half to three-quarters of an hour; take out and drain in colander, pressing down with a large spoon, so as to get all the water out. Dish and send to table to be eaten warm with vinegar, butter, salt and pepper.

BAKED BEETS.
Mrs. S. M. Guy.

Beets retain their sugary delicate flavor much better by baking instead of boiling; turn often in the pan while in the oven, using a knife, as a fork would cause the juice to flow; when done, remove skin, and season with butter, pepper and salt, after slicing, or if for pickle, slice into good cold vinegar.

STRING BEANS.

String, snap and wash two quarts beans, boil in plenty of water about fifteen minutes, drain off and put on again in about two quarts boiling water; boil an hour and a half, and add salt and pepper just before taking up, stirring in one and a half tablespoons butter rubbed into two tablespoons flour. For shelled beans boil in water enough to cover half an hour and dress as above.

BINA'S STEWED CORN.

Shave corn off the ear, being careful not to cut into the cob; to three pints corn add three tablespoons butter, pepper and salt, and just enough water to cover; place in a skillet, cover and cook rather slowly with not too hot a fire, from a half to three-quarters of an hour, stir with a spoon often, and if necessary add more water, for the corn must not brown; if desired, a few moments before it is done, add half cup sweet cream thickened with teaspoon flour; boil well and serve with roast beef, escalloped tomatoes and mashed potatoes.

DRIED CORN.

For a family of eight, take a pint of corn, wash through one water, and put to soak over night in clean cold water; (if impossible to soak so long, place over a kettle of hot water for two or three hours), when softened, cook five to ten minutes in water in which it was soaked, adding as soon as boiling, two tablespoons butter, one of flour, and a little salt and pepper. Another good way to finish is the following: Take the yolk of one egg, one tablespoon milk, pinch of salt, thicken with flour quite stiff so as to take out with a teaspoon, and drop in little dumplings not larger than an acorn; cover tightly and cook five or ten minutes; have enough water in kettle before adding dumplings, as cover should not be removed until dumplings are done.

DRYING CORN.

Select good ears of sweet corn, husk, take off silk carefully, but do not wash; shave with a sharp knife, not too close to the cob, into a large tin pan or wooden bowl, scrape cob to get all the milk of corn; when about three quarts are cut off, line a large dripping-pan with flour sack paper, being careful to have sides and edges covered, pour in corn, spread, and put at once in moderate oven; stir frequently and leave in oven fifteen or twenty minutes. Set a table out in the sun, cover with a cloth, pour the corn upon it and spread out evenly and thinly. Before sunset bring the corn in and spread on a table in the house; in the morning heat again in oven and spread in sun as before. If directions are closely followed, the corn will be thoroughly dried on the evening of the second day, and when shaken will rattle; store in paper bag as soon as cooled. Prepare in small quantities, because it must not stand long after being shaven, but should at once go into oven to heat. When all dried put in oven for final heating; place to cool, pour into the bag, tie closely, and hang in a cool, dry, dark place.

PRESERVING CORN.
Mrs. S. M. Guy.

Scald the corn just enough to set the milk, cut from cob, to every four pints of corn add one pint salt, mix thoroughly, pack in jars, with a cloth and a weight over corn; keep in any convenient place, and when wanted for use put in a stew pan or kettle, cover with cold water, as soon as it comes to a boil pour off and put on cold again, and repeat until it is fresh enough for taste, then add a very little sugar, sweet cream, or butter, etc., to suit taste.

BOILED CAULIFLOWER.
Mrs. W. P. Anderson.

To each half gallon water allow heaped tablespoon salt; choose close and white cauliflower, trim off decayed outside leaves, and cut stock off flat at bottom; open flower a little in places to remove insects which generally are found about the stalk, and let cauliflowers lie with heads downward in salt and water for two hours previous to dressing them, which will effectually draw out all vermin. Then put into boiling water, adding salt in above proportion, and boil briskly over a good fire keeping the saucepan uncovered. The water should be well skimmed; when cauliflowers are tender, take up, drain, and, if large enough, place upright in dish; serve with plain melted butter, a little of which may be poured over the flowers, or a cream dressing may be used.

STUFFED CABBAGE.
Mrs. W. A. Croffut, New York City.

Take a large, fresh cabbage and cut out the heart; fill the vacancy with stuffing made of cooked chicken or veal, chopped very fine and highly seasoned and rolled into balls with yolk of egg. Then tie the cabbage firmly together and boil in a covered kettle two hours. This is a delicious dish and is useful in using up cold meats.

STEWED CABBAGE WITH EGGS.

Slice down a head of cabbage, put in a stew-pan already prepared with a very little water; butter, salt and pepper; cover and stew about twenty minutes, taking care not to let it burn; beat and strain three eggs, add half cup good vinegar (beat while pouring in vinegar), then turn mixture on cabbage, stirring briskly all the time. Serve immediately. Sour cream may be used instead of eggs and vinegar. To fry, slice, season, cover, stir frequently and fry twenty minutes.

EGG PLANT.

Take the large purple kind, peel and cut in slices, put in salt water for fifteen minutes, drain and wipe dry; make a light batter with one egg, flour and a little water, dip the slices into it and fry in butter or lard. Eggs and cracker may be used instead of the batter.

ITALIAN MACARONI.
Mrs. Col. Clifford Thomson, New York City.

Place two pounds of beef, well larded with strips of salt pork, and one or two chopped onions in a covered kettle on the back of the stove, until it throws out its juice and is a rich brown; add a quart of tomatoes seasoned with pepper and salt, and allow this mixture to simmer for two or three hours. Take the quantity of macaroni desired and boil in water for twenty minutes, after which put one layer of the boiled macaroni in the bottom of a pudding dish, cover with some of the above mixture, then a layer of grated cheese and so on in layers till your dish is filled, having a layer of cheese on the top; place in the oven an hour or until it is a rich brown. Commence early in the morning to prepare this dish.

MACARONI.

Take about three ounces macaroni and boil till tender in a stew-pan with a little water; take a pudding dish or pan, warm a little butter in it and put in a layer of macaroni, then a layer of cheese grated or cut in small bits, and sprinkle over with salt, pepper, and small pieces of butter, then add another layer of macaroni, and so on, finishing off with cheese; pour on rich milk or cream enough to just come to the top of the ingredients, and bake from one-half to three-quarters of an hour. Rice may be used instead of macaroni by first cooking as follows: Pick and wash a cup of rice, put in a stew kettle with three cups boiling water and set over the fire, the boiling water makes the kernels retain their shape better than when cold water is used; when done, put a layer of rice, cheese, etc., alternately as you would macaroni, and bake in the same way.

BOILED ONIONS.

Wash and peel, boil ten minutes, pour off this water, again add water, boil a few minutes and drain a second time; pour on boiling water (each time it must be boiling), add salt and boil for one hour, drain in a colander, place in a dish to send to the table, and add butter and pepper. Or about half an hour before they are done, turn a quart of milk into the water in which they are boiling, and when tender season as above. Old onions require two hours to boil. To fry onions, slice and boil ten minutes each time in three waters, drain, fry, stir often, season and serve hot.

BOILED POTATOES.

Wash clean, cut off the ends if you like, let stand in cold water a few hours, put into boiling water, cover and keep boiling constantly; after fifteen minutes throw in a handful of salt and boil another fifteen minutes; try with a fork and if it does not quite run through the potato they are done, (this is called "leaving a bone in them.") Drain, take to door or window and shake in open air to make them mealy; return to stove and allow to stand uncovered for a moment. Or when washed bake in moderate oven fifty minutes—or place in a steamer for twenty minutes over water kept constantly boiling. Bake sweet potatoes one hour; or place in a steamer over a kettle of boiling water, steam until almost done, (if fire is hot it will take half an hour,) scrape or pare them, place in an old dripping-pan and bake half an hour or fry.

FRICASSEE OF OLD POTATOES.

Slice cold boiled potatoes, put into a dripping pan, add milk, salt, pepper, and small lump of butter, allowing half a pint of milk to a dozen potatoes; place in oven for about fifteen minutes, stir occasionally with a knife to keep from burning; should brown slightly on the top. To fry, slice and fry in butter or ham or beef drippings, using only enough fat to prevent sticking; sprinkle with salt, cover with tin lid so that they may both fry and steam.

FRIED RAW POTATOES.

Pare and slice thin lengthwise of potatoes, let stand in cold or ice water several hours, drain in a colander, drop into as much boiling lard or drippings as is used for doughnuts, fry a light brown; take out with a skimmer and lay in a dry colander, which place in a tin pan and set in open oven. Put in only as many as fry brown and not stick together, and use a deep basin or the fat will boil over; dredge with a little salt as you take them up, and they will be light and crisp. If not cooked enough at first, they are improved by dropping into fat for one minute, after standing in oven a while; serve in a napkin or fringed tissue paper laid within a hot dish and folded lightly over them, as a dish cover would make them "soggy."

MASHED POTATOES.

Pare and boil till done, drain, and mash in the kettle until perfectly smooth; add milk or cream and butter and salt; beat like cake with a large spoon and the more they are beaten the nicer they become. Put in a dish, smooth, place a lump of butter in the center, sprinkle with pepper; or to brown them dip a knife in sweet milk, smooth over, wetting every part with milk and place in a hot oven twenty minutes. Or beat smooth the yolk of an egg, spread over potatoes and then brown.

NEW POTATOES.

Wash, scrape, boil ten minutes, turn off water and add boiling hot enough more to cover, also add a little salt; cook a few moments, drain, and set again on stove, add butter, salt and pepper, and a little thickening made of two tablespoons flour in about a pint of milk; put on the cover, and when the milk has boiled, serve. Or, when cooked and drained put in skillet with hot drippings, cover, and shake till a nice brown. Young potatoes are nice for breakfast cooked in this way.

POTATO CAKES.

Mix thoroughly with cold mashed potatoes left from dinner, the well beaten yolk, not white, of an egg, flour the hands and make into cakes as you would sausages, place in skillet greased with hot beef drippings, cover tightly, and in five minutes when lower side is browned, turn, remove cover, fry until the other side is a nice brown; serve hot.

SARATOGA POTATOES.

Pare and cut into thin slices on a slaw-cutter four large potatoes (new are best); let stand in salt water while breakfast is cooking; take a handful of the potatoes, squeeze the water from them and dry in a napkin; separate the slices and drop a handful at a time into a skillet of boiling lard, taking care that they do not strike together, stir with a fork till they are a light brown color, take out with a wire spoon, drain well, and serve in an open dish.

BAKED PARSNIPS.

Put four thin slices salt pork in a kettle with two quarts cold water, wash and scrape, and if large slice parsnips, and as soon as water boils place in kettle, boil about half an hour, place meat, parsnips and gravy in a dripping-pan, sprinkle with a little white sugar, and bake in oven a quarter of an hour, or until they are a light brown, and the water is all fried out. Add a few potatoes if you like. Those left over fried in a hot skillet with butter, ham fat or beef drippings, make a nice breakfast dish. It is better to dip each slice in a beaten egg before frying. Parsnips are good in March and April, and make an excellent seasoning for soups.

GREEN PEAS.

Wash lightly two quarts shelled peas, put into boiling water enough to cover, boil twenty minutes, add pepper, salt, and two tablespoons butter, (add more hot water when needed to prevent burning,) let boil five minutes, add two tablespoons butter rubbed into two scant tablespoons flour, stir well, and boil five minutes.

PEAS STEWED IN CREAM.
Mrs. W. A. Croffut, New York City.

Put two or three pints of young green peas into a sauce-pan of boiling water; when nearly done and tender, drain in a colander quite dry; melt two ounces of butter in a clean stew-pan, thicken evenly with a little flour, shake it over the fire, but do not let it brown, mix smoothly with a gill of cream, add half a teaspoonful of white sugar, bring to a boil, pour in the peas, keep moving for two minutes until well heated, serve hot. The sweet pods of young peas are made by the Germans into a palatable stew by simply stewing with a little butter and savory herbs.

HOW TO BOIL RICE.

Rice should be carefully picked over, and washed first in warm water, and rubbed between the hands, then five or six times in a good deal of cold water. It will not be white until it is well washed. Put one teacupful in a tin pan or porcelain kettle, add one quart boiling water and one teaspoon salt; boil fifteen minutes, not stirring, but taking care that it does not burn; pour into a dish and send to the table, placing a lump of butter in the center. Cooked thus the kernels remain whole. The Southern rice cooks much quicker and is nicer than the Indian rice. To boil rice in milk, put a pint rice into nearly two quarts of cold milk an hour before dinner, add two teaspoons salt, boil very slowly and stir often; cook on back part of stove or range so as to avoid burning, and take it up into a mould or bowl wet in cold water a short time before serving.

SALSIFY OR VEGETABLE OYSTER.

Parboil after scraping off the outside, cut in slices, dip it into a beaten egg and fine bread crumbs, and fry in lard.

SUMMER SQUASH.

When young and tender, wash, and put on whole in boiling water; when thoroughly cooked, (half to three-quarters of an hour) drain through colander, pressing out all the water; put back in kettle, stir and cook till dry, dress with butter, salt, pepper, and cream if you have it. If old and tough, peel, take out seeds, cut up and boil.

WINTER SQUASH.

Cut up, take out inside, pare the pieces and stew in as little water as possible. A tin with holes in it, which will fit kettle and keep the squash from touching the water, is best to steam with; cook an hour, mash in kettle, and if watery let stand on the fire a few moments, mashing until it becomes dry: season with butter, salt and pepper; be careful that it does not burn. Winter squashes are also cut up and baked in the oven.

SUCCOTASH.

Take pint of shelled lima beans, (green) or string beans, cover with hot water, boil half an hour, have ready corn, cut from six good sized ears, and add to beans; boil fifteen minutes, add salt, pepper, and two tablespoons butter. Be careful in cutting down corn not to cut too deep,—better not cut quite deep enough and then scrape; after corn is added watch carefully to keep from scorching.

SUCCOTASH.

Wash one pint dried lima beans and one and a half pints dried corn; put beans in kettle and cover with cold water; cover corn with cold water in a tin pan, set on top of kettle of beans so that while the latter are boiling the corn may be heating and swelling; boil beans fifteen minutes, drain off, cover with boiling water, and when tender (half an hour) add corn, cooking both together for fifteen minutes; five minutes before serving add salt, pepper and a dressing of butter and flour rubbed together, or one-half teacup cream or milk thickened with one table-spoon flour.

BAKED TOMATOES.
Mrs. S. Watson, Upper Sandusky.

Twelve solid, smooth, ripe tomatoes, cut a thin slice from blossom side, with a teaspoon remove pulp without breaking shell; take a small, solid head of cabbage and one onion, chop fine, add bread crumbs rubbed fine, and pulp of tomatoes, season with pepper, salt and sugar, add a teacup good sweet cream, mix well together, fill tomatoes, put the slice back in its place, lay them stem end down in a buttered pie-pan with just enough water to keep from burning, bake half an hour. They make a handsome dish for a dinner table.

MOTHER'S SLICED TOMATOES.

Prepare fully half an hour before dinner, scald a few at a time in boiling water, peel, slice, and sprinkle with salt and pepper, set away in a cool place, or lay a piece of ice on them. Serve as a relish for dinner, either in their own liquor, or by adding vinegar and sugar.

STEWED TOMATOES.
Mrs. Judge Cole.

Scald by pouring boiling water over them, peel, and slice cutting out all defective parts; place a lump of butter in a hot skillet, put in tomatoes, season with salt and pepper, keep up a brisk fire and cook as rapidly as possible, stirring with a spoon or chopping up with a knife, (in the latter case wipe the knife as often as used or it will blacken the tomatoes). Serve at once in a deep dish lined with toast. When iron is used, tomatoes must cook rapidly and have constant attention. If prepared in tin or porcelain they do not require the same care.

TOMATOES IN BRINE.
Mrs. R. S. Wilcox, Madison.

Take enough smooth ripe tomatoes to fill a half barrel, wash carefully removing stems and blossoms, being very particular not to use any in which the skin is in the least broken; make a brine of one pint salt and water enough to cover the tomatoes; place on the top a board with heavy weight to keep them under the brine, but not enough to bruise them. Tie a cloth tightly over the tub to secure from flies. Will keep until the next summer, and are delicious to eat uncooked, with a little sugar only.

TOMATO TOAST.
Mrs. S. Watson.

A quart of ripe stewed tomatoes, run through a colander, place in a porcelain stew pan, season with butter, pepper and salt, and sugar to taste; cut slices of bread thin, brown on both sides, butter and lay on a platter; just as the bell rings for tea add a pint of good sweet cream to the stewed tomatoes, and pour them over toast.

TURNIPS.

Wash, peel, cut in slices, and place in kettle and keep well covered with water; boil from twenty to thirty minutes, or until you can easily pierce them with a fork; drain well, season with salt, pepper and butter and mash fine. Do not boil too long, as they are much sweeter when cooked quickly.

CENTENNIAL GOVERNORS.

It was the plan of the Committee to give in this department, a recipe from the households of the President and each of the Centennial Governors of the States and Territories, and the following have been received, with many kind wishes for the success of the enterprise. The States are arranged in the order of their admission into the Union.

LEMON CUSTARD.
Mrs. Gov. J. P. Cochran, Delaware, 1787.

One pound sugar, quarter pound butter, four eggs, cup sweet milk, two crackers, two lemons; beat butter and sugar together until light, add eggs beaten light, next grated crackers, then grated rind and chopped pith of lemon, and one cup milk, the juice of lemon to be added last.

SODA BISCUIT.
Mrs. Gov. J. D. Bedle, New Jersey, 1787.

One quart sifted flour, two large teaspoons cream yeast, one tablespoon lard, a little salt; mix thoroughly and add milk enough to stir nicely, roll out half an inch thick, cut the proper size, and bake in a hot oven.

POTATO PUDDING.
Mrs. Gov. Ingersoll, Connecticut, 1788.

Boil six good mealy potatoes, mash very fine, beat well with the yolks of five eggs, half pound white sugar, quarter pound butter; beat whites of eggs to stiff froth, add the grated rind and juice of one lemon, stir well and add a little salt and a pint of good milk or cream; bake an hour and a half; reserve some of the whites of eggs to ice the top.

RICE CAKE.
Gov. Rice, Massachusetts, 1788.

One pound sugar, a pound ground rice, half pound butter, nine eggs, rose water to your taste; add a little salt, beat butter and sugar together, add rosewater, salt and eggs, lastly the rice; bake in shallow pans.

BUFORD CAKE.
Mrs. Gov. D. H. Chamberlain, South Carolina, 1788.

One quart flour, a pint sugar, a cup butter, a cup sweet milk, four eggs, spices of all kinds in small quantities, teaspoon saleratus, half pound raisins, half pound currants; this quantity will make two large loaves.

SALAD DRESSING.
Mrs. Gov. Cheney, New Hampshire, 1788.

Yolks of two hard boiled eggs rubbed very fine and smooth, one tea-spoonful of English mustard, one of salt, the yolks of two raw eggs beaten into the other, dessert spoonful of fine sugar. Add very fresh sweet oil poured in by very small quantities, and beaten as long as the mixture continues to thicken, then add vinegar till as thin as desired. If not hot enough with mustard, add a little cayenne pepper.

TO KEEP CUT ROSES FRESH.
Gov. Kemper, Virginia, 1788.

Roses, camelias and all hard wooded flowers, such as are used for head-dresses, button-hole boquets, etc., may be kept fresh and their beauty preserved by the following plan: Cut stems off at right angles and apply hot sealing wax to the end of the stalk immediately; this prevents the sap flowing downwards, thereby preserving the flower.

VEAL LOAF.
Gov. Tilden, New York, 1788.

Chop fine a leg or loin of veal, roll one dozen crackers, put half of them in the veal, with two eggs, pepper, salt, and butter size of an egg;

mix all together and make into a solid form; then take the crackers that are left and spread smoothly over the outside; bake three-quarters of an hour and eat cold.

ISINGLASS JELLY.
Mrs. Gov. J. B. McCreary, Kentucky, 1792.

Two ounces isinglass, five pints water, one and a half pounds sugar, the whites of three eggs well beaten; season highly with cinnamon, orange peel, mace and good brandy; after dissolving isinglass and adding spices, let it boil fifteen minutes, strain through flannel bag, and when nearly cool add the brandy.

SILVER CAKE.
Mrs. Gov. Porter, Tennessee, 1796.

Three-quarters pound sugar, three-quarters pound butter, whites twelve eggs, yolks of two, one teacup sweet milk, three teaspoons yeast powder, flour to suit; beat yolks and half the sugar till very light, add whites and rest of sugar, butter, and flour enough to make a batter rather stiffer than pound cake.

FRENCH PICKLE.
Mrs. Gov. Hayes, Ohio, 1802.

One peck green tomatoes sliced, six large onions sliced; mix these and throw over them one teacup of salt, and let them stand over night; next day drain thoroughly and boil in one quart vinegar mixed with two quarts of water for fifteen or twenty minutes. Then take four quarts vinegar, two pounds brown sugar, one-half pound white mustard seed, two tablespoons ground allspice, and the same of cinnamon, cloves, ginger, and ground mustard; throw all together and boil fifteen minutes.

CUP CAKE.
Mrs. Gov. Hendricks, Indiana, 1816.

One pound flour, one pound sugar, half pound butter, eight eggs beaten separately, one nutmeg, one cup milk, two teaspoons yeast powder; cream butter with half the flour, mix the yeast powder with the remaining portion of the flour, sift it into the batter, add the sugar and eggs which have been beaten together, and put it all into the pans.

MAINE SPONGE CAKE.
Mrs. Gov. Conner, Maine, 1820.

Ten eggs, their weight in sugar and half their weight in flour; beat the yolks with the sugar and flavor with lemon; beat the whites to a stiff froth and add them to the yolks and sugar; sift the flour in and stir quickly; it must not be beaten after flour is put in; bake immediately. This will make two thick loaves in six by nine pans.

GOOD BREAD.
Mrs. Gov. Hardin, Missouri, 1821.

For four small loaves boil four large potatoes; when done, pour off the water, and when it cools add to it your yeast cake; mash the potato very fine, put through a sieve, pour boiling milk on as much flour as you will need, let stand until cool, add the potato and yeast, a large teaspoon of salt and one tablespoon of sugar; stir very stiff, adding flour as is needed. Let stand in a warm place until light, dissolve one teaspoon of soda in a little hot water, mix well through with the hands, mold into loaves and let rise again. When sufficiently raised place in a moderately hot oven, keeping up a steady fire.

ORANGE PIE.
Gov. Stearns, Florida, 1845.

Grated rind and juice of two oranges, four eggs, four tablespoons sugar and one of butter, bake only with a lower crust. In grating the rind of the orange use only outside or yellow part.

CHRISTMAS PLUM PUDDING.
Mrs. Gov. Coke, Texas, 1845.

One quart seeded raisins, pint currants, half pint citron cut up, quart of apples peeled and chopped, a quart of fresh and nicely chopped beef suet, a heaping quart of stale bread crumbs, eight eggs beaten separately, pint sugar, grated nutmeg, teaspoon salt; flour your fruit thoroughly from a quart of flour, then mix remainder as follows: In a large bowl or tray put the eggs with sugar, nutmeg and milk, stir in the fruit, bread crumbs and suet one after the other until all are used, adding enough flour to make the fruit stick together, which will take about all the quart; dip your pudding cloth in boiling water, dredge on inside a thick coating of flour, put in pudding and tie tightly, allowing room to swell, and boil from two to three hours in a good sized pot with plenty of hot water, replenishing as needed from teakettle. When done, turn out in a large flat dish and send to table with a sprig of holly, or any bit of evergreen with bright berries, stuck in the top. Serve with any nice pudding sauce. This recipe furnishes enough for twenty people, but if the family is small, one-half the quantity may be prepared, or it is equally good warmed over by steaming. For sauce, cream a half pound sweet butter, stir in three-quarters pound brown sugar, and the beaten yolk of an egg; simmer for a few moments over a slow fire, stirring almost constantly; when near boiling add a half pint bottled grape juice, and serve, after grating a little nutmeg on the surface.

BLACK CAKE.
Mrs. Gov. Kirkwood, Iowa, 1846.

One pound flour, one of currants, one of raisins, one of sugar, half pound citron, half pound chopped figs, three-fourth pound butter, ten eggs, leaving out two whites, one teacup molasses, one of sour cream and soda, one gill brandy or good whisky, one-half cup cinnamon, two tablespoons allspice and cloves, four tablespoons jam.

WHITE SPONGE CAKE.
Mrs. Gov. Ludington, Wisconsin, 1848.

Whites of ten eggs, a tumbler and half of pulverized sugar, one of flour, one heaping teaspoon cream-tartar, a pinch of salt; put all through the sieve twice, then stir in lightly the eggs beaten to a stiff froth, flavor with vanilla or rose.

DELICIOUS PUMPKIN PIE.
Mrs. Gov. Irwin, California, 1850.

Cut a pumpkin into thin slices and boil until tender in as little water as possible, watching carefully that it does not scorch; set the stew kettle on top of stove, mash the pumpkin fine, heaping it against the sides of the kettle so that the water may drain from it and dry away, repeat this process until the water has all evaporated, and the pumpkin will be quite dry. This will require from a half to one hour. Mash and rub through a sieve, adding while warm a good sized lump of butter; to every quart of pumpkin after it is mashed add three quarts of milk and six eggs, the yolks and whites beaten separately, sugar to taste, one teaspoon salt, tablespoon ground cinnamon, one grated nutmeg, teaspoon ginger; bake in a hot oven until well set and a nice brown. It is as well to heat the batter scalding hot, stirring constantly until it is poured into the pie dishes.

ORANGE CAKE.
Mrs. Gov. Pillsbury, Minnesota, 1858.

Two-thirds cup butter, two small cups sugar, one cup milk, three teaspoons baking powder, the yolks of five eggs, three small cups flour, bake in jelly tins. Whites of three eggs beaten to a stiff froth, juice and grated peel of one orange, sugar to consistency; put this between the layers with white frosting on the top.

ICED PLUM PUDDING.
Mrs. Gov. Grover, Oregon, 1859.

Take two dozen sweet and half a dozen bitter almonds; blanch in scalding water, throw into a bowl of cold water; pound one at a time in a mortar, till they become a smooth paste, free from the smallest lumps. As you proceed, add frequently a few drops of rose water or lemon juice to make them light and prevent their oiling. Seed and cut in half a quarter of a pound of the best bloom raisins; mix with them a quarter of a pound of Zante currants, picked, washed and dried, and add to the raisins and currants three ounces of citron, chopped; mix the citron with the raisins and currants, and dredge them all with flour to prevent their sinking or clodding. Take a half pint of very rich milk, split a vanilla bean, and cut it into pieces two or three inches long, and boil it in the milk till the flavor of the vanilla is well extracted, then strain it out and mix the vanilla milk with a pint of rich cream, and stir in gradually a half pound of powdered loaf sugar and a nutmeg grated. Then add the pounded almonds, and a large wine glass of either marasquino, noyau, curacoa or the very best brandy. Beat in a shallow pan the yolks of eight eggs till very light, thick and smooth, and stir them gradually into the mixture. Simmer it over the fire, (stirring it all the time), but take it off just as it is about to come to a boil, otherwise it will curdle. Then, while the mixture is hot, stir in the raisins, currants and citron. Set it to cool, and then add a large teacupful of preserved strawberries or raspberries, half a dozen preserved apricots or peaches, half a dozen preserved green limes, and any other very nice and delicate sweetmeats; whip to a stiff froth another pint of cream, and add it lightly to the mixture; put the whole into a large melon mould that opens in the middle, and freeze it in the usual way. It will take four hours to freeze it well. Do not turn it out till just before it is wanted, then send it to table on a glass dish.

CHARLOTTE RUSSE.
Mrs. Gov. Osborn, Kansas, 1861.

One ounce gelatine, one pint sweet milk, one of cream, four eggs, sugar to taste; beat the sugar and yolks of eggs together until light, boil the gelatine in the milk and strain over the eggs and sugar; whip the cream, which must be very cold, to a nice froth and add to the above; flavor with vanilla. Line the dish you wish to serve it in with sponge cake, and pour the mixture in, then set it on ice till wanted.

LEMON ICE.
Mrs. Gov. Silas Garber, Nebraska, 1867.

Juice one dozen lemons, one gallon water, four pounds sugar, strain all into freezer; for sherbet add the white of one egg beaten to a froth for each lemon. In making ices, if they are not well mixed before freezing, the sugar will sink to the bottom, and the mixture will have a sharp unpleasant taste.

ENCHILADAS.
Gov. Safford, Arizona, 1863.

Put four pounds of corn in a vessel with four ounces lime, or in a preparation of lye; boil with water till the hull comes off, then wash the corn (usually done by Mexicans on a scalloped stone made for grinding corn as was practiced by Rebecca), bake the meal in small cakes called "tortillas," then fry in lard; take some red pepper ground, called "chili colorad," mix with it sweet oil and vinegar, and boil together. This makes a sauce into which dip the tortillas, then break in small pieces cheese and onions, and sprinkle on top the tortillas, and you have what is called "enchiladas." Any one who has ever been in a Spanish speaking country will recognize this as one of the national dishes, as much as the pumpkin pie is a New England specialty.

SPICE CAKE.
Mrs. Gov. Potts, Montana, 1864.

Three pounds seedless raisins, one and a half pounds citron, one pound butter, two and a half coffee cups sugar, two of sweet milk, six eggs, two large teaspoons baking powder, three teaspoons cinnamon, two of mace, four cups flour.

SNOW CUSTARD.
Mrs. Gov. Thayer, Wyoming Territory, 1868.

One-half package of Cox's gelatine, three eggs, one pint milk, two cups of sugar, juice of one lemon; soak the gelatine one hour in a teacup of cold water, add one pint boiling water, stir until thoroughly dissolved, add two-thirds of the sugar and the lemon juice; beat the whites of the eggs to a stiff froth, and when the gelatine is quite cold, whip it into the whites, a spoonful at a time, for at least an hour. Whip steadily and evenly, and when all is stiff, pour into a mold previously wet with cold water, and set in a cold place. In four or five hours turn into a glass dish. Make a custard of the milk, yolk of eggs, and remainder of the sugar, flavor with vanilla or bitter almond, and when the meringue is turned out of the mold, pour this around the base.

TABLE OF WEIGHTS AND MEASURES.*

1	quart of wheat flour (if sifted, heaping) . .	weighs	1 lb.	
1	" Indian meal	"	1 lb.	2 oz.
1	" Soft butter	"	1 lb.	1 oz.
1	" Loaf sugar	"	1 lb.	
1	" White powdered sugar	"	1 lb.	1 oz.
1	" Best brown sugar	"	1 lb.	2 oz.
10	eggs average size	"	1 lb.	
8	eggs large size	"	1 lb.	
1	pint granulated sugar	"	1 lb.	
2	good sized cups of soft butter	"	1 lb.	
1	pint flour	"		8 oz.
1	large tablespoon (a very little rounded) of flour, loaf sugar, or butter	"		¼ oz.

LIQUIDS.

1 pint contains 16 fluid ounces (4 gills.)
1 ounce contains 8 fluid drachms (¼ gill.)
1 tablespoon contains about ½ fluid ounce.
1 teaspoon contains about 1 fluid drachm.

A teaspoonful is equal in volume to 45 drops of pure water (distilled) at 60 deg. Fah. Teaspoons vary so much in size that there is a very wide margin of difference in their containing capacity.

4 Teaspoonfuls equal 1 tablespoon or ½ fluid ounce.
16 Tablespoonfuls " ½ pint.
1 Wine glass full (common size) equals 4 tablespoons or 2 fluid oz.
1 Teacupful equals 4 fluid ounces or 1 gill.
4 Teacupfuls equal 1 quart.
A common sized tumbler holds ½ pint.

AVOIRDUPOIS WEIGHT.

Used in weighing coarse and heavy articles and groceries.

16 drams (dr.) make 1 ounce (oz.)
16 ounces make 1 pound (lb.)
25 pounds make 1 quarter (qr.)
Four quarters make one hundred weight (cwt.)
Twenty hundred weight make one ton (T.)

LIQUID MEASURE.

Four gills (gi.) make 1 pint (pt.)
Two pints make one quart (qt.)
Four quarts make one gallon (gal.)

* Allowance to be made for extraordinary dryness or moisture of the article to be weighed or measured.

COOKS' TIME TABLE.

	Mode of Preparation.	Time of Cooking.	Time of Digestion.
		H. M.	H. M.
Apples, sour, hard	Raw	. . .	2 50
Apples, sweet and mellow	Raw	. . .	1 50
Beans, (pod)	Boiled	1 00	2 30
Beans with green corn	Boiled	45	3 45
Beef	Roasted	* 25	3 00
Beefsteak	Broiled	15	3 00
Beefsteak	Fried	15	4 00
Beef, salted	Boiled	* 35	4 15
Bass, fresh	Broiled	20	3 00
Beets, young	Boiled	2 00	3 45
Beets, old	. . . .	4 30	. . .
Bread, corn	Baked	45	3 15
Bread, wheat	Baked	60	3 30
Butter	Melted	. . .	3 30
Cabbage	Raw	. . .	2 30
Carrot, orange	Boiled	1 00	3 15
Cabbage and vinegar	Raw	. . .	2 00
Cabbage	Boiled	1 00	4 30
Cake, sponge	Baked	45	2 30
Cheese, old	Raw	. . .	3 30
Chicken	Fricasseed	1 00	3 45
Codfish, dry and whole	Boiled	* 15	2 00
Custard, (one quart)	Baked	30	2 45
Duck, tame	Roasted	1 30	4 00
Duck, wild	Roasted	60	4 50
Dumpling, apple	Boiled	1 00	3 00
Eggs, hard	Boiled	10	3 30
Eggs, soft	Boiled	3	3 00
Eggs	Fried	5	3 30
Eggs	Raw	. . .	2 00
Eggs	Whipped	. . .	1 30
Fowls, domestic, roasted or	Boiled	1 00	4 00
Gelatine	Boiled	. . .	2 30
Goose, wild	Roasted	* 20	2 30
Lamb	Boiled	* 20	2 30
Meat and vegetables	Hashed	30	2 30

TIME TABLE. *(continued)*

	Mode of Preparation.	Time of Cooking.	Time of Digestion.
		H. M.	H. M.
Milk	Raw	. . .	2 15
Milk	Boiled	. . .	2 00
Mutton	Roast	* 25	3 15
Mutton	Broiled	20	3 00
Oysters	Raw	. . .	2 55
Oysters	Roasted	. . .	3 15
Oysters	Stewed	5	3 30
Parsnips	Boiled	1 00	2 30
Pig's feet	Soused	. . .	1 00
Pork	Roast	* 30	5 15
Pork	Boiled	* 25	4 30
Pork, raw or	Fried	. . .	4 15
Pork	Broiled	20	3 15
Potatoes	Boiled	30	3 30
Potatoes	Baked	45	3 30
Potatoes	Roasted	45	2 30
Rice	Boiled	20	1 00
Salmon, fresh	Boiled	8	1 45
Sausage	Fried	25	4 00
Sausage	Broiled	20	3 30
Soup, barley	Boiled	3 00	1 30
Soup, bean	Boiled	. . .	3 00
Soup, vegetable	Boiled	1 00	4 00
Soup, chicken	Boiled	2 00	3 00
Soup, oysters or mutton	Boiled	†3 30	3 30
Tapioca	Boiled	1 30	2 00
Trout, salmon, fresh, boiled or	Fried	30	1 30
Turkey, boiled or	Roasted.	* 20	2 30
Turnips	Boiled	45	3 30
Veal	Broiled	20	4 00
Veal	Fried	30	4 30
Vegetables and meat	Warmed	10	3 30
Venison steak	Broiled	20	1 35

* Minutes to the pound.

† Mutton soup.

The time given is the general average; may require a longer or shorter time, owing to the quality of the article to be cooked.

BILLS OF FARE.

SPRING BREAKFAST—Cold boiled ham, veal cutlets, boiled eggs, potatoes with cream, muffins, Graham bread, corn bread, oranges, coffee, tea, chocolate.

SPRING DINNER—Macaroni soup, baked fish with dressing and sauce, boiled ham, roast veal, asparagus, potatoes, spinach, lettuce, radishes, coffee. Dessert—Sponge cake pudding, lemon pie, cocoanut pie, lemonade.

SPRING SUPPER—Pickled tongue, pressed beef, waffles with maple syrup, spiced peaches, chow chow, canned fruit, preserves, cake, coffee, tea.

SUMMER BREAKFAST—Mutton chops, mackerel, beefsteak, potato balls, egg omelet, Graham toast, cold biscuit, rolls, tea, coffee, fruit.

SUMMER DINNER—Vegetable soup, roast lamb with mint sauce, currant jelly, broiled chicken, roast tongue, potatoes, peas, tomatoes, cauliflower, apple sauce, cucumber. Dessert—Snow pudding, cherry pie, sweet meat tarts, fruit, iced tea, iced coffee.

SUMMER SUPPER—Chicken salad, cold tongue, biscuit, tomato toast, baked sweet potatoes, mixed pickles, Charlotte russe, fruit, orange jelly, pine apple, ice cream, cake, iced tea.

AUTUMN BREAKFAST—Broiled beef, codfish balls, tomatoes, roast potatoes, hominy, biscuit, corn muffins, tea, coffee.

AUTUMN DINNER—Roast duck, roast beef, chicken pie, sweet potatoes, Irish potatoes, corn, squash, apple sauce, cold slaw, pickles. Dessert—Boiled fruit pudding, peach pie, cheese, ice cream, grapes, tea, coffee.

AUTUMN SUPPER—Broiled pheasant, chicken croquettes, bread, rusk, spiced peaches, fruit, preserves, cake.

WINTER BREAKFAST—Beefsteak, sausage, broiled ham, Saratoga potatoes, fried mush, buckwheat cakes, coffee, tea, chocolate.

WINTER DINNER—Oyster soup, roast turkey, boiled ham, oyster pie, onions, turnips, sweet and Irish potatoes, cranberry sauce, celery. Dessert—Queen of puddings, cheese, mince pie, plum pudding, fruit, nuts, coffee.

WINTER SUPPER—Fried oysters, chicken salad, raw oysters, chow-chow, biscuit, canned fruit, cake, tea.

LUNCH NO. 1.—Escalloped oysters, chicken salad, ham sandwich, biscuit, mixed pickles, cheese, basket of mixed cakes, ice cream, nuts, fruit, chocolate, tea, coffee.

LUNCH NO. 2.—Buttered bread, crackers, cold chicken, sardines with sliced lemons, cheese, olives, pickles, tongue, Saratoga potatoes, cake, jelly, jumbles, fruit, orange or lemon ice, tea, coffee, chocolate.

TEA FOR COMPANY—Escalloped oysters, cold tongue, chicken salad, muffins, bread, rusk, canned fruit, pickles, coffee, tea. Ice cream and cake later in the evening.

TEA FOR COMPANY—Warm biscuit, ham sandwich, sardines with sliced lemons, pickles, pressed beef, chicken, fruit, preserves and cream, cake in variety, tea, coffee, chocolate, lemon ice.

ECONOMICAL BREAKFAST NO. 1.—Ham and eggs, hash, baked potatoes, hominy, Graham gems, coffee.

ECONOMICAL BREAKFAST NO. 2.—Beefsteak or fish, fried Graham mush, tomatoes, potatoes, apple sauce, corn bread or toast, coffee.

ECONOMICAL DINNER NO. 1.—Spare ribs, roast potatoes, cabbage, fruit, rice pudding.

ECONOMICAL DINNER NO. 2.—Codfish, egg sauce, mashed potatoes, parsnips, horse-radish, pickles, bread, custard pie.

ECONOMICAL DINNER NO. 3.—Boiled pork, beans, potatoes, greens, apple pie.

ECONOMICAL DINNER NO. 4.—Fish, potato cakes, baked tomatoes, bread pudding.

ECONOMICAL DINNER NO. 5.—Boiled beef, lima beans, boiled potatoes, squash, sliced tomatoes, apple tapioca pudding.

ECONOMICAL DINNER NO. 6.—Roast beef and potatoes, macaroni with cheese, lemon pie.

ECONOMICAL DINNER NO. 7.—Broiled chicken, fricasseed potatoes, turnips, tomato toast, fresh fruit.

In preparing for a company of twenty, allow one gallon of oysters, four chickens and six bunches of celery for chicken salad, fifty sandwiches and six quarts of ice cream, two quarts wine jelly, two moulds Charlotte russe.

FRAGMENTS.

HOW MOTHER MAKES HASH.

Mother's hash doesn't taste of soap grease, rancid butter, spoiled cheese, raw flour, boarding house skillets, hotel coffee, garden garlics, bologna sausage, or cayenne pepper, neither is it stewed and simmered and simmered and stewed, but is made so nicely, seasoned so delicately, and heated through so quickly, that the only trouble is, "there is never enough to go round." Mother says cold meat of any kind will do, but that corned beef is best; always remove all surplus fat, and bits of gristle, chop fine, and to one-third of meat add two-thirds of chopped cold boiled potato, and one onion chopped very fine; place in your dripping-pan, season with salt and pepper, dredge with a little flour, and pour in at the side of the pan, enough water to come up level with the hash, place in oven and do not stir; when the flour is a light brown, and has formed a sort of crust, take out of oven, add a lump of butter, stir it through several times, and you will have a delicious hash. Or it may be made by cooking longer, of cold raw potatoes, which peel, slice, and let lie in salt and water a half hour before chopping; or meat and potatoes, always in the proportions given above, and before chopping, season with pepper and salt, add a chopped onion if you like, place in hot skillet, with just enough water to moisten, add a little butter or some nice beef drippings, stir often until warmed through, cover and let stand on a moderately hot part of the stove fifteen minutes. When ready to dish run your knife under and fold as you would an omelet; serve hot with tomato catsup. In making hash meats may be combined if there is not enough of a kind. Do not make hash or any other dish greasy. It is a mistaken idea to think that fat and butter in large quantities are necessary to good cooking. Butter and oils may be melted without changing their nature, but when cooked they become much more indigestible and injurious to weak stomachs. Mother says that

AFTER THANKSGIVING DINNER

Most excellent hash may be made thus: Pick meat off turkey bones, shred it in small bits, add dressing and pieces of light biscuit cut up fine, mix together and put into dripping pan, pour over any gravy that was left, add water to thoroughly moisten but not enough to make it sloppy, place in a hot oven for twenty minutes, and when you eat it, you will agree that the turkey is better this time than it was at first; or warm the remnants of turkey over after the style of escalloped oysters, (first a layer of bread crumbs, then minced turkey, and so on); or add an egg or two and make nice breakfast croquettes. The common error in heating over meats of all kinds, is putting into a cold skillet, and cooking a long time. This second cooking is more properly only heating, and should be quickly done. All such dishes should be served hot with some sort of tart jelly. Mother always saves a can of currant juice, (after filling all her jelly cups and glasses), from which to make jelly in the winter, and it tastes as fresh and delicious as when made in its season.

ALWAYS SAVE

All the currants, skimmings, pieces, etc., left after making jelly, place in a stone jar, cover with soft water previously boiled to purify it, let stand several days, in the meantime take your apple peelings without the cores, and put on in porcelain kettle, cover with water, boil twenty minutes, drain into a large stone jar; drain currants also into this jar, add all the rinsings from your molasses jugs, all dribs of syrup, etc., and when jar is full drain off all that is clear into vinegar keg, (where, of course, you have some good cider vinegar to start with), if not sweet enough add brown sugar or molasses, cover the bung hole with a piece of coarse netting, and set in the sun or by the kitchen stove. In making vinegar always remember to give it plenty of air, and it is better to have the cask or barrel (which should be of oak) only half full so that the air may pass over as large a surface as possible. Vinegar must also have plenty of material such as sugar, molasses, etc., to work upon. Never use alum or cream of tartar as some advise, and never let your vinegar freeze. Paint your barrel or cask if you would have it durable. Company, sickness or other circumstances may prevent making

SWEET PICKLES

in their season, but they can be prepared very nicely at any time by taking pear, peach, plum or apple preserves, and pouring hot spiced vinegar over them; in a few days they will make a delightful relish. It very often happens in putting up cucumber pickles that you can only gather or buy a few at a time; these can be easily pickled in the following manner: Place in a jar, sprinkle with salt, in the proportion of a pint salt to a peck cucumbers, cover with boiling water, let stand twenty-four hours, drain, cover with fresh hot water; after another twenty-four hours, drain, place in a jar and cover with cold, not very strong vinegar; continue to treat each mess in this manner, using the two jars, one for scalding and the other as a final receptacle for the pickles, until you have enough, when drain and cover with boiling cider vinegar, add spices, and in a few days they will be ready for use. Never throw away even

A CRUMB OF BREAD,

but save it and put with other pieces; if you have a loaf about to mold, cut in thin slices, place all together in a dripping-pan and set in oven to dry, and you will find that when pounded and rolled, it will be very nice for dressing, stuffing, puddings, griddle cakes, etc. Keep in a covered box, or in a paper bag tied securely and hung in a dry place. Mother thinks it is much more economical to prepare meats with a dressing of some kind, since they "go so much further."

STUFFED BEEFSTEAK

Is as nice for dinner as a much more expensive roast, and it can be prepared from a rather poor flank or round steak; pound well, season with salt and pepper, then spread with a nice dressing—may use some of the bread crumbs—roll up and tie closely with twine (which always save from the grocer's parcels), put in a kettle with a quart boiling water, boil slowly one hour, take out and place in dripping pan, adding water in which it was boiled, basting frequently until a nice brown and making gravy of the drippings; or you may put it at once into dripping pan, omitting the boiling process, skewer a couple slices salt pork on top, add a very little water, baste frequently and if it bakes too rapidly, cover with a dripping pan. It is delicious sliced down cold.

HOW TO MAKE NICE GRAVY

Is a problem many housekeepers never solve. Remember that grease is not gravy, neither is raw flour. Almost any kind of meat liquor or soup stock from which all fat has been removed, may be made into nice gravy by simply adding a little seasoning and some thickening; if browned flour is used for the latter the gravy will require but little cooking, but when thickened with raw flour it must cook until thoroughly done or the gravy will taste like so much gummy paste. It is best to brown a quart of flour at a time. Put in a skillet, set in the oven or on top of the stove, stir often until it is a light brown, put into a wide mouthed bottle, cork and keep for use. All gravies should be well stirred over a rather hot fire as they must be quickly made, and must boil not simmer. Mother says

THE CARE OF FAT AND DRIPPINGS

is as necessary in any family as the care of last year's garden seeds or the "Family Record." Especially when much meat is used, there is a constant accumulation of trimmings of fat, drippings from meats, etc., which should be tried out once in two or three days in summer—in winter once a week will do. Cut up in small pieces, put in skillet, cover, and try out slowly, stir occasionally, and skim well; add the cakes of fat, saved from the top of your meat liquor, slice a raw potato and cook in it to clarify it, drain all the clear part into a tin can or stone jar, and you will find it very nice to use either alone or with butter and lard in frying potatoes, dough-nuts, etc. The fat of mutton should always be tried out by itself, and used for chapped hands and such purposes. The fat which is not nice enough for any of the above uses, should be tried out and placed in a jar, kettle or cask of strong lye, to which all soap grease should be consigned. Observe never to use for this purpose lean meat or raw fat. Keep a stick with which to stir occasionally. It will need but little boiling to make the best of soft soap. Mother has many other valuable ideas on how to stop the numberless little "leaks" which keep many a family in want, whereas a little care and economy in these minor details would insure a fair competency, but she thinks it better to have the ideas she has already given thoroughly digested before clogging them with others. She says a neat, clean home, a tidy table, and well cooked, palatable meals, are safeguards against the evils of the ale house, the liquor saloon, and the gambling table, and whether or not this is wholly true, there seems reason in it. By the way she has just taken up a paper from which she reads this item by Prof. Blot: "Wasting is carried on so far and so extensively in American kitchens that it will soon be one of the common sciences." "Just as I told you," says mother, then folding her hands complacently together, she looks down at the bright figures of the carpet, and repeats in her slow measured way, "After all, whether we save or spend, the life is more than meat, and the body more than raiment."

HINTS FOR THE SICK ROOM.

Always keep the room carefully ventilated, since pure air is a great restorative of health and strength, but never allow a draft or current of air to pass directly over the bed of the patient. Everything should be kept in perfect neatness and order. Matting is better than a carpet on the floor of a sick room, though when the latter is used it may be kept clean by throwing a few damp tea leaves over only a part of the room at a time, then quietly brushing them up with a hand broom. The bed linen, also the linen next the person, should be frequently changed, always airing it well, either in the hot sun or by the stove. Wash and refresh the patient whenever suitable, brush the teeth and hair, bathing the latter with bay rum; all this to be modified, of course, by the strength of the patient and the directions of the medical attendant. Besides these, a table not liable to injury, a small wicker basket with compartments to hold the different bottles of medicine, and a small book in which to write all the physician's directions, two baskets made on the same plan to hold glasses or cups, screens to shade the light from the eyes of the patient, a nursery lamp with which to heat water, beef tea, etc., a quill tied on the door handle with which the nurse can notify others that the patient is asleep, by merely passing the feather end through the key-hole, several "ring cushions" to give relief to patients compelled to lie continually in one position, (these cushions are circular pieces of old linen sewed together and stuffed with bran), and a sick couch or chair, are a few of the many conveniences which ought to be in every sick room.

The following recipe makes a delicious refreshing and cooling wash in the sick room:

Take of rosemary, wormwood, lavender, rue, sage and mint, a large handful of each. Place in a stone jar, and turn over it one gallon of strong cider vinegar, cover closely, and keep near the fire for four days, then strain, and add one ounce of pounded camphor gum. Bottle and keep tightly corked.

There is a French legend connected with this preparation (called *vinaigre a quatre voleurs*). During the plague at Marseilles, a band of robbers plundered the dying and the dead without injury to themselves. They were imprisoned, tried, and condemned to die, but were pardoned on condition of disclosing the secret whereby they could ransack houses infected with the terrible scourge. They gave the above recipe. Another mode of using it is to wash the face and hands with it before exposing one's self to any infection. It is very aromatic and refreshing in the sick room; so, if it can accomplish nothing more, it is of great value to housekeepers.

FOOD FOR THE SICK

Should always be prepared in the neatest and most careful manner, and the dishes and articles used should be kept entirely by themselves. Never tempt the appetite of the sick, since the cessation of the appetite is nature's warning that food is not needed. When the appetite begins to return, surprise the patient with some nice delicacy properly prepared. Special wants of the body show themselves in special cravings for certain articles of food. These should be gratified whenever possible. Watermelons act on the kidneys and are good in many cases of fever, bowel complaint, etc. Celery also is good in some diseases of the kidneys. Fresh, crisp raw cabbage, sliced fine and eaten with good vinegar is easily digested, and often highly relished by a patient suffering from a "weak stomach." New cider is also excellent in many cases of nervous dyspepsia. Fruits and berries, raw, ripe and perfect, used in moderation, are admirable remedies in cases of constipation and its attendant diseases. The grape has a wide range of curative qualities. The seeds are excellent for costiveness, the pulp is very nutritious and soothing to irritated bowels, while the skin if chewed acts as an astringent. Raw beef is excellent in dysentery; it should be minced very fine, and given in doses of a spoonful at a time every four hours, the patient in the meantime eating nothing else. Bananas are good in chronic diarrhœa. A rind of bacon is good for teething children to chew. Rice water, or rice jelly are advisable in many cases of convalescence from acute fever, summer complaint and like diseases. Gelatine and isinglass are delicate and easily digested. Buttermilk is good in all bilious diseases. Vegetable acid drinks, herb teas, toast water, and all such drinks are often much relished. Buttered toast, either dry or dipped, though so generally given, is rarely a suitable article for the sick, as melted oils are very difficult of digestion. In quinsy, diptheria, inflammation of lungs, typhus and other putrid fevers, acids are of very great benefit. Take a handful of dried currants, pour over them a pint of boiling water, let them stand half a minute without stirring, then drain off the water, strain it through a cloth, and set it away to cool; when given to the patient dilute well, so that the acid taste is very slight.

ARROW-ROOT CUSTARD.—One tablespoon of arrow-root, one pint of milk, one egg, two tablespoons sugar; mix the arrow-root with a little of the cold milk; put the rest of milk on the fire and boil, and stir in the arrow-root, egg and sugar well beaten together; scald and pour into cups to cool; any flavoring the invalid prefers may be added.

ALUM WHEY.—Mix half ounce of powdered alum with one pint sweet milk, strain and add sugar and nutmeg: it is good in hemorrhages, and sometimes for colic.

BEEF TEA.—Cut pound best lean steak, in small pieces, place in glass fruit jar, (a *perfect* one) cover tightly and set in a pot of cold water; heat gradually to a boil, and continue this steadily three or four hours until the meat is like white rags and the juice thoroughly extracted; season with very little salt, and strain through a wire strainer; Serve either warm or cold. To prevent jar toppling over, tie a string around the top part, and hang over a stick laid across the top of pot. When done set kettle off stove and let cool before removing the jar and in this way prevent breakage. Or when beef tea is wanted for immediate use, place in a common pint bowl (yellow ware) add very little water, cover with a saucer, and place in a moderate oven; if danger of burning add a little more water.

BARLEY WATER.—Add two ounces pearl barley to half pint boiling water; let simmer five minutes, drain and add two quarts boiling water; add two ounces sliced figs and two ounces stoned raisins; boil until reduced to a quart; strain for drink.

CHICKEN BROTH FOR SICK.—Take the first and second joint of a chicken, boil in one quart of water till very tender and season with a very little salt and pepper.—*Miss M. R. Johnson.*

EGG GRUEL.—Beat the yolk of an egg with tablespoon of sugar, beating the white separately; add a teacup of boiling water to the yolk, then stir in the white and add any seasoning; good for a cold.

FEVER DRINK.—Pour cold water on wheat bran, let boil half an hour, strain and add sugar and lemon juice. Or pour boiling water on flax seed, let stand till it is ropy, pour into hot lemonade and drink.

GRAHAM GEMS FOR INVALIDS.—Mix graham flour with half milk and half water, add a little salt, beat, making the batter thin enough to pour; have the gem pan very hot, grease it, fill as quickly as possible and return immediately to a hot oven; bake about thirty minutes. Practice will teach just the proper consistency of the batter, and the best temperature of the oven. It will not be good unless well beaten.

JELLICE.—One-half teaspoon currant or cranberry jelly put into a goblet, beat well with two tablespoons water, fill up with ice water and you have a refreshing drink for a fever patient.

MULLED BUTTER MILK.—Put in good butter milk and when it boils, add the well beaten yolk of an egg. Let boil up and serve. Or stir into boiling butter milk thickening made of cold butter milk and flour. This is excellent for convalescing patients.

MILK PORRIDGE.—Place on stove in skillet one pint new sweet milk and a very little pinch of salt, when it boils, have ready sifted flour, and sprinkle with one hand into the boiling milk, stirring all the while with a spoon. Keep adding flour until it is about the consistency of thick molasses; eat warm with a little butter and sugar. This is excellent for children suffering with summer complaint. Or, mix the flour with a little cold milk, until a smooth paste, and then stir into the boiled milk. Or, break an egg into the dry flour and rub it with the hands until it is all in fine crumbs (size of a grain of wheat), then stir this mixture into the boiling milk.

OAT MEAL FOR THE SICK—Mix a tablespoon of meal with a little cold water till perfectly smooth, pour gradually into a pint of boiling water, and boil slowly for twenty or thirty minutes, stirring almost constantly; do not let it scorch; season with a little salt, sugar, spice of any kind if desired, and brandy or wine if the nature of the case will permit.

PANADA—Take two richest crackers, pour on boiling water, let stand a few minutes, beat up an egg, sweeten to taste, and stir all together; grate in nutmeg and add brandy or wine to suit the invalid. Or, boil a mixture of one-fourth wine and three-fourths water, and flavor with lemon, then break in toasted bread.

RASPBERRY VINEGAR—Pour over two quarts of raspberries in a stone jar, one quart of the very best vinegar; let stand twenty-four hours, strain, and pour liquor over fresh fruit, and let stand in the same way; allow one pound sugar to a pint of juice; put into a stone jar and set in pot of boiling water one hour; skim well, put into bottles, cork and seal tight. Diluted with water this is very nice for the sick. Toast bread may be eaten with it.

RASPBERRY RELISH—To each pint of berry juice add one pound of sugar. Let it stand over night; next morning boil ten minutes, and bottle for use.—*Mrs. W. G. Hillock, New Castle, Ind.*

CURRANT SHRUB.—Make the same as jelly, but boil only ten minutes; when cool, bottle and cork tight, (see directions for canned fruits). Raspberry, strawberry and blackberry shrubs are made in the same way; when used, put in two-thirds ice water.

SASSAFRAS DRINK—Take the pith of sassafras boughs, break in small pieces and let soak in cold water till the water becomes glutinous. This is good nourishment and much relished.

TOAST TEA—Toast bread very brown, pour on boiling water, strain and add cream and sugar, and nutmeg if desired.

TAMARIND WHEY—Mix an ounce of tamarind pulp with a pint of milk, strain and sweeten. Or, simply stir a tablespoon of tamarinds into a tumbler of cold water.

VEGETABLE SOUP—Two tomatoes, two potatoes, two onions, and one tablespoon rice; boil the whole in one quart of water for one hour, season with salt, dip dry toast in this till quite soft, and eat; this may be used when animal food is not allowed.

WINE WHEY—One pint of boiling milk, two wine glasses of wine, boil a moment stirring well, take out the curd, sweeten and flavor the whey.

WHEAT GRUEL—Take a double handful of flour, tie up tightly in a cloth and put in a kettle of boiling water, boil from three to six hours, take out, remove cloth and you will have a hard round ball. Keep in a dry cool place, and when wanted for use, prepare by placing some sweet milk (new always preferable) to boil, and grating into the milk from the ball enough to make it as thick as you desire, stirring it just before removing from the stove with a stick of cinnamon, this gives it a pleasant flavor; put a little salt into the milk. Very good for children having summer complaint.

EXCELSIOR BLACKBERRY WINE—To one quart of pure juice add two quarts of clear, cold water, and one and one-half pounds of coffee sugar (C or B grade.) The best berries make the best wine, the Lawton being preferred. Mash thoroughly, adding a small quantity of water to extract all the juice from the berries, first measuring and making a correct account of the water in order to ascertain the exact amount of juice obtained. It is safe to use one pint of water to one quart of berries for this purpose. When the fruit is all mashed and pressed, strain the juice, deduct the amount of water used in washing the pumice, and the remainder will be the exact quantity of juice. Knowing this you can add water in the proportion given above, including the water already in the juice. Measure the whole quantity of watered juice which is to be wine, add sugar as above, put it in an open vessel, (a stone jar is best for small quantities) cover with a thin cloth and skim once a day till the scum is all off and fermentation has ceased, for which stage watch closely. Bottle and lay away in a dark cool place; if put into kegs—brandy or gin and whisky kegs are best. The next spring rack off and add two ounces sugar to the gallon. Wine thus made has received commendation from the highest quarters including that of heavy dealers in New York City.—*E. R. Southwick.*

HINTS FOR THE WELL.

Don't eat too much. Don't eat late at night. Don't stuff the babies.

Little children require food oftener than adults, but it should be given them only in small quantities at a time.

Adults need to eat at regular intervals two or three times a day, allowing time for each meal to be fully digested before another is taken. It would spoil a loaf of bread, half baked, to poke a lump of cold dough into the middle of it.

Don't eat too fast; the digestive organs are something like a stove, which if choked up and out of order, burns slowly, and if you keep piling in fuel grows more and more choked. The wiser course is to let it burn down and put in fuel only when needed. It is a foolish notion that food always keeps up the strength. Only what we digest helps us; all beyond that is a tax upon the system, and exhausts the strength instead of increasing it.

Use good palatable food, not highly seasoned; vary in quantity and quality according to age, climate, weather, and occupation. Unbolted or partially bolted grains are good and sufficient food for dogs, horses, and men; but nature demands variety. As a rule, the flesh of meat eating animals is not wholesome food. Hot soft bread digests slowly.

Cooking may spoil good food. Pork, if eaten at all, should be thoroughly cooked. Avoid frying meat; boil, roast or broil it, beginning with a high heat; for soups begin lukewarm.

Three full meals daily are customary, but the number, the relative quantity and quality, and the intervals between them, are largely matters of opinion, habit and convenience; regularity is the important thing.

Eat something within an hour after rising, especially if obliged to labor or study; but avoid both these before breakfast if possible, and particularly exposure to malaria or contagion.

Let the amount of the meal bear some relation to future needs as well as present appetite; but it is better to carry an extra pound in your pocket than in your stomach.

Eat in pure air and in pleasant company; light conversation and gentle exercise promote digestion, but hard work of any kind retards it. Avoid severe bodily or mental labor just before and for two hours after a full meal.

Masticate well; eat slowly; five minutes more at dinner may give you better use of an hour afterward. Drink little at meals, and never a full glass of very hot or very cold liquid. Never wash down a mouthful. Avoid waste of saliva.

Remember that when the stomach is sour after eating, the food is actually rotting—that is a nauseating word but it expresses the absolute facts in the case, and it means that some of the rules above given have been violated.

Evacuate the bowels daily, and above all regularly; the best time is after breakfast; partly to be rid of a physical burden during the day, but chiefly to relieve the brain. Constipation is safer than diarrhœa. For the former, exercise, ride horseback, knead the belly, take a glass of cool water before breakfast, eat fruit and laxative food; for the latter, follow an opposite course—toast, crust, crackers and rice are best food. Pain and uneasiness of the digestive organs are signs of disturbance; keep a clear conscience; rest, sleep, eat properly; avoid strong medicines in ordinary cases.

Panaceas are *prima facie* humbugs; their makers and takers, their vendors and recommenders are knaves or fools, or both. Nature cures most diseases, if let alone or aided by diet and proper care. There are no miracles in medicine; remember that to keep and to get well generally require only a recognition of Nature's powers, with knowledge of anatomy, and physiology, experience, and common sense.

A DYSPEPTIC'S FIGHT FOR LIFE.

Judge W. was a fretful, irritable, depressed, despondent, discouraged, listless, moody, nervous, wretched dyspeptic for five weary years. He tried travel, but neither the keen air of the sea-shore nor the bracing breezes of the northern prairies brought him relief. He tried all the panaceas and all the doctors at home and abroad in vain. Some told him that he had heart disease, others thought it was inflammation of the spleen, gout, Bright's disease, liver complaint, lung difficulty or softening of the brain. Bottle after bottle of nostrums went down the unfortunate Judge's throat, and it was only when physicians and friends gave him up, and pronounced him to all intents a dead man, that he threw bottles, plasters, powders and pills to the four winds and with the energy of despair, set about disappointing his doctors, and getting ready to live despite their ghastly predictions. Then began a fight for life against dyspepsia, a fight which many have begun but few have won. He bathed the whole body every morning in cold water, summer and winter, not by a shower or a plunge, but by vigorously dashing the water on the body with the hands, and afterwards rubbing briskly with a coarse towel. This was continued without missing a single morning for a year. In the meantime the strictest diet was instituted. By experimenting, the patient found what he could eat without harm, and ate that only in very small quantities, measuring his food on his plate before beginning his meal, and limiting himself rigidly to that quantity. His principal food for nearly three years was cracked wheat and Graham mush, and the last meal was taken at two o'clock in the afternoon— not a particle of food passed his lips from that time until the next morning, thus giving the stomach complete rest and time to begin the work of recuperation. Special attention was given to eating slowly and thoroughly masticating the food, and not to eat too much, too fast, or too often were rules strictly and rigidly observed. Bathing, diet, rest, sleep, and gentle exercise in the open air did the work. It was a dreadful conflict—days of struggle and temptation, requiring more heroism and steady tenacity of purpose than would nerve a soldier for battle, for such a battle is for the hour or the day, but this fight was renewed every morning and continued every day for months and years. But patience, courage, intelligent judgment, and a strict adherence to the above regimen won the day without a grain or a drop of medicine, and Judge W. believes that the good Lord of us all has never permitted any man to discover or invent medicine that will cure dyspepsia. Nature is the only perfect physician. Cold water, fresh air, the natural grain (wheat), sleep, rest and gentle exercise make up the grand panacea. With these alone, and the self denial and moral courage to persist in the good fight, Judge W., the confirmed, nervous, miserable dyspeptic, became a well, strong, and hearty man in five days? No. In five months? No. In five years? Yes; and after the fight, when contemplating the victory won, he could say with that model philanthropist, Amos Lawrence, after his battle of fifteen long years with the same disease, "If men only knew how sweet the victory is, they would not hesitate a moment to engage in the conflict."

HINTS ABOUT MARKETING.

Very few housekeepers understand how to select meats wisely or how to buy economically. Most trust the butcher, or buy at hap-hazard with no clear understanding of what they want, and no consideration at all for economy; and yet a little knowledge of facts, with a moderate amount of experience and observation will enable any one to buy both intelligently and economically. It is best, when possible, to buy for cash. Ready money always commands the best in the market, at the lowest prices. It is also better to buy of the most respectable regular dealer in the neighborhood, than of transient and irresponsible persons. Apparent "bargains" frequently turn out the worst possible investments. If a dealer imposes on you, drop him at once. In buying beef, select that which is of a clear, cherry-red color after a fresh cut has been for a few moments exposed to the air. The fat should be of a light straw color, and the meat marbled throughout with fat. If the beef is immature, the color of the lean part will be pale and dull, the bones small, and the fat very white. High-colored, coarse-grained beef with the fat a deep yellow should be rejected. In corn fed beef, however, the fat is yellowish, while that fattened on grasses is whiter. In cow beef the fat is also whiter than in ox beef. Inferior meat from old or ill fed animals has a coarse, skinny fat and a dark red lean. Ox beef is the sweetest and most juicy, and the most economical. When meat pressed by the finger rises up quickly, it is prime, but if the dent disappears slowly, or remains, it is inferior in quality. Any greenish tints about either fat or lean, or slipperiness of surface, indicates that the meat has been kept so long that putrefaction has begun, and consequently is unfit for use, except by those persons who prefer what is known as a "high flavor." Tastes differ as to the choice cuts. The tenderloin which is the choicest piece, and is sometimes removed by itself, lies under the short ribs and close to the back bone, and is usually cut through with the porter-house and sirloin steaks. Of these the porterhouse is generally preferred, the part nearest the thin bone being the sweetest. If the tenderloin is wanted, it may be secured by buying an edgebone steak, the remainder of which after the removal of the tenderloin, is equal to the sirloin. The small porterhouse steaks are the most economical, but in large steaks the coarse and tough parts may be used for soup, or after boiling, for hash, which, in spite of its bad repute, is really a very nice dish when well made. A round steak, when the leg is not cut down too far, is sweet and juicy, the objection being its toughness, to cancel which it may be chopped fine, seasoned and made into breakfast croquettes. The interior portion of the round is the tenderest and best. The roasting pieces are the sirloin and the ribs, the latter being most economical at the family table, the bones forming an excellent basis for soup, and the meat, when boned, rolled up and roasted, being in good form for the carver, as it enables him to distribute equally the upper part with the fatter and more skinny portions. There are roasts and other meats equally good in the fore quarter of beef, but the proportion of bone to meat is greater.

Veal should be clear and firm and the fat white. If dark and thin with the tissues hanging loosely about the bone, it is not good. Veal will not keep so long as an older meat, especially in hot or damp weather, and when going, the fat is soft and moist, the meat flabby and spotted, and inclined to be porous like a sponge. Overgrown veal is inferior to that which is smaller but well fatted.

Mutton should be fat, and the fat clear and white. Be wary of buying mutton with yellow fat. An abundance of fat is a source of waste, but as the lean part of fat mutton is much more juicy and tender than any other, it should be chosen. After the butcher has cut off all he can be persuaded to remove, you will still have to trim it freely before broiling. The lean of mutton is quite different from that of beef. While beef is a bright carnation, mutton is a deep, dark red. The hind-quarter of mutton is best for roasting. The ribs may be used for chops and are the sweeter, but the leg cutlets are the most economical, as there is much less bone, and no hard meat, as on the ribs. Almost any part will do for broth. As much of the fat should be removed as practicable, then cut into small pieces and simmer slowly until the meat falls to pieces. Drain off and skim off any remaining fat, and thicken with rice or vermicelli.

Lamb is good at a year old, and more digestible than most immature meats. The meat should be light red and fat. If not too warm weather, it ought to be kept a few days before cooking. It is stringy and indigestible if cooked too soon after killing.

Great care must be taken in selecting pork. If ill-fed or diseased, no meat is more injurious to the health. The lean must be finely grained, and both fat and lean very white. The rind should be smooth and cool to the touch. If clammy, be sure the pork is stale, and reject it. If the fat is full of small kernels, it is indicative of disease. In good bacon the rind is thin, the fat firm and the lean tender. Rusty bacon has yellow streaks in it. Hams are tried by sticking a knife into them. If when drawn out it has no bad odor, the ham is good.

Meat should always be wiped with a dry clean cloth as soon as it comes from the butcher's, and in loins the pipe which runs along the bone should be removed as it soon taints. Never buy bruised meat.

When found necessary to keep meat or poultry longer than was expected, sprinkle pepper, either black or red, over it. It can be washed off easily when ready for cooking. Powdered charcoal is recommended to prevent meat from tainting. Meat which has been kept on ice must be cooked immediately, but it is much better to place meats, poultry, game, etc., by the side of, not on, ice, as it is the cold air, not the ice, which arrests decay. All meats except veal, are better when kept a few days in a cool place.

GAME AND POULTRY.

To Preserve game or poultry in summer draw as soon as possible after they are killed, wash in several waters, have in readiness a kettle of boiling water and plunge them in, drawing them up and down by the legs so that the water may pass freely through them; do this for five minutes, drain, wipe dry, and hang in a cool place; when perfectly cold rub the insides and necks well with pepper; prepared in this way they will keep two days in warm weather; when used wash thoroughly; or wash well in soda water, rinse in clear water, place inside several pieces of charcoal, cover with a cloth, and hang in a dark cool place. The most delicate birds can be preserved in this way. If game or poultry is at all strong, let it stand several hours in water with either charcoal or soda; the latter will sweeten when they are comparatively spoiled.

Sportsmen who wish to keep prairie chickens, pheasants, or wild fowl, in very hot weather, or to ship long distances, should draw the bird as soon as killed, force down the throat two or three whole peppers, tying a string around the throat above them, sprinkle inside a little powdered charcoal, and fill the cavity of the body with very dry grass. Avoid green or wet grass which "heats," and hastens decay.

A young turkey has a smooth black leg, and if male, a short spur. The eyes are bright and full, and the feet supple, when fresh. The absence of these signs denotes age and staleness.

In young geese, the bills and feet are yellow and supple and the skin may be easily broken; the breast is plump and the fat white; an old goose has red and hairy legs and is unfit for the table.

Young ducks feel tender under the wing and the web of the foot is transparent; those with thick, hard breasts are best. Tame ducks have yellow legs, wild ducks reddish ones.

Young fowls have a tender skin, smooth legs and comb, and the best have yellow legs. In old fowls the legs are rough and hard.

In pheasants and quails yellow legs and a dark bill are signs of a young bird. They are in season in autumn.

Pigeons should be fresh, fat and tender, and the feet pliant and smooth.

In prairie chickens, if fresh, the eyes should be full and round, not sunken, and if young, the breast bone is soft and yields to pressure. The latter test also applies to all fowls and game birds.

Plover, woodcock, snipe, etc., may be chosen by the same rules.

In venison the meat should be of a rich, reddish brown and fine grain, and if young the fat is thick, clear and close.

FISH.

The eyes of fish are bright, and the gills a fine clear red, the body stiff and the smell not unpleasant, when fresh. Mackerel must be lately caught or it is very indifferent fish, and the flavor and excellence of salmon depend entirely on its freshness. Lobsters when recently caught have some muscular action in the claws which may be excited by pressing the eyes. The heaviest lobsters are the best.

In fresh-water fish the same signs of freshness are good tests. Among the best of these are the Lake Superior trout and white fish, and coming from cold waters they keep best of all fresh-water fish; the latter is the best, most delicate, and has fewer bones, greatly resembling shad. The wall-eyed pike, bass and pickerel of the inland lakes are also excellent fish, and are shipped, packed in ice, reaching market as fresh as when caught, and are sold at moderate prices. California salmon is also shipped in the same way, and is sold fresh in all cities, with fresh cod and other choice varieties from the Atlantic coast, but the long distance which they must be transported makes the price high. The cat-fish is the staple Mississippi river fish, and is cooked in various ways. Lake Superior trout are the best fresh fish for baking. All fish which have been packed in ice should be cooked immediately after removal, as they soon grow soft and lose their flavor. Stale fish must never be eaten.

The best salt mackerel for general use are "English mess," but "bloaters" are considered nicer. In selecting always choose those which are thick on the belly and fat; poor mackerel are always dry. The salt California salmon is excellent, those of a dark rich yellow being best. To freshen, place *with scale side up.* Salmon boiled and served with egg sauce or butter dressing is nice. No. 1 white fish is also a favorite salt fish, and will be found in all markets.

A good deal of sturgeon is put up and sold for smoked halibut. The skin of halibut should be white; if dark it is more likely to be sturgeon. Smoked salmon should be firm and dry. Smoked white fish and trout are very nice, the former being a favorite in whatever way cured. Select good firm whole fish. White fish is very nice broiled. Each of the above is better than herring.

WOOD.

When wood is used for cooking, always buy that which is straight and solid. A cord of small crooked sticks does not contain one half as much solid fuel as straight coarse body wood. The best wood for fuel is hickory and maple.

HOW TO CUT AND CURE MEATS.

It is often economical for a family to buy beef by the quarter, and smaller animals whole, especially when wanted for winter use, and every housekeeper ought to know how to cut up meats and to understand the uses and relative value of the pieces. It is not difficult to cut up beef, and is very easy to reduce any of the smaller animals to convenient proportions for domestic use, and in order to make the subject clear we present the accompanying engravings, the first of which represents the half of a beef, including, of course, the hind and fore quarters. The letters indicate the direction

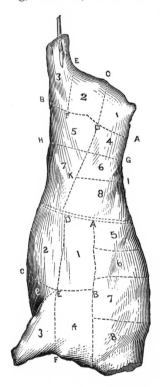

in which the cuts should be made, beginning in the order of the alphabet, cutting first from A to B, then from C to D, etc. In the fore quarter cut from A to B, from B to C, from D to E, etc. For cutting, use a sharp, long and pointed knife, and a saw of the best steel, sharp, and set for butcher's use. The beef should be laid on a bench or table with the inner side up. In hind quarter 1 represents the "rump" which is best corned; 2, "round," the under part of which makes steaks, the outside good corning pieces, or the whole may be used for dried beef; 3, "shank" for soups; 4, "rump steaks"; 5, "veiny piece" for dried beef or corning; 6, sirloin, the best steak; 7, flank for corning or stews; 8, porter house, the upper part of which is equal to sirloin. Cut in this way a part of the tenderloin, the choicest bit of the beef, lies in the sirloin and a smaller part in the upper part of the porter house steak. In the fore quarter 1 is the "rib piece" for boiling or corning; 2, the "plate" piece for corning; 3, the "fore shank" for soup; 5, the "rib roast," first cut; 6, "rib roast," best cut, and the best roast in the beef; 7, "chuck rib roast," commonly used for "pot roast;" 8, neck piece for corning or pie meat; 9, best cut for corn beef.

VEAL.

A—Loin, best end, for roasting.
B—Loin, chump end, for roasting.
C—Fillet, for baking or roasting.
D—Knuckle for stewing.
E—Fore knuckle, for stewing.
F—Neck, best end, for roasting.
G—Neck, scrag end, for stewing.
H—Blade bone.
I—Breast, for stewing.

PORK.

A—Back, lean part for roast.
B—Loin, for roast.
C—Bacon to be cured.
D—Shoulder, to be cured.
E—Ham, to be cured.

MUTTON.

A—Leg, for boiling piece.
B—Loin, for roast.
C—Rump piece, for roast.
D—Chops, frying or broiling.
E—Fore-shoulder, for boiling.
F—Neck, for stewing or roasting.
G—Brisket, for stewing.

BRINE FOR BEEF—To one hundred pounds beef, take eight pounds salt, five of sugar or five pints molasses, (Orleans best, but any good will do), two ounces soda, one ounce saltpeter, four gallons water, or enough to cover the meat. Mix part of the salt and sugar together, rub each piece, and place it in the barrel, having covered the bottom with salt. When the meat is all in, put the remainder of salt and sugar in the water. Dissolve the soda and saltpeter in hot water, add it to the brine and pour over the meat; place a board on top of meat, with a weight sufficient to keep it under the brine. Let the pieces intended for dried beef remain in the brine three weeks, take out, place in a tub, cover with water, let stand over night, string and dry. Boil brine, skim well, let cool, and pour over the bony pieces left. These are good boiled, and eaten either hot or cold, and they will keep good for several months. Tongue may be pickled with the beef. Brine made the same way, with the addition of two pounds more of salt, is good for hams and shoulders. Brine for pickled pork should have all the salt it will dissolve, and a peck or half bushel in bottom of barrel. If pork is salted in this manner it will never spoil, but the strength of the brine makes it necessary to salt the hams and side meat separately. Pork when killed should be thoroughly cooled before salting, but should not remain longer than one or two days. It should never be frozen before salting, as this is as injurious as salting before it is cooled. Large quantities of pork are lost by failing to observe these rules. If pickled pork begins to sour, take it out of the brine, rinse well in clear cold water, place a layer in a barrel, on this place charcoal in lumps the size of a hen's egg or smaller, add a layer of meat and so on, until all is in the barrel, cover with a weak brine, let stand twenty-four hours; take meat out, rinse off the charcoal, put it into a new strong brine, remembering always to have plenty of salt in the barrel (more than the water will dissolve). If the same barrel is used, cleanse it by placing a small quantity of quicklime in it, slack with hot water, and add as much salt as the water will dissolve, and cover tightly to keep the steam in.—*D. Buxton.*

To Cure Hams.—For every ham, half a pound of salt, same of brown sugar, half an ounce of cayenne pepper, half an ounce allspice, half an ounce saltpeter; mix and rub well over the hams, laying them in the barrel they are to be kept in with the skin side down; let them remain a week, make a pickle of water and salt strong enough to bear an egg, add to it half a pound of sugar, pour over the hams till they are thoroughly covered, let them remain four weeks, take out and hang up to dry for at least a week before smoking; smoke with corn cobs or hickory chips,—an old but a good way.—*Mrs. S. M. Guy.*

To Keep Hams.—For one hundred pounds of meat, take eight pounds salt, two ounces saltpeter and four gallons water; put hams in this pickle in the fall, keeping them well under the brine; in April take out, drain three or four days, slice as for cooking, fry nearly as much as for table, pack in stone jars, pressing down the slices as fast as they are laid in the jar; when full put on a weight, and when entirely cold, cover with the fat tried out. Prepared in this way they retain the ham flavor without being smoked. The gravy left from frying will be found very useful in cooking.

CARVING.

It is no trifling accomplishment to carve well, and both ladies and gentlemen ought to so far make carving a study that they may be able to perform the task with sufficient skill at least to prevent remark. There are no real difficulties in the way of mastering the accomplishment; knowledge simply is required. All displays of exertion are in bad taste because they indicate a want of ability on the part of the carver, or are a strong indication of the toughness of roast or the age of the bird. A good knife of moderate size and great sharpness is a necessity. Fowls are easily carved, and in roasts such as loins, breasts, forequarters, etc., the butcher should always have instructions to separate the joints. The platter should be placed so near to the carver that he has full control over it; if far off, nothing can prevent an ungraceful appearance. In carving a turkey, cut off the wing nearest you first, then the leg and second joint; then slice the breast until a rounded, ivory-shaped piece appears; insert the knife between that and the bone, and separate them; this part is the nicest bit of the breast, next comes the "merry-thought." After this, turn over the bird a little, and just below the breast you will find the "oyster," which you separate as you did the inner breast. The side-bone lies beside the rump, and the desired morsel can be taken out without separating the whole bone. Proceed in the same way upon the other side. The fork need not be removed during the whole process. An experienced carver will dissect a fowl as easily as you can break an egg or cut a potato. He retains his seat, manages his hands and elbows artistically, and is perfectly at his ease. There is no difficulty in the matter; it only requires knowledge and practice, and these should be taught in the family, each child taking his or her turn.

Chickens and partridges are carved in the same way. The trail of a woodcock on a bit of toast is the choicest bit of that bird; also the thigh of a partridge.

SIRLOIN OF BEEF.

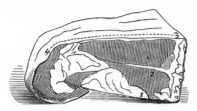

In carving beef, mutton, lamb, and veal, thin smooth and neat slices are desirable—*cut across the grain,* taking care to pass the knife through to the bones of the meat. There are two modes of helping a sirloin of beef; either by carving long thin slices from 3 to 4, and helping it with a portion of the fat underneath the ribs, or by cutting thicker slices, from 1 to 2, through the tenderloin.

SHOULDER OF MUTTON.

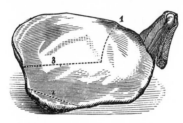

A shoulder of mutton should be cut down to the bone, in the direction of the line 1, and thin slices of lean taken from each side. The best fat is found at 2, and should be cut in thin slices in that direction. Several tempting slices can be cut on either side of the line 3, and there are nice bits on the under side near the flap.

HAM.

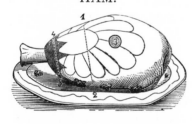

A ham may be carved in three ways: first, by cutting long delicate slices through the thick fat from 1 to 2, down to the bone; secondly, by running the point of the knife in the circle in the middle, and cutting thin circular slices, thus keeping the ham moist, and, thirdly, and most economically, by commencing at the knuckle at 4–5, and slicing upward.

LEG OF MUTTON.

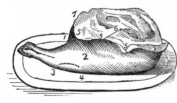

In carving a leg of mutton, the best slices are obtained from the center, by cutting from 1 to 2; and some very good cuts are found on the broad end from 5 to 6. Some epicures prefer slices nearer the knuckle, but they are dry. The cramp-bone is a delicacy, and is obtained by cutting down to the bone at

4, and running the knife under it in a semicircular direction to 3. The fat so esteemed by many lies on the ridge 5. By turning over the meat some excellent slices are found, and can be cut lengthwise.

TONGUE.

A tongue should be carved as "thin as a wafer;" its delicacy depending in a great degree upon that. A well cut bit tempts the most fastidious; and this applies, in fact, to all kinds of roast and boiled meats. A chunk of beef we turn from with disgust—an artistic slice we enjoy. The center slices of the tongue are considered the best, and should be cut across at the line 1, and the slices taken from each side, with a portion of the fat which is at its root, if it is liked. The question should be asked.

HAUNCH OF VENISON.

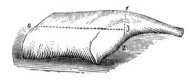

A haunch of venison should be cut across to the bone on the line 1–3–2, then turn the dish a little, and put the point of the knife at three, and cut down as deep as possible in the direction of 3–4, and continue to cut slices on the right and left of the line. The fattest parts are found between 4 and 2. A loin of veal and a loin of mutton should be jointed by the butcher before it is cooked, and the carver easily cuts through the ribs, and should serve a portion of the kidney and the fat on each plate.

A fillet of veal is cut in thin, smooth slices off the top, and portions of the stuffing and fat helped to each. In cutting a breast of veal, separate the breast and brisket, and then cut them up.

In serving fish, some practice is needful, for lightness of touch and dexterity of management are requisite to prevent the flakes from breaking. In serving mackerel, shad, etc., a part of the roe should be placed on each plate. The fins of the turbot are the most sought for; this fish is placed underpart uppermost on the platter, as there lies the primest part. In carving salmon, a portion of the back and belly should be served to each person. The choicest morsels are next to the head, the thin part comes next, and the tail is the least esteemed. The flavor of the fish nearest the bone is not equal to that on the upper part.

HOUSEKEEPING.

Housekeeping, whatever may be the opinion of the butterflies of the period, is an accomplishment in comparison to which in its bearing on woman's relation to real life and to the family, all others are trivial. It comprehends all that goes to make up a well ordered home, where the sweetest relations of life rest on firm foundations, and the purest sentiments thrive. It is an accomplishment that may be acquired by study and experiment, but the young and inexperienced housekeeper generally reaches success only through great tribulation. It ought rather to be absorbed in girlhood, by easy lessons taken between algebra, music and painting. If girls were taught to take as much genuine pride in dusting a room well, hanging a curtain tastefully, or broiling a steak to a nicety, as they feel when they have mastered one of Mozart's or Beethoven's grand symphonies, there would be fewer complaining husbands and unhappy wives. The great lesson is to learn that work well-done is robbed of its curse. The woman who is satisfied only with the highest perfection in her work drops the drudge and becomes the artist. There is no dignity in slighted work, but to the artist, no matter how humble his calling, belongs the honor which is inseparable from all man's struggles after perfection. No mother who has the happiness of her daughter at heart, will neglect to teach her first the duties of the household, and no daughter who aspires to be queen at home and in her circle of friends, can afford to remain ignorant of the smallest details that contribute to the comfort, the peace and the attractiveness of home. There is no luck in housekeeping, however it may seem. Everything works by exact rule, and even with thorough knowledge, eternal vigilance is the price of success. There must be a place for everything and everything in its place, a time for everything and everything in its time, and "patience, patience" must be written in blazing capitals all over the walls. The reward is sure. Your husband may admire your grace and ease in society, your wit, your school-day accomplishments of music and painting, but all in perfection will not atone for an ill-ordered kitchen, sour bread, muddy coffee, tough meats, unpalatable vegetables, indigestable pastry, and the whole train of horrors that result from bad housekeeping; on the other hand, success wins gratitude and attachment in the home circle, and adds lustre to the most brilliant intellectual accomplishments.

One of the first ideas the young housekeeper must divest herself of is that because she is able or expects sometime to be able to keep servants, it is therefore unnecessary to understand household duties, and to bear their responsibility. "Girls" are quick to see and note the ignorance or incapacity of the mistress of the house, and few are slow to take whatever advantage it brings them, while the capacity of the mistress at once establishes discipline. The model house should not be large, nor too fine and pretentious for daily use. The mistress of many a fine mansion is the veriest household drudge. A great house, with its necessary retinue of servants, is not in keeping with the simplicity of a republic where trained servants are not known, and is seldom pleasant for the family or attractive to friends. The furniture should be selected for comfort rather than show. Most modern chairs put their occupants to torture, and throw them into attitudes anything but graceful. Comfortable chairs should have broad seats, and a part at least, low seats for women and children. Carpets should as a rule be of small patterns. The stoves, if grates are not used, should be of the kind that may be thrown open or closed at pleasure, and burn either wood or coal. If a furnace is used great care must be taken that the rooms are not kept too hot in winter, and that there is most thorough ventilation, as the health of the family depends as much on the quality of the air they breathe as on the food they eat. There must be plenty of sunlight, floods of it in every room, even if the carpets do fade; the housekeeper must be quick to note any scent of decay from vegetables or meats in the cellar, or from slops or refuse carelessly thrown about the premises. Every room must be clean and sweet. In sickness care in all these respects must be doubled. In damp and chilly autumn and spring days a little fire is comfortable morning and evening. The food for the family must be fresh to be wholesome, and it is economy to buy the best, as there is less waste in it. No housekeeper ought to be satisfied with any but the very best cooking. Without it the most wholesome food is unpalatable and distressing, and no considerations of economy should ever induce her to place on the table bread with the slightest sour tinge, cake or pudding in the least heavy or solid, or meat with the slightest taint. Its use means disease and costly doctor's bills, to say to nothing of her own loss of repute as an accomplished housekeeper. If children and servants do work improperly, she should quietly insist on its being done correctly, and in self-defense they will soon do it correctly without supervision. Order and system mean the stopping of waste, the practice of economy, and additional means to expend for the table and for the luxuries and elegancies of life, and money in these things is well expended. It requires good food to make good muscle and good brain, and the man or woman who habitually sits down to badly cooked or scanty dinners, fights the battle of life at a great disadvantage.

THE PARLOR.

The dusting of a parlor seems simple enough but is best done systematically. All fragile movables should be stored away carefully in some neighboring closet, and the furniture protected as far as possible by covers, or removed from the room. Open the blinds and let in the light, and open the windows if it is not storming or too windy. Look on the ceiling for cobwebs, and sprinkle the carpet over with moistened bran, salt, damp coffee grounds, or tea leaves. Clean out corners and edges with a sharp pointed stick and stiff whisk broom, brush thoroughly under the heavy furniture with a parlor brush, then with a clean, fine and rather light broom make long, straight strokes the "right way" of the carpet. Short strokes dig into the carpet, wear off the nap, and raise more dust. Now leave the room until all dust is settled, then with a long feather duster, brush the dust from every piece of furniture, from the tops of windows and door casings, panels and knobs, upper edge of base-board, picture frames, etc. Next take a clean soft cotton cloth or an old silk handkerchief, or better a soft dusting towel with fleecy surface which is sold expressly for this purpose, and rub, not simply wipe the furniture. If any spot of dust is too firmly fixed, wash in lukewarm soapsuds, and immediately rub dry with chamois skin. If there is open work carving, draw the cloth through or dust with a paint brush, and it will be found more convenient to blow out some of the places which are difficult to reach, for which a small pair of bellows may be used. To clean and dust a piano, use a half yard best canton flannel with nap free from all specks and grit, brushing lightly over to remove the dust; if there are finger marks or spots, rub up and down over them, always keeping the nap next to the instrument; dust under the wires may be blown out with a pair of bellows. Keep the piano closed at night and in damp weather; open on bright days and if possible let the sun shine directly upon the keys, as the light will keep them from turning yellow. Tune every spring and fall. As a last finishing touch to the rearranging of the parlor, leave late papers, magazines, a volume of poetry, or a stereoscope and views where they will be readily picked up by callers.

THE SITTING ROOM.

The sitting room should be the pleasantest, because most used, of all in the house. Do not put down a Brussels carpet here, as it is too hard to sweep and holds too much dust. To prevent moths under the carpets, grind black pepper coarsely, mix with camphor gum, and strew thickly about the edges and wherever they are apt to be found. To clean the oilcloth, use warm water without soap, or what is much better, milk and water; to make it wear well give it one or two coats of linseed oil, dry thoroughly and then varnish. By keeping mats at the doors it will only be necessary to sweep the sitting room thoroughly once a week, but occasionally when very dusty it may be cleaned by setting a pail of cold water by the door, wet the broom in it, knock off the drops, sweep a yard or so, then wash the broom as before and sweep again, being careful to shake all the drops off the broom, and not to sweep far at a time. If done with care the carpet will be very nicely cleaned, and the quantity of dirt in the water will be surprising. The water must be changed several times. Snow sprinkled on a carpet and swept off before it has time to melt, is also nice for renovating a soiled carpet. A scrap bag hung on the sewing machine, for storing all bits of cloth and ravelings and ends of thread, will save much sweeping. In summer, wire doors and mosquito netting in windows will keep flies out and at the same time admit the air. Washing windows and wiping off doors once a week after sweeping and dusting, keeps all tidy. To remove finger marks, which are constantly appearing on doors about the knobs, use a damp cloth as soon as they are observed.

THE DINING ROOM.

At meals always make the table as attractive as possible—a boquet adds to its appearance. Make the dining room neat and tidy, and most important of all, wear a cheerful countenance. Gather up the fragments that nothing be lost or wasted. When each meal is over, if you do not have a crumb cloth under the table, which, when the chairs are removed, can be lifted carefully at the edges and the crumbs shaken into the centre, it is best to take a broom and sweep the crumbs lightly under the table until the dishes and victuals are removed, then brush on a dust pan. To clear the table, bring in a dish-pan, gather up all the silver, cups and saucers, butter and sauce plates, and glassware, carry to the kitchen, place them in the sink and return with the pan. Scrape the plates as clean as possible and put in, add platters and vegetable dishes, saving all the remnants of food that are to be kept, on smaller dishes, to be taken to the cellar or refrigerator. To wash the dishes, have clear hot water in the pan, and first wash the silver without soap or cloth, using only the hands; if any are greasy, wipe with a soft paper before putting in the water, rinse in clear hot water and wipe off immediately on a perfectly dry, soft, clean towel; in this way the silver is kept bright, and does not get scratched. Add some soap in the water, make a suds, wash the glass ware, rinse and wipe dry. Next take cups and saucers and so on, leaving those most greasy till the last. Always keep a clean dish-cloth. One lady writes, "I have smelled a whole housefull of typhoid fever in one sour, dirty dish-rag." Many prefer to use three dish cloths, one for the nicest articles, one for the greasy dishes, and one for pots and kettles, keeping each cloth perfectly sweet and clean, and, after using it, washing, rinsing, and hanging to dry on a small rack kept for this purpose. The towels for wiping dishes may also dry here. A dish mop or swab for washing small deep articles is convenient.

THE BEDROOM.

The family bedroom should be on the first floor if possible. Matting is better for the floor than carpet, because freer from dust, and this is the room used in case of sickness. If made properly it will wear several years. Canton mattings are made on boats in pieces about two yards long, and afterward joined on shore into pieces of fifty yards. It is easy to see where these short pieces are joined; after cutting into lengths, first sew these places across and across on the wrong side, then sew the breadths together and tack down like a carpet. Matting should never be washed with anything except moderately warmed salt and water, in the proportion of a pint of salt to a half pail of soft water. Dry quickly with a soft cloth. A bed room matting should be washed twice during the season, a room much used, oftener. In this room there should be a medicine closet, high above the reach of children, where are kept camphor, hot drops, mustard, strips of old linen, etc., for sudden sickness or accident. There should also be a large closet, a part of which is especially set apart for childrens' use, with low hooks where they may hang their clothes, a box for stockings, a bag for shoes, and other conveniences, which will help to teach them system and order.

THE GUEST CHAMBER.

The bed of the guest chamber should always stand so that when one opens the eyes in the morning, the light from the window will not be directly upon them, as it is trying to weak eyes and unpleasant to strong ones. Keep the bureau where the sun's rays will never strike the mirror, and where it will not be heated by the stove, as either will granulate the amalgam. Chambers should always be provided with transoms over the doors, and windows arranged so as to lower easily from the top. A light feather bed covered with a case like a pillow, may be either used over the mattress, or a comfort may be used over it and the feather bed under it. Tacked on the inside of the washstand doors, two crotcheted pockets are nice for bathing sponges, and there should be plenty of towels, especially of those coarse, rough ones which make a morning bath such a luxury. A broad oil cloth in front of the washstand is also a protection to the carpet in bathing, and is needed when there is no bath room up stairs.

THE KITCHEN.

It is almost impossible to give any directions excepting in a general way regarding the kitchen, as there is an endless variety of plans and arrangement. The main thing is to systematize everything, grouping such things as belong to any particular kind of work. For instance, in baking do not go to the china closet for a bowl, across the kitchen for the flour, and to the farther end of the pantry or store room for an egg, when they may all just as well be within easy reach of each other. Study and contrive to bring order out of the natural chaos of the kitchen, and your head will save your hands and feet much labor. There is an old and true saying that "a woman can throw out with a spoon faster than a man can throw in with a shovel." In cooking meats, for instance, unless watched, the cook will throw out the water without letting it cool to take off the fat, or scrape the dripping-pan into the swill-pail. This grease is useful in many ways. Bits of meat are thrown out which would make good hashed meat or hash; the flour is sifted in a wasteful manner, or the bread pan left with dough sticking to it; pie crust is left and laid by to sour, instead of making a few tarts for tea. Cake batter is thrown out because but little is left; cold puddings are considered good for nothing, when often they can be steamed for the next day, or, as in case of rice, made over in other forms. Vegetables are thrown away that would warm for breakfast nicely. Dish towels are thrown down where mice can destroy them. Soap is left in water to dissolve, or more used than is necessary; the scrub brush is left in the water, pails scorched by the stove, tubs and barrels left in the sun to dry and fall apart, chamber pails allowed to rust, tins not dried, and iron ware rusted; nice knives are used for cooking in the kitchen, silver spoons used to scrape kettles, or forks to toast bread; cream is allowed to mould and spoil, mustard to dry in the pot, and vinegar to corrode the castor; tea, roasted coffee, pepper and spices to stand open and lose their strength; the molasses jug loses the cork and the flies take possession; vinegar is drawn in a basin and allowed to stand until both basin and vinegar are spoiled; sugar is spilled from the barrel, coffee from the sack, and tea from the chest. Different sauces are made too sweet, and both sauce and sugar are wasted; dried fruit has not been taken care of in season, and becomes wormy; the vinegar on pickles loses strength or leaks out, and the pickles become soft; potatoes in the cellar grow, and the sprouts are not removed until they become worthless; apples decay for want of looking over; pork spoils for want of salt, and beef because the brine wants scalding; hams become tainted or filled with vermin, for want of the right protection; dried beef becomes so hard it can't be cut; cheese molds and is eaten by mice or vermin; bones are burnt that will make soup; ashes are thrown out carelessly, endangering the premises, and wasting them; servants leave a light and fire burning in the kitchen, when they are out all the evening; clothes are whipped to pieces in the wind; fine cambrics rubbed on the board, and laces torn in starching; brooms are never hung up, and are soon spoiled; carpets are swept with stubs hardly fit to scrub the kitchen, and good new brooms used for scrubbing; towels are used in place of holders, and good sheets to iron on, taking a fresh one every week; table linen is thrown carelessly down, and is eaten by mice, or put away damp, and is mildewed; or the fruit stains are forgotten, and the stains washed in; tablecloths and napkins used as dish-wipers; mats forgotten to be put under hot dishes; teapots melted by the stove; water forgotten in pitchers, and allowed to freeze in winter; slops for cows and pigs never saved; china used to feed cats and dogs on; and in many other ways a careless or inexperienced housekeeper wastes, without heeding, the hard earned wages of her husband. Economy counts nowhere so well as in the kitchen.

Use a cloth to wash potatoes. It is no trouble to keep one for this purpose, and it will save your hands and your time. Some prefer a brush. Tie a strip of muslin on the end of a round stick, and use to grease bread and cake pans, gem-irons, etc. Have two large pockets in your kitchen apron, and in one of them always keep a holder. A piece of clam or oyster shell is much better than a knife to scrape a kettle, should you be so unfortunate as to burn anything on it. If you use a copper teakettle, keep an old dish with sour milk and a cloth in it, wash the kettle with this every morning, afterwards washing off with clear water, and it will always look bright and new. Cut a very ripe tomato and rub over a kitchen table to remove grease. The juice will also remove stains from and whiten the hands. A piece of sponge fastened on the end of a stick or wire is the best thing with which to clean lamp chimneys.

If you use oil buy the best kerosene; to test it place a small quantity in a teacup, and if it does not easily ignite when brought in contact with a lighted taper or match, it is good; poor oil will ignite instantly. Keep oil in a ten gallon can with a faucet at the lower part, so as to draw off into a smaller can or lamp filler; set the large can in a cool dark place, keep all the articles used for cleaning, filling and trimming lamps by themselves. For these purposes provide an old waiter (to hold the things), a lamp filler, pair of scissors or a lamp trimmer, box of wicks, soap, washing soda, and several soft cloths and towels, also a wire hairpin with which to keep open the vent in the burner. When lamps need an extra cleaning, add one tablespoon soda to a quart of water, being careful that none of the bronze or gilding comes in contact with the soda. When the wick becomes too short to carry up the kerosene, and if you have not time to put in a new wick, a piece of cotton rag pinned on below will prove a good feeder. If a hole is broken in a glass chimney, paste on a piece of paper and it will answer its purpose until you get a new chimney. When the burners of lamps become gummy and prevent the wicks moving freely, boil them up in suds over the fire a short time, and they will become entirely clean and work well. Lamps may become incrusted inside with settlings from the oil, and ordinary washing will not remove it. Take soapsuds and fill the lamp about one-third full, then put in a little sharp sand, and shake vigorously. A few minutes will remove every particle of settlings. Always fill the lamps every day and in the day time. Never fill a lamp after dark near a lighted lamp. Never light an almost empty lamp, as the empty space is nearly always filled with a very explosive gas. In putting out a lamp turn the flame down low, and wave a fan, book or paper across the top of the chimney. Blowing down a chimney is very dangerous when a lamp is nearly empty and turned up high. Never start a fire with the oil.

If kitchen floors are simply oiled, two or three times a year, no grease spot is made when grease drops on them, for it can be easily wiped up,— carpet or paint is not advisable. Neither paint nor paper the walls, but once a year apply a coat of the good old fashioned white wash. Do not have the wood work painted, the native wood well oiled and varnished lightly, is much the best finish. A wide, roomy dresser is a great convenience. It should have two wide closets below and three narrower ones above, with a row of drawers at top of lower closets. Here should be kept all pots and kettles, sauce-pans, waffle-irons, kitchen crockery, tins, etc., all arranged and grouped together so as to be convenient for use. If possible have good sliding doors, and at top and bottom of same have a narrow sliding panel for a ventilator, which should be closed when sweeping. By this arrangement every article of kitchen ware can be enclosed from the dust and flies. A well appointed sink is a necessity in every kitchen—should be near both window and range, so as to have light, and also be convenient to the hot water. It should be provided with a "grooved" and movable dish drainer, set so as to drain into the sink. Always have lamps placed at each end, or at the sides, so that the room may be well lighted in the evening. Never place a range or cooking stove opposite a door or window if it can be avoided, as any draft will prevent the oven from baking well.

Not less than three large windows are desirable in every good sized kitchen. Have your kitchen cheerful, pleasant, well ventilated, convenient and clean.

Fill new tin pans with boiling water (having a little soda in it), let stand on a warm part of the range for a while, wash in strong soap suds, rinse and dry well. Scouring tins very often with whitening or ashes wears them out; if properly taken care of, washed in suds and thoroughly dried, they will not need scouring.

Boil ashes or a bunch of hay or grass in a new iron pot before cooking in it; scour well with soap and sand, then fill with clean water and boil one or two hours.

HOUSE CLEANING.

When mother earth summons the stirring winds to help clear away the dead leaves and winter litter for the coming grass and flowers, every housekeeper has a feeling of sympathy, and begins to talk of house cleaning. The first bright sunshine of spring reveals unsuspected dust and cobwebs, and to her imagination even the scrubbing brushes and brooms seem anxious to begin the campaign. In northern latitudes it is best, however, not to begin too soon. Do not trust entirely to appearances, for spring is almost certain to break her promises of pleasant weather, and give us a good many days when it will be anything but pleasant to sit shivering in a fireless room, while your children become unmanageable and your husband growls. So for the sake of health, peace and comfort do not remove the stoves before the middle of May. When you begin, do not upset all the house at once, driving your husband to distraction and your children to the neighbors. By cleaning one or two rooms at a time and using a little womanly tact, the whole house may be renovated with little inconvenience. Before the "trouble" begins have all tools on hand and in good order. Provide lime for whitewashing, carpet tacks, good soap, sawdust, carbolic acid and spirits of ammonia. Fold carpets by lifting one side, carrying it over to the other and laying down carefully, thus preventing the straw and dust from the under side from soiling the upper. Carry out and hang on a strong line over the grass, and beat thoroughly with a carpet whip such as are sold at all house furnishing stores, or a broom or stick, taking care not to use anything rough that will catch into the carpet. Take one or two pails of sawdust, wet thoroughly and scatter well over the floor; very little dust will arise when you sweep it off, and it will not be necessary to clean the floor before washing woodwork and windows. If you cannot get sawdust, use moist earth instead. After floors have been cleaned and dried, wash over with strong brine, which will destroy any insects that may be lurking in cracks and corners. Sinks, drains, and all places that become sour or impure, should be cleaned with carbolic acid and water. This is the best disinfectant known, and should be kept in every house, and used frequently in warm weather. While house cleaning, brighten up old furniture by rubbing well with kerosene oil; should it be marred or bruised use the "Magic Furniture Polish," given in the miscellaneous department. Take bedsteads to pieces and saturate every crevice with strong brine; nothing is better to purify and cleanse or to destroy bedbugs. To clean windows and mirrors take clean, warm rainwater, and put in just enough spirits of ammonia to make it feel slippery. If very dirty rinse, if not wipe dry, and you will be surprised at the effect. Do not polish stoves until fall if you are going to put them away during the summer, but to keep them or any iron utensils from rusting rub over with kerosene. When polishing, six or eight drops of turpentine added to blacking for one stove, brightens it and makes it easier to polish.

Always beat a carpet on the wrong side first; cover oil or grease spots with flour and then pin a thick paper over, repeat the process several times, each time brushing off the old flour into a dust pan and putting on fresh.

To remove mortar and paint from windows, rub spots of mortar with hot sharp vinegar; or if nearly fresh, cold vinegar will loosen them. Rub the paint spots with camphene and sand.

To clean paint use whiting on a damp cloth; it cleans nicely.

To remove spots from gray marble hearths, rub with linseed oil.

GENERAL SUGGESTIONS.

On Monday, wash; Tuesday, iron; Wednesday, bake; Thursday, give a part of the day to church or charitable work; Friday devote to general sweeping and dusting; Saturday bake and prepare for Sunday. When the clothes are folded off the frame after ironing, examine each piece to see that none are laid away that need a button or a stitch. Clean all the silver on the last Friday of each month, and go through each room and closet to see if things are kept in order, and nothing going to waste. Have the sitting room tidied up every night before retiring. Remember that man requires a variety of food, and it is just as cheap to make frequent changes of diet. Make the most of your brain and your eyes, and let no one dare tell you you are devoting yourself to a low sphere of action.

HOUSEKEEPER'S ALPHABET.

APPLES—Keep in dry place as cool as possible without freezing.

BROOMS—Hang in the cellar way to keep soft and pliant.

CRANBERRIES—Keep under water in cellar; change water monthly.

DISH of hot water set in oven prevents cakes, etc., from scorching.

ECONOMIZE time, health, and means, and you will never beg.

FLOUR—Keep cool, dry, and securely covered.

GLASS—Clean with a quart water mixed with tablespoon of ammonia.

HERBS—Gather when beginning to blossom; keep in paper sacks.

INK STAINS—Wet with spirits turpentine; after three hours rub well.

JARS—To prevent, coax "husband" to buy a Buckeye Cook Book.

KEEP an account of all supplies with cost and date when purchased.

LOVE lightens labor.

MONEY—Count carefully when you receive change.

NUTMEGS—Prick with a pin, and if good oil will run out.

ORANGE and lemon peel—Dry, pound, and keep in corked bottles.

PARSNIPS—Keep in ground until spring.

QUICKSILVER and white of an egg destroy bedbugs.

RICE—Select large with a clear fresh look; old rice may have insects.

SUGAR—For general family use, the granulated is best.

TEA—Equal parts of Japan and green are as good as English breakfast.

USE a cement made of ashes, salt and water for cracks in stove.

VARIETY is the best culinary spice.

WATCH your back yard for dirt and bones.

XANTIPPE was a scold. Don't imitate her.

YOUTH is best preserved by a cheerful temper.

ZINC lined sinks are better than wooden ones.

& Regulate the clock by your husband's watch, and in all apportionments of time remember the Giver.

THE LAUNDRY.

The first time black calicoes are washed, pour boiling rainwater over them, let stand about five minutes, then wash, rinse, starch, and hang out. This will set the color and prevent fading. Some treat all calicoes in this manner. Black percales, lawns, etc., starched in gum arabic water and ironed on the wrong side will look like new. Do not use soap in washing black or navy blue linens. Take instead two potatoes, wash, peel and grate into tepid soft water, add a teaspoon ammonia; wash the linens in this and rinse in cold bluing water. They will need no starch, and should be dried, and ironed on the wrong side. Bran water is nice for brown linens, also for flannel, merino or cashmere. Purple and black calicoes are very much improved by dipping them in sweet milk, (with a little water added). Use this in place of starch, as it not only stiffens, but improves the color of the calico. Calicoes and linens should be hung in the shade to dry; do not let them lie in the water, but wash, rinse, starch, and hang right out. Remember, in washing flannels, to use soft water, always boiling hot; use soft soap, and put it in the water, never rub it on the clothes. Use neither wash-board nor wringer, but let the entire work be done with the hands. On no account suffer flannels or calicoes to lie in a pile after they are wrung out; it is better to take each piece separately, wash, rinse and hang out; in the meantime the suds and rinsing waters must be kept boiling hot. When flannels are almost dry bring them in, pull into shape, fold loosely, roll up tightly in a clean towel, and iron after they have been folded a quarter of an hour. Flannels washed and ironed in the above manner will keep white and soft, and will not shrink. Never wash flannels on a stormy day, and never let them freeze. The washing fluids that contain turpentine, alcohol, ammonia, camphor gum, etc., ought never to be used, since they tend to open the pores of the skin, thus making the person more liable to take cold. Instead of these it is better to use borax, which not only whitens and cleans the clothes, but softens the water.

PROF. LIEBIG'S WASHING FLUID.

The very best known, as it saves in time, labor, clothes and soap. One pound sal-soda, one-half pound stone lime, five quarts soft water; boil a short time in copper or brass kettle, stirring occasionally, let settle and pour off the clear fluid into a stone jug and cork for use; soak white clothes over night in simple water, wring out and soap wristbands, collars and dirty or stained places; have boiler half filled with water, and when at scalding heat, put in one common teacup of fluid, stir and put in clothes, and boil half an hour, rub lightly through one suds only, rinsing well in the bluing water as usual, and all is complete. Instead of soaking clothes over night, they may soak in suds for a few hours before beginning washing. For each additional boiler of clothes add half a cup only of the fluid, of course, boiling in the same water through the whole washing. If more water is needed in the boiler for the last clothes dip it from the sudsing tub. This fluid brightens instead of fading the colors in calico, and is good for colored flannels. It does not rot clothes, but they must not lie long in the water; the boiling, sudsing, rinsing and bluing must follow each other in rapid succession, until clothes are hung on the line, which should be by ten o'clock in the morning.

SOAP FOR FAMILY USE.

Much of the toilet and laundry soaps in the market are adulterated with injurious, and, to some persons, poisonous substances, by which diseases of the skin are occasioned or greatly aggravated, and great suffering results, which is rarely traced to the real cause. The fat tried from animals which have died of disease, if not thoroughly saponified, is poisonous, and sometimes produces death. If in making soap the mass is heated to too high a degree, a film of soap forms around the particles of fat; if at this stage resin, salsoda, silicate and other adulterations are added, the fat is not saponified, but filmed, and if poisonous or diseased it so remains, and is dangerous to use. A bar of such soap has an oily feeling, and is unfit for use. If it feels sticky, it has too much resin in it. The slippery feeling which belongs to soap properly made cannot be mistaken. Another test of pure soft or hard soap is its translucent or semi-transparent appearance. Soft soap that is cloudy is not thoroughly saponified, or else has been made of dirty or impure grease. It is not only safer but more economical to buy pure soap, as the adulterations increase the quantity without adding to the erasive power. Some of the brown soaps sold in market are seventy-five per cent. resin, and the buyer gets only twenty-five per cent. of what he wants for his money. Fifteen per cent. of resin improves the quality, but any excess damages it, and is worse than useless. Almost every family may make excellent soft soap with very little expense by saving grease, and using lye from hard wood ashes or pure potash. Never use concentrated lye. Melt the grease and boil with the lye if possible; if not, put cold lye into cask, melt the grease and pour into the lye. Twenty-five pounds of grease will make a thirty-two gallon cask of soap. Stir thoroughly occasionally for a day or two. If the lye is too weak or too strong, it will not cut the grease; if too strong, add water, if too weak, add lye. To test, take out some in a dipper and experiment with it. The lye should bear up an egg so that only a part as large as a ten cent piece is exposed. The soap when done should be almost transparent and free from any cloudy appearance. It will not pay any family to make hard soap, but great care should be taken to get only that which is perfectly pure. "Dobbin's Eclectic" is the only pure brand I know of that is widely sold.—*I. F. Fletcher, Minneapolis, Minn.*

BLUING.

Take one ounce of Prussian blue, one-half ounce of oxalic acid, dissolve in one quart of perfectly soft rain water; insert a quill through the cork of bluing bottle to prevent waste, or putting too much in clothes, and you will be pleased with the result. One or two tablespoons of it is sufficient for a tub of water, according to the size of tub. Chinese blue is the best and costs twelve and a half cents an ounce, the acid will cost three cents. This amount will last a medium sized family one year.

FLOUR STARCH.

Have kettle or pan on stove with one quart boiling water, into which stir three heaping tablespoons flour, previously mixed smooth in a little cold water; stir steadily until it boils, and then often enough to keep from burning. Boil about five minutes, strain while hot through a crash towel. The above quantity is enough for one dress, and will make it nice and stiff. Flour starch is considered better for all calicoes than fine starch, since it makes them stiffer, and the stiffness is longer retained.

TO MAKE FINE STARCH.

Wet the starch smooth in a little cold water, in a large tin pan, pour on a quart boiling water to two or three tablespoons starch, stirring rapidly all the while; place on stove, stir until it boils, and then occasionally; boil from five to fifteen minutes, or until the starch is perfectly clear. Some add a little salt, or butter or pure lard, or stir with a sperm candle; others add a teaspoon kerosene to one quart starch; this prevents that stickiness sometimes so annoying in ironing. Either of the above ingredients is an improvement to flour starch. Many, just before using starch, add a little bluing. Cold starch is made from starch dissolved in cold water, being careful not to have it too thick; since it rots the clothes, it is not advisable to use it—the same is true of potato starch.

ENAMEL FOR SHIRT BOSOMS.

Melt together with a gentle heat, one ounce white wax, and two ounces spermaceti; prepare in the usual way a sufficient quantity of starch for a dozen bosoms, put into it a piece of this enamel the size of a hazel nut, and in proportion for a larger ironing. This will give your clothes a beautiful polish.

HOW TO DO UP SHIRT BOSOMS.

Take two tablespoons best starch, add a very little water to it, rub and stir with a spoon into a thick paste, carefully breaking all the lumps and particles. Add a pint of boiling water, stirring at the same time; boil half an hour stirring occasionally to keep it from burning. Add a piece of starch polish the size of a large pea; if this is not at hand use a tablespoon of gum arabic solution (made by pouring boiling water upon gum arabic and standing until clear and transparent), or a piece of clean mutton tallow half the size of a nutmeg and a teaspoon of salt will do, but is not as good. Strain the starch through a strainer or a piece of thin muslin. Have the shirts turned wrong side out; dip the bosoms carefully in the starch and squeeze out, repeating the operation until the bosoms are thoroughly and evenly saturated with starch; proceed to dry. Three hours before ironing dip the bosoms in clean water; wring out and roll up tightly. First iron the back by folding it lengthwise through the centre; next iron the wristbands, and both sides of the sleeves; then the collar band; now place the bosom-board under the bosom, and with a dampened napkin rub the bosom from the top towards the bottom, smoothing and arranging each plait neatly. With a smooth, moderately hot flat-iron, begin at the top and iron downwards, and continue the operation until the bosom is perfectly dry and shining. Remove the bosom-board, and iron the front of the shirt. If the irons become rough or smoky lay a little fine salt on a flat surface and rub them well; it will prevent them from sticking to anything starched, and make them smooth; or scour with bath-brick before heating, and when hot rub well with salt, and then with a small piece of beeswax tied up in a rag, after which wipe clean on a dry cloth.

TO WASH FLANNELS.

Make a strong suds of boiling water and soft soap—hard soap makes flannels stiff and wiry—put them in, pressing them down under the water with a clothes stick; when cool enough rub the articles carefully between the hands, then wring—but not through the wringer—as dry as possible, shake, snap out, and pull each piece into its original size and shape, then throw immediately into another tub of boiling water, in which you have thoroughly mixed some nice bluing. Shake them up and down in this last water with a clothes stick until cool enough for the hands, then rinse well, wring, shake out and pull into shape—the snapping and pulling are as necessary as the washing—and hang in a sunny place where they will dry quickly. Many prefer to rinse in two waters with the bluing in the last, and this is always advisable when there are many flannels.

HOW TO WASH BLANKETS.

All that is necessary is abundance of soft water, and soap without resin in it. Resin hardens the fibres of wool, and should never be used in washing any kind of flannel goods. Blankets treated as above will always come out clean and soft. A little bluing may be used in washing white blankets.— *North Star Woolen Mill, Minneapolis, Minn.*

Blankets should be shaken and snapped until almost dry; it will require two persons to handle them. Woolen shawls, and all woolen articles, especially men's wear, are much improved by being pressed with a hot iron under damp muslin.

TO WASH LACE CURTAINS.

Shake the dust well out of the lace, put in tepid water, in which a little soda has been dissolved, and wash at once carefully with the hands in several waters, or until perfectly clean; rinse in water well blued, also blue the boiled starch quite deeply and squeeze, but do not wring. Pin some sheets down to the carpet in a vacant airy room, then pin on the curtains stretched to exactly the size they were before being wet. In a few hours they will be dry and ready to put up. The whole process of washing and pinning down should occupy as little time as possible, as lace will shrink more than any other cotton goods when long wet. Above all it should not be allowed to "soak" from the mistaken idea that it washes more easily, nor should it ever be ironed. Every housekeeper should have a pair of frames, made very like the old fashioned quilting frames, thickly studded along the inside with the smallest size of galvanized tenter hooks, in which to fasten the lace, and having holes and wooden pins with which to vary the length and breadth to suit the different sizes of curtains. The curtains should always be measured before being wet, and stretched in the frames to that size to prevent shrinking. Five or six curtains of the same size may be put in, one above the other, and all dried at once. The frames may rest on four chairs.

TO WASH THREAD LACE.

Cover a bottle with white flannel, baste the lace carefully on the flannel and rub with white soap; place the bottle in a jar filled with warm suds, let remain two or three days, changing the water several times, and boil with the finest white clothes on washing day; when cooled a little, rinse several times in plenty of cold water, wrap a soft dry towel around it and place in the sun; when dry, unwind, but do not starch.

TO WASH A SILK DRESS.

To wash a silk dress with gall soap, rip apart and shake off the dust, have ready two tubs warm soft water, make a suds of the soap in one tub, and use the other for rinsing, wash the silk, one piece at a time, in the suds, wring gently, rinse, again wring, shake out, and iron with a hot iron on what you intend to be the wrong side. Thus proceed with each piece, and when about half done throw out the suds and make suds of the rinsing water, using fresh water for rinsing.

GALL SOAP.

For washing woolens, silks, or fine prints liable to fade: One pint of gall, two pounds common bar soap cut fine, and one quart boiling soft water; boil slowly, stirring occasionally until well mixed; pour into a flat vessel, and when cold cut into pieces to dry.

TO PREVENT BLUE FROM FADING.

To prevent blue from fading, put an ounce of sugar of lead into a pail of water, soak the material in the solution for two hours, and let dry before being washed and ironed; good for all shades of blue.

TO BLEACH MUSLIN.

For thirty yards of muslin, take one pound of chloride of lime, dissolve in two quarts rain water; let cloth soak over night in warm rain water, or long enough to be thoroughly wet; wring out cloth and put it in another tub of warm rain water in which the chloride of lime solution has been poured. Let it remain for about twenty minutes, lifting up the cloth and airing it every few moments, and rinse in clear rain water. This will not injure the cloth in the least, and is much less trouble than bleaching on the grass.

Or, scald in suds and lay them on the clean grass all night, or if this cannot be done, bring in and place in a tub of clean soft water. In the morning scald again and put out as before. It will take from one or two weeks to bleach white. May be bleached in winter by placing on the snow. May is the best month for bleaching. To whiten yellow linens or muslins, soak over night or longer in buttermilk, rinse thoroughly and wash the same as other clothes. This will also answer for light calicoes, percales, lawns, etc., that will not fade. Some use sour milk when not able to procure buttermilk. To whiten yellow laces, old collars, etc., put in glass bottle or jar in a strong suds, let stand in sun for several days, shaking occasionally.

BROWN LINEN

May be kept looking new until worn out if always washed in starch water and hay tea. Make flour starch in the ordinary way. For one dress put on the stove a common sized milk pan full of timothy hay, pour on water, cover, and boil until the water is of a dark green color; then turn into the starch, let the goods soak in it a few minutes, and wash without soap; the starch will clean the fabric, and no rinsing is necessary.

TO CLEANSE ARTICLES MADE OF WHITE ZEPHYR.

Rub in flour, changing it as often as it looks soiled. Shake the flour from it and hang in the open air a short time.—*Mrs. A. S. C.*

FLORAL.

MY MORNING GLORIES.

Doubtless we all have a great respect for our mother Eve, whom a well known author, in utter defiance of Blair or Murray, has called the "fairest of all her daughters," but it may be we have felt at times that but for her early experiments in pomology, our lives would have been very different from what they are, and that cooks and cook books would have been unnecessary; that we should have roamed, at our own sweet will, among lovely flowers and odorous shrubs, satisfying our hunger with fruits, fresh and perfect, right from God's own hand, never suffering pain or sorrow, reposing when weary on soft couches of moss and fragrant flowers, lulled to slumber by the sweet songs of birds and the soft rustling of leaves above our heads, and awakening refreshed to new pleasures and enjoyments in this blissful Arcadian life, which would have gone on forever. And this train of thought came into my mind this morning from seeing a lovely morning glory vine adorning the plain fence which surrounds my garden, glorifying it with its bewitching grace and brilliant color, illuminating the whole landscape, giving sweet thoughts to the working man as he goes forth to his toil, lighting up with pleasure the faces of the little children as they pass along to school, and warming and brightening wonderfully the heart of the careworn anxious mother with recollections of her merry girlhood time, when *her* precious mother took the responsibilities of housekeeping, and she sang merrily as she trained the vines and arranged the vases and bouquets to make the dear home bright and beautiful. And as I admire the freshness of the new-made blossoms, I wonder if Eve had anything in Eden more lovely and delicate, and if she, surrounded by a wealth and luxuriance of flowers, with Adam to dress and train them for her, appreciated them as much, or looked upon them as lovingly as we do our floral beauties, for which we labor and toil. I can hardly believe she did, and thinking it all over, it seems to me that it is our duty and should make a large part of our enjoyment to cultivate these beautiful vines which grow so readily and reward us so well, in greater profusion so that all who pass by them on their way to daily toil, may inhale large draughts of pleasure from their coronets of many colored blossoms, arrayed in such wondrous beauty as far surpasses Solomon in all his glory, and may be led by their silent unintrusive teachings to thank God for His beautiful gifts, and to love Him sincerely for strewing the rough paths of life with such perfect unsullied loveliness.—*Mrs. Gen. Van Cleve, Minneapolis, Minn.*

HOUSE PLANTS.

Plants that require a high or low temperature, or a very moist atmosphere, and plants that bloom only in summer are undesirable. Procure fresh sandy loam, with an equal mixture of well rotted turf, leaf mold and cow yard manure, with a small quantity of soot. In repotting use one size larger than they were grown in; hard burned or glazed pots prevent the circulation of air. Secure drainage by broken crockery and pebbles laid in the bottom of the pot. An abundance of light is important, and when this cannot be given, it is useless to attempt the culture of flowering plants. If possible they should have the morning sun, as one hour of sunshine then is worth two in the afternoon. Fresh air is also essential but cold chilling draughts should be avoided. Water from one to three times a week with soft lukewarm water, draining off all not absorbed by the earth. Do not permit water to stand in the saucers, as the only plants thriving under such treatment are calla lilies, and even for these it is not necessary unless while blooming. Dust is a great obstacle to the growth of plants; a good showering will generally remove it, but all the smooth leaved plants such as camellias, ivies, etc., should be occasionally sponged to keep the foliage clean and healthy. Plants succeed best in an even temperature ranging from sixty to seventy degrees during the day, with from ten to twelve degrees lower at night. If troubled with insects put them under a box or barrel and smoke from thirty to sixty minutes with tobacco leaves. For the red spider, the best remedy is to lay the plants on the side and sprinkle well or shower. Repeat if necessary. The soil should be frequently stirred to prevent caking. If manures are used give in a liquid form. Some of the most suitable plants for parlor culture are pelargoniums, geraniums, fuchisas, palms, begonias, monthly roses, camellias, azaleas, oranges, lemons, Chinese and English primroses, abutilons, narcissus, heliotrope, stevias, bouvardias, petunias and the gorgeous flowering plant *poinsettia pulcherrima*. Camellias and azaleas require a cooler temperature than most plants, and the *poinsettia* a higher temperature. Do not sprinkle the foliage of the camellias while the flower buds are swelling, as it will cause them to droop, nor sprinkle them in the sunshine. They should have a temperature of about forty degrees and more shade. By following these rules, healthy flowering plants will be the result.—*J. S. R.*

IF HOUSE PLANTS

Are watered once a week with water in which are mixed a few drops of ammonia, they will thrive much better. Sometimes small white worms are found in the earth; lime water will kill them. Stir up the soil before pouring it on to expose as many as possible. For running vines burn beef-bones, pulverize and mix with the earth.

TO KEEP PLANTS WITHOUT A FIRE AT NIGHT,

Have made of wood or zinc, a tray about four inches deep, with a handle on either end, water tight—paint it outside and in, put in each corner a post as high as the tallest of your plants; and it is ready for use. Arrange your flower pots in it, and fill between them with sawdust; this absorbs the moisture falling from the plants when you water them, and retains the warmth acquired during the day, keeping the temperature of the roots even. When you retire at night spread over the posts a blanket or shawl, and there is no danger of freezing. The tray may be placed on a stand or table and easily moved about.

WINDOW GARDENING.

All the varieties of English ivy, the hoya carnosa, the passion flower, the jasmine, the pilogyne suavis, and begonias are especially suitable for window culture. Very pretty effects may be produced at the cost of a few cents, by planting verbenas, morning glories, cobea scandens, and the maurandias in baskets or flower-pots, which may be concealed behind statuary or bronzes. The best fertilizer for them or any other house plants is that afforded by the tea pot; the cold teagrounds usually thrown away, if poured as a libation to these household fairies, will produce a miracle of beauty and perfume.

SURE SHOT FOR ROSE SLUGS.

Make a tea of tobacco stems and a soap-suds of whale oil or carbolic soap, mix and apply to the bush with a sprinkler, turning the bush so as to wet the under as well as the upper part of the leaves; apply before the sun is up three or four times.

ANOTHER.

About the first of June, small worms make their appearance on the rose bushes, and in a very few days eat every leaf on them; to destroy these pests take four gallons water, add one tablespoon paris green, stir thoroughly and apply to the bushes with a garden syringe or watering pot, early in the morning; keep the water well stirred or shaken while applying, or the last in the pot will be too strong and kill the leaves of the bushes.— *Mr. C. Phellis, Sr.*

TO PREPARE AUTUMN LEAVES AND FERNS.

Immediately after gathering, take a moderately warm iron, smear it well with white wax, rub over each surface of the leaf once, apply more wax for each leaf; this process causes leaves to roll about as when hanging on the tree. If pressed more they become brittle and remain perfectly flat. Maple and oak are among the most desirable, and may be gathered any time after the severe frosts; but the sumac and ivy must be secured as soon after the first slight frost as they become tinted, or the leaflets will fall from the stem. Ferns may be selected any time during the season. A large book must be used in gathering them, as they will be spoiled for pressing if carried in the hand. A weight should be placed on them until they are perfectly dry; then, excepting the most delicate ones, it will be well to press them like the leaves, as they are liable to curl when placed in a warm atmosphere; these will form beautiful combinations with the sumac and ivy.

TO PREPARE SKELETON LEAVES.

When properly prepared, skeleton leaves form a companion to the scrap book or collection of pressed ferns, fronds, etc. This is a tedious operation, and requires skill and great patience to obtain satisfactory results. Some leaves are easier to dissect and make better specimens than others, and as a rule a hard thin leaf should be chosen; that is, when a special variety is not required. Among those which are skeletonized most successfully, are the English ivy, box elder, willow, grape, pear, rose, etc. They should be gathered during the month of June, or as soon as the leaf is fully developed. The leaves should be immersed in a vessel of rain water and allowed to remain till decomposed; when this takes place, press the leaf between pieces of soft flannel and the film will adhere to the flannel, leaving a perfect net work; dry off gradually and clean the specimen with a soft hair pencil, place between folds of soft blotting paper, and when perfectly dry, place in your collection. To bleach the leaves, dissolve one-half pound chloride of lime into three pints of rain water, strain and use one part of solution to one of water. For ferns use the solution full strength. When perfectly white remove to clear water, let stand for several hours, changing water two or three times, float out on paper and press between blotting paper in books. In mounting use mucilage made of five parts gum arabic, three parts white sugar, two parts starch; add very little water, boil and stir till thick and white.

DRYING FLOWERS.

Take clean sand, wash in several waters, dry thoroughly in the stove, weigh and to every twelve pounds take one ounce of stearine scraped fine, heat sand over a fire and scatter stearine over it, stir constantly until sand is thoroughly coated; take a box six inches deep, ten inches wide, and fifteen inches long; bore a half dozen half-inch holes in bottom, paste strong paper over them, sift a layer of sand a quarter of an inch deep into box, lay as many flowers and leaves on sand as you can, sift upon them another layer of sand, knocking the sides of the box gently until every little space between and under the flowers is well filled, put in another layer of flowers, and so on until box is full; put on lid securely, place box under or near the stove or where it will be constantly warm, and they will be done in four days, if only exposed to the sun it will take longer. To remove flowers, cut through the bits of paper at the bottom and let the sand run out, place open box in a cool, moist cellar for a few hours, and then take out the flowers. If these directions are followed carefully the natural color of the flowers will be preserved, and if protected from dust and the sun, will keep for a long time.

TO CRYSTALIZE GRASSES.

Dissolve two pounds of alum in one quart of boiling water, and let cool nearly down to blood heat; pour over the grasses which have previously been suspended over a basin or jar; let stand in the shade twenty-four hours.

TO MAKE A RUSTIC FLOWER STAND.

Take a stump up by the roots, turn it upside down, put firmly in the ground and sow flower seeds in it. The rustic sticks used by nurserymen for hanging baskets, urns, etc., are the knotted roots of the bush known as greenbrier, common in the woods in northern Ohio.

TO PROTECT DAHLIAS FROM EARWIGS.

Soak a piece of raw cotton in kerosene and slightly tie it round the stem and stakes, if any, about a foot from the ground; as the oil dries apply more.

TO CLEAR ROSE TREES FROM BLIGHT (GREEN FLY).

Take sulphur and tobacco dust in equal quantities and strew over the trees early in the morning when the dew is on them. When the insects disappear syringe the trees with a decoction of elder leaves.

TO FREE BEDDING PLANTS FROM LEAF LICE.

Mix an ounce of flour of sulphur with one bushel of sawdust; scatter this over the plants and the insects will soon disappear, though a second application may possibly be necessary.

AN EXCELLENT SHADING FOR A GREENHOUSE.

Mix one pound of salt with ten pounds of unslacked lime, cover with boiling water, stirring briskly; when cold, thin with buttermilk to the consistency of paint, and apply with a common whitewash brush on the outside of the glass.

FARM AND GARDEN.

APPLES.

This kind of fruit may be grown on almost any farm or lot by judicious selection of varieties and proper culture and training. A sloping hillside contiguous to a well defined valley, forms the choicest orchard site, not only for the apple, but also for pears and all other fruits. In any case secure good surface drainage, and if the soil is heavy and tenacious it should be underdrained. Low situations and heavy soil should be avoided. Cold air settles in the valleys, forcing the heated air upon the more elevated portions, so that frosts are more frequent and severe on low ground. In planting an orchard get good strong healthy trees of three or four years' growth. As to varieties, those which do well in one locality are not certain to thrive in another, and it is always best to ascertain what sorts have been tested and approved in the neighborhood. Hardy and productive kinds of second quality are more satisfactory than fruits of greater excellence which lack in these qualities. For the commercial orchard, where a large quantity of fruit is to be produced for market, it is best to plant only a few varieties, and these should be productive, hardy, of the "iron clad" class, and of such a character as to bear transportation and to command a ready market. In planting, let the soil be in the condition, and prepared in the manner as for good crop of potatoes or other hoed crop. A hole should be dug only large enough to admit the roots in a natural position, and at a depth not greater than they had in the nursery. The earth to fill in about the roots should be well pulverized, that it may be worked thoroughly in with the hands; when nearly filled up, enough water should be poured in to settle the earth firmly about the roots. When the water has sunk away, fill up immediately to prevent baking. This system obviates the necessity of tramping in trees with the feet, a vicious practice. When planted in the fall, a mound of six or eight inches high should be thrown up about the tree to secure it against frost and surplus water. In the spring the mound should be removed. No manure should be placed in contact with the roots of a tree in planting, especially an evergreen. Newly planted trees are much benefitted by mulching, if they do not have careful cultivation.

THE CHERRY.

Soils naturally adapted to the chestnut appear to be the most suitable for cherries. They should receive no stimulating manures, and but little culture, as a luxuriant growth causes the bark to burst, injuring the tree. The best results have been secured from trees grown in grass with a moderate, sound, healthy growth. Some hardy varieties seem to do equally well on clay or sand, hill or valley, timber or prairie. These are called the Dukes and the Morellos. The most valuable is the large Montmorency, Early Richmond and May Duke. Cherries may be planted from twelve to twenty feet apart and not deeper than they were in the nursery. Trees two or three years from bud are old enough. They should be headed back and grown in their natural, conical form. Prune while young, as stone fruits do not readily heal over the stump of a large limb.

PEARS.

At least a few pear trees should be planted in every orchard. The crop is certain and any surplus may be readily and profitably disposed of. The force of the old saying "planting pears for one's heirs" has been lost by the advance of pomology, for many varieties now in cultivation are early and productive bearers, and we have the means of forcing early fruitage upon varieties that formerly wore out the patience of the orchardist before they reached the bearing stage. The pear will grow in a variety of soils, but attains the greatest perfection in a strong, clayey loam. Even heavy tenacious clay soil, well underdrained, is adapted to it. Light, sandy or gravelly soil is unsuitable. The three points essential to security from blight and the successful growing of pears, are, 1st. Sound, healthy trees, three years from bud; 2d. Ground with a predominance of clay, sufficiently rolling to secure perfect surface drainage; 3d. Thorough underdrainage; with these give only a moderate degree of cultivation early in the season, as a late growth is an invitation to the attack of disease. Fifteen or twenty feet is wide enough apart for most sorts, and many will succeed if planted much closer. The trees should be trained in a conical, or pyramidal form, by causing them to branch low, by curbing, thinning out and shortening the upper limbs so as to keep the lower branches always the longest. If blight appears, or there is a failure of crop, it means that the soil is exhausted and needs to be supplied with pear tree food. This must be supplied artificially, and chemical analysis shows what ingredients are needed, and that wood ashes, crushed and uncrushed bones, and common salt, furnish the necessary potash, lime, phosphate of lime and soda needed by the exhausted soil. In applying these and all other fertilizers, the golden rule is moderation; too much may prove fatal. This is particularly true of alkalies. In all cases rich, unfermented stable manure is to be avoided. Trees of a moderately vigorous growth, perfectly matured before winter, are so seldom blighted as to be for all practical purposes exempt. A safe practice is to cover the body and all the principal branches of the tree with a wash made by placing a peck of lime and two pounds of sulphur in a vessel and adding sufficient boiling water to slack the lime. An ounce of carbolic acid may be added. Where the trees have attained size the sulphur may be applied by boring a hole with a three-quarter auger in the trunk of the tree, inserting a tablespoon of the mixture and plugging.

THE QUINCE.

Is hardy, compact in growth, and requires but little space, and with proper attention is very productive. It flourishes in any good garden soil, but prefers moist situations. If set in clumps in a lawn and kindly cared for it is highly ornamental. No fruit pays better for attention and manuring. Coal and wood ashes and the refuse suds of the washing are very beneficial, and salt is one of its best fertilizers. Apply about one quart to the ground under each tree early in the spring and another quart when the quinces are half grown.

TO RAISE PLANTS OF CURRANTS AND GOOSEBERRIES.

As soon as the leaf drops in autumn, trim out the new growth into cuttings four to six inches long; open a trench with one side perpendicular and set the cuttings along the perpendicular side, having the top bud come about even with the surface; pack the soil against them firmly. Cover just as winter sets in with a deep mulch of some coarse material to prevent hard freezing and "heaving;" remove mulch in the spring and keep the ground mellow.

To prevent mildew on gooseberry bushes, sprinkle the bushes with a weak solution of saleratus well mixed with alum.

THE RASPBERRY.

Flourishes in almost any soil, and will thrive in neglected fence corners, but a good loam, well cultivated, gives the best results. It bears liberal manuring, and should be planted in fall or early spring, three feet apart in rows from six to nine feet wide, or for garden planting much closer.

Summer pruning is now practiced by all good cultivators, which consists in pinching or cutting off the shoots as soon as they are two feet high, which causes them to branch out with strong laterals; these are cut back according to their strength in the winter. In autumn or winter the old cones and the weak new ones should be cut away and only the strong and healthy left for the next crop. Trained thus no support is needed. Leaf and woods mold, crushed sugar cane stalks, straw, grass, chips, ashes and rotted tanbark are all good mulching material, and placed close around the roots insure big crops.—*J. S. Robinson.*

REMEDY FOR THE PLUM CURCULIO.

Prepare a muslin spread large enough to cover the ground under the tree as far out as the branches extend; give the tree a vigorous shake or two, and the insects will drop off upon the sheet, and may be readily gathered up and dispatched. In the few first hot days of spring the insect begins its work of destruction in earnest and the process of shaking should then begin and be carried on vigorously morning, noon and evening, and kept up as long as any curculios are found, seldom over a period of twenty-five days, unless the season is cool and backward. Of course there will be a stray insect now and then till the plum changes color for ripening, but the damage will be slight. The writer has tried many remedies but all have failed miserably except this, which has repeatedly saved his crop of plums when all other trees in the neighborhood have failed.—*J. H. Shearer.*

TO PREVENT RABBITS FROM EATING THE BARK OF YOUNG FRUIT TREES.

Saturate a woolen cloth well with common soft soap and rub the trees two or three times each winter. It not only protects them from rabbits, but is excellent for the tree, making the bark smooth and healthy.

PROTECTING CABBAGE FROM WORMS.

Mix wheat bran and buckwheat flour together and sprinkle dry over cabbage. It does not matter about quantity.—*Miss Abbie Phellis Baker.*

TO RAISE CELERY.

Make the ground as rich as possible with old well rotted pulverized manure, set the plants in rows six inches apart with twelve inches space between rows, without trenching. As the plants grow and require handling, earth them up by filling dirt in between the rows. Make rows about twenty feet long, and after filling in between the first two, lay a board on the dirt so filled in, and run the wheelbarrow on it to fill in the next space, and so on till all are filled. By this process six times the amount of celery may be raised on a given space of ground, and with much less labor than by trenching. By this plan you have the rich warm surface soil for the plants to grow in; the heavy rains do not wash the dirt in and swamp the young plants, and you economize space. Great care should be taken not to let the dirt sprinkle in between the stalks of the plants as you fill between the rows. After filling in the dirt, hold the stalks firmly together with one hand and press the dirt around them with the other; twice or three times filling up will do; and two wagon loads of dark rich dirt is enough to earth up six hundred plants.—*Major W. D. Hall, Minneapolis, Minn.*

HOW TO RAISE INDIAN CORN.

Plow as early in the spring as the season will permit with three horses abreast, seven or eight inches deep; harrow and roll until the ground is thoroughly pulverized; plant from the first to the fifteenth of May, with Dickey drill, three or four inches deep in rows three and one-half feet apart. As soon as the corn begins coming up, harrow again with a light harrow thoroughly, giving no attention to rows. When the plants are about three or four inches high, plow with a walking or double-shovel plow, with shovels about two inches wide, close to the corn—the closer the better—and quite deep. For the rest of the culture use common sized shovels, and plow about every eight days until the corn is about three and a half or four feet high.—*Mr. C. Phellis, Sr., Darby Plains.*

REMEDY FOR SMUT IN WHEAT.

Soak the seed wheat in brine and then dust it with unslacked lime. This is a sure preventive.

THE HORSE.

The secret of breaking and managing a horse is contained in the Good Book: "He that hath mercy on his beast, hath mercy on himself." Study the disposition of the animal, remembering that the horse is an intelligent creature, and will study yours. He forms strong attachments, accommodates himself so far as his nature will permit, to the disposition and habits of his master. The horse, like the man, must be curbed in the start, and this stage of breaking is the most important and perilous. To gain the confidence of the untutored colt is the first thing. To do this take an ear of corn in your hand, walk around and around him, coming closer and closer, until he can reach and nibble the corn, do not grab at him or attempt to do anything but caress him. Next time take a halter with you, and slip over his head, coaxing him with the corn and taking care not to pull, letting go rather than to force him. Next put a surcingle about his body, fasten a strap to his off fore foot, double up the near foreleg and strap it up; draw the strap which is fastened to the other foot through the surcingle over the back on the off side, cause the colt to step, and draw this also up to the body, push him over, and five minutes of struggling while you remain cool and quiet, petting, but not striking him, will teach him his first lesson that man is stronger than he. Harness him with a steady horse without hitching to any load, drive him for ten minutes, and turn him out again, be quiet, gentle, cautious and firm, and you will succeed. No colt should be considered broken, until he will hold back a buggy without breeching, while it is crowding up on his hind legs. The most perilous accident that can occur in driving is the breaking of the harness in going down hill, and with a little care a colt may be broken so that the sudden pushing of the vehicle upon him will not frighten him. Begin by pushing it gently upon him while standing until he gets accustomed to the sensation, then make him back the vehicle, until he does it without timidity, and finally push it against him with force. Remember that a horse needs to learn a lesson but once and he never forgets it. Balky horses are made, as a rule, by balky men, who impose heavy burdens on colts before they know how to draw.—*J. W. Starr.*

GOOD FEED FOR HORSES.

A new and favorite kind of mash for horses is just coming into use, composed of two quarts of oats, one of bran, and half pint of flax seed. The oats are first placed in a bucket over which is placed the flax seed and boiling water, then the bran; cover the bucket with a rug, and let sweat, stir well, feed once a day.—*J. W. Starr.*

FOR COLIC IN HORSES.

Give salt freely. For wounds on horses, use carbolic acid and glycerine in proportion of one to twenty. For botts in horses, turn the horse on his back, give one pint flax seed oil and keep him on his back a few minutes. Loss of appetite in horses.—Two quarts of sour apples is the best medicine to improve the appetite of a horse.

CURE FOR BLOAT IN CALVES.

When a calf that is being raised by hand is overfed and becomes bloated, give it, if two months old, a tablespoon of good tar, if three months old, a half teacupful. This is also good for bloat in horses. If cows give bloody milk, polk root sliced or grated and mixed with bran will cure.

CHOKED CATTLE.

May sometimes be quickly relieved by throwing a quantity of snuff up the nostrils; the coughing that follows usually throws out the obstruction. Driving the cattle rapidly often has the same effect.

LICE ON CATTLE.

May be removed by rubbing plentifully the neck, back and other parts where the lice are found with lard oil, or other soft grease.

HOG CHOLERA.

If the hog is not too far gone the following will cure in every instance: Mix equal parts of finely powdered ginger and allspice with any kind of ground feed, giving two or three tablespoons three times a day to a full grown hog. There is no danger of giving too much. Wood ashes thrown around and in the pen is a good preventive.

TO KILL TICKS ON SHEEP.

Fill a dredging-box with scotch snuff, and when sheep are sheared, sift it plentifully along the back-bone and wherever there seem to be ticks give them a good supply. This is also good for lice on cattle, etc.

TO CURE GRUB IN SHEEP.

Mix one quart of whisky and two ounces of yellow snuff, heat to a blood-heat and inject into each nostril. To cure stretches in sheep. Make a tea of red pepper, and give two doses a day.

TO CURE FOOT-ROT IN SHEEP.

As soon as sheep become lame, pass them through a trough containing a warm solution made of four ounces of arsenic, four ounces of potash in one gallon of water; boil till dissolved. Keep it about three inches deep so as to cover the feet as the sheep walk through. The trough should be about twenty feet long and just wide enough to admit of one sheep walking after another. This will cure in every instance and a thousand may be run through in one hour.

CHICKEN CHOLERA.

Dissolve in one gallon of water a piece of alum size of a walnut, shut chickens up and set this alum water before them and leave no other water in their reach.—*A. Houghton Morey.*

CHICKEN CHOLERA.

Clean the chicken house every spring and wash the perches with coal oil, use copperas dissolved and sprinkled around plentifully as a disinfectant. As soon as any signs of cholera appear, feed the chickens the following: A good teaspoon saleratus or soda to every quart of corn meal mixed with water; give this once every two or three days, and oftener if badly affected. This has been tried where they have had the disease for several successive seasons, and proved effectual.—*Mrs. E. T. Carson.*

GAPES IN CHICKENS.

The way to cure gapes in chickens is to take the worms out of their windpipes. Take a blue-grass stem, strip off the seed, leaving the branches of the head about an inch in length; open the chicken's mouth, insert the stem in the windpipe, turn it softly around between the thumb and finger, then draw it out. If you have the worms out, the chicken is cured; if not, try again. Be particular to twist the stem down, not push, as that might force the worms down and the chicken be choked. Gapes may be prevented as well as cured by mixing asafoetida or red pepper with the food of the chickens.

TO REMOVE LICE ON FOWLS.

Let them dust themselves in sand to which some sulphur has been added, also put sulphur in their drink, and if some of it is burned in a pan (the hen house closely fastened), it will purify the hennery. Place tobacco stems under hens while setting and they will come off their nests clear of lice and remain so all summer.

CHICKEN FEED.

Corn meal not sifted, sour milk and soda (one teaspoon to a quart of milk) mixed together and baked in a pan, then crumbed up and soaked (when it becomes hard) makes most excellent chicken feed.

TO PREVENT CATS KILLING CHICKENS.

When a cat is seen to catch a chicken, tie it around her neck (firmly, for she will do her best to rid herself of it). Be firm for that time, and the cat is cured; she will never again touch a chicken or bird.

MEDICAL.

ANTIDOTES TO POISONS.

The first thing to do is to cause their ejection by vomiting, to do which place mustard mixed with salt on the tongue, or give large quantities of lukewarm water, or tickle the throat with a feather. These failing, instantly resort to active emetics like tartar emetic, sulphate of copper, or sulphate of zinc. After vomiting has taken place with these, continue it if possible by copious draughts of warm water till the poison is entirely removed. Of course, if vomiting cannot be induced, the stomach pump must be employed, especially if arsenic or narcotics have been taken. A brief table formulated as follows may be useful for emergencies.

POISONS.	ANTIDOTES.
Acids.	Alkalies—Soap and milk, chalk, soda, lime-water.
Alkalies.	Vegetable Acids—Vinegar, oil in abundance.
Alcohol.	Common salt, moderately.
Arsenic.	Send for the doctor and his stomach pump.
Antimony.	Oak bark, strong green tea.
Baryta or Lime.	Epsom salts, oils and magnesia.
Bismuth.	Whites of eggs, sweet milk.
Copper.	Whites of eggs, or strong coffee.
Gases.	Cold douche, followed by friction.
Iodine.	Starch, wheat flour in water.
Creosote.	Whites of eggs, sweet milk.
Lead.	Lemonade strong, epsom salt.
Opium and other Narcotics.	Emetics—cold douche, exercise and heat.
Phosphorus.	Magnesia in copious draughts.
Zinc.	Whites of eggs, sweet milk.
Mad Dog Bite.	Apply fire in some form to the wound thoroughly and immediately.
Bite of Insect.	Ammonia applied freely.
Bite of Serpent.	Same as for mad dog, followed by whisky to intoxication.

The foregoing are the more common and more important poisons and their antidotes.—*P. L. Hatch, M. D., Minneapolis, Minn.*

DIPHTHERIA.

For this place it must be presumed that the symptoms of the disease are sufficiently distinct in a given case to be rightly interpreted by nonprofessional persons. At once give of Proto-iodide of Mercurius, third decimal trituration, from half to three grains every one to three hours according to the age of the patient and the severity of the attack, always leaning strongly toward the longer intervals, and never failing to lengthen them with the improvement; use no external applications except dry flannel. At the same time, without regard to the inclinations of the patient, give as often (in severe cases as every two hours) as every three hours, the best beef tea or extract of beef in generous quantities. In this terrible disease, if a choice were to be made between the medicine or the nourishment, by all means retain the latter. The best medication may arrest the local effects of the blood poison but cannot resupply the waste of blood, upon which, after all, recovery depends. Spend no precious time trying other remedies. Leave this to the physician after he assumes the case.—*P. L. Hatch, M. D.*

SCARLET FEVER.

Like small pox, spreads by infection and contagion. The first symptom is generally vomiting; fever soon sets in; the throat is slightly sore; there is headache, thirst, restlessness, and slight delirium at night. These symptoms continue about forty-eight hours, when the rash makes its appearance over the lower part of the neck and upper part of the chest. This rash is of a bright scarlet in healthy persons, having a velvety appearance, but not raised or rough. On the second day of the rash it spreads over the body, and on the third over the limbs. At this period it begins to fade on the chest and body, and about the third day from its appearance on the hands and feet, it disappears altogether. It returns, however, as a light blush for several days, with more or less fever. With the subsidence of the eruption there appears over the body a dandruff-like scurf. This stage is very dangerous, from the fact that the removal of this outer coating renders the patient peculiarly liable to suppression of perspiration on the slightest exposure to cold. Judicious nursing is far more important than medicines, but no case should be without a competent physician. The room should have a uniform temperature day and night of about 68° to 70°; should be well aired, without exposure to drafts. In this room the patient should remain until thoroughly well, unless it be in the summer season. The clothing should be light during the rash, and increased after it until convalescence is established. Give cold drinks very sparingly. When the skin is hot, sponge the body frequently. It is well to bind a piece of fat salt pork on the throat, or put around it a light flannel scarf, rubbing the throat daily and freely with camphorated oil. The diet should consist of light gruels and liquids until the eruption subsides, when it may be solid but still simple. After the early stages are passed, the danger will depend upon the exposure of the new tender surface to cold and the resulting dropsy. The change of an article of clothing, lowering of temperature in the room at night, stepping into a cold room, are but few of the many ways of so chilling the skin as to suppress perspiration and induce dropsy. There are two simple methods of rendering patients less liable to dropsy after scarlet fever. First, rub them over frequently with fatty substances, as lard or oil. Second, frequent warm baths during convalescence. After the bath great care should be taken to remove the refuse water beyond the reach of exposure, or disinfect it.—*By an Eminent Physician.*

CHOLERA MIXTURE.

Take one ounce each of the following ingredients; tincture opium, capsicum or red pepper, rhubarb, peppermint and camphor; put in large bottle, with a pint best brandy. Dose is ten to twenty drops in two or three teaspoons water. Good in any case of diarrhea.—*Mrs. Dr. Thomson.*

PIGS FEET OIL.

Let the liquor in which they have been boiled stand over night; in the morning skim off the fat (will be formed in a cake on top) put in a tin pan, boil until all water is evaporated, bottle and keep for use. No family where there are small children should be without it. A celebrated physician said that a child could not have the croup if pigs feet oil was freely given at the first symptoms.

CURE FOR CORNS.

The worst corn or bunion can be removed by keeping cotton on it saturated with opodeldoc. No pain.

GOOD CROUP REMEDIES.

To one half cup molasses add a teaspoon of saleratus or soda, beat to a white froth, give a spoonful every few minutes. Or take four or five hollyhock blossoms, boil and apply wet around the throat. Or wring a towel out of ice water, and wrap quickly around the throat and on the chest with a dry one or flannels over it.

CONSTIPATION.

Two ounces of senna, simmer the strength out in one quart of water, strain the tea; one pound prunes cooked soft with half teacup white sugar. Several times a day, take first one tablespoon of the senna tea, then eat one prune fasting as much as possible.

SURE CURE FOR CHOLERA INFANTUM.

One ounce pulverized rhubarb, one ounce peppermint herb, one ounce soda. Pour one pint of boiling water on these three and let stand on the hearth two hours. Strain, and add one pint best brandy, one half pound best white sugar, and one ounce paregoric. Dose: one teaspoon every half hour until the discharge shows the color of the medicine; then only every three or four hours. Good also for adults in diarrhea.

BLACKBERRY CORDIAL.

Put a half bushel of blackberries in a preserving kettle and cook until scalded through well; strain and press out all the juice; put juice in kettle with the following spices well broken up and put into a bag: one-quarter pound allspice, two ounces cinnamon bark, two ounces cloves, and two nutmegs; add loaf sugar, about one pound to every quart of juice or more if preferred, and cook slowly ten or fifteen minutes, remove from the fire, let cool a little and add good pure brandy in the proportion of one pint to every three pints of juice. A smaller quantity may be made, using the same proportions. This is an excellent remedy for diarrhea and other diseases of the bowels.

EYE WASH.

Sulphate of zinc two grains, sulphate of morphine one-half grain, distilled water one ounce; mix and bottle. Drop in the eye (a drop or two at once), then wink the eye several times, so that the wash may reach all the parts and keep quiet and do not use the eyes for about an hour. This wash is for bloodshot eyes, and when used it will produce quite a smarting sensation.—*Dr. D. W. Henderson.*

FOR SORE MOUTH IN NURSING BABIES.

A teaspoon each of pulverized alum and borax, half a saltspoon of pulverized nut-galls, a tablespoon of honey; mix and pour on it half a teacup boiling water; let settle and with a clean linen rag wash the mouth four or five times a day, using a fresh piece of linen every day.

GOLDEN OINTMENT.

One pound lard, eight ounces beeswax, one ounce camphor gum in five ounces alcohol, one ounce origanum, one ounce laudanum; let all dissolve while melting the lard and beeswax, then stir together until cold or the camphor will go off in a steam. Do not mix too hot. This will cure pain in the side by applying as a plaster. For enlarged neck or goitre dilute with one-fourth iodine. For salt rheum apply externally and take cathartics to cleanse the blood. For scald head rub together one ounce golden ointment and three drachms of red precipitate, remove the hair and rub with this twice a day, each day washing with castile soap suds. For catarrh, rub the ointment up in the nose profusely, and let it remain all night. In the morning draw cold water up the nose and throw it back two or three times to clean the tubernated bones. Also bathe the face and ears with cold water.

HEALING SALVE.

Pint olive oil, half ounce common resin, half ounce beeswax; melt well together and bring oil to boiling heat; add gradually of pulverized red lead—three eighths of a pound; (for summer use a trifle more lead) in a short time after it is taken up by the oil, and the mixture becomes brown or a shining black, remove from the fire and when nearly cold add two scruples pulverized camphor. It should remain on the fire until it attains a proper consistence for spreading, which may be known by dipping a splint or knife in the mixture from time to time and allowing it to cool. When used spread thinly on a piece of tissue paper or old fine linen. Excellent for frost sores or any kind that are hard to heal.—*Mrs. W. G. March.*

ITCH OINTMENT.

Two tablespoons lard, one of black pepper, one of ground mustard; boil all together and when taken off and nearly cold, add one tablespoon sulphur. Anoint with this three evenings successively just before going to bed.

Do not change bed clothes or wearing clothes during the time. After this wash with castile soap suds, and change all the clothing that has been worn or touched.

SALVE FOR CUTS AND BURNS.

To one half pound of sweet lard, add one fourth pound of beeswax and the same of resin; heat all together till well mixed, pour in a little tin box. Apply to the wound a little on a soft cotton cloth.—*Mrs. Ford.*

LINIMENT.

The common May weed blossoms put in alcohol are much superior to arnica for the same uses.

The white of an egg and salt mixed to a thick paste is one of the best remedies for sprains or bruises or lameness for man or beast. Rub well the parts affected.

SALT RHEUM.

A minister who hates quacks and all patent medicine humbugs, had a child very sick with the above disease for four years. The child's face was covered with the eruption, and the parents could not leave it five minutes night or day for all these weary years. They tried sulphur springs, and not a few physicians of both schools in vain. All such cases can be cured for 25 or 50 cents, by using "Fowler's Solution," a preparation found in all the drug stores. Medicine to be given after eating, at first one drop (carefully measured) after each meal for a week. Then two drops for a week, then three drops for a week, then give none for a week and begin as at first. The best way is to give this remedy under the eye of a physician. Not only was the above child cured, but others have been who are now residing in Marysville. This recipe alone to one afflicted with this disorder is worth the price of twenty books.

TETTER OINTMENT.

Put one ounce nitric acid in a two ounce vial, add one-half ounce quicksilver; let stand until the acid eats up the silver. Take pure sweet lard seven ounces, put in a new earthen dish. Warm the lard until nearly melted, pour all together, acid, quicksilver and lard, and stir until cold when it is fit for use. Wash the parts affected with pure white castile soap and warm water, wipe dry and anoint with the salve twice a day. Avoid using cold water while using the salve. I know this recipe to have cured a bad case of salt rheum in the hands of ten years standing.—*Mrs. M. B. F.*

Catnip tea is good for colic in young children.

Sage tea is excellent for the hair.

Rue tea is good for worms in children.

Pennyroyal tea is most excellent for a cold.

FOR SORE THROAT.

Take five cents' worth chlorate of potassa, dissolve and take teaspoon every hour, and also gargle with it.—*Estelle Woods Wilcox.*

TO PREVENT A CHILD COUGHING AT NIGHT.

Take one cup of powdered white sugar and make into a stiff molasses, add ten cents worth of "Seneka snake root;" dose one teaspoon on retiring.

TO PREVENT TAKING COLD.

If out in cold weather with insufficient clothing or wrappings, fold a newspaper and spread across the chest. Persons having weak lungs can in this way make for themselves a very cheap and perfect lung protector. Large papers spread between quilts at night add much to the warmth.

To cure a felon. On the first appearance, apply a poultice of the common fleur de luce root well mashed. It will cure in a short time.

To stop bleeding at the nose. Bathe the feet in very hot water, drinking at the same time a pint of cayenne pepper tea.—*Miss J. B.*

To stop bleeding. Apply wet tea leaves or scrapings of sole leather to a fresh cut and it will stop the bleeding.

WHOOPING COUGH.

Mix one lemon sliced, half pint flax seed, two ounces honey, and one quart water, and simmer, not boil, four hours; strain when cool, and if there is less than a pint of the mixture, add water. Dose; one tablespoon four times a day, and one also, after each severe fit of coughing. Warranted to cure in four days.

To remove warts. Touch the warts with caustic potassa or liquor potassa.

The operation is not painful, does not discolor the skin and removes the warts in a short time leaving the skin perfectly smooth.

Cure for wounds from rusty nails. Dip fat pork in turpentine and bind it on the wound.

To remove cinder from the eye. Dirt usually lodges under the upper lid; take hold of the lashes firmly, draw out and downward quickly and let go, and the lashes of the underlid will catch and retain the foreign substance, which may then be wiped off.

MISCELLANEOUS.

CANARY BIRDS.

CANARY BIRDS—Do not keep in a room that is being painted or has odor of new paint. Do not hang over a stove or grate which contains fire. Do not set cage in a window, and shut it down upon it; the draft is injurious. Do not wash cage bottom, but scrape clean with a knife, and then put on some fresh gravel; the moisture breeds red mites, and is injurious to the bird. Do not keep the birds you intend to breed in the spring together during the winter. Do not keep single birds in a room where others are breeding, or males and females in mating season in the same room in separate cages, as it is likely to cause pairing fever. Feed canary and rape seed, but no hemp. For diarrhea put a rusty piece of iron in water dish, changing water not oftener than twice a week, and bread boiled in milk as for the asthma; boil it well in this case, so that when cold it will cut like cheese; give freely with plenty of vegetables.

Moulting is not a disease, yet during this period all birds are more or less sick, and some suffer severely. They require plenty of nourishing food. Worms, insects, and fruit to those which eat them; and to those which live upon dry seeds, bread dipped in milk, fruit and vegetables.—*Mrs. Mary Winget.*

TEETH—Many, while attentive to their teeth, do more injury than good by too much officiousness, daily applying some dentrifice tooth powder, often impure and injurious, and rubbing them so hard as not only to injure the enamel by excessive friction, but also to hurt the gums even more than by a toothpick. Tooth powders advertised in newspapers are to be suspected, as some of them are not free from corrosive ingredients. Charcoal, (which whitens the teeth very nicely) pumice stone, cuttle fish, and similar substances, are unfit for use in tooth powders, as all are to a certain extent insoluble in the mouth and are forced between the margin of the gums, forming a nucleus for a deposit. Below will be found a few good formulas for dentrifices:

Creta preparata lb s. ii. j.; powdered borax lb i.; powdered orris root lb i.; cardamom seeds z. i. j.; white sugar lb i.; flavor as you wish, either with wintergreen, rose or jasmine. If color is desired, one pound of rose pink and as much less of creta preparata is used.

The following is a simple and cheap preparation, and is pretty good. Take of prepared chalk and fine old Windsor soap pulverized well, in proportion of about six parts of the former to one of the latter. Soap is a very beneficial ingredient of tooth powder.—*H. W. Morey, D. D. S.*

CUTTING TEETH—The time the first teeth make their appearance varies, but the following dates approximate the time: Central incisors from five to eight months after birth; lateral incisors from seven to ten; first molars from twelve to sixteen; cuspids, or eye teeth from fourteen to twenty; second molars from twenty to thirty-six. The first teeth should be protected from decay as far as possible by careful cleaning daily; if decay makes its appearance, the cavity should be promptly filled, and the tooth saved until displaced by the permanent teeth. About the sixth year the first molars of the permanent teeth make their appearance. They are generally supposed to belong to the first or milk teeth and are frequently lost for want of care. A little more attention given to the first teeth would save parents and children sleepless nights and suffering.—*B. L. Taylor, D. D. S., Minneapolis.*

QUEEN BESS COMPLEXION WASH—Put in a vial one drachm of benzoin gum in powder, one drachm nutmeg oil, six drops of orange blossom tea, or apple blossoms put in half pint rainwater and boiled down to one teaspoonful and strained, one pint of sherry wine. Bathe the face morning and night; will remove all flesh worms and freckles, and give a beautiful complexion. Or, put one ounce powdered gum of benzoin in pint whisky; to use put enough in the water in wash bowl till it is milky.

COLOGNE WATER—One quart alcohol, three drachms oil lavender, one drachm oil rosemary, three drachms oil bergamot, three drachms essence lemon, three drops oil cinnamon.

CLEAN HAIR BRUSHES by pouring on the brush a teaspoon of ammonia, wash thoroughly in cold or tepid water, and expose to sun about two hours. The same process cleans tooth brushes.

BOSTON BERNETT POWDER FOR THE FACE—Five cents worth of bay rum, five cents worth of magnesia snow flake, five cents worth of bergamot, five cents worth of oil of lemon; mix in a pint bottle and fill up with rain water. Perfectly harmless and splendid.—*Emma Collins.*

FOR CHAPPED HANDS, FACE OR LIPS.—Ten drops carbolic acid in one ounce glycerine; apply freely at night.

INDELIBLE INK.—Two drams lunar caustic, six ounces distilled or rain water; dissolve and add two drams gum water. Wet the linen with the following preparation: dissolve one-half ounce prepared natron in four ounces water, add half ounce gum water (recipe below); after smoothing it with a warm iron, write with the ink, using a gold, quill, or a new steel pen. The writing must be exposed to a hot sun for twelve hours, do not wash for one week, then be particular to get out the stain which the preparation will make. If this is followed in every particular there need never be a failure. Gum water for the above is composed of two drams gum arabic to four ounces water. One teaspoon makes two drams, two tablespoons make one ounce. If at any time the ink becomes too pale add a little of pure lunar caustic. Never write without using the preparation, as it will rot the cloth.

MAGIC FURNITURE POLISH—Half pint alcohol, half ounce resin, half ounce gum shellac, a few drops aniline brown; let stand over night and add three fourths pint raw linseed oil and half pint spirits turpentine; shake well before using. Apply with cotton flannel, and rub dry with another cloth.— *O. M. Scott.*

TO CLEAN SILVERWARE EASILY—Save water in which potatoes have been boiled with a little salt, let it become sour, which it will do in a few days; heat and wash the articles with a woolen cloth, rinse in pure water, dry and polish with chamois leather. Never allow a particle of soap to touch silver or plated ware.

TO MAKE RAG RUGS—Cut rags and sew hit and miss, or fancy striped as you choose; use wooden needles, round, smooth and pointed at one end, of any convenient length. The knitting is done back and forth (like old fashioned suspenders), always taking off the first stitch.—*Anna F. Hisey.*

TO DESTROY WEEDS IN WALKS—Boil ten pounds stone lime, five gallons water and one pound flour of sulphur, let settle, pour off clear part and sprinkle freely upon the weedy walks.

TO KEEP AWAY MOTHS—Dust your furs with powdered alum, working it well in at the roots of the hair. Do not air woolen articles and furs in the summer sunshine. They should be put aside in the early spring and left untouched until October.

TO PRESERVE BOOKS—Bindings may be preserved from mildew by brushing them over with spirits of wine. A few drops of any perfumed oil will secure libraries from the consuming effects of mold and damp. Russia leather which is perfumed with the tar of the birch-tree, never molds or sustains injury from damp. The Romans used oil of cedar to preserve valuable manuscripts. Russia leather covered books, placed in a stationers' window will destroy flies and other insects.

BLACK FOR WOOLENS—One ounce vitriol, one ounce extract logwood to two pounds goods; color in iron. Dissolve the extract over night in warm water. Pulverize the vitriol, put it into boiling water sufficient to cover the goods. Wash the goods well, rinse in warm water, then simmer a few minutes in vitriol water. Take out, wash thoroughly in clear water, then dip in boiling logwood dye till the color is good, stirring often and lifting up so it will get the air. Dry, then wash in suds and rinse. In renovating black alpaca that has become rusty, dissolve the logwood only, as nothing is needed to set the color. Wash the goods well in suds, rinse, dip in logwood dye, boil a few minutes, stirring and lifting to air. When dry wash again in suds and rinse in water in which a little gum arabic has been dissolved and press smoothly on the wrong side while damp. Dyed in this way the color will not rub off more than from new goods, and looks as good as new. When extract of logwood is used, it is only needful to boil enough to dissolve before putting in the goods.

UNFERMENTED WINE FOR COMMUNION—Weigh the grapes, pick from the stems, put in a porcelain kettle, add very little water and cook till stones and pulp separate; press and strain through a thick cloth, return juice to kettle, add three pounds sugar to every ten pounds grapes; heat to simmering, bottle hot and seal. This makes one gallon, and is good.

TO PRESS SATIN—All satin goods should be pressed upon the right side. To press and clean black silk, shake out all dust, clean well with a flannel cloth, rubbing it up and down over the silk; this takes out all dust that may be left; take some good lager beer and sponge the silk, both on the wrong and right side, sponging across the width of the silk, and not down the length, and with a moderately warm iron press what is intended for the wrong side. After sponging it is better to wait a few moments before pressing, as the irons will not be so apt to stick.

TO TAKE OUT MILDEW—Wet the cloth and rub on soap and chalk mixed together, and lay in the sun. Or, lay the cloth in buttermilk for a short time, take out, and place in the hot sun. Or, put lemon juice on and treat in the same way.

A GOOD CEMENT for mending almost anything, may be made by mixing litharge and glycerine to the consistency of thick cream or fresh putty. This cement is useful for mending stone jars, stopping leaks in seams of tin pans or wash boilers, cracks and holes in iron kettles, fastening on lamp tops; in all cases the article mended should not be used till the cement has hardened. This cement will resist the action of water, hot or cold, acids, and almost any degree of heat. Cement for attaching metal to glass. Mix two ounces of a thick solution of glue with one ounce of linseed oil varnish, and half an ounce of pure spirits of turpentine; boil the whole together in a close vessel. After it has been applied to the glass and metal, clamp together for two or three days, till dry. Cement for china. To a thick solution of gum arabic add enough plaster of paris to form a sticky paste; apply with a brush and stick edges together. To paste paper on tin. Make a thin paste of gum tragacanth and water, to which add a few drops of oil of vitriol. Mix a pound each of transparent glue and very strong vinegar, one quart alcohol, a small quantity of alum, and dissolve by means of a water bath. This is useful for uniting horn, pearl, shell and bone.—*B. H. Gilbert.*

LIGHTNING CREAM FOR CLOTHES OR PAINT—Four ounces white castile soap, four ounces ammonia, two ounces ether, two ounces alcohol, one ounce glycerine; cut the soap fine, dissolve in one quart soft water over the fire, and when dissolved add other ingredients.

COCHINEAL COLORING—To a pound of wool take two gallons rain water, one ounce cream tartar, one and a half ounces cochineal, two ounces solution tin, one-fourth ounce turmeric; first put the water in a copper kettle and let it boil, put in the cream tartar, in five minutes the cochineal, in five minutes solution tin, in five minutes turmeric, in five minutes yarn, boil an hour, stir all the time. Rinse in cold water.

The following recipes and advertisement were received too late for insertion in the proper place.

OLD-FASHIONED LOAF CAKE.

Three pounds flour, one and one-fourth pounds butter, one and three-fourths pounds sugar, five gills new milk, one-half pint yeast, three eggs, two pounds raisins, one teaspoon soda, one gill of brandy or wine, two teaspoons cinnamon and two of nutmeg. All the butter and part of the sugar should be rubbed into the flour at night. Warm the milk, and pour the yeast into it; then mix together, and let rise until light. It is better to set the sponge over night, and in the morning add the other ingredients, (flouring raisins,) and let rise again. When light, fill your baking pans, and let rise again. Bake in a moderate oven. This recipe makes three large loaves.—*Mrs. John J. Bagley, Michigan, 1837.*

CHILI COLORAD.

Take two chickens; cut up as to stew; when pretty well done, add a little green parsley and a few onions. Take one-half pound large pepper pods, remove the seeds, and pour on boiling water; steam for ten or fifteen minutes; pour off the water, and rub them in a sieve until all the juice is out; add the juice to the chicken; let it cook for half an hour; add a little butter, flour and salt. Place a border of rice around the dish before setting on the table. This dish may also be made of beef, pork or mutton; it is to be eaten in cold weather, and is a favorite dish with all people on the Pacific coast.—*Mrs. Gov. Bradley, Nevada, 1864.*

REVOLUTIONARY CREAM PIE.

One pint rich cream, one tea cup sugar, two tablespoons flour, and one teaspoon lemon. Line pan with crust; pour in cream, and bake with an upper crust.—*Mrs. S. W. Hubbard, Madison.*

CEMENT FOR RUBBER OR LEATHER.

Dissolve one ounce of gutta percha in one-half pound chloroform. Clean the parts to be cemented; cover each with solution, and let them dry twenty or thirty minutes; warm each part in the flame of a candle, and press very firmly together till dry.

HIT AND MISS.

Baking Powder—Eight ounces flour, eight of soda, seven of tartaric acid; mix thoroughly by passing several times through a sieve.—*Mrs. Trimble, Mt. Gilead.*

Baking Powder—Cream of tartar two parts, bicarbonate of soda one part, corn starch one part; mix.—*Mrs. B. H. Gilbert, Minneapolis.*

Bread—First use good flour and Gillett's cream yeast, which is always sure, and to be preferred to any other; two tablespoons are sufficient for four large loaves of bread; soak it in a little warm water, but do not scald it; take two quarts of warm water (water that potatoes have been boiled in, or milk and water, is preferable), add the yeast and a little salt; stir in sufficient flour to knead without sticking to the board; knead well fifteen minutes, and set to rise in a warm place over night. In the morning knead well again, make into loaves and set to rise till full of holes the size of a pin point, then bake in a moderate oven from three-fourths to one hour.—*Mrs. Frank M. Rockwell, Chicago.*

Soda Biscuit—Put one quart of flour, before sifting, into sieve with one teaspoon soda and two of cream tartar (or three of baking powder), one of salt, and one tablespoon white sugar; mix all thoroughly with the flour, run through the sieve, and then rub in one level tablespoon of lard or butter (or half and half), wet with a half pint sweet milk, roll on board about an inch thick, cut with biscuit cutter, and bake in a quick oven fifteen minutes. If you have not milk, use a little more butter, and wet with water. Handle as little and make as rapidly as possible.—*M. Parloa.*

The admirable recipes for cooking cranberries, on pages 153 and 191, are taken from the circular of Messrs. C. G. & E. W. Crane, of Caldwell, N.J., accompanying each package of their celebrated "Star Brand" cranberries, which have attracted so much attention. See advertisement. Their fruit is remarkable for its fine quality, and the care with which it is put up, and needs only to be cooked in accordance with the simple directions given, to be fully appreciated. The peck boxes are particularly desirable for family use. Don't fail to try the first and principle recipe—that for cranberry sauce—with the next cranberries you cook.

Japanese Paperware—Jennings Brothers, 352 Pearl St., New York City, have a fine display of their Paperware at the Centennial Exposition.

The pails, pans, basins, bowls, foot-baths, cuspudores, pitchers, fruit dishes, etc., etc., are durable and cheap. While papier machie has been in use for ornament for centuries, it has not been applied successfully for household articles until this firm produced it from their factory in Connecticut. No house furnishing establishment is complete without paperware.

MARYLAND BISCUIT—Three pounds flour, one-half cup each butter and sweet lard, a little salt, water enough to mix; work an hour, roll, cut into cakes and bake.—*Mrs. G. W. Hensel.*

LEBANON RUSK—One cup mashed potatoes, one of sugar, one of home made yeast, three eggs; mix together, when raised light add half cup butter or lard, and flour to make a soft dough, and when quite light mould into small cakes, and let them rise again before baking. If wanted for tea, set about nine o'clock A. M.—*Mrs. J. S. Stahr.*

SAUER KRAUT—Slice cabbage fine on a slaw cutter; line the bottom and sides of an oaken barrel or keg with cabbage leaves, put in a layer of the sliced cabbage about six inches in depth, sprinkle lightly with salt and pound with a wooden beetle until the cabbage is a compact mass; add another layer of cabbage, etc., repeating the operation, pounding well each layer, until the barrel is full to within six inches of the top; cover with leaves, then a cloth, next a board cut to fit loosely on the inside of barrel, kept well down with a heavy weight. If the brine has not raised within two days add enough water, with just salt enough to taste, to cover the cabbage; examine every two days, and add water as before, until brine raises and scum forms, when lift off cloth carefully so that the scum may adhere, wash well in several cold waters, wring dry and replace, repeating this operation as the scum arises, at first every other day, and then once a week, until the acetous fermentation ceases, which will take from three to six weeks. Up to this time keep warm in the kitchen, then remove to a dry cool cellar, unless made early in the fall, when it may be at once set in the pantry or cellar. One pint of salt to a full barrel of cabbage is a good proportion; some also sprinkle in whole black pepper. Or, to keep until summer: In April squeeze out of brine, and pack tightly with your hands in a stone jar, with the bottom lightly sprinkled with salt; make brine enough to well cover the kraut in the proportion of a tablespoon salt to a quart of water; boil, skim, cool, and pour over; cover with cloth, then a plate, weight, and another cloth tied closely down; keep in a cool place and it will be good in June. Never pound nor salt the cabbage too much, watch closely, keep clear from scum, for good sauer kraut.—*Mrs. Mary Weaver, Darby Plains.*

THE

FRUGAL HOUSEWIFE:

OR

Complete Woman Cook.

WHEREIN

The Art of dressing all Sorts of VIANDS, with
Cleanliness, Decency, and Elegance,

IS EXPLAINED IN

Five Hundred approved RECEIPTS, in

GRAVIES,	PASTRIES,
SAUCES,	PIES,
ROASTING,	TARTS,
BOILING,	CAKES,
FRYING,	PUDDINGS,
BROILING,	SYLLABUBS,
STEWS,	CREAMS,
HASHES,	FLUMMERY,
SOUPS,	JELLIES,
FRICASEES,	JAMS, AND
RAGOUTS,	CUSTARDS.

TOGETHER WITH THE BEST METHODS OF

POTTING,	DRYING,
COLLARING,	CANDYING,
PRESERVING,	PICKLING,

AND MAKING DOMESTIC WINES.

TO WHICH ARE ADDED,

VARIOUS BILLS OF FARE,

And a proper Arrangement of Dinners, two Courses, for every
Month in the Year.

BY SUSANNAH CARTER,

OF CLERKENWELL, LONDON.

PHILADELPHIA:
PRINTED BY JAMES CAREY, 83 N. SECOND STREET.

1796.

To KEEP BUTTER FRESH—Work until solid, make into rolls, take two
gallons water; one pint white sugar, one level tablespoon saltpetre; make
the brine strong enough with salt to bear an egg, boil and skim. Let cool,
pour over butter and keep under brine with a weight. Butter will keep for
a year as sweet as when churned.—*Mrs. Mary Weaver.*

CLOVER VINEGAR—Put a large bowl of molasses in a crock, and pour
over it nine bowls of boiling rain water; let it stand until milk warm, and

put in two quarts of clover blossoms, and two cups of bakers yeast. Let this stand two weeks, and then strain through a towel. I think it is better than cider vinegar. I never had anything even mould in it.—*Mrs. McAlaster, Goshen, Ind.*

TO ROAST VENISON.

After the haunch of venison is spitted, take a piece of butter, and rub all over the fat, dust on a little flour, and sprinkle a little salt; then take a sheet of writing paper, butter it well, and lay over the fat part; put two sheets over that, and tie the paper on with small twine. Keep it well basted, and let there be a good soaking fire. If a large haunch, it will take near three hours to do it. Five minutes before you send it to the table, take off the paper, dust it over with a little flour, and baste it with butter; let it go up with a good froth; put no gravy in the dish, but send it in one boat, and currant jelly, melted, in another.

A FOWL OR TURKEY ROASTED WITH CHESTNUTS.

Roast a quarter of a hundred of chestnuts, and peel them; save out eight or ten, the rest bruise in a mortar, with the liver of a fowl, a quarter of a pound of ham, well pounded, and sweet herbs and parsley, chopped fine; season it with mace, nutmeg, pepper, and salt; mix all these together, and put them into the belly of your fowl; spit it, and tie the neck and vent close. For sauce, take the rest of the chestnuts, cut them in pieces, and put them into a strong gravy, with a glass of white wine; thicken with a piece of butter rolled in flour. Pour the sauce in the dish, and garnish with orange and water cresses.

TO JUG PIGEONS.

Truss and season the pigeons with pepper and salt; and having stuffed them with a mixture of their own livers, shred with beef suet, bread crumbs, parsley, marjoram, and two eggs, sew them up at both ends, and put them into the jug, the breast downwards, with half a pound of butter. Stop up the jug, so that no steam can get out; then set them in a pot of water to stew. They will take two hours and more in doing, and they must boil all the time. When stewed enough, take them out of the gravy, skim off the fat clean; put a spoonful of cream, a little lemon peel, an anchovy shred, a few mushrooms, add a little white wine to the gravy, and having thickened it with butter and flour, and dished up the pigeons, pour the sauce over them. Garnish with sliced lemon.

A STEAK PUDDING.

Make a rich paste of a quartern of flour and two pounds of suet shred fine, mixed up with cold water, seasoned with a little salt, and made stiff. The steaks may be either beef or mutton, well seasoned with pepper and salt. Roll the paste out half an inch thick. Lay the steaks upon it, and roll them up in it. Then tie it in a cloth, and put it into boiling water. A small pudding will be done enough in three hours. A large one takes five hours boiling.

These pages, selected from an old cook book, now in the possession of Mrs. Dr. Thompson, Marysville, O., are given as a curious relic of the olden time.

The Delaware Wrought Iron Fence.

CHEAP, BEAUTIFUL AND DURABLE

Received First Premium at the Indiana and Ohio State Fairs.

The *DELAWARE FENCE COMPANY* are now prepared to deliver and set up their fences in any part of the country at the following low prices:

Prices for Fence Delivered and set up.--No Extras.

No. 1. With Wrought Iron Posts, Braces and Stools, per lineal foot,...........$ 1 75
" 2 Same style, strength and appearance as No. 1. but less weight—suitable for stone wall, ... 1 50
" 3 Fully ornamented,...................$2 50 Partially Ornamented............... 2 20
" 4   "   "   .... 2 50   "   " 2 20
" 4½ "   "   .... 2 00   "   " 1 50
" 5   "   "   .... 2 50   "   " 2 25
" 6   "   "   .... 2 75   "   " 2 25
" 7   "   "   .... 3 00   "   " 2 25

Parties taking their fence here, on cars, will be allowed 25 cents per foot off the above rates. Any mechanic can set these fences as we furnish full directions for setting. We now make an entire Wrought Iron Fence, below as well as above ground, having discarded cast iron in our Posts, Braces, and Stools, making them entirely of wrought iron, thus rendering breakage impossible.

We also furnish here, on cars, Single, Double, and Carriage Gates, together with their Posts. These Gates and Posts are suitable for any kind of wood fence or hedge. A Single Gate, straight top, and two Posts, everything complete, including our self-acting latch, $18.00; Rounded top Gate and Posts, $22.00; Carriage Gate and Posts, $33.00. The Gates and Posts to be all wrought iron. Carriage Gates fill a space of 10 feet, Single Gates, 4 feet.

The height of Fence No. 1 is 3 feet 8 inches; No. 2, 2 feet 8 inches; No. 3, 3 feet 8 inches; No. 4, 3 feet 7 inches; No. 5, 3 feet 7 inches; No. 6, 4 feet 2 inches; No. 7, 4 feet 2 inches. No. 4½, 2 feet 8 inches. In sending an order enclose diagram noting distance from end of Fence to center of space for 1st Gate, from there to center of space for 2d Gate (should there be one), and then to the other end or corner of Fence. Sides of premises measured by same rule. Note grade, if any, state to which Post the Gate should hang, and mark which is front on diagram. Grounds should be prepared by time of arrival of Fence, so as to occasion no delay in setting.

Orders Solicited.

DELAWARE FENCE CO.,

Delaware, Ohio.

WAY'S IMPROVED

PATENT LEVER

CLOTHES WRINGER.

If you were to be asked what in your judgment was the best way to secure peace, long life, and happiness in your family, by one who was a new beginner, what would you say, Mrs. Smith ?

I would first ask, " have you a clothes wringer ?" if not, I would then be ready to give my advice.

Taking care to let conscience rule, I would say, get as one of the first and most essential things, **Way's Patent Lever Clothes Wringer,** and then give my reasons, which are many:

ADAMS - CB,CIN,O,

1st. It is the most durable and simple in its construction.

2d. Its superiority of rolls.

3d. No thumb screws, cogs or springs to rust and get out of order.

4th. Its rolls adjust themselves to any thickness of cloth, from a bed quilt to thinest lace, merely by the pressure of the foot.

Next, your tub cannot tip over as it is not fastened to the wringer, but on one of the best commodities that can grace a laundry, a bench neat and handy, so that a child can readily work it. And in fact, time nor space would not allow the naming of all there is to be said in praise of this the **woman's friend.**

It has taken the premium and two prize medals at the Cincinnati Exposition, 1873-'74, also Medal at the Indianapolis Exposition, 1874, and first premium at the State Fairs of Ohio. In fact it gives splendid satisfaction. Everybody likes it. It is the common sense wringer.

TRY ONE AND YOU WILL LIKE IT.

E. F. LANDIS'

Fourfold Self-Supporting

CLOTHES HORSE or DRIER,

An article of real merit and value to every housekeeper.

PATENTED JUNE 30, 1874.

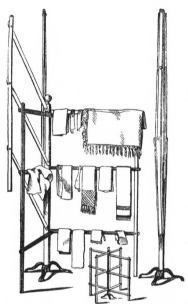

It can be used for out-door drying but is especially adapted for in-door use on cloudy or rainy days, and the snowy season of winter, when it is unpleasant to stretch a line, and especially for putting clothes on after ironing, to thoroughly dry them before putting away.

The cut illustrates the drier. On the left it is shown with two sections let down for use, one in the act of being closed, and one raised or closed. On the right it is shown closed for setting away after use, in which way it occupies *very little space.* It differs from most others in this, that you can use it with either one, two, three or the four sections at a time. Nos 1, 3, 5 and 6 give 40 feet of drying surface, and by using cords through the perforations in the uprights, it gives 96 feet of drying surface. The capacity of Nos. 2 and 4 is one-fourth less Height, when folded, of Nos. 1 to 4, is 7 feet 2 inches; 5 and 6, 8 feet 2 inches.

Liberal Discounts, and Profitable Employment for Agents.

REDUCED PRICE LIST.

No. 1. Oiled Walnut or Cherry, 16 Rails $3 75
" 2. " " " 12 " 3 50
" 3. Plain Ash, 16 " 3 25
" 4. " " 12 " 3 00
" 5. Oiled Walnut or Cherry, 16 " 4 25
" 6. Plain Ash, 16 " 4 00

For further particulars, address,

EZRA F. LANDIS,

Sole Proprietor and Manufacturer, LANCASTER, PA.

N. B.—Agencies solicited everywhere. State or County Rights can be had on easy terms, and without risk of loss.

CANCERS.

TUMORS,

CANCERS CURED

And warranted to be satisfactory to any one, without Cutting or the use of Caustics. No blood ; no pain. Call and read the testimony from hundreds that have been cured.

W. M. PARK. M. D., In Charge of Cancer Department·

We treat all other diseases with perfect success, and guarantee entire satisfaction to all. We invite all to call and see and read for themselves the many testimonials we have, and we are daily in receipt of letters from all parts of the country, from persons under our treatment, telling us of the benefits they have received from using

DR. TOWNSEND'S OXYGENATED AIR !

We are weekly in receipt of hundreds of just such letters. If a person calls on us for treatment, and we say to them it will take three or four months to cure you, and they promise faithfully to follow our instructions, and then go home with our treatment and only follow our instructions one or two weeks, and because they are not decidedly improved, leave it off, it is no fault of ours or our treatment ; it is simply their own fault But to all that will follow our instructions we will guarantee perfect satisfaction. We thoroughly understand all the different schools of practice, the Old School, the Homœopathic School and the Eclectic School, and we give our patients such treatment as they need, regardless of any particular School of practice. We wish to say to all that OXYGENATED AIR will purify the blood in one-third the time that any other known remedy can possibly do. Dr. Townsend has connected with him in his business some of the most thorough and skillful physicians and surgeons in America, as our cures will show. Address all letters to

Dr. E. F. TOWNSEND,

No. 122 High St., between Fenner and Stewart Streets, Providence, R. I.

Patients at a distance can be just as successfully treated as those who consult Dr. Townsend personally, by writing full statement of their case Be sure to write plainly your name and Postoffice address, and send stamp for our illustrated paper. Direct all letters to my principal office, 122 High St., Providence, R. I.

1½ Horse Power, upright style, combined Engine and Boiler ready for immediate use, with Governor, Pump and Heater $175
Ditto without Governor.. 160
4 Horse Power, style as above, with Boiler and all complete with Governor,
Pump and Heater 325
Other sizes and styles will be furnished portable or stationary. In all cases satisfaction guaranteed. For circular, terms, and further particulars address as above.

The Excelsior Meat Chopper is superior to any of equal price now in use. Will
mince, ready for market, 40 to 50 pounds of meat in 10 to 15 minutes. For hand or
steam power, price $45—guaranteed. Send for circular to

B. MUSSER, Strasburg, Lancaster Co., Pa.

RECIPE FOR GOOD TEMPER.

This celebrated recipe, which has been tested in numerous households, with the most satisfactory results is to be found in no other cook book ; but if strictly followed, is guaranteed to produce a perfectly sweet temper, which will keep in any climate until the next " Centennial." It is this :

BUY ONLY THE "ST. JOHN" SEWING MACHINE.

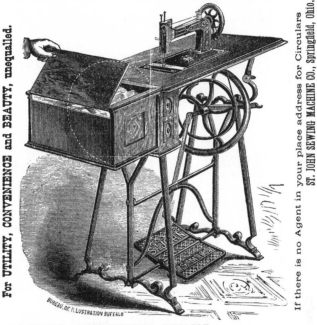

It is SIMPLE ; LIGHT RUNNING ; DURABLE.
It runs either FORWARD or BACKWARD without change of stitch or feed.
It has a CLOSED SHUTTLE, without holes to thread through.
It winds the BOBBIN, without running the machine.
It does the greatest range of work, of any machine made.
It is what you want. Buy the "St. John."

PROSPECTUS

OF THE

Housekeeper's Companion.

————

THE HOUSEKEEPER'S COMPANION is a new monthly illustrated paper, ɔ legantly printed, and devoted to the economical management of the Household in all its branches.

It will make an effort to discuss, from time to time, every Department of Housekeeping.

New preparations of food and improved methods of cooking will receive particular attention.

New inventions in Household Implements will be noticed and illustrated as opportunity may offer.

Recipes, contributed and selected. will form one of its prominent features.

Another of its aims will be to popularize Housekeeping and to dispel the pernicious notion, so widely entertained, that a knowledge of its important duties is debasing

Every issue will contain information worth the entire cost of a year's subscription.

Terms, 50 Cents a Year, in Advance, Including Postage.

☞ An agent wanted in every town to solicit subscriptions, to whom a ib eral commission will be paid.

Address,

M. T. RICHARDSON, Publisher,

Union Building, Brooklyn, N. Y.

P. O. Box165.

————

"THE UNION COUNTY JOURNAL,"

MARYSVILLE, OHIO.

————

Published Every Friday.

————

C. M. KENTON, Editor & Proprietor.

————

A Democratic Newspaper, Devoted to General and Local News.

————

☞ ALL KINDS OF JOB PRINTING NEATLY EXECUTED. ☜

THE HARRISON PATENT COMBINATION KITCHEN SAFE.

The most useful household invention of the nineteenth century. A Kitchen Safe, Flour Bin, Kitchen, Bread Table, Rolling Pin, Bread Pan, Spice Drawers are all combined and contained in a handsome piece of furniture, made of the best seasoned black walnut or white wood oak grained.

With this Safe a person need not move one step on making bread, cakes or pastry, for all the necessary machinery and ingredients are centered within reach.

PRICES AT THE FACTORY.

No. 1.	All Walnut, paneled, moulded ends and front, capacity one barrel................................$22 00
" 1.	" " " " " " " half " 20 00
" 2.	Walnut, paneled moulded front, paneled and stained end, capacity one barrel................ 20 00
" 2.	" " " " " " " " half " 18 00
" 3.	Oak grained and varnished, plain, capacity one barrel.. 17 00
" 3.	" " " " " half " 15 00
" 3.	" " carved and moulded, capacity one barrel 18 00
" 3.	" " " " " half " 17 00

BOXING AND CARTAGE TO DEPOT 50 CENTS.

Address, MISSOURI VALLEY NOVELTY WORKS,
SOLE PROPRIETORS AND MANUFACTURERS, ST. JOSEPH, MO.

The Recipes for Making Coffee

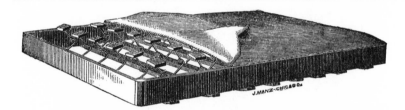

APPENDIX 1.

Short-Title List of Ohio Cookery Works Published or Written through 1900.

Prepared by Andrew F. Smith.

ABBREVIATIONS.

AAS   American Antiquarian Society, Worcester, Massachusetts

BGSU   Bowling Green State University, Ohio

BKW   Works located by Barbara K. Wheaton

CS   William R. Cagle and Lisa Killion Stafford, *American Books on Food and Drink*. New Castle, Delaware: Oak Knoll Press, 1998

EBB   Eleanor Brown and Bob Brown, *Culinary Americana: Cookbooks Published in the Cities and Towns of the United States of America during the Years from 1860 through 1960*. New York: Roving Eye Press, 1961

EL   Eleanor Lowenstein, *Bibliography of American Cookery Books, 1742–1860*. Worcester: Antiquarian Society, 1972

JW   Johnson and Wales University, Culinary Archives and Museum, Providence, Rhode Island

KSU   Kent State University, Kent, Ohio

LC   Library of Congress, Washington, D.C.

MC   Margaret Cook, *America's Charitable Cooks: A Bibliography of Fund-Raising Cook Books Published in the United States (1861–1915)*. Kent, Ohio: n.p., 1971

MHS   Minnesota Historical Society, St. Paul

MU   Miami University, Oxford, Ohio

NYHS   New York Historical Society, New York

NYPL   New York Public Library, New York

OHS   Ohio Historical Society, Columbus

OSU   Ohio State University Library, Columbus

OWU   Ohio Wesleyan University, Delaware, Ohio

PC   Private Collection

SL   Schlesinger Library, Radcliffe College, Cambridge, Massachusetts

SLO   State Library of Ohio, Columbus, Ohio

UI   University of Iowa, Iowa City

VW   Virginia M. Westbrook, "Introduction to the Reprint Edition," Estelle Woods Wilcox, ed., *Buckeye Cookery and Practical Housekeeping*. St. Paul: Minnesota Historical Society Press, 1988.

WK   Wheaton, Barbara Ketcham, and Patricia Kelly. *Bibliography of Culinary History: Food Resources in Eastern Massachusetts*. Boston: G. K. Hall and Company, [1987?].

1820

See Josephson, Bertha E., ed., "Ohio Recipe Book of the 1820s," *Mississippi Valley Historical Review* 36 (June 1949): 97–107. [From a handwritten manuscript at the Ohio Historical Society]

1830

Mackenzie, Colin. *Five Thousand Receipts in All the Useful and Domestic Arts, Adapted to the Western States*. Hamilton, Ohio: Taylor Webster at the Telegraph Office. [EL]

1831

Barnum, H. L. *Family Receipts, or Practical Guide for the Husbandman and Housewife*. Cincinnati: Published by A. R. Roff; Lincoln and Company Printers. [EL]

1840

Templin, James D. *The Baker's and Cook's Oracle*. Oxford, [Ohio]: Printed for the Author, c. 1840. [MU; EL]

White, Daniel T. *White's New Cook-Book, Embracing Temperate and Economical Receipts*. Cincinnati: n.p. [CS; WK]

1841

Bryan, Lettice. *The Kentucky Housewife*. Cincinnati: Stereotyped by Shepard and Stearns. [EL]

Girardey, George. *Manual of Domestic Economy, or House-Keeper's Guide*. Dayton, Ohio: John Wilson. [SLO; EL]

1842

Girardey, G[eorge.] *Höchst nützliches Handbuch über Kochkunst.* Cincinnati: Stereotyped by F. U. James. [MU; EL]

Hardin, Philomelia Ann Maria Antoinette. *Every Body's Cook and Receipt Book: But More Particularly Designed for Buckeyes, Hoosiers, Wolverines, Corncrackers, Suckers and All Epicures Who Wish to Live in Present Times.* [Cleveland]: Printed for the Author. [EL]

1844

Girardey, George. *The North American Compiler Containing a Large Number of Selected, Approved, and Warranted Recipes.* Rossville, Ohio: Printed for the Author. [AAS]

200 Receipts on the Art of Cookery, Preserving Meats and Vegetables; and Other Interesting Matters. Chardon, Ohio: Published by Joseph W. White. [EL]

1845

Howland, E. A. *The American Economical Housekeeper, and Family Receipt Book.* Stereotyped edition. Cincinnati: Published by H. W. Derby and Company. [JW; OHS]

1852

Bradley, J. S. *Mrs. Bradley's Housekeeper's Guide.* Cincinnati: H. M. Rulison. [LC]

1853

Bradley, J. S. *Mrs. Bradley's Book of Cookery and Housekeeper's Valuable Receipts.* Cincinnati: Edwards and Goshorn. [EL]

Bradley, J. S. *Mrs. Bradley's Housekeeper's Guide.* Cincinnati: H. M. Rulison. [EL]

1854

Crowen, Mrs. Thomas. *Every Lady's Cook Book.* Toledo, Ohio: Sawyer, Brother and Company. [EL]

The Family Cyclopædia or Domestic Library; in One Book. Cleveland, Ohio: H. B. Skinner. [EL]

The Family Token, or Book of Practical Arts. Hudson, O[hio]: D. Marshall and Company. [EL]

The House-keeper's Almanac. Cleveland: Baer and Cotter. [EL]

The Kitchen Directory, and American Housewife. Cincinnati: Moore, Anderson, and Company. [EL]

Witt, B. F., comp. *Family Receipts being a Collection of One Hundred.* Cincinnati: Published by Applegate. [EL]

1855

Campbell, Sylvia. *The Practical Cook Book.* Cincinnati: Longley Brothers. [EL]

The Kitchen Directory, and American Housewife. Cincinnati: Moore, Wilistach, and Keys. [EL]

Scott, Marion L. *The Practical Housekeeper, and Young Woman's Friend.* Toledo, Ohio: Blade Steam Printing. [EL]

1856

The Family Manual; Containing Several Hundred Valuable Receipts for Cooking Well at a Moderate Expense. Louisville, Kentucky, or Cincinnati, Ohio: Barclay and Company. [CS; WK]

1857

Simmons, John H. *The Confectioner and Fancy Cake Baker.* Bucyrus, Ohio: J. A. Estill, Simms' Block. [CS]

The House-keeper's Almanac. Cleveland: C. S. Bragg and Company. [EL]

1858

The Kitchen Directory, and American Housewife. Cincinnati: Moore, Wilistach, Keys, and Company. [EL]

1859

Bradley, J. S. *Mrs. Bradley's Housekeeper's Guide.* Cincinnati: H. M. Rulison. [EL]

The Kitchen Directory, and American Housewife. Cincinnati: Moore, Wilistach, Keys, and Company. [EL]

1860

Bradley, J. S. *Mrs. Bradley's Housekeeper's Guide.* Cincinnati: H. M. Rulison. [EL]

The Kitchen Directory, and American Housewife. Cincinnati: Moore, Wilistach, Keys, and Company. [EL]

1861

Evans, Mary I. T. *Recipes in Cookery, for the Sick and Convalescent, in hospitals and families.* Cleveland, Ohio: Ingham and Bragg. [OHS]

The Volunteer's Cook-book: For the Camp and March. Columbus, Ohio: Joseph H. Riley and Company. [NYHS]

1864

The House-Keeper's Guide and Everybody's Hand-Book: Containing over Five Hundred Recipes. Rev. and corr. ed. Cincinnati, Ohio: Smith and Swinney. [PC]

1867

Cox, Ann C. *Family Directory.* Columbus, Ohio: Printed for the Author. [LC]

1868

Howe, Ann. *The American Kitchen.* Cincinnati: Howe's Subscription Book Concern. [OHS]

1871

The Household Companion for 1871. Cincinnati: Bradley and Power. [EBB; JW]

The House-Keeper's Guide and Everybody's Hand-Book: Containing over Five Hundred Recipes. 10th ed. Cincinnati, Ohio: Smith and Swinney. [LC]

1873

First Presbyterian Church. *Presbyterian Cook Book.* Dayton, Ohio: Crooke and Company. [LC]

First Presbyterian Church. *Presbyterian Cook Book.* 2nd ed. Dayton, Ohio: Historical Publishing Company. [MC]

Hamilton, W. C., and Company *Family Receipt Book.* [Cincinnati, W. C. Hamilton and Company, c. 1873]. [LC]

1874

Congregational Cook-Book. 2nd ed. Columbus, [O.]: First Congregational Church. [MC]

First Presbyterian Church. *Presbyterian Cook Book.* 3rd ed. Dayton, Ohio: J. H. Thomas. [MC]

Follett, Eliza G. *The Young Housekeeper's Assistant.* Sandusky: Register Steam Printing Establishment. [EBB]

Ladies of the Seventh Presbyterian Church of Cincinnati. *Practical Recipes of Experienced Housekeepers.* Cincinnati: n. p. [EBB; MC]

Jermain, Fannie D., and the Ladies of Toledo and Other Cities, comp. *Tried and True Recipes: The Home Cookbook.* Toledo: Toledo Commercial Company. [MC; PC]

Portsmouth Soldiers' Aid Society. *Portsmouth Monumental Cook Book.* Portsmouth, [Ohio]: J. W. Newman, printer. [LC; MC]

Sauvert. *The Parisian Cook Book, or French Culinary Directory.* Columbus, Ohio: Smythe and Company. [OHS]

1875

The American Household Advisor. New York and Cincinnati: E. C. Bridgeman, 1875. [LC] [Note: This includes a copy of Eliza Ann Wheeler's *The Frugal Housekeeper's Kitchen Companion, or Guide to Economical Cookery.*]

Hawhe, H. J. *"The Eclipse": for Hotel and Home Cooking: Suitable for Rich and Poor.* Columbus, Ohio: Glenn, printer and binder. [OHS]

Ladies of the First Presbyterian Church. *Presbyterian Cookbook.* Dayton, Ohio: John H. Thomas and Company, 1875. 5,000 printed. [JW; OSU; MC] [Note: A facsimile of this work was published by Arno Press, New York, in 1973.]

1876

Buckingham, Jane W. *The Housekeeper's Friend: a Practical Cook-Book Compiled by A lady of Zanesville and Sold for the Benefit of the Home of the Friendless.* Zanesville, Ohio: Sullivan and Parsons. [LC; MC]

Campbell, A[rchibald] J. *American Practical Cyclopædia, or, Hoe Book of Useful Knowledge.* Cleveland, Ohio: A. J. Campbell. [UI]

Jermain, Frances Delavan Page, comp. *Tried and True Recipes. The Home Cook Book.* Toledo: T. J. Brown, Eager and Company. [LC; BGSU; MC]

Ladies of the First Presbyterian Church. *Presbyterian Cookbook.* Dayton, Ohio: John H. Thomas and Company. 6,000 printed. [EBB; JW; MC]

[Wilcox, Estelle Woods, comp.]. *Centennial Buckeye Cook Book.* Marysville: J. H. Shearer and Son. [JW; LC]

1877

[Wilcox, Estelle Woods, comp.]. *Buckeye Cookery and Practical Housekeeping. Compiled From Original Recipes.* 2nd ed. Marysville, Ohio: Buckeye Publishing Company. [LC]

[Wilcox, Estelle Woods, comp.]. *Buckeye Cookery and Practical Housekeeping.*

Compiled from Original Recipes. 3rd ed. Marysville, Ohio: Buckeye Publishing Company. [OSU]

[Wilcox, Estelle Woods, comp.]. *Buckeye Cookery and Practical Housekeeping. Compiled from Original Recipes.* Minneapolis, Minn.: Buckeye Publishing Company. 25,000 printed.

[Wilcox, Estelle Woods, comp.]. *Buckeye Cookery and Practical Housekeeping. Comp. from Original Recipes.* Marysville, Ohio: Buckeye Publishing Company. 27,000 printed.

1878

Brown, Frank. *Brown's Excelsior Recipe Book.* Macedonia, [O]: Brown Brothers. [LC]

Ladies of the First Presbyterian Church. *The Youngstown Cook Book.* Youngstown, Ohio: n.p. [MC]

Ladies of Toledo and Other Cities, comp. *Tried and True Recipes: The Home Cookbook.* 2nd ed. Toledo: Toledo Commercial Company. [LC; MC]

St. Francis Street Methodist Episcopal Church, South Mobile, Alabama. *Gulf City Cook Book.* Dayton, Ohio: United Brethren Publishing House. [JW; LC]

1879

Ladies of the Presbyterian Church, Paris, Ky. *Housekeeping in the Blue Grass. A New and Practical Cookbook Containing Nearly a Thousand Recipes.* New and enl. ed. Cincinnati: Robert Clarke and Company. 10,000 printed. [JW]

Quinn, C. L. *The Practical Recipe Book for Families, Confectioners and Bakers.* Cincinnati: [Central Book Concern]. [LC]

1880

Cook and Receipt Book. Leetonia, Ohio: Eng. Lutheran Church. [MC]

[Jermain, Frances Delavan Page, comp.]. *Tried and True Recipes: The Home Cook Book.* 3rd ed. Toledo: T. J. Brown, Eager and Company. [JW; MC]

Ladies of the First Presbyterian Church. *Presbyterian Cookbook.* Dayton, Ohio: Thomas. [MC]

Shumway, D. *Shumway's Universal Recipe Book.* Cuyahoga Falls, Ohio: Shumway's Cough Compound Cough Syrup, [1880?]. [OHS]

Young Ladies of Christ Church. *Revised Edition of the Valuable Recipes.* Warren, Ohio: Press of Warren Record. [MC]

1881

Carlin, William. *Old Doctor Carlin's Recipes*. Toledo, Ohio, and Boston, Massachusetts: The Locke Publishing Company. [LC]

The Cleveland Herald Cookbook. [Cleveland, Ohio]: The Herald Publishing Company. [OSU]

Kirkpatrick, Thomas Jefferson, comp. *Farm and Fireside Practical Cook Book*. Springfield, Ohio: Farm and Fireside Company. [LC]

Our Cooks in Council. A Manual of Practical and Economical Recipes for the Household. Jefferson, Ohio: The Ladies of the Congregational Church. [LC; MC]

1883

Kirkpatrick, T. J., comp. *The Housekeeper's New Cook Book, Embracing Nearly One Thousand Recipes and Practical Suggestions to All Young Housekeepers in Regard to Cooking and the Utensils Used*. Springfield, Ohio: Mast, Crowell and Kirkpatrick. [OHS; BGSU]

Ladies of the First Presbyterian Church. *Presbyterian Cookbook*. Dayton, Ohio: n.p. [EBB; MC]

1884

The Hunter Sifter Cook Book. Cincinnati and New York: The Hunter Sifter Manufacturing Company. [LC; OHS; JW]

Ladies' Social Society of the Euclid Avenue Presbterian [*sic*] Church. *Cooks in Council*. Cleveland, Ohio: William W. Williams. [JW; MC; UI]

1885

Murrey, Thomas J. *What to Buy and How to Use Cereals*. Akron, Ohio: Akron Milling Company, [1885?]. [OHS]

1886

Ladies of the First Presbyterian Church. *Presbyterian Cook Book*. Dayton, Ohio: Historical Publishing Company. [JW]

Ladies of the First Presbyterian Church. *Presbyterian Cook Book*. 10th ed. Dayton, Ohio: Historical Publishing Company. [JW; LC; OSU; MC]

1887

Buell, Maria Nye, comp. *Centennial Cookery Book. Sold for the Benefit of the Woman's Centennial Association of Marietta, Ohio*. Marietta, Ohio: Times Print. [LC; MC]

Chase, Alvin Wood. *Dr. Chase's Family Physician, Farrier, Bee-Keeper and Second Receipt Book.* Toledo, Ohio: Chase Publishing Company. [CS]

[Wilcox, Estelle Woods, comp.]. *The Buckeye Cook Book.* Subscription edition. Minneapolis, Minn., Dayton, Ohio: Buckeye Publishing Company. [LC]

1888

First Reformed Church. *The Housekeeper's Guide.* Dayton, Ohio: Reformed Publishing Company, [1888?]. [MC]

Kenton Cook-book Company. *The Kenton Cook-book.* Kenton, Ohio: W. M. Beckman, [c. 1888]. [LC; UI]

Ladies' Library Association of Sandusky. *The Sandusky House-Keeper.* Sandusky, Ohio: I. F. Mack and Bro. [JW; MC]

Ladies of the Miles Avenue Church of Christ. *The Tried and True Cook Book.* Cleveland: n. p. [MC]

Ladies of the Presbyterian Church, Paris, Ky. *Housekeeping in the Blue Grass. A New and Practical Cookbook Containing Nearly a Thousand Recipes.* New and enl. ed. Cincinnati: Robert Clarke and Company. 18,000 printed. [PC]

Pulte, Mary J. *"Mrs. J. H. Pulte." Domestic Cook Book.* Cincinnati: G. W. Smith. [LC]

Season, Eva A., comp. *The Ohio Farmer's Home Guide Book : A Complete Manual of Practical Instruction in Every Department of Household Economy : Including the Kitchen, the Laundry, the Dining-room, the Parlor, the Sleeping Rooms, Fancy Work, Home Decoration, Parental Duty.* Cleveland, Ohio: The Ohio Farmer. [LC; OHS; UI]

The Weekly Bee Cook Book. The Largest Collection of New and Valuable Receipts Ever Embodied in One Volume. Toledo, Ohio: The Toledo Bee Company. [LC]

Western Reserve Book of Recipes; a Manual of Cooking, Pickling and Preserving, and Other Useful Information for the Housekeeper. Garrettsville, Ohio: Will W. Sherwood, Art Printer, Binder and Stationer. [MC]

1889

Kramer, Bertha. *"Aunt Babette's" Cookbook: Foreign and Domestic Receipts for the Household.* 4th ed. Cincinnati, Chicago: Bloch Publishing and Printing Company. [OSU]

Ladies of the First Presbyterian Church, Dayton, Ohio. *Presbyterian Cookbook.* Wheeling, West Va.: F. H. Cargo. [EBB; JW; MC]

1890

Abel, Mary White Hinman. *Practical Sanitary and Economic Cooking Adapted to Persons of Moderate and Small Means.* Columbus, Ohio: American Public Health Association. [CS]

Kirkpatrick, T. J., comp. *The Housekeeper's New Cook Book, Embracing Nearly One Thousand Recipes and Practical Suggestions to All Young Housekeepers in Regard to Cooking and the Utensils Used.* Springfield, Ohio: Mast, Crowell and Kirkpatrick. [EBB; JW; NYPL]

Kramer, Bertha F. *Aunt Babette's Cook Book: Foreign and Domestic Receipts for the Household.* 6th ed. Cincinnati: Bloch Publishing Company. [PC]

Richardson, Anna Martin. *Home Made Candies and Other Good Things Sweet and Sour.* Cincinnati: R. Clarke and co. [OSU; LC]

The Weekly Bee Cook Book. The Largest Collection of New and Valuable Receipts Ever Embodied in One Volume. Toledo, Ohio: Toledo Bee Company. [OHS]

1891

Gebhart, Mrs. George P. *Gilt-Edged Cook Book. A Careful Compilation of Recipes.* Dayton, Ohio: Press of the United Brethren Publishing House. [JW; MC]

Stewart, Isabella G. D., et al. *The U.S. Cook Book: A Comprehensive Cyclopedia of Information for the Home.* Toledo, Ohio: Merrill Pub. Company. [BGSU]

1892

Warren, Jane. *The Handy Reliable Cook Book.* Coshocton, Ohio: Tuscarora Advertising Company. [OHS]

1893

The Adelaide Cook Book. By a Leader of Society and a Most Noted Entertainer. Cincinnati: L. Wise and Company. [LC]

"Aunt Babette's" Home Confectionary. Chicago and Cincinnati: Bloch Publishing and Printing Company. [JW]

Ladies of the Main Street M. E. Church, Akron, Ohio. *The Columbian Recipes: A Publication of the Methodist Cook-Book.* Rev. ed. Akron, Ohio: Capron and Curtice. [JW; MC; PC]

Ladies of the M. E. Church, Bloomington. *Fayette County Business Directory and Cook Book.* Columbus, Ohio: Ruggles-Gale Company. [MC]

Ladies of the M. E. Church. *Madison County Business Directory and Cook Book.* [Sedalia, Ohio]: Asher and Shaffer. [OHS; MC]

1894

Crowell, John S. *The Standard Cook Book. Embracing More than One Thousand Recipes and Practical Suggestions to Housekeepers.* Springfield, Ohio: Mast, Crowell and Kirkpatrick. [OHS; LC]

Dayton Evening Herald. *The Dayton Evening Herald Cook Book: Embracing More than One Thousand Recipes and Practical Suggestions to Housekeepers.* Dayton, Ohio: Herald Pub. Company. [LC]

Ladies' Aid Society of the First Presbyterian Church. *Recipes Tried and True.* Marion, Ohio: Press of Kelley Mount. [BGSU; JW; LC; MC]

Ladies of the Collingwood Avenue Presbyterian Church. *Culinary Conceits for Good Housekeepers.* Toledo: Barkdull Printing House. [JW; MC]

New Process Catalogue and Cook Book. Cleveland, Ohio: Standard Lighting Company, [c. 1894]. [BGSU; JW; UI]

1895

Boyd, Mrs. William Hart. *The Queen Cook Book.* Cincinnati, Ohio: W. H. Ferguson Company.

Columbus Retail Grocers. *The Home Guide: A Volume of Useful Information to Each Home.* Columbus: C. K. Dalgarn and E. H. Deaton for Columbus Retail Grocers. [BKW]

The Dodekas, Trinity Baptist Church. *The Dodeka Recipes.* [Cleveland, Ohio: Press of Whitworth Bros.] [MC]

Ladies Aid Society of the Friends' Church. *Friends' Cook Book.* Wilmington, Ohio: Friends' Church. [PC]

Ladies Aid Society of the Friends' Church, Wilmington, Ohio. *Friends' Cook Book.* 2nd edition. Norwalk, Ohio: Laning Printing Company. [OHS; MC]

Ladies of Beckwith Memorial Presbyterian Church. *Up-to-Date Cook Book.* [Cleveland, Ohio: n. p., 1895?.] [MC]

Ladies of Raper M. E. Church. *Kitchen Echoes. A Careful Compilation of Tried and Approved Recipes.* Dayton: n.p. [EBB; MC]

Ladies of Raper M. E. Church. *Kitchen Echoes. A Careful Compilation of Tried and Approved Recipes.* 2nd ed. Dayton: Walker Lithographing and Printing Company. [JW]

Women of St. Timothy's Church. *The Massillon Cook Book.* [Massillon: Lookout Pub. Company]. [JW]

1896

Ladies and Their Friends of the First Methodist Episcopal Church. *The Oberlin Common-Sense Cook Book.* [Oberlin, Ohio?]: Pearce and Randolph. [NYPL; MC]

Ladies of the Canton, O., First Baptist Church. *The Canton Favorite Cook Book.* Canton, Ohio: Roller Printing Company. [LC; MC]

Ladies of St. Paul's Methodist Episcopal Church. *The Delaware Cook Book: A Careful Collection of Tried and Approved Recipes.* Delaware, Ohio: St. Paul's Methodist Episcopal Church. [PC]

Mitchell, Mrs. Wm. C., ed. *Handy Recipes Furnished by the Ladies and Friends of the Covington M. E. Church.* Greenville, Ohio: Tribune Publishing House. [OHS; MC]

Painesville Branch of the Alumnae Association of Lake Erie Seminary. *Painesville Cook Book.* Painesville, Ohio: Telegraph Publishing Company. [JW; MC]

St. Paul's Methodist Episcopal Church. *The Delaware Cook Book.* Delaware, Ohio: F. T. Evans. [BGSU]

Ziemann, Hugo. *The Presidential Cook Book. Adapted from "The White House Cook Book."* Akron, Ohio *et al.:* Saalfield. [KSU]

1897

The Alturian Cook Book. Favorite Recipes Contributed by the Wives and Daughters of Troy. Troy, Ohio: Kessler's Printery. [MC]

Ladies of Cedar Avenue Disciple Church. *Everyday Cook Book.* Cleveland, Ohio: J. B. Savage Print, [c. 1897]. [MC]

Ladies of Cleveland Dorcas Society. *The Dorcas Cookery. Local and Contemporary Ads.* Cleveland: Plain Dealer, Job Rooms. [EBB]

Ladies of the Church of the Good Shepard. *The Cook Book: What to Eat and How to Cook It.* Cleveland, Ohio: Blumberg Printing Company. [PC]

Ladies of the First Methodist Episcopal Church. *Our Own Cook Book.* Norwalk, Ohio: Laning Printing Company. [MC]

Ladies Guild of Trinity Church, Fostoria, Ohio. *Trinity Guild Cook Book.* Norwalk: Laning Printing Company. [EBB; JW; MC]

Ladies of the Methodist Church and the Ladies of the G. A. R., eds. *Berea Cook Book.* Berea, Ohio: Advertiser Print, December 25. [MC; JW]

Ladies of the Unity Church. *Choice Recipes.* [Cleveland, Ohio: n.p.] [JW; MC]

Markscheffel, Louise. *Hints on Coffee Making for the Use of Housekeepers Who Aim for the Best.* Toledo: Woolson Spice Company, Blade Printing and Paper Company. [PC]

Members and Friends of the Ladies' Auxiliary and King's Daughters of the W. F. M. S. of Third Street Methodist Episcopal Church. *The Domestic Echoes: a Careful Consideration of the Tried and Approved Recipes.* Columbus, Ohio: Press of Nitschke Bro's. [JW; OHS]

The New American Cook Book. Springfield, Ohio: Mast, Crowell and Kirkpatrick Company. [CS; JW; OHS]

Standard American Cook Book. Springfield, Ohio: Crowell and Kirkpatrick Company. [JW]

Young Ladies' League. *A Daily Remembrance.* Fostoria, Ohio: First Presbyterian Church. [BGSU]

1898

Friends Cook Book. Norwalk, Ohio: Laning Printing Company. [MC]

Ladies' Aid Society of the First M.E. Church. *The Methodist Cook Book.* Xenia, Ohio: W. B. Chew. [MC; OHS]

Ladies' Aid Society. *The Crawford County Cook Book: A Collection of Valuable and Reliable Recipes in All Departments of Cookery.* Bucyrus, Ohio: First Methodist Episcopal Church. [OHS; MC]

Ladies' Bible Class [of the First Methodist Episcopal Church]. *Culinary Arts for All Housekeepers.* Bowling Green, Ohio. Toledo: B. F. Wade. [EBB; UI]

Ladies of the St. Joseph's Orphan Society. *Pearl of the Kitchen. A Careful Compilation of Tried and Approved Recipes.* Dayton, Ohio: Reformed Publishing Company. [MC]

Vern, Dollie. *The Young Women's League Cook Book.* Dayton, Ohio: Groneweg Printing Company. [LC]

The Young Women's League Cook Book. Dayton, Ohio: n.p. [MC]

1899

Epworth League Cook Book of Port Jefferson, Ohio. [Lima, Ohio: The Parmenter Printing Company.] [MC]

Hatch, Mrs. Arthur E., comp. *Choice Receipts from the Members of the Cleveland Health Protective Association.* Cleveland, Ohio: [Williams Publishing and Electric Company, Printers]. [JW; MC]

Ladies of the Ebenezer Society of the Evangelical Church. *Pickaway County Business Directory and Cook Book.* Circleville, [O]: R. P. Dresbach. [OHS; MC]

The Mixicologist. Cincinnati: Lawlor and Company, [c. 1897 (1899)]. [JW]

Neff, Israel Howard. *A Text Book of Cookery for the Use of Schools.* Cincinnati: n. p. [EBB]

The New American Cook Book. Springfield, Ohio: Crowell and Kirkpatrick Company. [JW]

Pechin, Mary Shelley. *The 3-6-5 Cook Book, for Use 365 Days in the Year.* Cleveland: Helman-Taylor Company. [LC; JW]

St. Paul's M. E. Church Directory for 1899 and Cook Book. Toledo: B. F. Wade Printing Company. [EBB; JW; MC]

Sargent, Kate. *100 Receipts about Mushrooms.* Cleveland: Charles Orr. [EBB]

Ladies of the First Presbyterian Church of Napoleon, Ohio. *Daily Remembrance.* Napoleon: L. L. Orwig and Son, Printers. [PC]

1900

Ladies' Benevolent Society, of the Case Avenue Presbyterian Church. *Case Avenue Presbyterian Cook Book.* [Cleveland, Ohio: Britton Printing Company, [1900?].] [JW; MC]

Ladies' Home and Foreign Missionary Society of the First Presbyterian Church. *Book of Favorite Recipes.* East Liverpool, Ohio: n.p., [c. 1900]. [MC]

Ladies of the First Presbyterian Church of Logan. *Tried, Tested, Proved: The Logan Cook Book.* [Logan, Ohio?: n.p., c. 1900.] [MC]

Ladies of the Presbyterian Church. *A Book of Tested Recipes. A Cook Book.* Orwell, Ohio: n. p., [c. 1900]. [MC; UI]

Woman's Christian Association, Department of Domestic Economy. *Sandwiches, Salads and Other Good Things.* [Dayton, Ohio]: Pirsch Press, [1900?]. [UI]

Women of St. Timothy's Church. *The Massillon Cook Book.* 2nd ed. [Massillon: Lookout Pub. Company]. [JW]

APPENDIX 2.

Editions of Buckeye Cookery Book.

[Wilcox, Estelle Woods, comp.]. *Centennial Buckeye Cook Book*. Marysville: J. H. Shearer and Son, 1876. [LC; JW]

[Wilcox, Estelle Woods, comp.]. *Buckeye Cookery and Practical Housekeeping. Compiled from Original Recipes*. 2nd ed. Marysville, Ohio: Buckeye Publishing Company, 1877. [LC; PC]

[Wilcox, Estelle Woods, comp.]. *Buckeye Cookery and Practical Housekeeping. Compiled from Original Recipes*. 3rd ed. Marysville, Ohio: Buckeye Publishing Company, 1877. [OSU]

[Wilcox, Estelle Woods, comp.]. *Buckeye Cookery and Practical Housekeeping. Compiled from Original Recipes*. Minneapolis, Minn.: Buckeye Publishing Company, 1877. 25,000 printed.

[Wilcox, Estelle Woods, comp.]. *Buckeye Cookery and Practical Housekeeping*. Marysville, Ohio: Buckeye Publishing Company, 1877. 27,000 printed. [PC]

[Wilcox, Estelle Woods, comp.]. *Buckeye Cookery and Practical Housekeeping. Compiled from Original Recipes*. Minneapolis, Minn.: Buckeye Publishing Company, 1879. [UC]

[Wilcox, Estelle Woods, comp.] *Buckeye Cookery and Practical Housekeeping, Compiled from Original Recipes*. Minneapolis, Minn.: Buckeye Publishing Company, 1879. 58,000 printed.

[Wilcox, Estelle Woods, comp.]. *Buckeye Cookery and Practical Housekeeping. Compiled from Original Recipes*. Minneapolis, Minn.: Buckeye Publishing Company, 1880. 80,000 printed. [WK]

[Wilcox, Estelle Woods, comp.]. *Practical Housekeeping. A Careful Compilation of Tried and Approved Recipes*. Minneapolis, Minn.: Buckeye Publishing Company, 1880. [UC]

[Wilcox, Estelle Woods, comp.]. *Buckeye Kochkunst und Praktisches Haushalten*. Minneapolis: Buckeye Publishing Company, 1880. [MC]

[Wilcox, Estelle Woods, comp.]. *Buckeye Cookery and Practical Housekeeping. Compiled from Original Recipes*. Minneapolis, Minn.: Buckeye Publishing Company, 1881. 80,000 printed. [WK]

[Wilcox, Estelle Woods, comp.]. *Practical Housekeeping. A Careful Compilation of Tried and Approved Recipes*. Minneapolis, Minn.: Buckeye Publishing Company, 1881. 110,000 printed. [UC]

[Wilcox, Estelle Woods, comp.]. *Buckeye Cookery and Practical Housekeeping. Compiled from Original Recipes.* Minneapolis, Minn.: Buckeye Publishing Company, 1883. [UC]

[Wilcox, Estelle Woods, comp.]. *The Dixie Cook-book. Carefully Compiled from the Treasured Family Collections of Many Generations of Noted House-keepers; Largely Supplemented by Tested Recipes of the More Modern South-ern Dishes, Contributed by Well-known Ladies of the South.* Rev. ed. Atlanta, Ga.: L. A. Clarkson and Company, 1883. [LC; UC]

[Wilcox, Estelle Woods, comp.]. *Practical Housekeeping: A Careful Compila-tion of Tried and Approved Recipes.* Minneapolis: Buckeye Publishing Company, 1883. 180,000 printed. [WK; PC]

[Wilcox, Estelle Woods, comp.]. *Practical Housekeeping. A Careful Compilation of Tried and Approved Recipes.* Minneapolis, Minn.: Buckeye Publishing Company, 1884. [UC]

[Wilcox, Estelle Woods, comp.]. *Buckeye Cookery and Practical Housekeeping. Compiled from Original Recipes.* Minneapolis, Minn.: Buckeye Publishing Company, 1885. [UC]

[Wilcox, Estelle Woods, comp.]. *The Dixie Cook-Book; Carefully Compiled from the Treasured Family Collections of Many Generations of Noted House-keepers; Largely Supplemented by Tested Recipes of the More Modern South-ern Dishes, Contributed by Well-known Ladies of the South.* Rev. ed. Atlanta: L. A. Clarkson and Company, 1885. [VW; PC]

[Wilcox, Estelle Woods, comp.]. *Practical Housekeeping. A Careful Compilation of Tried and Approved Recipes.* Denver: Perry and Baldy, 1885. 250,000 printed. [PC]

[Wilcox, Estelle Woods, comp.]. *Practical Housekeeping. A Careful Compilation of Tried and Approved Recipes.* Minneapolis, Minn.: Buckeye Publishing Company, 1886. 250,000 printed. [LC; PC]

[Wilcox, Estelle Woods, comp.]. *Practical Housekeeping. A Careful Compilation of Tried and Approved Recipes.* Denver: Perry Publishing Company, 1886. 250,000 printed. [PC]

[Wilcox, Estelle Wilson, comp.]. *Tried and Approved Buckeye Cookery.* German Title: *Geprüft und gutgeheissen Buckeye kochkunst: und praktisches haushal-ten.* Edition: Rev. und vergrössert. Publisher: Minneapolis, Minn. : Buck-eye Verlags-Gesellschaft, 1887. 80,000 printed. [MHS]

[Wilcox, Estelle Wilson, comp.]. *Buckeye Cookery with Hints on Practical Housekeeping.* Minneapolis, Minn.: Buckeye Publishing Company, 1887. [PC]

[Wilcox, Estelle Woods, comp.]. *Buckeye Cookery with Hints on Practical Housekeeping; Tried and Approved Recipes.* Minneapolis, Minn.: Buckeye Publishing Company, 1887. 250,000 printed. [NYPL]

[Wilcox, Estelle Woods, comp.]. *Practical Housekeeping. A Careful Compilation of Tried and Approved Recipes.* Dayton, OH.: Buckeye Pub. Company, 1887. [NYPL]

[Wilcox, Estelle Woods, comp.]. *The Buckeye Cook Book.* Subscription edition. Minneapolis, Minn., Dayton, Ohio: Buckeye Publishing Company; 1887. [LC]

[Wilcox, Estelle Woods, comp.]. *The New Dixie Cook-book and Practical Housekeeper, Carefully Compiled from the Treasured Family Collections of Many Generations of Noted Housekeepers.* Rev. and enl. ed. Atlanta, Ga.: L. A. Clarkson and Company, 1889. [LC]

[Wilcox, Estelle Woods, comp.]. *The New Practical Housekeeping. A Compilation of New, Choice and Carefully Tested Recipes.* Subscription edition. Minneapolis, Minn.: Home Publishing Company, 1890. [LC]

[Wilcox, Estelle Wilson, comp.]. *New Buckeye Cookery with Hints on Practical Housekeeping.* Rev. and enl. ed. Dayton, Ohio, and Minneapolis, Minn.: Home Publishing Company, 1891. [PC]

[Wilcox, Estelle Wilson, comp.]. *Buckeye Cookery with Hints on Practical Housekeeping.* Rev. and enl. ed. Chicago: H. J. Smith and Company, and Minneapolis: Buckeye Pub. Company, 1891. [UC]

[Wilcox, Estelle Wilson, comp.]. *Buckeye Cookery with Hints on Practical Housekeeping.* Rev. and enl. ed. Chicago: H. J. Smith and Company, and Minneapolis: Buckeye Pub. Company, 1892. 755,000 printed. [PC]

[Wilcox, Estelle Woods, comp.]. *The New Dixie Cook-book and Practical Housekeeper, Carefully Comp. From the Treasured Family Collections of Many Generations of Noted Housekeepers.* Rev. and enl. ed. Atlanta, Ga.: Dixie CB Pub. Company, 1893. [VW]

[Wilcox, Estelle Woods, comp.]. *The Housekeeper Cook Book.* Minneapolis: Housekeeper Publishing Company, 1894. [LC; WK]

[Wilcox, Estelle Woods, comp.]. *The New Buckeye Cook Book. A Revised and Enlarged Edition of Practical Housekeeping.* Minneapolis: Housekeeper Publishing Company, 1896. [VW]

[Wilcox, Estelle Woods, comp.]. *The New Buckeye Cook Book. A Revised and Enlarged Edition of Practical Housekeeping. A Careful Compilation of Tried and Approved Recipes for All Departments of the Household.* 9th ed. St. Paul, Minn.: Webb Publishing Company, 1904. [LC]

[Wilcox, Estelle Woods, comp.]. *The New Buckeye Cookery with Hints on Practical Housekeeping.* [Minneapolis, Minn.: Housekeeper Corp.] Trade Edition, [c. 1905]. [LC; NYPL]

[Wilcox, Estelle Woods, comp.]. *The Original Buckeye Cookery and Practical Housekeeping.* Chicago: Trade Supplied by Reilly and Britton Company, St. Paul, Minn.: Webb Publishing Company, 1905. [NYPL; PC]

REPRINTS.

Wilcox, Estelle Woods, comp. *Buckeye Cookery and Practical Housekeeping.* Introduction by Dorman H. Winfrey. Minneapolis, MN: Buckeye Publishing Company, 1877. Reprint. Austin, Texas: Steck-Warlick Company, 1970.

[Wilcox, Estelle Woods, comp.]. *Buckeye Cookery and Practical Housekeeping, Compiled from Original Recipes.* Minneapolis: Buckeye Publishing Company, 1879. Introduction by King Willson. 58,000 printed. Reprint. Lawndale, California: Willson Publishing Company, 1971.

[Wilcox, Estelle Woods, comp.]. *The Buckeye Cookbook; Traditional American Recipes as Published by the Buckeye Publishing Company in 1883.* Minneapolis, Minnesota: Buckeye Publishing Company, 1883. An unabridged republication of the cookery sections. New York: Dover Publications, Inc., 1975.

Wilcox, Estelle Woods, ed. *Buckeye Cookery and Practical Housekeeping: A Nineteenth-Century Best Seller.* Introduction by Virginia M. Westbrook. Facsimile of the 1880 edition. St. Paul: Minnesota Historical Society Press, 1988.